SLEEP IN EARLY MODERN ENGLAND

Sleep

IN EARLY MODERN ENGLAND

Sasha Handley

YALE UNIVERSITY PRESS
NEW HAVEN AND LONDON

Published with assistance from the Annie Burr Lewis Fund

For information about this and other Yale University Press publications, please contact:
U.S. Office: sales.press@yale.edu   yalebooks.com
Europe Office: sales@yaleup.co.uk   yalebooks.co.uk

Typeset in Minion Pro by IDSUK (DataConnection) Ltd
Printed in Great Britain by Gomer Press Ltd, Llandysul, Ceredigion, Wales

Library of Congress Cataloging-in-Publication Data

Names: Handley, Sasha.
Title: Sleep in early modern England / Sasha Handley.
Description: New Haven : Yale University Press, 2016. | Includes
    bibliographical references.
LCCN 2016016541 | ISBN 9780300220391 (cloth : alkaline paper)
LCSH: Sleep—Social aspects—England—History—17th century. |
    Sleep—Social aspects—England—History—18th century. | Sleeping
    customs—England—History. | Sleep—England—History. | Social
    change—England—History. | England—Social life and customs. |
    England—Social conditions. | BISAC: HISTORY / Europe / Great Britain. |
    HISTORY / Modern / 17th Century. | SOCIAL SCIENCE / Customs & Traditions.
    | HISTORY / Social History.
Classification: LCC GT3000.4.G7 H36 2016 | DDC 306.40942/06—dc23
LC record available at https://lccn.loc.gov/2016016541

A catalogue record for this book is available from the British Library.

10 9 8 7 6 5 4 3 2 1

For Christine, Michael, Sarah and Stuart

CONTENTS

LIST OF ILLUSTRATIONS

ACKNOWLEDGEMENTS

THE HISTORY OF sleep has exercised my mind for almost a decade now and in that time I have accumulated debts to many friends and colleagues. Fellow sleep specialists that have generously shared their thoughts and expertise with me include Bill MacLehose, Mike Greaney, Garrett Sullivan Jr, Claire Durant and Penny Lewis. My first thoughts about this project took shape at the University of Warwick during stimulating conversations with Colin Jones, Matthew Thomson and Carolyn Steedman. My former PhD supervisors Carolyn Steedman and Peter Marshall continue to be an immense source of practical support and creativity even though I am now officially in the mid-stage of my career. Since leaving their watchful care I have enjoyed fruitful working environments at the University of Northumbria and at the University of Manchester, where my colleagues have indulged and often fuelled my obsession with sleep.

This book has of course demanded a great investment of time, thought and hard labour, and I am particularly grateful to the institutions and funding bodies that have supported different stages of the project and enabled its completion. Thanks are due to the University of Manchester for the award of a Simon Postdoctoral Fellowship; to McGill University for the award of a fellowship on the 'Making Publics' project, funded by the Canadian Social Sciences and Humanities Research Council; to the Arts and Humanities Research Council for the award of an Early Career Fellowship; to the Victoria and Albert Museum for the award of a Visiting Research Fellowship; to the Lewis Walpole Library for the award of a Visiting Fellowship; and to the British Academy for the award of a Mid-Career Fellowship. Whilst researching this book I have delved into an exciting mixture of archives and collections. I received especially valuable advice from Julianne Simpson at the John Rylands Library; Hilary Davidson and Beatrice Behlen at the Museum of London; Victoria Bradley at Ham House; Lucy Aynsley at Lyme Park; Hanne Faurby at the Victoria and Albert Museum's Clothworkers' Centre; and Adam Koszary at the Museum of English Rural Life. The Victoria and Albert Museum proved to be a particularly inspiring place to complete this book, which has been enriched by their copious and beautiful collections.

Sleep is a subject that encourages strong opinions and personal stories of pleasure and pain. I have learned a great deal from conversations with friends and colleagues including Charlotte Alston, Hannah Barker, Erin Beeston, Catherine and Oliver Boote, Andrew Davies, Kate Dossett, Josie Firmin, Peter Garratt, James Grover, Joseph Hardwick, Vicky Holmes, Steven Johnson, Robert Jones, Daniel Laqua, Clark Lawlor, Anita O'Connell, Neil Pemberton, Rosie Peppin Vaughan, Gareth Prosser, Julie-Marie Strange, Richard Terry, Leigh Wetherall Dickson, Rachael Wiseman and Ed Wouk. Others have been kind enough to share their thoughts and to read different parts of the manuscript. Special thanks go to Alasdair Raffe who offered wise counsel on an early draft of this book at a very difficult time. Anthony Fletcher's comments on a later draft were equally enlightening. Friends and colleagues who have been kind enough to trawl through its pages include Alice Dolan, Claire Durant, Jennifer Evans, Victoria Gardner, Matthew Grant, Stephen Gordon, Leif Jerram, Hannah Newton, Susan North, Matthew Potter, Pedro Ramos Pinto, Janine Rivière, Jennifer Spinks, Garrett Sullivan Jr, Elaine Tierney and Selina Todd. Jenny Spinks is, without doubt, the best colleague that I could wish for, a terrific historian, and a great friend. Selina is an equally wise and inspiring historian and she has also been a fabulous friend and mentor.

Colleagues at the North West Early Modern Seminar and participants at the John Rylands Seminar on Print and Materiality in the Early Modern World have given me considerable food for thought since 2012, as have my fellow early modernists Joanne Bailey, Mary Brooks, Flora Dennis, Angela McShane, Rosamund Oates, Sara Pennell, Naomi Pullin, Tim Reinke-Williams, Laura Sangha, Bill Sherman and Anna Whitelock. My own MA and PhD students have been a constant source of inspiration and indeed of references.

Preparing this book for publication has been much less stressful than I had once imagined, which is thanks in large part to my good fortune in working with an astute and supportive editor in the shape of Robert

Baldock, to whom Joe Bergin kindly introduced me. My manuscript editor Rachael Lonsdale also offered flawless and cheerful support throughout the revision process. My final thanks, as ever, go to my family, who continue to encourage me in everything I do and to indulge my quirky fascinations. I am very lucky to have them.

INTRODUCTION

O N THURSDAY, 9 October 1712 a contributor to the fashionable daily periodical the *Spectator* styled himself as an interpreter of dreams named
'*Titus Trophonius*'. He observed, 'There are many whose waking Thoughts are
wholly employed on their sleeping ones.'[1] The satirical essay from which his
comment was drawn was directed against people who put too great store on
the portentous or prophetic qualities of their sleep and dream states. Titus's
complaint may have been driven by the controversial appearance in London
in 1706 of the millenarian group known as the French Prophets, whose
dreamlike predictions of the world's end had been roundly censured in press
and pulpit alike. The group's leaders stood trial at the Court of Queen's Bench
in 1707, accused of publishing 'False and Scandalous Books', and of orches-
trating 'Tumultuous' assemblies. The French Prophets certainly caused a stir,
yet the sleepy visions of the Dutch seaman Nicholas Hart may have been even
fresher in Titus's mind after they made a splash in the national press, and
indeed in the *Spectator*. On 5 August 1711 Hart fell into a deep and continuous sleep for five days and five nights whilst being treated for kidney stones
at the capital's St Bartholomew's Hospital. This slumberous trance was an
annual event for Hart, who always succumbed on the same day each year
(which also happened to be his birthday). It was Hart's custom upon waking
to narrate colourful reports of his sleepy adventures in the other world, and
to reveal the postmortem fates of named individuals, which captivated the
crowds of people who gathered around his bedside.[2]

Whatever Titus's motivation was for satirising these events, his observation neatly illuminates the thesis of this book – that early modern people
were acutely conscious of the unconscious. We can hardly blame them for
this obsession. Alongside breathing and eating, sleep was an essential

support to human life that no man, woman or child could live without. Peaceful rest was a treasured respite from the day's labours and an unparalleled restorative of vital energy, health and happiness. Sleeping well, or poorly, touched on every aspect of life, determining physical strength and appetite and shaping distinct states of mind, mood and emotions. Sleep's importance to early modern life and culture can hardly be overstated and yet the history of this vital and ubiquitous human experience has barely been told. This book reveals how early modern English people tried to secure peaceful sleep on a daily basis, what methods and materials they used, and the powerful motivations that persuaded them to focus so much time and energy on this seemingly mundane practice.

This book uncovers a deep-seated link between daily practices of sleep and its cultural value. For early modern people, sleep was not a purely functional act since its quality was believed to shape their fortunes on both sides of the grave. The distinctive culture of sleep revealed in the following pages shows that the quality of an individual's nightly slumber was imbued with the power to give or to destroy life, to craft or to ruin reputations, and to smooth or to obstruct the path to heaven. People reflected on their own sleeping habits, and on those of others, as a means of acquiring self-knowledge and of locating themselves in the world around them. Sleep was the single most time-consuming activity within daily life and its quality helped to define an individual's life trajectory. The vast array of sleep-related practices and preparations that took place within the home underline the vital role that sleep played in everyday settings and open a new window onto the physical, spiritual and emotional lives of men, women and children in this period, whose deepest hopes and insecurities were laid bare as they prepared themselves for sleep's approach.

This book makes a case for the vital importance of cultural forces in shaping sleep's physical experience. At the same time, it argues that perceptions and practices of sleep underwent an extraordinary set of changes from the mid-seventeenth to the mid-eighteenth century in English society. People's nocturnal habits attracted unprecedented interest as sleep's meanings, timings and physical environments were transformed. Sleep's physical causes and effects were fiercely debated in these years as new connections were made between sleep quality and the operation of the brain and nerves. Sound and restorative sleep had always been prized as an essential support to life but it became more highly valued than ever before for safeguarding the faculties of human reason. Sleep's timing, duration and quality became a critical health concern for individuals and for wider society, sparking countless investigations, discussions and treatments that sought to understand and to control its physical effects and defects. Early modern people clearly understood the benefits of a good night's sleep for the health of their bodies and minds and they went to great lengths to try and secure it. Their individual and collective efforts represent an early and neglected phase of sleep's medicalisation – a process that scholars have assumed began in the late nineteenth century and intensified in the twentieth century with the 'discovery' of REM sleep.[3] A good night's sleep was understood to enrich physical and mental well-being and its value as a guardian of the soul's health was strongly championed at the same time. The confessional divisions that had emerged within English religious culture in the wake of the Reformation were firmly cemented from the late seventeenth century, which gave a renewed spiritual vitality to sleeping habits and to sleeping environments within the homes of faithful Christians. Emerging social, economic and cultural forces such as sociability and sensibility also offered a different set of motivations and vocabularies that men and women could draw on to think about sleep's value in relation to their own bodies and minds, and to the progress of civil society more generally. This cluster of socio-economic, cultural and religious transformations was unique to English society in these years. The way that people responded to them offers a particularly compelling case study within sleep's broader history and indeed within the history of early modern England.

Sleep's unrivalled importance to the health of body, mind and soul in these years was manifested in its daily practice and material dimensions. Bedsteads, bedding textiles and sleeping environments occupied distinct spaces within many households, where they were understood as sites of physical and spiritual transformation, and as cherished sanctuaries that promised security and relief. People kept many of their most intimate and meaningful objects in and around their bedsteads and those with sufficient resources lavished time, money and energy on making, maintaining and personalising their sleeping environments to create a familiar, secure and comfortable set of associations and sensations that were uniquely designed to ease their bodies and minds into a peaceful state of relaxation. These changes fostered a vibrant and unique culture of sleep that aligned its successful practice with physical, mental and spiritual health to an unprecedented degree.

Being Asleep

At the heart of this book is an understanding of sleep as an embodied process with unique sensory dimensions and cultural meanings. Sleep is an organic physical state that renders the human body largely immobile. The brain remains active, vital respiratory functions continue and some muscle and eye movements persist, but the heart rate slows, the muscles relax, and the sleeper's consciousness of the world around them gradually recedes.[4] These characteristics have persisted across time and space. No consensus yet exists, however, on sleep's principal biological cause or purpose, or on the origin and meaning of the ideas and sensations that pulse through body and mind in this state.[5] The desire to resolve this dilemma and to understand how and why sleep is so vital to human health and well-being has triggered numerous investigations of sleeping practices and bedtime behaviours that open windows onto the physical and emotional lives, cultural preoccupations and intimate thoughts of people in different periods and places.[6]

Sleep's physical effects played a central role in moulding early modern sleeping habits. The sleep physiology traced in this book involves three intersecting phases: falling asleep, being asleep, and waking up. All three are shaped by a mixture of biological, sensory, cultural and environmental cues that differ between individuals and across cultures. Distinctive rituals signal these differences and mark the unique thoughts and sensations associated with each sleep phase and the transitions between them.[7] Scholars from the natural sciences, neurosciences, social sciences and humanities acknowledge this heady mix of causes, but they differ markedly in the weight attached to each one.[8] Chronobiologists study the biological causes of sleep's timing and duration. Their work highlights important differences in sleep preferences that seem to be driven by the unique calibration of individual biological clocks. People may be genetically predisposed to sleep at different times, for variable lengths of time, and at different depths of consciousness.[9] Neuroscientists have identified two separate yet interlinked brain processes that are crucial to sleep's onset, duration and structure: the homeostatic process (physiological need for sleep) and the circadian process (internal biological clock). The homeostatic process helps promote sleep's onset and it is closely associated with the deep, slow-wave and restorative sleep that most people experience in the early hours of slumber. The specific time at which the homeostatic process kicks in is largely determined by the number of hours that a person has remained awake since they last slept – it may therefore perform a compensatory role by extending sleep's length to make up for a previous deficit. As the effects of the homeostatic process start to wear off, usually in the early hours of the morning, the circadian process takes over and keeps the sleeper at rest for another three to five hours. The circadian process drives sleeping and waking activity within the body according to a 24-hour cycle but its rhythms are also sensitive to light and darkness, which helps to synchronise the circadian clock. The circadian process thus appears to play an important role in promoting waking.[10]

The operation of these neurological processes has been extensively documented in modern sleep research yet primarily according to a one-phase sleep cycle and often by modelling human sleep on animal behaviour. The influence of these internal bodily processes on early modern sleeping habits is of course much more difficult to trace. It is also methodologically fraught given the prevalence of biphasic sleeping patterns, which is to say that many early modern people appear to have slept in two separate phases during the night, rather than in one single consolidated phase of sleep, which they termed their 'first' and 'second' sleeps.[11] These historical and cultural variations question the seemingly 'natural' status of sleep preferences and patterns, which are in fact acutely sensitive to different cultural and physical environments. Sleep may appear to be an entirely natural activity but its boundaries are heavily shaped by time, place and culture.

This book is largely concerned with the third key ingredient that is believed to determine the nature and quality of human sleep, and whose influence modern sleep scientists have recently begun to acknowledge on a wider scale. This is the 'allostatic' process, defined as 'the mechanism by which sleep timing and duration can be controlled by external forces such as social and ecological cues'.[12] Early modern bodies and brains cannot be put under the microscope to view their inner biological functions, but it is possible to uncover the cultural, sensory and environmental cues – the habitual routines, familiar sounds, visions, smells and tactile sensations – that converged at bedtime, and which early modern people associated with the drowsy state that signalled sleep's approach. The expectations of 'sleep-hopeful bodies' – a modern phrase used to describe the thoughts, feelings and sensations that immediately precede sleep – thus form a critical focus in what follows.[13] I do not attempt to universalise early modern sleeping habits but instead to understand how the biological need for sleep was negotiated within a particular cultural and physical environment in which sleep's meanings and practices were being transformed.

Embodied Sleep

Early modern sleeping practices are plotted here through embodied experiences, which fuse nature and culture on a linked spectrum. By 'embodied experience' I mean something that embraces the entire person: body, mind, sensations, thoughts and emotions. These experiences were expressed in verbal, textual and material form and they bear testimony to the way that sleep was perceived and practised on a daily basis.

Thoughts, feelings and sensations converge at sleep's onset.[14] We fall asleep because we are tired and because we expect sleep to come at certain times and in certain places. Whilst it may be tempting to believe the opposite, sleep isn't something that just happens – people prepare and plan for it in ways that involve their rational minds and memories, their bodily sensations and movements, and the objects with which they choose to surround themselves. Sleep's approach is intimately associated with particular vistas, smells, sounds, rituals and feelings, which may convey a sense of familiarity and relaxation.[15] Early modern people anticipated, summoned and reflected on their sleep in very particular ways, and this was a process over which they could and did exercise partial control. By focusing on the habitual sleeping environments of home I reconstruct how men, women and children understood the balance between nature, culture and environment in influencing their sleep routines. This book explains how and why they tried to take charge of sleep's timing and duration, the routines that surrounded it, and its material apparatus. These individual habits formed a microcosm of sleep's broader cultural meanings and they reveal the symbolic categories with which sleep was most closely associated – most notably with the need for safety, familiarity and refreshment, and the specific forms they took in seventeenth- and eighteenth-century England.

Sleeping in Safety

Safeguarding the integrity of body, mind and soul was the chief ambition that shaped early modern sleeping practices. People sought first and foremost to protect themselves from potential dangers, which stemmed from the sense of fragility and anxiety that sleep's onset produced. Sleep evokes unique feelings of vulnerability that cut across cultures (and even across species) and these feelings are heavily shaped by the dulled consciousness imposed by this state of repose. Those on the verge of sleep become less aware of their sensory environments and anxious to defend themselves against threats that they cannot detect. The idea of sleep, and its physical practice, thus generates a unique set of human emotions that require explanation. Evidence of sleep-related anxiety has surfaced in clinical observations when the brain appears to remain partly aware of its environment and alert to potential threats in more superficial sleep states such as REM sleep.[16] Feelings of submersion, sinking and loss of control surface time and time again in people's descriptions of falling asleep, which mark its distinctiveness from all other sensory experiences.[17]

Similar sensations and feelings of anxiety characterised early modern perceptions of falling asleep but the apparent sources of danger, and the methods chosen to repel them, were culturally distinct. Sleep was understood as a state of transition between day and night, between degrees of consciousness, between the earthly and spiritual realms, and between life and death. The forces of nature moulded its boundaries, as did supernatural agents and human action. All three of these forces presented potential dangers, which varied from the mundane to the transcendental. Sleep could endanger the household's security and the physical and spiritual lives of its occupants by exposing them to fires, floods, malicious intruders, bedbugs, disease, mental disorder, sexual assault, or even death and damnation.[18] The anxieties associated with sleep were reinforced by classical texts, Holy Scripture, didactic literature, cumulative household wisdom, conversation and by daily experience, which all furnished evidence of the unfortunate fates that could be met during the slumberous hours of darkness. This book traces the cultural roots of these fears and responses to them in four ways: through the creation of enclosed, comfortable and familiar sleeping environments; through the selection of trusted sleeping companions; through the careful observation of sleep regimens; and through the practice of protective bedtime rituals. These habits were underpinned by a common concern to sleep in 'safety' and 'security' – two concepts that stimulated efforts to attain physical, psychological and spiritual protection during the hours of sleep.

Sleep Comfort

Alongside 'safety' and 'security', many people also used the term 'comfort' to express their desire for pleasurable physical sensations and modes of relaxation at bedtime.[19] 'Comfort' is a term with particular resonance in the eighteenth-century world of goods that has sparked contentious debates about its meaning. The definition of 'sleep comfort' used here is, however, distinct, and I use it to refer to the feelings of physical and psychological ease that were keenly sought as part of the quest to secure sound sleep. My definition of 'sleep comfort' thus merges the well-established early modern meaning of 'comfort' as spiritual solace, or emotional relief, with the material definition advanced by John E. Crowley, who defined comfort in relation to bodily sensibilities and their material environments.[20] Bedsteads, bedding textiles and sleeping chambers could offer all of these things simultaneously to their occupants. Spiritual consolation was sought by reading parts of Holy Scripture or devotional texts at bedtime, by looking at religious images that hung on the walls, that were carved onto the wooden frame of the bedstead or that were embroidered onto the bed's textiles. These materials were in turn believed to offer physical, spiritual and emotional satisfaction to the sleeper: a theme that is developed in Chapter 3. The desire to sleep well was a powerful motivation for filling sleeping chambers with pleasing, comfortable and clean furnishings, images and objects. These goods were less subject to the same criticisms of excessive consumption that applied to other parts of the early modern household – perhaps because they were understood as necessities rather than luxuries. The specific bodily needs that attended sleep thus circulated in a different register from other physical sensibilities. They must be considered independently from more generalised demands for physical comfort within the home, which acquired ideological support and a new vocabulary in these years.[21] A state of physical and psychological comfort, however it was achieved, was judged to be most conducive to procuring peaceful rest.

Early Modern Sleep

This book offers new insights into an essential yet neglected feature of early modern life and culture. At the same time, it intervenes in lively contemporary debates about sleep's nature, purpose and experience by revealing the importance of distinct historical ideas and environments in moulding sleep's daily practice. Despite sleep's ubiquity, its cultural meanings and daily practice have yet to receive sustained scrutiny in early modern societies and cultures. One important exception is the work of A. Roger Ekirch who reflected on sleeping habits as part of his influential analysis of pre-industrial night-time culture in Europe and America. The characteristic biphasic pattern of 'segmented sleep' that he identified involved the division of each night's sleep into two distinct cycles.[22] These cycles were interspersed by a short period of waking where a range of activities might take place – from household chores to meditative prayer, or even beer-brewing. These habits, and their eventual decline, have been largely explained by the importance of nature's rhythms in shaping bedtimes and especially by the availability of natural light to illuminate waking activities. These forces were diluted by the onset of industrialisation, urbanisation and by new lighting technologies that changed the timetables of daily life and transformed the material culture of ordinary households.[23] Neat as this story of change is, there are important questions that remain unanswered. Recent research has, for example, questioned whether the linguistic meanings of 'first' and 'second' sleep do in fact correspond to a pattern of segmented slumber.[24] The patchy survival and inconsistencies of early modern source materials also caution against accepting a universal model of sleep's practice that covers a diverse range of individuals and communities over a long period of time. Early modern bedtimes, as far as they are recoverable, form a complex jigsaw that combines individual opportunities for determining sleep's timings with personal preferences and religious sensibilities. The contentious debates that emerged around bedtimes in early modern England underline their lack of uniformity. I do not offer an alternative 'system' of sleeping habits in the pages that follow but insist instead on a more flexible and multilayered understanding of sleep's timings that could vary on a daily basis, according to key transitions in the individual life cycle, and that took account of a diverse range of personal and religious sensibilities. Early modern scholars have described the variety of nocturnal leisure activities that impacted upon bedtimes and sleep quality in many urban centres. Craig Koslofsky has described how the 'nocturnalisation' of early modern culture – the widespread extension of waking activities into the hours of darkness – began to blur the accepted frontiers between day and night.[25] Much remains to be said however about the influence of nocturnal culture, and especially of night-time sociability, on everyday sleeping practices. Sleep thus has a history that is related to, yet distinct from, cultures of night-time activity, and this is traced in the pages that follow.

This book moves inside the household to examine the ideas, routines, objects and environments that shaped sleep's daily practice. The seasonal rhythms of nature were of course central to the timing and duration of sleep, as human geographers have shown, but these ecological factors were not the only forces that shaped bedtimes.[26] This book presents a more holistic vision of early modern sleep culture, which combines the forces of nature with cultures of healthcare, devotional practices, wider social and cultural influences, and with the sleeping environments of home. In taking this approach I draw inspiration from sociologists and anthropologists who have shown how sleep's practice shifted according to social status, gender, age, occupation, religious belief and socio-economic structures.[27] The phrase 'dormatology' has recently been coined to capture the outpouring of influential sleep research in the fields of human geography, sociology, medical anthropology and neuroscience.[28] Historians have much to add to this conversation by uncovering the material environments and cultural influences that moulded sleep behaviours and sleep quality in different historical contexts and by revealing the distinctive emotions that accompanied sleep and shaped its everyday practice. Put simply, sleeping habits are as much a product of culture as they are of physiology.

Sleep's daily practice was a practical support to human life and an essential component of individual identity. Managing sleep's physical arrangements, and reflecting on its quality, helped early modern people to locate themselves in the world around them, and they drew on a variety of cultural resources to help them do this – from classical literature and medical philosophies, to the words of Holy Scripture. Garrett Sullivan and Bill MacLehose have investigated how sleep's cultural meanings were forged in relation to medieval and early modern literature, concepts of bodily function, emotional health and theories of cognition.[29] Anna Whitelock's fascinating study of Queen Elizabeth I's bedfellows also describes the unique feelings of insecurity and anxiety associated with sleep, which shaped demands for stable and familiar surroundings and trustworthy sleeping companions at bedtime.[30] I take note of these influences and explain how they defined the sleeping lives of less illustrious men and women in similar ways.

As well as tracing sleep's cultural significance, this book also asks a new set of questions about the content, arrangement and use of sleeping environments. The kinds of bedsteads that people slept in were determined in part by their socio-economic power, and increasingly by fashion, taste and commerce. We already know a lot about what early modern bedsteads and bedding textiles looked like, but much less about how they felt, why certain materials, textures and sensations were prioritised, and how they helped to trigger particular memories and to create unique feelings and states of mind linked to sleep. The practical and symbolic role of bedsteads in staging the emotional dramas of family life has also been well documented, which tied these objects to the most intimate moments of early modern life. The emphasis of scholarship to date has nevertheless been focused on conscious waking activities such as sex, marital relations and childbirth. My focus here is on the principal activity that ordered people's relationships with their bedsteads – namely, the needs and expectations associated with sleep. Sleep's multisensory dimensions and affective qualities structured the material dimensions of household life. Sleep-related objects, from pillow-cases to bedsheets, played a particularly important role in structuring physical and emotional experiences of slumber. The sensations and thoughts sparked by these objects could offer soothing reassurance and it was psychologically important to surround oneself with meaningful and personal objects.[31] These feelings were especially prized at bedtime, which could be fraught with worldly and spiritual anxieties.

The surprising lack of focus on sleep in histories of everyday life is mirrored by its neglect within early modern medical culture, even though refreshing sleep was widely acknowledged to maintain health and well-being. Pedro Gil Sotres briefly examined sleep's importance as one of the six non-natural principles that shaped preventative healthcare advice in medieval and early modern Europe. I trace the powerful influence of these healthcare principles within daily life.[32] Another key part of this history is the emergence of influential medical philosophies that reshaped understandings of sleep's physiology in the decades after 1660.[33] The philosophies discussed here tied sleep's practice more firmly than ever before to the operations of the brain and nerves – the relationship between sleep and the life of the mind is one that had enormous repercussions within English society and culture and it continues to inspire sleep research in the modern world.

My focus on household sleeping practices also uncovers the importance of religious beliefs as an essential motivation for the careful regulation of sleep's timing, its routines and its material environments. Attending to these details was, I argue, an embodied method of devotion that was designed to protect both body and soul from corruption. Alec Ryrie and Erin Sullivan have traced the influence of Holy Scripture on sleep's day-to-day management amongst Protestants in the post-Reformation British Isles.[34] Phyllis Mack has also identified sleep management and dream interpretation as key devotional practices within Methodist communities in eighteenth-century Britain.[35] I examine these practices within a new chronology, and in relation to a different set of religious priorities to explain how and why they intensified within many households after 1660. The household devotions that surrounded sleep assumed unprecedented importance in these years as England's Protestant communities fragmented at an alarming rate. These devotional habits were also firmly grounded within the changing material dimensions of household life. The spiritual meanings of sleeping environments, bedsteads and bedding textiles take centre stage here, alongside the bedtime routines, prayers and reading habits that bookended and sanctified the hours of sleep for a wide range of Protestants, and indeed Catholics, who understood their sleep routines as an essential part of their Christian duties.

The nature and practice of sleep has been briefly sketched in analyses of early modern dream cultures and states of consciousness. Contentious debates about the causes of dreams and their emotional effects have been prominent and they parallel disputes about sleep's origins within and outside of the physical body.[36] This book forms a bridge between shifting understandings of sleep and dreams in these years by uncovering formative debates about the influence of different sleep states upon non-conscious visions and dreams – different sleep postures were believed to be crucial, as were the climatic conditions of sleeping environments. The cultural revaluation of sleep traced in this book stimulated growing interest in, and investigation of, non-conscious states of mind. Different sleep and dream states, nightmares and sleep disorders such as sleepwalking were carefully distinguished from each other and investigated in relation to operations of body, mind and personal identity.

Sources and Methodology

Accessing sleep's multisensory dimensions has determined my selection of source materials and methods. Sleep's daily practice within the household is traced through an original sample of 115 probate inventories that were proved in the Prerogative Court of Canterbury (hereafter PCC) between January 1660 and December 1760. The PCC had jurisdiction over the estates of deceased men and women in England and Wales from 1383 to 1858. Its holdings are particularly strong between 1660 and 1782 when it was a mandatory requirement for executors and administrators of personal estates to return an inventory of the deceased's possessions to the court registry. The inventories vary in length and detail but they include lists of goods, chattels, cash, crops, livestock and debts owed and owing. The data set analysed here is based on the contents of selected households sampled evenly at ten-year intervals to examine long-term shifts in chamber location, labelling and content. The content of all chambers has been examined but specific focus falls on those that contained bedsteads and sleep-related goods. The Appendix contains details of the size, complexity and location of the households in the sample. The conclusions drawn from the inventories are considered in relation to analyses of English household inventories that number in the thousands, which are drawn from existing scholarship. Taken together, this evidence reveals the vertical relocation of bedsteads to the upper floors of many households, which were accompanied by a rich variety of personalised and meaningful objects.

A number of methodological challenges must be confronted when using probate inventories. Inventories are incomplete records of household content that are restricted in their social, geographical and gender range. The executors of individual estates, administrators and court officials that compiled the inventories may have lacked personal knowledge of the properties they surveyed. Their attention was focused on household goods that had a significant resale value, which led to the selective recording or omission of particular possessions.[37] The descriptive detail of inventories varied widely and could be generic. However, when used cautiously these records still offer unparalleled evidence of long-term structural changes in sleeping environments, especially their location within the household and their material dimensions. The relative stability of this body of evidence is partly due to the high value of bedsteads and bed furnishings, which could account for approximately one third of the total cost of household goods, and were therefore more likely to be listed.[38] The PCC inventories have been selected because of their relative consistency of form and composition across this period and because they are typical of household inventories in other English regions.

The City of London is best represented in the geographical spread of households examined and it accounts for approximately 30 per cent of the total (see Appendix). The sample is weighted towards the southeast of England with a substantial number of households located in Surrey, Kent, Essex and the counties of Buckinghamshire and Berkshire. This geographical bias is partly justified by the fact that London and its environs were at the forefront of the earliest changes in the expansion and reorganisation of household space. Fruitful comparisons can nonetheless be drawn between these regions and households in other parts of England, including Oxfordshire, Herefordshire, Cheshire, the Midlands and the southwestern counties of Somerset, Devon and Cornwall. The social and occupational range of the men and women whose possessions have been examined is again restricted yet broad enough to draw useful comparisons of experience. Occupations are listed in one quarter of the inventories and they include blacksmiths, butchers, carpenters, clergymen, clerks, coachmakers, grocers, husbandmen, merchants, millers, packers, painters, saddlers, tailors, tanners and yeomen. The sample is completed by the inventories of a few minor gentry and widows. The total value of individual estates has not been systematically analysed since this offers only a partial guide to personal wealth. Nonetheless, the size of individual households and the estimated resale value of their contents suggest that the sample contains a mixture of wealthy individuals and people of more modest means, some of whom resided in temporary lodgings or with borrowed furnishings that were later reclaimed by their owners.

The inventories provide a flexible framework within which to plot the daily sleeping habits of early modern people who exercised considerable control over their own sleep routines and environments. The time, money and thought that they invested in sleep are illuminated by an extensive body of personal testimonies, which includes diaries, correspondence and autobiographies in both manuscript and print. These records cover the same timeframe as the inventories and they compensate for the overly static and impersonal nature of those records. They give unparalleled evidence of where people slept, for how long, who they slept with, how they explained periods of disturbed sleep and how their subjective experiences of sleep were structured by different bedsteads, sleeping environments and emotions. These records paint a colourful picture of why some people deliberately chose to sleep in rudimentary bedsteads; why they bookended their sleeping hours with prayers and protective rituals; and why some people chose, on occasion, to sleep beside trusted friends and servants. Methodological constraints nevertheless apply equally to these records. Their mode of production, purpose, genre and representativeness all present limitations. These records are, by their very nature, socially restricted – generally created by men and women who had the literacy skills, leisure time and motivation to put pen to paper. Spiritual autobiographies feature prominently, which were created for distinct personal reasons that may only partly represent the views and practices of the wider population. These documents nevertheless afford the most intimate glimpses of habitual sleeping practices and how individual men and women translated sleep's shifting cultural meanings into their daily routines.

Surviving objects are invaluable for understanding the embodied and sensory dimensions of early modern sleep, yet the verbal expression of how these materials structured sleep's experience can only be captured by examining how users related to these objects, which is often revealed in their letters and diaries. The content of personal testimonies highlight a further methodological difficulty: reflections on the nature, quality and meaning of sleep were usually triggered by a disturbed night's sleep. When sleep went smoothly it was taken for granted and subsumed within the ordinary rhythms of household life. Such familiar experiences probably formed part of daily discussions within the home but they rarely prompted written comment.[39] I have tried to offset this problem by reading against the grain, focusing closely on those moments when sleep went wrong and when ordinary expectations of its practice were overturned.

Sleep's nonverbal perception and practice similarly justifies my focus on its material dimensions. Bedsteads, beds and bedding textiles feature prominently in the following chapters. Textiles created a unique sense of homeliness and belonging that was particularly valued within sleeping environments. One of the more striking conclusions of this book is just how much emotional investment people poured into the paraphernalia of sleep, and into their bedding in particular. Bedding textiles were extensions of bodily sensations and they were potent repositories of personal meanings, memories and sensations, being closely bound up with feelings of love, loss and comfort. They were also the materials that lay closest to sleeping bodies and created feelings of warmth, reassurance, cleanliness and security at bedtime. This was especially true of bedding textiles that were handmade and personalised by their owners or by those close to them. These materials also signalled broader socio-economic, cultural and religious meanings, which illustrate shifting understandings of sleep across this period.[40] These objects feature here for the specific ways in which they ordered embodied experiences of sleep rather than as further evidence of the explosion of new textile goods in early modern homes.

Attitudes to sleep that circulated beyond the household, but which shaped its routines, are traced in manuscript and printed sources that track long-term shifts in medical, philosophical, religious and cultural attitudes towards sleep. They include architectural treatises, medical regimens, handbooks of domestic medicine, household recipe books, guides to household management, sermons, devotional guides, educational treatises, periodicals, poems, novels, operas and visual images of different sleep states in portraiture, prints, etchings and engravings. This rich variety of materials underlines the powerful interest that sleep attracted in these years and the overlapping genres that shaped its understanding and practice.

Structure

Sleeping practices are charted in relation to the main locations and cultural influences that shaped them. Flows of continuity and change are signalled within each chapter, which illustrate the effects of social, cultural, religious, medical and philosophical developments across the period. Sleep's essential role in supporting human life is the subject of the first two chapters. Chapter 1 explains how sleep was believed to operate within the body, and how its quality could be shaped by individual lifestyles, by the natural environment, and by a vibrant world of supernatural forces. It charts shifting medical understandings of sleep and explains how and why peaceful slumber was judged essential to physical and psychological well-being. Chapter 2 reveals how these ideas shaped habits within the home, where sleep was safeguarded by a rich culture of preventative healthcare practices – from the selection of healthy bedding textiles, to vigorous cleansing routines and the preparation of sleep-inducing medicines. Both chapters are framed by sleep's ever-closer alignment with the health of the brain and nerves.

Sleep's role in securing spiritual health is the subject of Chapter 3, which identifies healthy and well-regulated sleep routines as central features of Christian practice and identity. The chapter reveals sleep's intrinsic Christian meanings, its connections to death, resurrection and salvation, and why bedtime routines and sleeping chambers were so heavily shaped by these spiritual meanings in the years after 1660 as household devotions were strongly promoted.

Chapters 4 and 5 examine sleeping environments within and outside of the household and how they structured the sleeping practices of its members. The location, content and arrangement of sleeping environments were crucial in ordering nocturnal habits. The terms 'sleeping environment' and 'sleeping chamber' are used to refer to any household space in which sleep was likely to take place. I use 'bedchamber' only when it was used in its original context – this label was not routinely used until the nineteenth century. Chapter 4 maps the relocation of bedsteads from multifunctional ground-floor chambers to semi-specialised chambers on the upper floors of many households. This development satisfied commonplace desires for security and enclosure during sleep. The importance of resting in stable, familiar and satisfying surroundings is strongly emphasised since it was judged essential for securing physical and psychological relaxation. The familiar sleeping environments of home are deliberately contrasted with the unfamiliar sleeping environments that feature in Chapter 5. Reports of these displacements show the dissatisfaction that could be produced by sleeping away from home in unfamiliar and potentially unsafe bedsteads and chambers. This was a reality that increasingly confronted men and women who slept in different households, lodging houses, inns and taverns to create and maintain their social networks. The chapter examines the diverse places in which people slept, the range of bedfellows who they slept beside, and the erratic bedtimes that often ensued from the pursuit of public and household sociability. These habits sparked fierce debates about sleep's moral boundaries and its social utility. The second part of the chapter shows how these migratory sleeping habits were managed and the unique codes of civility that informed them. The physical dangers that were associated with sleeping in unfamiliar bedsteads and in particular chambers were offset in a variety of ways. Satisfying desires for security, cleanliness and comfort proved once again to be of paramount importance in ordering people's expectations of sleep.

The relationship between sleep and personal identity is continued in the book's final chapter, which shows how and why sleep experiences were framed and understood as ciphers of individual identity. This development was shaped by the spread of neurological understandings of sleep and by the cult of sensibility that had taken hold of English imaginations by the mid-eighteenth century. The chapter examines how widely circulating cultural representations of sleep, sleep disorders and dreams were absorbed within models of selfhood by the close of the eighteenth century. This final chapter thus has a slightly longer chronology to encapsulate the long-term consequences of sleep's cultural revaluation.

Sleep's history, both as an idea and as a practice, has fluctuated dramatically across time and space. This book is a vital chapter in a bigger story about how different historical environments and cultures can and have influenced people's understanding of sleep and its perceived importance to their health and well-being. Sleep's cultural value is fundamental to the degree of time, labour and thought that people invest in its daily practice, which in turn has a powerful effect on how it is experienced. This book reveals how sleep's meanings and practices shaped multiple dimensions of human life as well as the agency of individual men and women to influence seemingly inexorable biological processes. A great deal of work remains to be done in uncovering the unique features of sleep's history, but I hope that fellow historians and researchers across the humanities, social sciences and life sciences will be encouraged to place cultural understandings of sleep and individual agency at the heart of future enquiries.

CHAPTER I

Sleep, Medicine and the Body

"THE BENEFIT OF sleepe, or the necessity rather needeth no proofe, for that without it no living creature may long endure, according to that saying of the Poet *Ovid*".[1] The words of physician, clergyman, and chief master of Manchester grammar school, Thomas Cogan, pronounced sleep's unique importance to human life in his *The haven of health*. Cogan designed this practical healthcare guide chiefly for the instruction of his students but it gained a much wider readership thanks to seven printed editions published between 1584 and 1636. For Thomas Cogan the benefits of a good night's sleep were almost incalculable; it revived weary bodies, refreshed tired minds, and was essential to the long-term health and happiness of body and soul. Cogan credited sound sleep with the power to allay anger and sorrow, and to bring human bodies into harmonious balance with God and the natural world that He had created. The sleep that Cogan described involved, at its very core, a profound process of metamorphosis in which bodies and souls were translated between different physical and mental states and even between different worlds. Sleep's power to transform human life was so potent that Cogan imbued it with supernatural qualities by citing the epic verse of Roman poet Ovid for his readers. In his classic work *Metamorphoses*, which chronicles the history of the world up to the formation of Julius Caesar's Roman empire, Ovid presents sleep as a unique state of alteration that has supported and threatened human life since the universe was created. In his verse, sleep can radically transform human beings by transporting them between the ordinary realms of nature and an enchanted world of magical power. Here, the tranquil and troubled sleep of humans lies in the hands of the gods. Somnus, the gentle god of sleep, quietens the world with the gift of peaceful slumber, whilst the Roman god

Mercury commits rape and murder by drawing a veil of sleep over the eyes of his victims with a magical sleep-procuring wand.[2] This characterisation of sleep as a fragile state of existence, in which humans can be restored to vitality or extinguished from life, had strong appeal for Thomas Cogan and his contemporaries, who believed that human health was determined by a heady mixture of material and spiritual forces. The body's motions were thus ever changing, driven by its inner flows, by the external forces of nature, by the movements of the planets and by the will of divine and diabolical agents.[3]

Sleep was an inherently unstable process and its ability to carry men and women between the mundane waking world and a realm of supernatural power was echoed in plays and poems, in Holy Scripture and in the concept of the Great Chain of Being, which established an influential framework for understanding how matter and spirit interacted.[4] This chain was described and depicted as a divinely ordained structure in which all organic matter, animals, humans and supernatural beings were linked together in a hierarchy of association whose layers stretched from the flora and fauna of the natural landscape right up to God in heaven. Human bodies were believed to be perfect microcosms of this expansive and interactive universe whose operations were sustained and endangered by an array of natural and supernatural powers. This combination of influences was especially pronounced during sleep, which was understood as a fluid and vulnerable state of existence that marked the midway point on the path of transformation between life and death.

Bodily knowledge about sleep was shaped by a culture in which health and sickness were explained by a combination of the body's internal operations and by the material and spiritual environments with which it interacted on a daily basis. This chapter probes why a sound night's sleep was judged so important for physical and mental well-being, how sleep was believed to operate within the body, and the range of advice offered by medical practitioners about how peaceful slumber was best secured. Early modern men and women unwaveringly accepted the health-giving properties of sound sleep throughout this period and its connection to a God who worked through nature. The way that sleep was believed to affect the body's faculties nevertheless underwent important changes. For much of the sixteenth and seventeenth centuries, sleep's operation within the body was principally focused on the lower organs, namely the stomach, liver and heart. This was underpinned by the humoral physiology of the ancient world, which was the foundation of an influential healthcare system known as the 'six non-natural things' in which healthy patterns of sleeping and

waking were highly prized. Medical understandings of sleep were transformed after the 1660s, however, as sleep's physiological operation became
increasingly focused on the body's upper regions, especially the brain and
nerves. English physicians pioneered 'neurological' models of sleeping and
waking patterns that prioritised these areas. Their work spread rapidly
across the British Isles and it had wide-ranging consequences for perceptions and practices of sleep. Healthy sleep became more highly prized than
ever before, not only for supporting digestion and providing essential
refreshment, but also for preserving the faculties of human reason and
keeping the nerves in good working order. This shift in emphasis from
stomach to brain had far-reaching effects. Sleep's knowledge economy
turned more decisively towards the body's internal operations as physicians, anatomists and philosophers mapped its effects on body and brain in
acute detail. The ready admittance of supernatural agencies as key agents
within sleeping and waking patterns was re-examined, as bodily knowledge
about sleep was firmly located within the visible boundaries of the material
world. Here, a powerful ideal of peaceful sleep emerged as this essential
period of nourishment became more highly valued than ever before for
refreshing the bodies and minds of rational and productive citizens. This
shift has yet to be examined in detail and so the following pages constitute
a missing early chapter within the story of sleep's medicalisation, which
became a pressing healthcare concern for individuals and wider society.

Sleep, the Humours and the Six Non-Natural Things

God and Nature were the chief overseers of restorative sleep. Nature was
understood not only as the tangible physical environment, but also as an
active agent within the body that battled disease at God's behest.[5] Since God
was the original author of sickness and the ultimate guardian of health and
restoration, sleep quality depended on the individual's relationship with
Him and the physical world that He had created. Men and women could
not guarantee a good night's sleep without God's help but they played a
critical role in maintaining the quality of their own slumber by carefully
regulating their daily habits according to the order of nature, and by
attending to their Christian duties. The need to preserve the body in
harmony with the natural world was nowhere more pronounced than in
the humoral system of physic that dominated medical thinking in medieval
and early modern Europe. Humoral physiology was popularised by the
medical theories of the Greek physicians Hippocrates (c. 460–c. 370 BC)
and Galen of Pergamon (AD 129–c. 200), whose work was widely translated

and published across Europe from the thirteenth century and established the foundation for most printed health regimens, which offered a step-by-step guide to healthcare.

According to this corpus of knowledge, the balance of four bodily humours (or fluids), determined health, sickness and temperament: blood, which was warm and moist; choler, or yellow bile, which was warm and dry; melancholy, or black bile, which was cold and dry; and phlegm, which was cold and moist. Each of these four humours corresponded to one of the earth's four natural elements of air, fire, earth and water, and to the planet with which each element was associated.[6] The make-up, or 'complexion', of the humours in any individual body differed according to age and gender, and each person's qualities also varied according to weight and lifestyle. Children were generally characterised as warm and moist beings, whilst those of advanced age were described as cold and dry since the body's life-sustaining heat and moisture was believed to dissipate gradually over time. Those in between these two extremes enjoyed a more temperate body heat, although men were judged to have hotter and drier bodies than women because they were conceived from warmer seed on the right-hand side of their mother's womb. This way of categorising the body extended to its individual organs and physiological processes, and medical prescriptions were also devised with these principles in mind. The healthcare advice offered by medical practitioners, and the therapeutic wisdom that featured in health regimens and household recipe books, was thus carefully calibrated to suit individual needs and changed throughout the life cycle.

Careful management of sleeping and waking habits was a core element in prescribed rules of health preservation that were key to regulating the body's humours for people of all ages and complexions. 'Sleep and waking' was the third category within the *sex res non naturales*, or the 'six non-natural things', which sat alongside five other environmental and dietary elements that comprised air, food and drink, motion and rest, excretion and retention, and the passions of the mind. A healthy and long life depended on the body's careful interaction with all six non-natural factors, in combination with God's grace. Moderate intake of food and regular habits of sleeping, exercising, excretion, taking the air and soothing the passions helped to keep the humours in check and to prevent their corruption, which invited disease.

This collection of medical advice circulated widely through conversation, letters and printed regimens of health, which encouraged a proactive culture of health preservation and disease prevention amongst their readers. Maintaining a strong and well-managed body required self-discipline and it was thus an essential component of personal and Christian identity, being understood as a sign of decency, wisdom and moral virtue. Health regimens grew in size, number and form across early modern Europe and by the late seventeenth century they had been transformed from individualised regimens, largely designed for high-ranking men, into accessible and affordable handbooks of healthcare that catered for different ranks, ages and lifestyles of men and women.[7] Peaceful sleep was thus essential to life. It nourished the whole body by balancing the humours and by restoring its levels of heat and radical moisture that had dissipated with the day's labours, but it also had a more specific function in supporting the process of nutrition.

Sleep and the Stomach

For much of the medieval and early modern period temperate sleep was primarily valued for supporting the process of digestion. Medical practitioners, drawing on the ancient wisdom of influential Greek philosophers like Aristotle (384–322 BC), taught that food consumed during waking hours was heated, broken down and purified in four separate phases during sleep. When darkness fell and sleep approached, the body's innate heat was drawn into its core where it intensified and warmed the stomach and liver. This process was likened to the effect of flames beneath a cooking pot. The heat from the flames triggered a two-phase process of digestion, or 'concoction', in which the food in the stomach began to soften and disperse its nutritional benefits. Hot vapours rose up from the stomach during this process, which transported a sweet and pleasant humidity through the veins up to the cold and moist brain. As the vapours cooled they produced condensation that descended through the body in a heavy mass, moistening its internal organs and obstructing the ordinary flow of animal spirits that enervated the body's senses, which were lulled into sleep. When this process was complete the purified substance that remained in the stomach aided the reproduction of blood in the liver, and so was an essential support to life.[8]

This strong relationship between sleep and digestion was especially prominent in early English health regimens. In 1539 Sir Thomas Elyot, lawyer, humanist scholar and ambassador to King Henry VIII, published an accessible healthcare guide based on the principles of humoral physic that he had translated from the works of Hippocrates and Galen. Elyot's *Castel of Helthe*, first published in 1539, explained sleep's unique ability to promote healthy nutrition, regulate body temperature and preserve humoral balance: 'The commoditie of moderate slepe, appereth by this, that naturall heate, which is occupied about the matter, wherof procedeth nouryshment, is comforted in the places of digestion, and so digestion is made better, or more perfite by slepe, the body fatter, the mynde more quiete and clere, the humours temperate'.[9] Elyot calculated the optimum number of sleeping hours to be taken each night according to the efficiency of individual digestive systems and the heaviness of the supper consumed, as well as by age and natural complexion. Healthy people with a strong constitution required a small amount of sleep, generally between six and eight hours each night, but sleeping hours were extended for those with 'weake stomakes' who digested more slowly. People of advanced age were encouraged to eat soup, broths and 'panadoes' – a sweet meal of boiled bread mixed with fruit and spices – which were moistening and easy to digest.[10] They were encouraged to eat in small quantities, three or four times a day, and they might be permitted to take a brief nap after meals to speed digestion. Pregnant women were allowed to take between nine and ten hours of sleep each night because they took longer to digest the food in their stomachs due to the added compression of the foetus.[11] Elyot's work proved extremely popular with further editions and adaptations published in every subsequent decade of the sixteenth century.[12]

Similarly popular was the work of English physician and former Carthusian monk Andrew Boorde. He echoed Thomas Elyot's sleep-advice in his Compendyous Regyment, or a Dyetary of Healthe, which offered a comprehensive guide to individual healthcare. Boorde praised the virtues of moderate sleep for perfecting digestion, for nourishing the blood, and for sharpening the memory since it eased the transit of the body's vital fluids and prevented the build up of malignant humours. He believed that healthy sleep offered protection for the whole body since 'it dothe restore nature, & doth quyet al ye humours & pulses [of] man, & dothe animate & co[m]forte all ye naturall & anymall & spyrytual powers'.[13] Thomas Cogan agreed and judged that wholesome sleep was essential to prevent 'undigested and raw humours' that bred a wide range of illnesses.

Durham physician and former clergyman William Bullein combined Galenic advice with the medical theories of Persian polymath Avicenna (c. 980–1037), Swiss German physician Paracelsus (1493–1541) and Aristotle in his popular healthcare guides. Aristotle wrote three short yet influential treatises on the physiology of sleep and dreams that form part of the collection of his works known as the Parva Naturalia. In his De Somno et Vigilia, the process of digestion took centre stage in explaining how sleeping and waking occurred within the body. Sleep was here described as a seizure of the heart, also known as the 'primary sense-organ'. After food was ingested, a mass of hot vapours rose up from the stomach to the cold brain; here they condensed, cooled and descended back down through the body. This cooling process made the head heavy, the eyelids droop, and it immobilised the heart, which became unable to perform its ordinary functions, including the exercise of perception. Aristotle judged sleep's chief value to lie in speeding the process of nutrition, which strengthened the body, supported its growth and allowed it to exercise its powers of perception upon waking. Sleep was thus vital to the continued existence of all human and animal species.

William Bullein was similarly convinced of the health benefits conferred by restful sleep, which again centred on the digestive process. His pocket-sized health guides designed for everyday use include *The Government of Health* (1558) and *Bulleins Bulwarke of Defence Againste All Sicknes, Sornes, and Woundes that dooe daily assaulte mankinde* (1562), which advised readers how to prepare the stomach before bedtime to achieve peaceful sleep. The moderate intake of approved foods and drinks at appropriate times of day was crucial. Large quantities of liquor were censured, as was the 'ryotous' consumption of meat, both of which overheated the stomach and impeded the digestive process.[14] The intimate connection between sleep and the stomach was likewise reflected in manuscript and printed health regimens that paid careful attention to the time allowed to lapse between meal times and bedtimes. Thomas Cogan spoke for many when he recommended that bedtime should be postponed for one to two hours after supper, and ideally after a leisurely walk had been taken to help the food descend to the pit of the stomach where it could be more easily heated and digested.[15]

Whilst peaceful sleep promoted healthy digestion, sleep loss was routinely ascribed to infirmities of the stomach and greedy feasts of rich food and drink. Erratic sleeping hours could, by the same measure, generate digestive malfunctions. In the mid-seventeenth century, Nicholas Culpeper, the London-based apothecary and author of popular healthcare guides, believed that troublesome sleep was the likely result of overheated bellies inflamed by incomplete digestion. Culpeper recommended a range of affordable herbs, grains, flowers and leaves to combat this problem in his *Pharmacopoeia Londinensis, or, The London Dispensatory*, first published in 1653.[16] The sleep-advice of London physician and surgeon John Pechey similarly centred on diet and digestion, and he adapted his wisdom for those with distinct healthcare needs, such as pregnant women, babies and young children, and people of advanced age. Children were judged particularly susceptible to humoral imbalance and thus to sleep disturbances because they had weak stomachs, watery organs, and were prone to a gluttonous intake of breast milk. When the stomach struggled to digest this avalanche of milk, the liquid began to putrefy and produced toxic vapours that either kept the child awake, or provoked distressing nightmares. Pechey blamed the 'terrible Phantasms' experienced by some children on the 'ill concoction' of milk in their delicate bellies, which was caused by the child being put to bed on a full stomach, by having drunk too much milk, or by drinking milk that had become 'hot, sharp, and distasteful' by the erratic sleeping patterns of mothers and nursemaids.[17]

Nicholas Culpeper and John Pechey deliberately tailored their health-care advice to a wide audience. They published accessible, practical and user-friendly guides to health management and offered advice and personal consultations at reasonable prices. Pechey distributed free healthcare advice to the poor within his own London parish and his paid services could be obtained for less than one shilling in person, or by completing a health questionnaire by post.[18] John Archer, who claimed to be a physician to King Charles II, also aimed to teach ordinary men and women how best to care for their long-term health. He reserved special praise for moderate sleep that 'sweetly moistned' the bowels, and condemned the habits of gluttonous people who 'dig their Graves with their Teeth' by ordering their diets according to their palates rather than to principles of good health. Archer's advice could be gleaned from his popular healthcare guide *Every Man his own Doctor*, first published in 1671 and reissued in 1673 and 1678, or in person at his business premises near Charing Cross.[19] Beyond London, the Somerset physician John Allen, an extra-licentiate of the Royal College of Physicians, confirmed that 'Moderate Sleep much conduces to Health, in perfecting Digestions, and recruiting Strength'.[20] Allen's *Synopsis Universae Medicinae Practicae* (1719) blended classical precepts of healthcare with more current concerns. The work proved popular and was published in three Latin editions, with translations in English, German and French. For children and adults alike, managing the motions of the stomach held the key to a restful night's sleep. A consensus of medical opinion firmly linked healthy digestion with restful sleep and with bodily vitality into the late seventeenth century and beyond.

The link between sleep and digestion dominated advice about the optimum body posture to adopt in bed.[21] Thomas Elyot echoed the opinions of earlier physicians by advising his readers to raise their heads in bed to create a gentle downwards slope towards the stomach. This prevented the regurgitation of food during sleep, sped digestion and ensured that the sleeper rested without unnecessary interruption. This elevation was probably accomplished by stacking pillows and bolsters beneath the head and upper

back, or, as Thomas Cogan put it, by sleeping 'well bolstered up'.[22] Andrew
Boorde agreed that sleepers should 'lye with your heade som what hygh, lest
that ye meat whiche is in your stomacke thorow eructuacions or some other
cause asce[n]de to ye oryfice of the stomacke'. Those more advanced in age,
and with slower digestive systems, were especially encouraged to adopt an
upright posture to keep food at the pit of the stomach where it could be more
quickly digested. They were occasionally permitted to sleep sitting upright in
a chair, rather than in bed, to achieve this ambition.[23]

Sleepers were encouraged to alternate their posture during the night to
support the process of 'concoction' in which food was broken down and its
essential nutrients absorbed. Resting first on the right side, which was
hotter than the left, allowed food to descend more easily into the pit of the
stomach, close to the liver, where it generated heat during the initial stage of
digestion.[24] Turning onto the cooler left side of the body after a few hours
released the stomach vapours that had accumulated on the right and spread
the heat more evenly through the body. This advice was prominent in both
printed and manuscript healthcare guides and in recipe books, which were
familiar household objects that contained a combination of culinary and
medical recipes for everyday use.[25] References to sleep posture were,
however, rarely worthy of note in diaries or letters. English folk beliefs
nevertheless suggest that there was a widespread perception of a right and
a wrong way to lie in bed, and to rise from it. Rising on the right rather than
the left side of the bed was considered by some to be an unlucky omen for
the day ahead. Church of England clergyman John Gaule poured scorn on
this notion in an astrological text of 1652, deeming it folly 'to bode good or
bad luck, fortune, successe, from the rising up on the right, or left side'.[26]
Despite Gaule's objections, this familiar idiom had antecedents stretching
back to ancient Rome and the health implications of poor sleep posture
may well be the cultural root of the modern expression 'to get out of the
wrong side of bed', which is generally associated with waking up in a bad
mood. Since physicians encouraged sleepers to spend the second part of the
night on their left side, rising on the right may suggest that body and mind
had become disordered by a failure to heed this advice.

The practice of turning from right to left during sleep was recommended in most health regimens but the same was not true of lying directly
on the stomach. Thomas Cogan declared that to lie 'groveling' on the belly
was unhealthy since it impeded digestion. Cogan's choice of words also
suggests that this posture was regarded as unseemly since it may have
evoked sinful biblical imagery of the serpent in the Garden of Eden, which
was condemned by God to grovel on its belly in the dust as a punishment

for tempting Eve to eat the apple from the Tree of Knowledge.[27] The combined physical and spiritual dangers of sleeping on the belly ensured that it was firmly discouraged, except for children, and those individuals that suffered from 'feble digestion'. They were permitted to lie directly on the stomach, or better still to lay their hands, or the hands of their bedfellows, on their stomachs to increase its inward heat and speed digestion.[28] The healthcare guide *Aristotle's Secret of Secrets* deliberately invoked the wisdom of the ancient philosopher in recycling similar advice for a new reading public in 1702. Its author referred to the routine use of stomach-coverings and hot thick cloths to warm this vital body part during sleep. Night waistcoats, soft leather pillows tied around the waist, or even small dogs were sometimes used to perform the same function, whilst the judicious use of bed-warmers was recommended for easing digestion and drying excess moisture from the body.[29]

Perfecting digestion largely determined sleep posture throughout this period but the effects of poor sleep posture on other parts of the body became more pronounced in later works as they absorbed fresh knowledge of human physiology. Nicolas Andry de Bois-Regard, a French physician and pioneer of orthopaedic medicine, warned in his two-volume *Orthopaedia* (1743) that children should not be allowed to rest on high bolsters lest their bodies be made crooked at this fragile stage of life.[30] The special developmental needs of children, both physically and psychologically, were increasingly recognised from the late seventeenth century. The author of *The Art of Nursing* (1733) believed that the delicate rib-bones and weak ligaments of young children 'may give way, and bend inward, under the Weight of the whole Body' if they were laid to sleep on their sides, as was customary for adults. It was much better at this tender age for them to be laid in the cradle on their backs; this position was likened to 'the Keel of a Ship ... upon which the Child may therefore rest with Safety and Ease'.[31] Safeguarding the delicate limbs of children may have likewise informed a commonplace proverb from Somerset that condemned the practice of letting children sleep on the laps of their nursemaids.[32]

Bearing in mind this important exception, sleeping on the back was near universally condemned.[33] The objections of most medical practitioners were based on a mixture of humoral physiology and knowledge of brain function. Thomas Cogan spoke for many when he wrote that sleeping on the back drew phlegm and other toxic humours into the base of the brain where they pooled and generated nightmares, epileptic fits, or apoplexy.[34] An excess of moisture in the brain, which was the body's coldest organ, was further aggravated if the sleeper's uncovered head lay in the direct line of the moon's rays since the moon was understood to be a cold and moist planet. This was one very practical reason for the widespread use of nightcaps in bed, which moderated the brain's heat and helped to prevent it from flooding.

Sleeping on the back was also closely linked to physiological explanations of nightmares. Dreams of all varieties had three possible causes, coming either directly from God, from other supernatural agents or, more commonly, from an internal bodily imbalance. Humoral explanations of nightmares, which described them as the products of overly moist brains, were widely accepted yet many physicians were quick to distinguish ordinary nightmares from the phenomenon known as 'the Mare' – a terrifying dream that was commonly associated with a diabolical agent. They dismissed customary fears that lying on the back invited a visit from an 'incubus', which was portrayed as a type of demon that preyed on sleepers by sitting on their chests and impeding their breath, speech and movement.[35] William Bullein acknowledged that lying on the back could generate dangerous passions by disturbing the balance of the humours, but he scorned those people who tried to protect themselves from diabolical attacks by hanging conjuring charms and sacred 'relickes' around their necks when they went to bed. As a devout Protestant, Bullein was offended by the idea that objects made by human hands could perform God's work by protecting sleepers from harm. His opinions on this subject were tinged by a virulent anti-Catholicism and he insisted that a careful diet, a clean bed and a firm faith in Jesus Christ were the only effective methods of securing a good night's rest.[36] London physician Thomas Willis was slightly more circumspect on this point. He conceded that the Devil might be the cause of the pain and immobility associated with the incubus on some extraordinary occasions, but that these symptoms were much more likely to be a fantasy of the imagination produced from an overfull stomach, from imperfect respiration caused by sleeping on the back, or from an excess of fluid in the brain.[37] The Italian physician and medical writer Giovanni Borsieri de Kanifeld firmly identified the physiological origins of nightmares within the ordinary course of nature. An eighteenth-century translation of his work rejected the idea that a 'spectre, or frightful object' was somehow to blame for these disturbances. Nightmares were much more likely to result from morbid states of the brain that prevented the healthy flow of blood through that vital organ.[38] Physicians and philosophers from across Europe thus advanced natural physiological explanations of nightmares in the late seventeenth and eighteenth centuries. Chapter 3 nevertheless reveals the persistent fusion of natural and supernatural explanations of sleep, which was especially marked within the home, where a variety of rituals and protective objects (some invested with magical powers) were used to keep sleepers safe from harm.

Supernatural Sleep

There was a diverse spectrum of opinion about the natural and supernatural causes of different sleep and dream states, which could sometimes coexist and overlap. The principle that divine and diabolical agents could enter the body and govern its operations was foundational to accounts of revelatory sleep in which God revealed his will to faithful Christians, and to accounts of demonic possession and witchcraft. In John Milton's epic poem *Paradise Lost* (1667) Satan initiates the fall of humans when he plants the sinful idea of eating the forbidden apple into Eve's mind as she slumbers peacefully beside Adam in their heavenly bower.[39] Milton's poem, and this scene in particular, resonated throughout the seventeenth and eighteenth centuries and sparked a rich variety of critical commentaries and visual depictions.[40]

Reports of great sleepers who slumbered for several days or weeks at a time also found a ready audience throughout this period. These expansive sleeps were usually interpreted as communications from God or as miscellaneous curiosities that were published principally for entertainment. The former was typified by a short chapbook entitled *The true relation of two wonderfull sleepers* (1646) that related the fate of Elizabeth Jefkins, the 36-year old wife of a London clothworker. Elizabeth was possessed by a sleep so strong that she could not be roused by her husband's voice or touch, by cold water poured over her body, or by local physicians who tried to unblock her senses by letting blood from her nostrils. In spite of these efforts, Elizabeth died after sleeping continuously for over 100 hours and no explanation could be found for her fatal sleepiness in her humoral complexion, in her constitution, or in her lifestyle, which was reported to be exemplary. Her death was instead presented as a miraculous call to repentance by God, who used Elizabeth's body to show his anger at the civil wars that were devastating the British Isles at this time. The unnaturalness of these conflicts was dramatically paralleled by the unnaturalness of Elizabeth's sleep, which resulted in her premature death rather than in the nourishment and refreshment for which sleep had first been ordained.[41] Sleep was thus understood as a characteristically protean state, which exposed human beings to the will of unpredictable supernatural forces; it thus had the potential to transform human life in radically different ways.

Sleep's power to transport men and women between the earthly kingdom and a transcendent magical world of spirits was also represented in familiar literary and theatrical forms. William Shakespeare was a devotee of Ovid's poetry, at the heart of which lay the principle of metamorphosis.[42] Shakespeare's admiration for Ovid may well have kindled his fascination with sleep. He certainly recognised its dramatic potential to frame key moments of transition in his plays, and its capacity to fuse the spiritual and material dimensions of his protagonists' lives. Shakespeare's plays link sleep quality to lifestyle, temperament, and to the tumultuous passions of the soul. Yet, for those characters that overstep the accepted boundaries of natural and divine law, punishments are visited upon them in the form of dramatic sleep disturbances or total sleep deprivation, which are sometimes accompanied by supernatural agents. Shakespeare condemns the crimes of Henry Bolingbroke, who usurps the throne of his cousin King Richard II (and most likely murders him) to crown himself as King Henry IV in 1399, by depicting him in his nightgown, mourning the loss of his slumber:

> O sleep! O gentle sleep!
> Nature's soft nurse, how have I frighted thee,
> That thou no more wilt weigh my eyelids down
> And steep my senses in forgetfulness?[43]

This scene suggests that Henry's guilty conscience prevents him from sleeping, or that God, who works through Nature to impose his judgments, has ordered Henry's restlessness. The palpable distress that Henry suffers reveals the physical and psychological trauma that sleep loss could produce, however it came about.

The murderous intrigues of King Richard III are punished in similar fashion. Richard, crowned king of England in 1483, is widely suspected of having murdered his two young nephews in his scramble to seize the throne for himself. In Shakespeare's play, Margaret of Anjou, the widow of the Lancastrian King Henry VI, who has been deposed and imprisoned by the House of York, curses her husband's murderous successor thus: 'No sleep close up that deadly eye of thine, / Unless it be while some tormenting dream / Affrights thee with a hell of ugly devils!' Margaret's wish is granted when the ghosts of Richard's suspected murder victims (including her husband) visit him the night before the Battle of Bosworth Field and force him to confess his crimes. Richard's guilt is confirmed by his defeat in the decisive battle of the Wars of the Roses, marking the end of Plantagenet rule in England.[44]

That sin could be sleep's thief, whether brought on by feelings of guilt or by God's judgment, is most vividly illustrated in Shakespeare's *Macbeth*. Macbeth is deprived of sleep after stabbing King Duncan with a dagger whilst he sleeps peacefully in his bed, yet the greater punishment is reserved for Lady Macbeth who urged her husband to commit this unnatural act of regicide. A physician is called to attend Lady Macbeth and he watches her as she walks and talks in her sleep. The physician has treated sleepwalkers whose malady stemmed from bodily ailments before, but he discerns an otherworldly origin for Lady Macbeth's agitated wanderings:

Foul whisperings are abroad: unnatural deeds
Do breed unnatural troubles: infected minds
To their deaf pillows will discharge their secrets:
More needs she the divine than the physician. God, God forgive us all![45]

The powerlessness of natural medicaments to treat Lady Macbeth's sleep-walking identify its supernatural origin and reveal the monstrous corruption of her soul. These dramatic devices are effective methods of characterisation precisely because they reflect the variety of sleep's known causes, which extended from the body's inner cavities up to God in heaven. Shakespeare and his contemporaries Philip Marlowe, Philip Sidney and Edmund Spenser understood only too well the negative moral implications associated with disturbed sleep, which they exploited to considerable dramatic effect.[46]

These examples of extreme sleepiness or sleeplessness were nevertheless atypical, and their dramatic power relied on the fact that they lay outside the ordinary course of daily life. Whilst a handful of people may have yearned to experience revelatory sleep and dreams as a sign of divine favour, most wished to avoid such dramatic episodes and simply desired the kind of restorative slumber that was God-given and that was partly within their own power to procure by careful attendance to their bodily habits and Christian duties. Divine and supernatural explanations for disturbed sleep certainly persisted into the eighteenth century but medical practitioners continued to favour natural explanations for intermittent periods of wakefulness unless some extraordinary circumstance suggested that the cause lay elsewhere.

Sleep, Brain and Nerves

Sleep's purpose and internal causes remained closely linked to the stomach throughout this period but the operations of the brain and nervous system became increasingly prominent in explanations of sleep's bodily origins from the 1660s. Health regimens and books of household medical recipes began to link sleep's healthy practice more strongly with the vitality of the brain and nerves, which became just as important as sleep's ability to perfect digestion. The influence that peaceful sleep played in soothing the mind and passions had long been noted in non-natural health regimens. The role that healthy sleep was believed to play in sharpening the intellectual faculties and soothing the nerves nonetheless became the main preoccupation of medical practitioners and the men and women who they advised. John Archer encouraged the readers of his accessible healthcare guide to carefully moderate their sleeping hours both as an aid to digestion and to ensure that 'the mind enjoys more tranquility'.[47] Similar emphases emerged in the health regimens of late Renaissance Italy where the head began to be prioritised alongside the stomach in medical advice about sleep as physicians increasingly stressed the brain's importance as the site of memory, sensation and motion.[48] In mid-eighteenth century England the health of the brain and nerves dominated the agendas of medical practitioners and wider society. Church of England clergyman John Trusler took an avid interest in neurological medicine during his studies at the University of Leiden, and he produced a self-help guide for the use of his London parishioners. In it, Trusler likened the powers of the mind to a watery current whose force weakened over the course of the day but whose potency was restored by sleep, which enlivened the brain and nerves with a flood of invigorating liquid.[49] Trusler's analogy was repeated many times and in many different forms, with sleep's virtues revered as an essential restorative to the faculties of judgement and imagination. Sleep and its associated disorders had become topics of intense interest as the balance of sleep-advice slowly shifted from the stomach to the brain.

The prioritisation of the brain and nerves in sleep regimens owed a substantial debt to the anatomical investigations of Dr Thomas Willis, whose work transformed understandings of sleep's operations within the body. Willis was a fellow of the Royal Society of London and in 1660 he was appointed Sedleian professor of natural philosophy at Oxford. Willis identified the motions of the brain and nerves as the key to all bodily operations, including sleep, and he coined the term 'neurologie' to explain how they interacted. His most influential text, Cerebri anatome or The Anatomy of the Brain and Nerves, was first published in 1664, and by 1681 it had been translated from Latin and published in English for the first time.[50] Thomas Willis aimed to 'unlock the secret places of Mans Mind' and he elevated the primacy of the brain and nerves in regulating sleep above all other bodily organs.[51]

One of Willis's most important achievements was to map the blood's circulatory paths by injecting coloured ink into a network of arterial veins at the base of the brain, now known as the 'Circle of Willis'.[52] He observed continuous blood flow between the brain and body and thereby was able to identify the specific parts of the brain that controlled sleeping and waking patterns, alongside its other principal functions. Thomas Willis situated the nerves that controlled sleep in the cerebellum at the back of the brain between the cerebrum and the medulla oblongata. Sleep occurred when the animal spirits that enervated the body were drawn away from their activities in the external parts of the brain and came to rest in the medulla oblongata.[53] The blood flowing through the arterial network and into the medulla oblongata refreshed the animal spirits. Once this restorative process was complete, the spirits could once again move to the external parts of the brain and nerves and wake the body from slumber. As well as describing how healthy sleep operated within brain and body, Thomas Willis also classified and described the pathologies of individual sleep disorders in close detail. Unnatural sleep states and interim states of consciousness had attracted some interest from medieval physicians and philosophers, but in Thomas Willis's hands they gained full independent status.[54] He explained that the imperfect sleep states of Lethargy, Coma and Carus all resulted from extreme pressure on the medullary nerves. Mild sleep disorders resulted from pressure on the peripheral parts of the brain but more serious conditions could penetrate into its core. If left untreated they could reach the cerebellum and destroy all sense and motion. Disorderly sleep was thus a symptom and a potential cause of a disordered brain and nervous system.

In his explorations of brain function, Thomas Willis identified a second corporeal or 'brutish' soul in addition to the superior rational soul, which had further consequences for understandings of sleep. Willis declared that the brain was 'the chief seat of the Rational Soul in a man' as well as the 'chief mover in the animal Machine'.[55] He distinguished between these two roles in his *De Anima Brutorum* (1672), which was translated and published by Samuel Pordage as *Two Discourses Concerning the Soul of Brutes* in 1684. The text described the existence and functions of this second soul in intricate detail. The corporeal soul was active alongside the superior rational and immaterial soul but their spheres of action were very different. The rational immaterial soul was always conscious, but the brutish soul that regulated the nerves was not, and so a range of bodily states, including sleep, could disturb it. In explaining the functions of the brutish soul, Willis drew a direct connection between the motions and disorders of the body and the health of the brain and nerves. This model of brain function exposed the vulnerabilities of the intellectual faculties and at the same time heightened the value of their natural guardian: peaceful sleep.

Thomas Willis's conclusions circulated widely in print. *Cerebri anatome* ran to nine editions in the British Isles and extracts from the text were included in medical compendia across Western Europe. Willis's anatomical research likewise informed his lucrative clinical practices in Oxford and London and the lectures that he delivered to medical students at Oxford, which influenced the young student and budding philosopher John Locke. The principles raised by Willis's work prompted a series of responses from physicians that showed the growing acceptance of sleep's neurological foundations. Dutch physician and botanist Herman Boerhaave combined a keen interest in botany, anatomy and the relationship between mind and body. He observed that healthy sleep depended on the 'Presence of the Spirits that are good and plentiful, in the Brain, its *Medulla*, Nerves and Muscles'.[56] The necessary conditions to procure sound sleep consisted of 'the Quiet of a contented Mind' and an absence of external stimuli. Boerhaave's conception of human physiology was notably different from that of Thomas Willis, but both men identified the brain and nerves as the primary seat of sleeping and waking. They encouraged physicians and patients to procure sound rest to strengthen the nerves and thereby preserve sharp judgement. Both men recognised the pernicious effects of immoderate sleep for the health of individual minds and, more importantly, for the health of the social organism.

Physician and chemist William Cullen was the chief proponent of neurological medicine in mid-eighteenth century Britain. Cullen was a leading light in Scotland's medical enlightenment, a fellow of the Royal College of Physicians, and a fellow of the Royal Societies of London and Edinburgh. He worked for a London apothecary in the early 1730s before returning to Scotland, where he studied medicine and later became professor of chemistry, professor of the institutes of medicine, and professor of the practice of physic at the University of Edinburgh. Cullen saw an important link between the theory and practice of medicine. He applied his physiological and botanical experiments to his lucrative private clinical practice, much of which was conducted by the exchange of letters with his patients who came from all corners of the globe.

In Cullen's influential volume on medical theory the *Institutions of Medicine*, he explained that the nervous system corresponded to 'the medullary substance of the brain, cerebellum, medulla oblongata, and spinalis', which mapped onto the physiological locus of sleep identified by Thomas Willis.[57] Cullen placed the nervous system at the centre of his physiological enquiries because it was pivotal to the functions of body and mind. He played a leading role in reinforcing medical understandings of the relationship between sleep, brain and nerves.[58] Cullen made no reference to digestion when he explained the causes of sleeping and waking to his students and instead gave primacy to the brain. He described natural sleep as a 'partial collapse' of brain activity and he identified the motion of the nervous fluid within the brain as the root cause of sleeping and waking. This motion fluctuated according to the composition of the nerves, the passions, and the role of external stimuli such as temperature, noise and degrees of excitability. All of these factors varied subtly according to age, status, gender, intellect and environment.[59]

Cullen included sleep and its associated disorders within the class of diseases that he defined as 'Neuroses'. The ailments included here were distinguished by the impairment of sense and motion. Subcategories of disease that admitted some form of sleep disturbance or drowsiness included 'Comata', 'Apoplexia', 'Carus', 'Catalepsis', 'Lethargus', 'Paralysis' and 'Oneirodynia': all of which involved the suspension of voluntary sense and motion. Cullen concluded that the head was most directly affected by these conditions and he described how overstretched brain fibres caused 'Agrypnia', the symptoms of which included long periods of sleeplessness.[60] Cullen cited the work of German physician Hieronymus David Gaubius and of Giambattista Borsieri de Kanifeld to support his conclusions. Borsieri de Kanifeld's work, which Cullen translated into English, argued that 'the extreme delicacy of the nervous medulla', which was the seat of sleep-related nerves, was liable to frequent disturbance. If these nerves lost tension the hurtful consequences that ensued included 'dulness of the external and internal senses, imbecility, confusion of ideas, disturbed sleep, watching, a morbid imagination' and even 'delirium'. In these circumstances vital powers of reasoning were thus likely 'to become deranged before the proper period'.[61]

Cullen believed that the ordinary powers of human perception were similarly constrained by disorderly sleep. Patients suffering from sleepwalking, or 'somnambulism', were subject to sensory deprivation, usually of sight, even though some remained capable of performing familiar waking activities. He discerned different degrees of somnambulism: 'common', 'furious' and 'complicated', which were distinguished by the degree to which the mind was agitated. Cullen believed that they might be caused by external stimuli such as excess food or wine, by too many bedclothes, by incorrect sleep posture, or by extreme mental exertion. Brain disorders also featured strongly in his list of potential causes.[62] William Cullen thus gave sleep and its disorders prominent positions within his systematic neuropathology of body and mind. The local origins of sleep in the brain were prioritised alongside in-depth knowledge of the structure, symptoms and effects of sleep's malfunctions. Cullen's publications and teaching provided a spur to further medical and philosophical enquiries into different states of consciousness and his work established a platform for broader speculations about the relationship between sleeping patterns and personal identity, which is explored in Chapter 6.

Neurological understandings of sleep circulated widely in print and networks of correspondence, which extended the importance of healthy sleep beyond a narrow medical elite. The work of Scottish physician George Cheyne was among the most significant contributions to the corpus of texts that classified sleep as a neurological condition. His popular healthcare books applied neurological understandings of the body to the lifestyles of the patients that he tended in the fashionable spa resort of Bath.[63] Cheyne's advice on sleep drew on principles of Newtonian physics and on the research of medical schools across eighteenth-century Europe that formulated new categories of nervous disease and related psychological conditions from the 1730s.[64] The schools at Leiden and Edinburgh fleshed out the parameters of the mind–body relationship and this became a central theme in Cheyne's *Essay on Regimen* (1740) and his *Natural Method of Cureing the Diseases of the Body, and Those of the Mind Depending on the Body* (1742). The non-naturals formed the organising principle of Cheyne's *Essay of Health and Long Life* (1724), which reached its seventh edition within the first year of publication. This preventative healthcare advice was given new impetus by its integration with nerve-centred medicine. The *Essay*'s third chapter explicitly addressed 'Sleeping and Watching'. Cheyne reaffirmed the familiar principle that regular and peaceful sleep was crucial for digestion and for nourishing the blood but he added to this by praising its ability 'to restore the weakned *Tone* of *nervous Fibres*'.[65] Cheyne also instructed his readers that it was both a Christian duty and a civic responsibility to sleep well to secure bodies and souls for purposeful action in the world.

Cheyne's role in framing the social aesthetics of nervous sensibility has been well established in studies of gout, consumption and melancholy. Sleep and its associated disorders have, however, been overlooked. Cheyne aligned the causes of troublesome sleep with an excess of nervous sensibility, which he famously defined as the 'English Malady' in his 1733 treatise of the same name.[66] This label encompassed several debilitating illnesses that were framed as signifiers of a prosperous and civilised individual.

Cheyne identified wealthy and intelligent men and women as the principal sufferers of these disorders whose worldly success, luxurious lifestyles and late-night studies made their nerves particularly sensitive to disturbance. Neurological understandings of sleep could thus enhance the status of those who suffered from sleep disturbances – a paradox that is more fully explored in Chapter 6. Cheyne's advice is significant, however, for fusing nerve-centred understandings of sleep with well-established emphases on digestion and for facilitating wider social engagement with neurological concepts of sleep. George Cheyne's interest in sleep's nervous origins and effects was widely echoed. They seeped into widely circulating handbooks of household physic and educational treatises that underlined the value of well-regulated sleep for maintaining the mind's vigour. Hugh Smythson's *Compleat Family Physician*, which claimed to offer 'A Compleat Body of Domestick Medicine' for family use, warned that too little sleep dulled the mind's faculties, whilst too much sleep could 'affect the mind with heaviness, want of apprehension, and inactivity: and weak nerves'.[67] Smythson claimed that he had been educated at Leiden and he seemed only too aware of the role that sleep played in maintaining the vitality of the nerves and thus the mind's faculties. Smythson's work, which was first issued in 1781 and reprinted in 1785, revealed the extent to which neurological explanations of sleep had diffused beyond a narrow band of anatomists and physicians to shape bodily knowledge in the wider medical marketplace and in the household, which was the principal hub of sleep's daily management.

Getting a good night's sleep was vital for the continued existence of all human life. This truism was a law of God and Nature that was confirmed by the wisdom of the ancient world, by Holy Scripture and by daily experience. The importance of healthy sleeping patterns was unquestioned throughout the early modern period; they were strongly linked to longevity and they were held to determine people's quality of life since they strengthened the body, soothed its passions, and supported the performance of Christian duties. The essential human need for sleep was unequivocal, yet physiological explanations of how sleep worked within the body, and what effect it had on mind, body and soul, were widely debated. The decades after 1660 saw a transformation of bodily knowledge about sleeping and waking patterns, which became more intimately linked to the health and vitality of the brain and nerves than ever before. Peaceful sleep remained critical for maintaining the body's strength, for restoring its levels of heat and moisture, and for supporting digestion on a daily basis. These essential functions nevertheless began to be upstaged by sleep's role as the principal guardian of rational, productive minds that relied on well-balanced nerves. The neurophysiology of sleep was made visible by the anatomical investigations and illustrated publications of Dr Thomas Willis, by the acclaimed classifications of nervous diseases by Dr William Cullen, and by the publications of 'nerve doctor' George Cheyne and other authors of self-help medical guides in the late seventeenth and eighteenth centuries. These texts popularised sleep's neurological foundations for a wide and curious range of audiences that extended from the fashionable spa resort of Bath to more modest households where health preservation was a central concern. Growing awareness of sleep's unique role in securing physical and mental health intensified the degree of time and attention that was focused on its daily practice, and it expanded the range of preventative measures and medicaments that were devised and used in pursuit of a good night's sleep. The following chapter traces these changes, yet it also shows that emerging neurological explanations of sleep did not completely undercut tried and tested ways of inviting slumber within many households, nor did it destabilise the overarching Christian framework within which healthy patterns of sleeping and waking made sense to early modern men and women. Sleep quality was understood as a product of God's will and of the motions of the natural world that He created, yet ordinary men and women were increasingly judged to have the means and the knowledge to harness nature's power to regulate their sleeping habits, to control their sleeping environments, and to preserve the health of their minds, bodies and souls.

CHAPTER 2

Healthy Sleep and the Household

IN 1608 GERVASE Markham, a Nottinghamshire poet, playwright and author of popular advice books, revered quiet sleep as 'the nourisher of life' in his historical comedy *The Dumbe Knight*. The Knight in question is Philocles, chief aide to the king of Cyprus, who cannot sleep because of his love for the Sicilian noblewoman Mariana. Philocles' longing for Mariana inflames his passions and his blood, and deprives him of the 'soft repose' that he describes as 'the juice of happinesse'. Sleep loss was a romanticised and useful dramatic device in Gervase Markham's play, yet in daily life it was a threat to the health of mind, body and soul that had to be avoided at all costs. Fifteen years after his play was first published, Markham laid down some practical advice about how to procure this treasured state of refreshment in his guide to household management, *Countrey Contentments, or The English Husvvife* (1623), which was revised and republished in different forms into the 1680s.[1] Recipes for securing peaceful sleep were noteworthy features within Markham's work and in comparable guides to household economy and health management that poured from English printing presses in the late seventeenth and eighteenth centuries. These texts, which varied in size, price and format, collectively affirmed that restful sleep was a gift of both God and Nature that was essential to the health and longevity of human life, to the health of individual households and increasingly to the health of civil society. The motivation to marshal sleep's boundaries stemmed from these objectives, from a powerful Christian impulse to live temperately and from first-hand experience of sleep's power to restore the vitality of mind and body.

An active culture of sleep management governed the rhythms of daily life. Healthy sleep was managed at home by the moderation of bedtimes and sleeping hours, by vigorous cleansing of bedsteads, bedding textiles and sleeping environments, and by the preparation of medicaments to prevent and to treat sleep loss.[2] All of these habits were shaped by non-natural principles of healthcare and by neurological understandings of sleep that were traced in the previous chapter. They reveal the care with which men and women attended to their sleeping lives and how they blended healthcare principles with their spiritual and domestic priorities on a day-to-day basis. These practices show that natural and supernatural methods of securing peaceful sleep were often used interchangeably within the home and that there was a pragmatic fusion of trusted homemade sleep-advice with new methods and medicaments that became widely available in the medical marketplace. Safeguarding sleep's daily practice, and its material environments, was prioritised as a key strategy in long-term health preservation. This pragmatic goal lay at the heart of a subtly shifting set of household sleeping practices that were gradually reshaped by new physiological explanations of sleep and by strong encouragement for individuals to take control of their sleeping lives for the benefit of their personal health and that of the social organism.

Healthy Sleeping Environments

Diaries, letters and guides to household management and physic reveal that sleeping well depended heavily on securing the right location, arrangement, content, cleanliness and sensory familiarity of sleeping environments. Bed furnishings and other sleep-related goods were selected and purchased to suit individual tastes but also in the hope of securing peaceful slumber, which was essential for health and happiness. The virtues of clean, airy and comfortable sleeping environments were increasingly prized in the late seventeenth and eighteenth centuries as the material guardians of restful sleep, as was the control of external stimuli that might distract or overexcite men, women and children at bedtime. The sensitive minds and nerves of sleep-hopeful bodies were judged especially vulnerable to overstimulation, disease and other potential dangers at bedtime and they thus had to be carefully managed. Exhaustive efforts to exert control over sleep's practice mark out its special status within the home. No other daily activity was so heavily governed by principles of good health, nor consumed as much time, money and labour as did sleep.[3] The bedstead, its textiles and its immediate surroundings thus represented the frontline in the battle to secure a peaceful night's rest.

There was consensus amongst medical practitioners and ordinary householders that a cool and fresh environment was essential for inducing sleep, and for ensuring its healthy progress during the night. Sleep was understood in physiological terms as a process in which the body's extremities were cooled as its heat was drawn inwards to the body's core organs. A cool sleeping environment was thus a natural support to sleep's onset. Ensuring access to fresh air was also the first healthcare principle of non-natural medicine and it was particularly important during sleep because it strengthened the body's internal organs, and regulated its inner heat and humours, which stopped the body from overheating and waking prematurely. Fresh air was equally prominent in neurological healthcare advice because it helped to subdue the sensibility of the body's nerves and to maintain the vital tension of the muscles, joints and nerves that kept bodies and brains in good order. Ayrshire physician James Makittrick Adair trained at the University of Edinburgh, where he may well have been influenced by the teaching of William Cullen, who was professor of chemistry and delivered clinical lectures at the Edinburgh Royal Infirmary. Adair became a keen advocate of neurological healthcare practices when he established his own clinical practices in Andover, Guildford and Bath. Adair echoed William Cullen's belief that healthy sleep was essential for regulating the nerves. To give a practical illustration of this truism, Adair published the testimonial of one of his patients, Mr Lucas, who regularly stayed at the York Hotel in Bath to restore his health. Mr Lucas believed that the nervous symptoms under which he had laboured for many years were only relieved when he began to ventilate his sleeping chamber. Another of Adair's correspondents, whom he described as 'an eminent physician', confirmed the wisdom of Lucas's advice:

> having for many years been occasionally subject to palpitations of the heart, shortness of breathing, great anxiety and depression of spirits, universal tremor, and other symptoms of the kind, usually called nervous; after trial of many medicines of the antispasmodic kind, I found nothing so effectual as a strict attention to preserving a due temperature of body during the night, at which time the above symptoms were most apt to recur. In order to preserve this temperature, I found it necessary to use only a moderately thin quilt in the summer, with an addition of a moderately warm blanket in the winter, and no fire in the room; one window of which was kept open all night in the summer, and the whole of the day in cold weather. This regimen produced sound and refreshing sleep . . .[4]

This testimonial advertised Adair's medical services to potential customers but it also revealed how the careful management of sleeping chambers was believed to secure perfect and unbroken sleep. Securing fresh and cool air was vital in achieving this ideal.

A constant flow of fresh air had the power to protect the body's internal functions but it was also essential for purifying sleeping environments, which presented countless health hazards. The toxic air associated with urban areas and other air pollutants such as flowers and vegetation presented particular challenges. The botanical experiments of Dutch physician Jan Ingen-Housz, who studied at the University of Leiden and tended to members of the Habsburg royal family, offered a practical demonstration of how the night air became poisonous. He undertook many of his experiments in England, which were published in the *Philosophical Transactions of the Royal Society*, and he was elected a fellow of the Royal Society of London in 1769. The respiratory motions of sleepers' lungs presented the most serious threat to health. Heightened sensitivity to the dangers of night-time pollution transformed sleeping environments into sites of technological experimentation. Yorkshire-born physician William Alexander studied medicine under the nerve-doctor William Cullen in Edinburgh, and he used this education to explain that air 'loses its spring, by want of circulation, but likeways by being repeatedly taken into, and thrown out of the lungs; for every time it is so taken in and thrown out again, it loses something of that principle which renders it necessary to animal life'. Alexander recommended an experiment for those who wished to test this conclusion at first-hand:

> ... by taking a large bladder full of air, and breathing backwards and forwards into it, through a small pipe, when he will find, that, after he has breathed the air a few times over, it will neither fill up the bladder nor his own lungs; so that he must be absolutely suffocated, if he does not soon breathe fresh air from another source. One single person sleeping in a small room breathes the whole air in it more than once over in a night; hence it is less pure than air that has not been breathed; and hence a person coming from the fresh air, into a bed-room in the morning, is sensible that the air in the bed-room is disagreeable. If two or more sleep in the same room, it becomes thereby still more unwholesome; and this unwholesomeness increases every night, if the room is not well ventilated and cleared of its bad air through the day ...[5]

Scottish baronet Sir John Sinclair similarly declared that nothing was more important to preserve good health 'than the admission of a free circulation of air into their bed-chambers'.[6] Sinclair was far from alone in voicing his concern about the effects of polluted air in homes and public institutions. The dangers of 'miasma' – a term used to describe the putrid vapours emitted by bodies and other organic matter, pervaded the writings of eighteenth-century medical practitioners who proclaimed that fresh air during sleep was essential.[7] James Makittrick Adair was a prominent voice in this chorus and he declared in his *Essay on fashionable diseases* that 'the admission of cold air into bed-chambers is of use in preserving health, cannot be doubted . . . for if foul air weakens and destroys the springs of life, pure air must necessarily support and invigorate them'.[8] Adair's medical works circulated widely in Britain and continental Europe and in them he used the investigations of natural philosophers Joseph Priestley and Stephen Hales to reveal the damaging effects that bodily effluvia could have on sleep quality, and consequently upon health. Adair praised a ventilator invented by Hales that was specially designed to filter fresh air into confined spaces. Adair was convinced that this kind of device could help sleepers to rest in the kind of pure 'dephlogisticated' air that Joseph Priestley had produced in his chemical experiments. Accessing this refined air was crucial if sleepers were to avoid being distempered by the concentration of foul stale breath that they exhaled in the night and that depleted the energy of their nervous systems.[9] Stephen Hales's ventilator was composed of small moveable wheels that could be attached to windowpanes and set in motion by the pressure of external airflow. He described his invention in his lengthy treatise, *A Description of Ventilators* (1743), which he dedicated to the Royal Society of London. The ventilator was initially designed to be installed in naval ships, but it was soon being recommended for domestic use.[10] A letter of 1750 from politician, historian and novelist Horace Walpole to his friend the diplomat Sir Horace Mann suggests that this kind of technology may have caught on in some wealthy households. Walpole told Mann that 'I was lately told by a person who saw it, that Bolinbroke and his wife used to have two silver tubes stand by their bedside, which they took in when they had any bad air to convey out: I have heard the Duchess of Shrewsbury had such an one. I tell you this, because I love the history of refinements'.[11] Horace Walpole may have considered such equipment a 'refinement', yet its central purpose in surrounding sleepers with fresh air was widely shared and it was increasingly framed as a necessity that was essential to secure individual and social health.

Access to fresh air during sleep could be achieved by simpler and more accessible means than the purchase of a silver ventilator. Purer air was associated with height, which shaped advice about the optimum location of bedsteads within the household, and the location of homes within the physical landscape. Bedsteads located on the upper floors of homes had access to cleaner air that was free of the hurtful dampness of ground-floor chambers. The advice of health regimens on this point again varied according to age, gender and complexion. Those with hot and dry complexions were advised to sleep in cooler chambers at the foot of the house, whilst those with cold and wet complexions would benefit from the warmer air of the upper floors. Chapter 4 shows that opportunities to sleep upstairs grew significantly across the early modern period. Space constraints and differences of wealth and status also played a role in determining sleep's locations, but a preference for resting on the upper floors of households remained commonplace. In his healthcare guide *A treatise on diet, or the management of human life*, physician Francis de Valangin complained that London's inhabitants were 'very careless about the Places or Rooms they sleep in; many Houses having Beds, from the Cellars to the Garrets, upon every Floor'.[12] Valangin recommended instead the practices of the ancients who slept in cool, dark chambers to invite restful slumber. For those that could afford it, care could also be taken to acquire a house on higher ground, away from damp marshy areas, and to locate sleeping chambers in an easterly direction so that the morning sunshine could filter quickly into the room and dispel the poisonous night air.

The need to secure fresh and temperate air during sleep similarly shaped advice about the healthiest position of bedsteads within sleeping chambers. Secluding oneself in a curtained alcove bed enclosed by thick and heavy curtains was no longer an approved ideal.[13] This arrangement afforded warmth, partial enclosure and protection from the draughts of windows and doorways, but it also impeded the free circulation of air during the night. Thomas Tryon, a London merchant and pioneering campaigner for vegetarianism, fostered an interest in health and well-being throughout his early apprenticeship as a hatter, but became a prolific author of popular lifestyle guides at the age of 48. In *A treatise of cleanness* (1682) Tryon expressed his firm belief that bedsteads were ideally placed 'in the most Airie Places of your Rooms' rather than in dark, damp corners.[14] John Trusler agreed that sleeping in a 'high room, dry, sweet and well-aired' was the most wholesome arrangement.[15] Bedsteads that stood in confined chambers with low ceilings could nevertheless be made more 'healthful' by minimising the use of drapery. Household recipes show that a fresh climate could also be achieved by sprinkling cooling plants and herbs like lettuce, purslane, willow leaves and water lilies between the bedstead and the chamber walls.[16]

Opinions about the ideal position of bedsteads began to change as mechanical models of the body gained traction in the eighteenth century.

The anonymous author of *The Art of Nursing* sought chiefly to prevent physical deformities in children, rather than humoral imbalance, by recommending that their cradles were 'turn'd directly to that Side of the Room from whence the Light comes; or else he will be in Danger of learning to squint . . . if the Light does not come to the Child in a strait Line, he will turn on both Sides to enjoy it; and this frequent Contortion of his Eyes, will at length grow into a Habit; so that if he accustoms himself to turn his Eyes always on one Side, he will be sure to squint; but if he turns them sometimes on one Side and sometimes on the other, he will contract a Manner of perpetually winking and twinkling with them'. These dangers could be offset by the commonplace practice of making 'a great Arch or Arcade of Twigs on the Top of the Cradle' from which a curtain could be suspended to protect the infant's eyes from direct light and their bodies from cold drafts. The curtain, which should ideally be made of a light, breathable textile such as dimity or muslin to produce 'an air of comfort and cleanliness', had the added benefit of shielding the child's eyes from objects that might distract them from sleep.[17] The physical and emotional development of children was thus uppermost in the minds of medical writers and philosophers who issued such advice and who advised parents and carers never to leave children surrounded by darkness for longer than was necessary in case irrational fears took hold of them.[18]

The easiest way to access fresh air at night was simply to open windows and doors. Judicious use could likewise be made of window shutters and curtains. Opening the window of a room adjacent to the bedchamber offered a solution for those who preferred not to sleep in a direct draught, or who had no window to open in their own chamber. James Makittrick Adair nevertheless warned that curtains should still be partially drawn to stop cold air blowing directly onto the sleeper.[19] He also drew on the botanical work of Jan Ingen-Housz to warn people not to keep fresh flowers near the bedside, which polluted the night air. This was a notable change from earlier health regimens that encouraged the liberal use of flowers and herbs to sweeten the air and linen of sleeping chambers. The popular household book of translator and poet John Partridge instructed householders to gather red roses in the summer, dry them and lay them on the bed to scent the linen. Natural philosopher Robert Boyle, who was renowned for his experiments with the healthful properties of air, noted the powerful sensory effects of rose-scented sleeping chambers in the summer months.[20] When the leaves turned moist in winter the flowers could then be dried and used to fill pillowcases or to be placed on the bed 'betweene the coverlet & the blanket at night'. The soporific qualities of roses were enhanced by their pleasant fragrance and household recipes for rose-based perfumes were widely recommended for making sleeping chambers 'sweet, and wholsome'.[21] There was then an unresolved tension between the habitual use of flowers and other foliage to sweeten the air of sleeping chambers, which may have hastened relaxation, and the damaging consequences that they might have on sleep quality. Opinions differed on how cool and clean air could be achieved at bedtime, and how it affected sleeping bodies, but medical practitioners and householders all agreed on its health-giving qualities.

The desire to rest in a cool and fresh environment at night was closely linked to the regulation of heat during sleep, which disordered the body's humours and its nerves. Overheated sleeping chambers were just as effective in spreading disease as those that lacked fresh air. Householders might avoid this by ensuring the free egress of air and by the sparing use of fires in their sleeping chambers, which burned wood or coal. This recommendation marked an important shift in attitudes towards sleep practice. Sixteenth-century health regimens praised the use of fires in bedchambers for purifying noxious vapours yet by the eighteenth century these benefits were offset by a firm conviction that fires, and other sources of intense heat, increased the corruption of the night air and destroyed the body's nervous tension. Lying too long in warm bedsheets was termed 'soaking' by Methodist leader John Wesley, who encouraged health preservation amongst his followers as an essential facet of Christian duty. Wesley claimed that textiles that generated excessive heat 'parboiled' the flesh and made both body and mind 'soft and flabby'. The resulting loss of nervous tension opened the door to a host of ailments including 'faintness, tremors' and 'lowness of spirits'.[22] Wesley's sermons and accessible devotional guides offered practical advice about how to prevent such dangers, which threatened health and hampered the effective practice of Christian devotions.

Like John Wesley, the healthcare advice of Thomas Tryon blended seamlessly with his religious faith. Tryon's Reformed Protestant beliefs had been shaped over many years by close contact with Baptists, Quakers and mystics, who all believed that the body's careful governance was essential for long-term spiritual health. The damaging effects of excessive heat were many and varied for Tryon, who blended an appreciation of non-natural medical wisdom with mechanistic models of bodily health. Tryon tailored his advice for the practicalities of daily life where attention had to be given not only to the flow of air but also to the kinds of textiles and materials used for sleeping in. He was convinced that 'hot soft Feather-Beds', in which bodies sumptuously sank, sucked natural strength from the organs, disordered the nerves and opened the pores of the skin so wide that the sweaty vapours that the body gave off during sleep were given free access to disturb its delicate inner humours. If that weren't bad enough, Tryon noted that feather beds often retained the excrement of the birds with whose feathers they had been stuffed. The feelings and sensations that these materials could excite might also encourage excessive sexual activity between bedfellows who sacrificed some of their sleeping hours in pursuit of pleasure. These fleeting moments of delight had damaging long-term consequences, however, leading to weak limbs, joints and to 'poor low effeminate Spirits'.[23] Physician and philosopher John Locke turned his attention to babies and young children but he expressed similar anxieties about overheated sleeping environments. Beds stuffed with expensive down and feathers might be coveted as a sign of luxury, but they threatened to melt the bodies of weak young infants in an excess of heat. Cheaper fillings of chaff or horsehair were cooler and more absorbent, which was particularly useful for children who were prone to bed-wetting.[24] Parents and nursemaids could also protect their young charges by sleeping, wherever possible, in a separate bed from the infant as early as was practicable. Very 'happy effects' might be produced if children were laid to sleep in small beds of their own as soon as they had been weaned. The child's body temperature could then become self-regulating at an early age and this precaution also reduced the risk that he or she might be accidentally smothered during the night by their bedfellow.[25]

Healthy sleeping environments had become a matter of intense concern that was by no means limited to the commercial world of medical goods and practice. In 1777 the journal known as *The Annual Register*, which surveyed the year's most important events, inventions and trends, documented the latest solutions for moderating room temperature whilst retaining a healthy flow of clean air.[26] James Makittrick Adair was again foremost amongst those physicians who complained about the over-use of fires, which made sleeping chambers 'almost intolerable'.[27] Thomas Tryon claimed that the 'fulsome Steams and thick Vapours' produced by fires would 'much disorder' anyone that lay in them for more than a few hours.[28] Similar objections were raised about the use of coal-filled bed-warmers that were frequently listed in the PCC household inventories. In the battle to keep out the cold, Adair instead recommended the use of 'hot sand, or jars filled with hot water' that warmed the bed without emitting any fumes.[29] This was a significant change from earlier medical advice that recommended the judicious use of bed-warmers as an aid to digestion. In an ideal world, sleepers should eschew all artificial sources of heat and aspire instead to the austere habits of Wiltshire gentleman Sir John Astley, who reputedly slept in a bed without curtains, and in a bedchamber without a fire, during his eighty-year-long life – even in the harshest of winters.[30]

The extent to which this kind of advice shaped daily practice probably varied according to the attitude and means of individual householders, and in line with seasonal weather conditions. Fireplaces and fire-tending equipment were present in nearly all the principal sleeping chambers listed in the PCC inventory sample, and in many of the subsidiary sleeping chambers. These sources do not of course reveal when or how often fires were lit, but it seems likely that a careful balance was struck between achieving a comfortable degree of warmth and clean, breathable air at bedtime. Reverend James Woodforde was a confirmed bachelor and a Church of England clergyman from Weston Longville in Norfolk who kept a detailed diary of his daily activities for over forty years. Woodforde was very protective of his own sleep quality and he kept a record of thermometer readings in his bedchamber because he was anxious to ensure a free circulation of cool air during the night.[31] He noted down those occasions when the cold winter months forced him to use bed-warmers, to light a fire, or to close the chamber windows due to the freezing temperatures that prevented him from sleeping.[32] This kind of close confinement proved especially unpleasant because his rest was still disturbed by the 'intolerable smoke and stink', which the night candles in his chamber threw off.[33] Woodforde's household candles were probably made from cheap yellow tallow, rather than from more expensive wax. Tallow candles were often prepared from the cast-off fat of sheep or cows, which was extremely smelly when burned.[34] A surviving household recipe for 'special good rose vinegar' suggests that James Woodforde's anxieties about the dangers of excessive heat may not have been uncommon. If a fire had to be made then this vinegar could be sprinkled on the green wooden boughs that were set alight to temper the hot air and to emit 'a cool and fresh s[c]ent, all over the chamber'.[35] Moderating body temperature and sleeping in clean, fresh air may well have become ordinary expectations by the mid-eighteenth century precisely because they offered a vital means of securing the health of body and mind.

Bedding textiles that moderated airflow and body temperature, and which looked and felt healthy, were prized possessions within early modern homes. Clergyman William Cole was one of many householders who valued the bright, neat and clean appearance of his bedding textiles. When Cole moved to a new home and a new parish in Waterbeach near Cambridge, he replaced the forty-year old 'gloomy blackish Bed' that his predecessor, Bishop Benson, had left behind. Cole may well have wished to offset the melancholy feeling that the dark bed produced to lift his mood at bedtime, but he was certain that its removal would also secure his health because the bishop's bed was 'Moth eaten, full of Holes and dirty'. In its place, he merrily described the installation of 'an almost new Blew & White Cotton Bed which I had at College, new made about 2 years before I left it'.[36] Cole was eager to stamp his personal mark on his new home and to safeguard his sleep by introducing cheerful, fresh and familiar bedding to his place of rest and regeneration.

Cole's investment of time and money mirrored a more widespread growth in the ownership of light and breathable bedsheets. The PCC inventories show a notable increase in the number of bedsheets possessed by householders between 1660 and 1760, which also diversified in textile range and quality.[37] Increased volume allowed more regular cleaning and changing of sheets. In these years, ideals of cleanliness applied equally to physical bodies and to the textiles that enclosed them at night. The purchase of breathable and easily laundered textiles for use next to the skin, usually made from linen, and less often from cotton, may well have been guided by a deep-seated desire to safeguard the body's internal operations and to secure its outer borders during sleep. White cotton counterpanes and quilts like those manufactured in Bolton, Lancashire, from the mid-eighteenth century were notable exceptions to a general preference for linen bedsheets, yet they shared a common trait with linen since both materials looked and felt healthy.[38] Cheap, colourful and readily available cottons were remarkably popular in the market for fashionable clothing in the eighteenth century, yet householders largely overlooked them when making their beds.[39] The PCC inventories and John Styles's analysis of textile thefts in the Old Bailey court records reveal an overwhelming preference for linen bedsheets.

With little difference in price between linen and cotton, linen's practical advantage probably lay in the greater strength and durability of its fibres, better able to withstand intensive laundering and thus having a longer shelf life.[40] This benefit was nevertheless enhanced by linen's unique sensations and by its broader cultural meanings, which forged an obvious link between this natural, organic fibre and the ideal of peaceful, healthy sleep. Linen had been aligned with concepts of order, purity, comfort and cleanliness since medieval times. It was particularly recommended for use next to the skin because it was exceptionally smooth, cool and fresh to the touch and it was also extremely absorbent. These qualities may well have generated feelings of cleanliness and purity for the user, which were reinforced by linen's habitual use in making clerical vestments and as a protective wrapping to preserve cherished personal belongings.[41] The fragment of linen depicted on the next page, which dates from c. 1680–c. 1699, very likely had overlapping uses as an altar sheet and as a bedsheet.

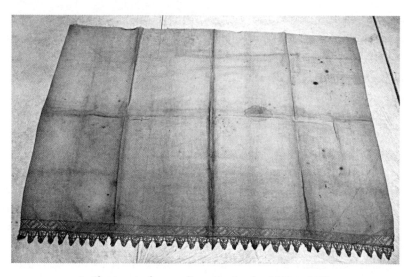

1. Sheet part of woven linen, England, *c.* 1680–*c.* 1699.

It is ornately decorated along one edge and bears characteristic signs of wear, tear and repair work close to the central panel, which would have had the most direct contact with the body that lay beneath it. When the sheet was no longer fit to grace a bedstead it was preserved by its owners alongside a silver-gilt chalice and paten – objects that held the consecrated bread and wine during Holy Communion. Once the sheet was no longer fit to sleep under, it may well have been used as a protective wrapping for these precious and sanctified objects of Catholic worship, or even as a way of concealing them. The chalice, which was made in England between *c.* 1630 and *c.* 1650, unscrews into three separate pieces, which would have given a distinct advantage to those who wished to hide this illicit object of Catholic worship if their homes were searched by state authorities.[42] The well-established cultural contexts in which linen circulated, which linked this cool and absorbent textile to physical and spiritual cleanliness, made this bedsheet a particularly apposite material with which to cover sleeping bodies and in which to preserve precious devotional objects.

On a day-to-day basis the sight, smell and feel of linen sheets undoubtedly conveyed feelings of wholesomeness to their users. As well as being cool to the touch, they were stiff and crisp in appearance, especially when starched, and they could be easily bleached in shades of white and cream to reinforce their associations with purity and cleanliness.[43] The smooth surface of some linen sheets, which depended on the density and weave of their threads, may have also offered a comfortable layer of protection from the scratchier surfaces of the bed's warmer top layers. Neurological explanations of sleep strengthened linen's value still further since meeting the sensory expectations of individual men and women was vital in lulling their bodies and minds into a state of peaceful relaxation. James Makittrick Adair explained that the body's 'sense of feeling' or 'sensibility' had to be satisfied to allow people to fully unwind and feel secure at bedtime. In practice this meant that some people were unable to 'sleep in any sheets coarser than those of cambric', which was a fine type of linen originally made in Cambrai, France, whilst others 'cannot bear the touch of velvet; [or] ... of the downy peach'.[44] Adair recognised the importance of personalising sleeping environments to satisfy different levels of nervous sensibility and varying expectations of what sleep was supposed to *feel* like; this could be achieved by catering for individual wishes about the most suitable type of bedding textile. The linen bedsheets examined in Chapter 4 show that there were wide variations in the texture of different linens to which individual sleepers were no doubt acutely attuned.

The heightened vulnerability associated with being asleep probably reinforced cultural preferences for linen sheets, whose cool stiff fibres were called on to regulate the body's inner functions and to secure its visible surfaces from infiltration by bedbugs, disease or diabolical forces. Linen sheets helped maintain a moderate body heat that supported digestion, regulated the motion of its fluids, and preserved the tension of muscles, joints and nerves. They safeguarded its external boundaries by absorbing sweaty excretions and nocturnal emissions, and by closing the skin's pores against contagion. It was a common practice when making linen bedsheets to join together two separate loom-widths of linen into a complete whole by a central panel of crochet, as depicted in Figure 2.

This open style of stitching served a combined practical and decorative function. The crochet panel was visually appealing but it could also be easily unpicked and the two linen widths turned to extend the sheet's life and ensure that it was evenly worn. This porous central panel may have had the added benefit of admitting greater airflow to the sleeper's body.[45] Sleeping between linen was judged akin to washing the body and this textile was a central feature in the early modern culture of cleanliness described by Georges Vigarello, which intertwined bodily sensations and the mind's perceptions.[46] The value of linen bedsheets was thus realised in both sensory and cultural registers; they gave assurances of protection to those who clutched them next to the skin and they helped maintain a stable sensory environment that was conducive to good health, psychological ease and sound sleep.

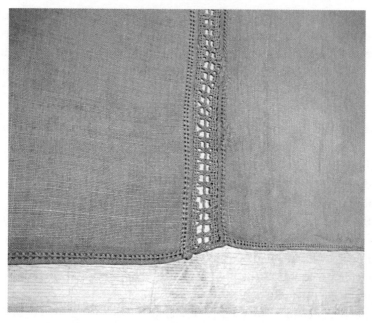

2. Linen sheet with bobbin lace insertions, England, seventeenth–eighteenth century.

Dressing for Bed

A rare engraved plate by London artist William Marshall, depicted in Figure 3, appeared as the frontispiece of *Ar't asleepe husband? A boulster lecture* (1640), a popular collection of moral lectures about female comportment that was penned by the prolific Westmorland poet and writer Richard Braithwaite. Marshall's image offers a playful reproof to wives who seized the quiet moments before sleep as an opportunity to chastise their husbands. The scene is likely imagined, although Marshall often worked from live models or portraits, yet it still offers a rare depiction of the kind of bedclothes that men and women may have worn to bed in the seventeenth century. The husband and wife depicted here each wear a head covering and a loose-fitting garment that covers their arms and torso. The wife's shoulders are also covered with a decoratively edged 'night rayle', a kind of shawl that was often made of linen. The shawl was designed to tie at the neck so that it could keep women warm as they sat up in bed to read, or, in this instance, to complain.[47] These garments were commonly listed in account books and inventories, and they were described in letters and diaries but what were they made of and how widespread was their use?

The desire to sleep beneath clean and fresh textiles applied equally to the clothes worn in bed as it did to bedsheets. Specialist garments for sleep may

3. Richard Brathwaite, *Ar't asleepe husband? A boulster lecture; stored with all variety of witty jeasts, merry tales, and other pleasant passages; extracted, from the choicest flowers of philosophy, poesy, antient and moderne history*, London, 1640.

have been rare commodities before the seventeenth century but they became more widely available and affordable by the mid-eighteenth century. The same preferences for cotton and linen fabrics emerge in relation to these garments as they do in relation to bedsheets. The terms most often used to describe items of clothing worn to bed include 'night gear', 'night shirts', 'shirts', 'shifts', 'smocks' and 'nightcloaths', some of which also doubled as general undergarments. They should not be confused, however, with 'nightgowns' that were often elaborate full-length items of daywear worn at home, or with loose, waist-length 'bedgowns' typically made from cotton, linen or wool that were used for work or leisure.[48]

Uncovering the precise use of certain items of clothing based on their labels alone is tricky since many garments had multiple functions during

day and night. Excise officer John Cannon surprised two female maidservants that his wife had taken for her bedfellows in 1720 when she slept at her
brother-in-law's house. When her husband appeared unexpectedly in their
chamber, the maids 'jumped out of bed in their smocks & ran into another
chamber affrighted'. Smocks were loose-fitting and washable garments,
often made of linen. Smocks or 'shifts' were the most typical female undergarments in this period, but they could also be worn during the daytime
both inside and outside of the home.[49] In spite of these difficulties, important research by Susan North points to a growing distinction between
garments worn during the daytime and those that were specifically dedicated to sleep from the seventeenth century.[50] This distinction may have
been driven, at least in part, by healthcare concerns, but it seems reasonable
to speculate that most people had access to some form of sleeping garment,
even if they had a number of different functions. The number of bedclothes
owned, their quality and appearance, varied according to wealth; these
distinctions applied to most types of early modern clothing and indeed to
bedding textiles. Some people did of course choose to sleep naked, either by
force of habit or to regulate their body temperature at different times of the
year.

Those body parts that were not covered by sheets and blankets, or by
bedclothes that encased the torso, remained exposed to external air and
required additional protection. Children that had a tendency to kick off
their sheets during the night might be dressed in a flannel or calico night-
vest to stop them from catching cold, especially during the cold winter
months.[51] More commonly worn to bed, however, were the 'nightcaps', 'caps',
'night coifs' and 'night croscloths', which played a crucial role in protecting
the brain at night.[52] The terminology associated with these garments is
again complex, with 'nightcaps' often referring to a head covering worn
informally at home during the daytime. The benefits of wearing nightcaps
in bed were nevertheless widely affirmed in health regimens. A collabora-
tive publication by medical practitioners Felix Platter, Abdiah Cole and
Nicholas Culpeper recommended that heads should neither be too warm
nor too cold at night; excessive exposure to cold air and the north wind
'may cause a great Stupidity', whilst overheating generated harmful
vapours.[53] Neurological explanations of sleeping and waking also acknowledged the brain's weakness at night. The layer of protection offered by
nightcaps may have assumed greater significance when sleepers were more
frequently surrounded by a flow of cool air and less enclosed by thick bed
hangings. James Makittrick Adair praised the value of nightcaps to allay his
patients' concerns that they might catch cold from the air that circulated

whilst they slept. He noted reassuringly that 'the danger of catching cold from such current is more apparent than real, for if the head and body are properly covered, there is no hazard'. Cosmetic reasons may also have shaped the selection and use of nightcaps since a cap made of a dense material was judged to impede the escape of excess vapours from the head, which in turn caused the hair to turn grey at an early age.[54]

Nightcaps were listed occasionally in the PCC inventory sample but this is likely to be a huge underestimate of the real number in regular use and it is difficult to disentangle the flexible use of these items during the day and during sleep, although a cut-out pattern book from the early nineteenth century suggests that caps for sleeping in were distinguished by being slightly longer in length and fitting more closely to the head. The combination of aesthetic and practical purposes that nightcaps served is underlined by the wide range of textiles from which they were made and in their ornate patterns. Some nightcaps were richly decorated with linen and silk and they were usually worn informally in company during the daytime.[55] These elaborate and expensive items were outnumbered, however, by large collections of simpler plain or quilted nightcaps, night coifs or night croscloths – the latter usually worn to bed by women.[56] Some of these caps have survived alongside pattern books with different designs and materials for men, women, children and servants that were made in different materials and adapted according to age, constitution and seasons of the year.[57] The use of Marseilles stitching on quilted nightcaps in the eighteenth century, which was distinguished by its raised white needlework, similarly combined fashion and practicality and mirrored the taste for Marseilles quilts in eighteenth-century England.[58] The lifespan of these simpler nightcaps may have been extended by the use of linen linings that were slipped inside the thicker outer layer for additional warmth and cleanliness. Cap linings could be easily removed and washed and their practicality was enhanced by the addition of earflaps and linen tapes that could be tied under the chin to keep them in place during the night, as shown in Figure 4.[59]

This is most likely a linen cap liner that was designed to fit inside a man's nightcap. Its size, earflaps and ties, and the gathered fabric of the roundel at its crown, ensured that this liner could fit snugly to the head's contours during sleep. The fine hand-stitching on the liner and the dense weave of the linen gave strength to this highly practical textile. This plain item is a very rare survival, which is probably explained by the embroidered letter 'C' that was stitched beneath the cap's turned-up edge. The Chafyn-Grove family from Wiltshire were staunch supporters of the Royalist cause during the civil wars and they appear to have treasured the liner as a relic of King

4. Cap liner, *c.* 1630–*c.* 1650.

Charles I, who stayed at their family home in Chisenbury prior to his execution in 1649.[60]

Simple nightcaps and their linings were frequently laundered and replaced due to habitual use. Those made from rudimentary materials that were subject to heavy use had a negligible resale value and potentially harboured diseases, which partly accounts for their limited survival. Visual sources, personal testimonies and account books nevertheless reveal their widespread use, with some being sewn or even knitted at home.[61] Tradesmen's ledgers list regular payments for nightcaps and owners took care to maintain them.[62] William Payne, the rector of Barnack near Peterborough from 1706 to 1751, kept a careful record of his household expenditure in his memorandum book and account book. In 1719 his account book listed three plain nightcaps valued at 4s. 6d. and six quilted nightcaps for colder nights valued at 10s., which he kept in a chest of drawers.[63] The schoolmaster, clergyman and bachelor Henry Mease, from rural Cheltenham, possessed 'a couple of night-caps' for use in winter when his accounts were taken in 1712. By 1725 he had replenished his stock with four more caps.[64] William Cole prepared for the winter of 1767 by commissioning local woman Mrs Goodwin to make him '6 Callico Night Caps'.[65] He added ten more linen caps to his supply just a month later.[66] Lady Anne Brockman was a mother of three and responsible for the day-to-day running of her family's household in Beachborough in Kent. Her account book shows that she commissioned a variety of fine holland and cambric nightcaps for different members of her household including children and servants. The caps ranged widely in cost and fabric and their use probably varied according to season and in line with principles of good health.[67] Nightcaps were also essential when sleeping away from home; James Woodforde took two on a visit to Oxford in October 1762, perhaps to regulate his body temperature in an unfamiliar environment.[68] A practical joke played by the young Elizabeth Raper also suggests that carrying a nightcap was a routine precaution for travellers, especially in winter. Elizabeth was the daughter of John Raper, a supercargo for the East India Company. She remained unmarried and kept house for her parents at Twyford House in Hertfordshire for much of her twenties and early thirties. During this period, which spanned the years 1756 to 1770, she kept a personal journal in which she recorded her household duties alongside many of her romantic entanglements. When Mr Hotham, one of Elizabeth's many suitors, stayed overnight at Elizabeth's parents' house in November 1758, she slipped unobserved into his chamber and playfully sewed up the nightcap that lay on the bed.[69] Elizabeth meant to disturb the familiar bedtime routine of her suitor and perhaps to keep her image fresh in his mind as he lay his head down to sleep. The humour implicit in Elizabeth's joke relied on the fact that nightcaps were staple parts of sleep's material apparatus and thus of habitual bedtime routines. They helped to secure physical comfort and peace of mind at bedtime, whether at home or abroad.

Cleaning the Bed

Practicality and cleanliness were then key incentives in the purchase, care and use of bedsheets, bedclothes and other sleep-related goods. Household recipes, printed guides to household management and surviving objects present an array of cleansing methods and materials that show the diligence with which sleeping chambers were maintained against dirt, dampness, disease and unwanted pests. Sleeping chambers routinely played host to scenes of childbirth but the precious bedstead, its mattresses and the staple bedding textiles might be secured from ruin by the use of separate mattresses and sheets that could be destroyed after use. One such mattress, made of carex – a coarse rush-like plant – is depicted in Figure 5. It is densely plaited from one continuous piece of carex, looped eight times and fastened by thick string of the same material, which suggests highly skilled manufacture. Robert Hooke, founder member of London's Royal Society and curator of experiments, depicted and remarked on the use of a very similar straw-like material that he called 'Taffety-riband' which was used for making robust 'Bed-matts' in many parts of England.[70]

At 1828mm long and 685mm wide, the mattress could easily accommodate a single recumbent body and the unplaited matting on the underside of the mattress could absorb a great deal of fluid during the birth. Once the child was born the mattress was probably burned since it was not fit to be recycled. This mattress is thus a very rare survival, being found walled up in the ceiling of a cottage in Titchfield, Hampshire, in 1961. The cottage, built in the sixteenth century, was likely converted from a barn warehouse that originally served Titchfield Abbey. The mattress may well have been purchased or made by a local craftsperson in anticipation of a birth but never used for this purpose; it was utilised instead as roof insulation for the cottage. Visual sources indicate the overlapping uses of similar plaited mattresses for childbirth and for laying out dead bodies from the sixteenth through to the eighteenth century in England, which will be explored in the following chapter. The existence and purpose of this type of mattress underlines the critical importance of cleanliness during sleep, since it was intended to protect the bedstead and to secure its staple mattresses and textiles from damage.

Extensive precautions were taken during pivotal moments of the life cycle but warding off bedbugs, flies and fleas proved to be a central preoccupation for householders on a more regular basis. The Irish-born journalist and novelist Oliver Goldsmith believed that bedbugs had an unrivalled capacity to 'banish that sleep, which even sorrow and anxiety permitted to approach.'[71] Diaries, correspondence and travel accounts from

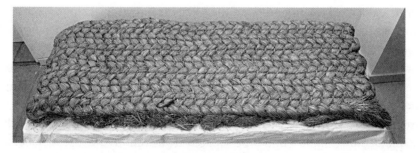

5. Carex mattress from Titchfield, Hampshire.

this period teem with references to the pains that these creatures caused: they were a constant cause of broken sleep. Expressions of disgust at the bites and revolting smell produced by bedbugs were inflected by discourses of class and ethnicity.[72] Securing a peaceful night's sleep nevertheless provided the most consistent explanation for the growing sense of frustration that their incursions provoked. The specific sensibilities associated with sleep offer the most compelling motivation for ridding sleeping environments of these unwelcome visitors, which was by no means an easy task.

Thomas Tryon believed that the problem of bedbugs was endemic: it could be traced to the very fabric of houses whose walls were plastered with a mixture of hog's hair and lime that attracted bugs. Wooden bedsteads were similarly believed to offer a hospitable environment for bedbugs of various types to prosper. Wooden bedsteads nevertheless predominated in early modern households until the nineteenth century when iron bedsteads began to appear with greater frequency. Early modern bedsteads had a particularly long lifespan. They were often expensive and could date back many generations, being routinely gifted as cherished heirlooms or as practical and symbolic gifts from parents to children when setting up home. There was also a vibrant second-hand trade in bedsteads that extended their life still further. Bedsteads represented the symbolic heart of the household but their physical make-up made them an appealing home for insects that endangered health. The warm and excretory bodies of sleepers exacerbated this problem and it was particularly acute in the much-traversed beds of lodging houses and inns. Thomas Tryon believed that such beds were a dangerous source of contagion since 'Beds suck in and receive all sorts of pernicious Excrements that are breathed forth by the Seating of various sorts of People, which have Leprous and Languishing Diseases, which lie and die on them'.[73] Lady Hertford wrote to Horace Walpole in anticipation of a visit to his Strawberry Hill home and begged him not to favour her by accommodating her in 'your best chintz bed, as I am in the secret, and know Sir Robert died in it'.[74] Her attempts to avoid sleeping in the bed of Horace's dead father may have been motivated by a combination of superstition and by a concern to protect her own health. Farmer Richard Latham and clergyman William Cole each guarded against these dangers by paying local tradespeople to renew their bed- and bolster-ticking on a regular basis. Others used cheap homemade fillings of straw, horsehair, beech leaves, chaff or flock that could be easily replaced, beaten and cleaned. Household recipes provided advice on the best materials to use for good economy and cleanliness alongside directions on prolonging the life of mattresses by rubbing the ticking with brown soap.[75] Chaff was especially prized as a filling for its absorbency, whilst being 'cool and pleasant' to sleep on during the summer months. Children's mattresses could also be protected from damp and decay by the use of rubber or leather sheets. Bolsters stuffed with a mixture of down feathers and small pieces of torn paper were similarly judged to be comfortable and cool to sleep on.

Unpleasant encounters between sleepers and bugs saw the emergence of specialised commercial services in the eighteenth century.[76] John Southall's *Treatise of Buggs* (1730) offered a range of practical guidelines about how to prevent and exterminate bedbugs. The treatise also included an advertisement for Southall's 'Nonpareil Liquor for destroying Buggs and Nits'.[77] Southall's advice could be sought at his home in Southwark and in his publication, priced at one shilling. The treatise was dedicated to Sir Hans Sloane, president of the Royal Society and the College of Physicians. This illustrious patron lent authority to Southall's claim that the destruction of bedbugs represented both a private good and a civic duty. Southall was one of many who titled themselves 'exterminators' and cashed in on a ready market for bug expulsion in the eighteenth century. Those less able or less willing to pay for these professional services were nevertheless well served by a wide repertoire of recipes for keeping beds free of bugs that were staple features of household notebooks and guides.[78] A family 'Booke of divers recipes' that spanned several generations from 1660 to 1750 included a comprehensive set of instructions for washing and cleaning wooden bedsteads with soap, aqua fortis and a homemade paste of quicksilver, black soap and tobacco dust that was to be left in the holes and joints of the bedstead where bugs were believed to congregate.[79] Hannah Glasse's *Servant's Directory, or House-Keeper's Companion* (1760) included no less than eight recipes for keeping bedchambers and bedsteads free from flies, fleas, bedbugs, gnats and silkworms. Glasse's concoctions included natural products that could be cheaply sourced and her publication boasted a long list of subscribers. The hot summer months posed particular difficulties for controlling bug infestations. At this time of year Glasse advised servants and householders to place a garland of 'Ash-boughs and Flowers' at the bed's head, whilst others advocated placing springs of the aromatic plant tansy at the bed's head, or sewing pieces of camphor to the mattress. These remedies were cheap, attractive, fragrant and practical. Glasse's garland also formed 'a pretty Ornament', whilst its floral scent attracted flies and gnats away from the body. Glasse catered for a diverse readership and she tailored her advice according to locality: those who lived in marshy or fenny areas were advised to burn a piece of fern in the chamber or to hang pieces of cow dung at the foot of the bedstead to keep bugs at bay. Country-dwellers were directed to bathe their hands and face in a mixture of wormwood, rue and water before retiring to bed to gain similar protection.[80] These parts of the body, which lay unprotected by bedsheets and bedclothes, required additional protection.

The cleansing regimes that aimed to eradicate bedbugs and noxious effluvia varied in the cost of their ingredients, in potency and in frequency of use. Anne Barker's *Complete Servant Maid* (1770) encouraged the daily airing of bedchambers by opening windows and uncovering beds, 'which will be a great help against bugs and fleas'.[81] Mattresses should be shaken daily and turned weekly, and the bedding textiles brushed and whisked. The servants responsible for these tasks moreover were sometimes required to wear pinafores when making the bed to prevent the linen being soiled by the dust and unpleasant liquids accumulated by emptying slops, cleaning fires and dusting.[82]

The most comprehensive remedy for bedbugs was even more time-consuming and very messy: in extreme cases the bedchamber had to be completely repainted afterwards. The dramatic nature of this recipe, which was replicated elsewhere, underlines its importance, and the number of recipes that Hannah Glasse included allowed readers to personalise her advice to suit their particular needs and pockets.[83] There was moreover a productive interaction between homemade recipes for cleansing bedsteads, textiles and bedchambers and those that circulated in print. One of the recipes that Glasse included was recommended by a 'Lady' that claimed to have 'cleared a Hundred Beds from those troublesome Vermin'.[84] The importance of a healthy sleeping environment had reached new heights by the mid-eighteenth century, which heightened sensitivity to bedbugs that routinely disturbed rest. Remedies to remove them were a core feature of household cleansing practices. They combined practical and aesthetic functions and they played a central role in shaping the sensory dimensions of sleeping environments.

Treating Sleep Loss

For most people sleep loss was usually sporadic and of short duration and the household was the natural arena for its prevention and treatment. Occasional interruptions to rest were anticipated, and carefully prepared for, revealing a strong desire to avoid the painful and potentially damaging effects of sleep loss. Recipes for preventing or treating sleep loss, disturbed sleep or nightmares were commonplace features of manuscript and printed recipe books, and the latter enjoyed a publication boom in England from the 1650s and into the eighteenth century.[85] A book of household recipes that spanned the years 1650–1739 was typical in interspersing culinary recipes with preparations designed 'To cause one to sleep'.[86] Sleep loss was generally treated with a mixture of tried and tested recipes, drawn from family recipe books, from the recommendations of friends and neighbours, or from published recipes: all of which could be prepared in a well-stocked kitchen. Recourse to paid medical services for sleeping problems was rare, or a last resort for those unfortunate individuals that suffered from prolonged and endemic sleep loss. Surviving manuscript recipe books show that many households anticipated and prepared for occasional periods of sleep loss by producing a stock of syrups, conserves and distillations of herbs, flowers and vegetables that were believed to provoke sleep.[87]

A recipe that had been used or recommended by family members or by esteemed friends and neighbours conveyed an unrivalled sense of authority, trust and safety to its users. In her will dated 10 April 1705, the Yorkshire gentlewoman Alice Thornton bequeathed to her beloved daughter Alice Comber 'all my Phisicall books and Recepts, together with my stock of salves and oyntments, desireing her to give unto her sister Katherine Danby what she may have occasion to use for her selfe or her children'.[88] Alice wished to protect her children and grandchildren after her death by furnishing them with her own knowledge and homemade medicaments that had kept her family safe under her watchful care. An important relationship of trust already existed between the donor and recipient and the latter was able to align an amicable personal relationship with the anticipation of physical relief. The expected efficacy of a particular remedy was strengthened by this personalisation, which could not be fully replicated by commercial treatments. The physical state of vulnerability induced by sleep may have rendered these relationships of trust particularly important.[89]

Trust was paramount in deciding which recipes, and from which sources, should be included in treasured collections that were intended to secure the health of multiple generations of one family. The first leaf of Martha Hodges's recipe book identified its original author as 'Our Great Grandmother Hodges' and it may not have been untypical in stretching across five decades. These ties of affection ensured that individual recipes drew on sleep's prophylactic vocabulary. The recipe book to which Elizabeth Okeover gave her name included a recipe 'To make Sirrup of Poppies to procure slepe Safelye' in which the poppy leaves had to be carefully cut, stilled and strained over twenty-four hours. The same collection included a recipe 'To cause sleepe safe and shure' by using gentler ingredients including the moss of an ash tree.[90] Concern to protect the health of loved ones was also evident in the customisation of individual recipes that were adapted to suit different members of the household according to gender, age, constitution and stage of life. A recipe to procure sleep signed by Elizabeth Jacobs could be adapted to different age groups by mixing the key ingredient of poppy with fortified wine 'for an old body'; with white wine 'for the middle'; and with beer for the younger generation.[91] The heat that each liquor generated within the body explained this variation: those of more advanced years were believed to benefit from the warmth of strong, vintage wines whilst the young profited from weaker, cooler fluids. Time was of paramount importance in preparing sleep recipes, with many preparations requiring several hours or even days to create. The conscientious preparation of these medicaments was nevertheless invaluable since they safeguarded the long-term health of cherished family members. Soporific syrups and conserves could moreover be stored for months or even years, and they thus offered a comforting resource for intermittent use. Preserving the health of family members in this way was a practical duty expected of a good housewife and it was also supported by a pervasive culture of Christian ethics.

Powerful motivations for safeguarding sleep thus existed and householders called on a rich body of healthcare knowledge that combined the cumulative wisdom of previous generations, trusted friends and neighbours and local physicians with commercial advice in recipe books and healthcare guides that were deliberately designed for regular daily use.[92] The years after 1660 saw considerable growth in the market for practical healthcare guides, and especially recipe books. Mary Fissell estimated that between 150 and 180 works of this kind were published in every decade between 1660 and 1740.[93] Sleeping and waking were staple features within this flourishing genre. Nicholas Culpeper's *Physicall Directory* and *English Physician* topped the list of best-selling medical books between 1641 and 1740. He was committed to educating ordinary men and women how best to preserve their own health, prevent disease, and treat everyday ailments at minimal expense and without recourse to the professional services of licensed medical practitioners.[94] Culpeper recommended moderate and sound sleep as part of a holistic health regimen because it aided digestion, refreshed the spirits and promoted general well-being. He recommended similar ingredients to those found in manuscript recipes for sleep, advocating the use of violet, which could be made into cakes, candies, conserves and syrups to cool and moisten hot and dry complexions. Medical writer Hannah Wolley learned the value of kitchen physic from her mother and sisters. When she reached adulthood she gave healthcare advice and medicaments to her neighbours and to the children of the free grammar school at Newport in Essex where her husband was schoolmaster. Her knowledge of cookery and household medicine was also offered up for a wider audience in a range of popular texts. An unauthorised version of Wolley's recipe book *The Accomplish'd lady's delight in preserving, physic, beautifying, and cookery* was published pseudonymously in 1675 and it instructed readers how to make a syrup of violet flowers.[95] Violet's soporific effects had the added benefit of infusing the air with a pleasant and sweet aroma that was prized for its health benefits. Herbalist John Gerard praised violet's 'odiferous' scent for calming the mind and for stimulating 'good and honest' contemplations that may have been especially welcome at bedtime.[96]

Most recipes for preventing or for treating sleep loss, disturbed sleep and nightmares came in a cooling liquid form, either as syrups, conserves or distillations, which could be consumed or applied externally, usually to the head, neck and temples. The key ingredients of these recipes, which were commonly interspersed with household cookery recipes, varied widely in form and cost. They included, though were not restricted to, aniseed, chamomile, cucumbers, houseleek, mandrake, deadly nightshade, poppy, purslane, rose, violet, lavender, cowslips, endive, eringo roots, lettuce, saffron, tobacco, wormwood, henbane, lily, parsley, nutmeg, dandelion, onions, rushes and sweet reed.[97] Many of these ingredients were believed to induce sleep by dissipating excess heat in both stomach and brain, and by slowing the vibrations of the nerves by cooling them down. Distillations of lettuce and cucumber had well-established cooling properties, whilst eringo roots (a sweetmeat delicacy found in coastal regions of southeast England) were associated with the sea and were valued – especially when preserved and candied – for moistening elderly bodies. Some of these ingredients were recommended for cultivation in kitchen gardens, whilst others could be readily purchased from groceries, apothecaries and local herb sellers.[98]

Essex clergyman Ralph Josselin employed the cooling properties of a 'carduus possett' – a hot drink steeped with *Carduus* thistle to bring on sleep. On other occasions he bathed his face with rose oil and took 'above 2 ounces sirrup roses' that allowed him to rest in comfort.[99] Waters, syrups and conserves made of roses were recommended for their calming properties and they were judged particularly effective when applied to the temples at bedtime.[100] Ralph Josselin tried to enhance the effects of these treatments by combining their use with solemn bedtime prayer.[101] Red, white, black, wild and yellow (or 'horned') poppies were believed to have a cooling and somniferous effect similar to that of roses. Thomas Willis recommended wild poppy as a remedy for an anxious mind, which was a common cause of sleep loss.[102] This herbal therapy was not new but Willis's comments on its properties underline how the preservation of a healthy mind and nerves was subtly prioritised in medical advice relating to sleep. Comparable recipes included filling pillowcases with hops, which was thought to lull the senses to sleep. A collection of medical recipes based on the wisdom of Elizabeth Grey (née Talbot), countess of Kent, included instructions for making a smelling-bag of sleep-inducing herbs that operated in similar ways.[103] Considerable overlap between homemade recipes and published advice was evident in the recipe book that belonged to the family of natural philosopher Robert Boyle. It included a recipe for bathing the feet and legs in chamomile water at bedtime, whilst a concoction of aniseeds and rose water placed in a string bag was believed to give 'a cold smell and procureth sleep' when tied to the upper lip so that its fumes could enter through the nostrils and infuse the brain during sleep.[104]

The use of 'Cabbage-Lettice' was especially recommended for bringing on the sleep of young children and old people, whose body heat could fluctuate dramatically and interrupt their rest. Most medical practitioners agreed that lettuce encouraged peaceful sleep but the way that it operated was increasingly debated as physiologies of sleep diversified. *The Ladies Dispensatory* (1652), a medical self-help book aimed at women and compiled by Leonard Sowerby, the son of a farrier from St Martin's in the Fields, hinted at disagreements about whether lettuce simply cooled the stomach or whether it also calmed the nerves by slowing the movement of the arterial blood.[105] Explanations of precisely *how* lettuce procured sleep certainly differed but there was no question of its effectiveness. The growing association between sleep, brain and nerves reinforced the authority of this familiar medicament rather than undermining it. The longevity of natural cooling therapies to treat sleep loss was not simply due to the stubborn persistence of non-natural medical precepts but to their productive fusion with emerging neurological explanations of sleep.

Trust was still firmly placed in tried and tested homemade remedies for disrupted sleep but they were subtly infused with, and indeed accompanied by, more commercial sleep-advice and remedies as the eighteenth century wore on. These overlapping spheres offered a wide choice of strategies and therapies to suit the needs and pockets of people suffering from temporary or long-term sleep loss. Gentlewoman Elizabeth Freke drew on household advice about sleep loss and on remedies that were available for purchase. In 1711 she compiled an inventory of her household medicines that totalled nearly 200 cordial waters, syrups and distilled waters and which featured a recipe made from boiled garden poppies that was believed to induce sleep. Alongside her homemade medicaments, Elizabeth maintained a lively interest in the wider medical marketplace.[106] Her inventory included '1 book of the family phisition', which was likely Gideon Harvey's *The family physician, and the house apothecary* (1676), which included detailed instructions on how to make simple yet essential medicaments for the home. Harvey included a recipe for red poppy water and one for conserve of roses that were each recommended as soporifics. Harvey underlined the wise economy of making these remedies at home by directly comparing the price of their ingredients with the higher cost of ready-made medicinal water that could be purchased from an apothecary.[107]

Elizabeth Freke was not alone in combining homemade and commercial advice and therapies. Oxfordshire gentlewoman Anne Dormer suffered from prolonged periods of sleep loss throughout her life. She attributed this infirmity to her delicate constitution and to the emotional distress caused by her unhappy marriage to Robert Dormer. She came to despise her marital bedchamber, which she described as a 'hatefull roome ... which is so like an oven that I could never sleep in it'. She described in a letter to her sister how she was forced to sit up in a chair through the night since the heat of the bed was so intense that 'there I lost my sleepe, and health and those somers I have layn there this last seven yeare I lived in a manner without sleepe; to stay in it was worss then Death'.[108] Anne finally managed to move her bedstead from an upstairs chamber to a cooler ground-floor chamber next to the dining room, though only with the support of her relatives who forced her disgruntled husband to accept this relocation. Aside from changing her sleeping environment, Anne tried different therapies to improve the quality of her rest. She drank chocolate, ran and played with her children at bedtime to invite pleasure and exhaustion, and she prayed and read the published sermons of Isaac Barrow, bishop of St Asaph.[109] The relief that Anne received was intermittent and so she turned on occasion to water-based therapies, which included visits to the spa at Tunbridge, which is examined in Chapter 5. In a letter of 1686 Anne wrote to her sister, Lady Elizabeth Trumbull, to tell her that 'since bathing am come to better sleepe then I used to have'.[110] These effects were nevertheless short-lived and when Anne returned home she turned to patent medicine for relief. Anne used a preparation known as the 'King's Drops' when her sleepless nights became unbearable and which she believed 'always relieve me when I take them'.[111] Her sparing use of this medicine was likely due to its high cost, but perhaps also to its powerful effects. This was an expensive distillation containing powdered human skull, also known as 'spirit of skull', or 'Goddard's Drops'. The drops were named after their probable creator, Jonathan Goddard, professor of physic at Gresham College, from whom King Charles II most likely purchased the recipe for £6,000. The medicine became known as the 'King's Drops' due to Charles's personal use of it, and because his royal chemist prepared the drops in the king's private laboratory.[112] The reputed effects of the drops were wide-ranging: it was touted by some as a general panacea but was judged particularly effective against disorders of the brain and nerves.[113] Anne Dormer directly linked her own use of the drops to her sleeping problems for which she may have perceived a neurological origin. She was highly sensible of the debilitating effects that living 'so many years with very little sleepe' had on both her body and mind.[114] Her choice of medicament may also have been guided by persuasive advertisements. In 1709 the single-sheet daily newspaper *The Daily Courant* ran an advertisement from a Holborn apothecary who declared that the King's Drops were 'famous against apoplectic fits, and all nervous complaints': a category that now admitted sleep disorders. Maladies of the brain and nerves were increasingly cited as a cause of disturbed sleep by medical practitioners and sufferers alike.

The medical wisdom that shaped understandings of healthy sleep and responses to sleep loss had thus diversified by the late seventeenth century. The treatments to which people resorted to procure restful sleep fused well-established homemade remedies and commercialised therapies. The former were given new vitality as they became associated with nerve-calming properties as well as with regulating humoral balance. William Ellis recommended lavender drops to the readers of his *Country Housewife's Family Companion* to relieve nervous debilities. This was based on the advice of an acquaintance who purportedly 'took Lavender Drops every Night he went to Bed, to the Number of sixty, in Water, Ale, or Wine; but best of all dropt on Loaf Sugar, letting it gradually dissolve in the Mouth, because by that Means it soaks more immediately into the Nerves'.[115] This updated use of a familiar medicament underlined the subtle influence of neurological classifications of sleep in the medical marketplace and in many households. A vibrant mixed economy of homemade and commercial recipes to preserve sleep and remedy sleep loss thus existed and signalled a common commitment to secure sound slumber and good health. As motivations for safeguarding sound sleep grew stronger, people were able to choose from a wider range of strategies and therapies than ever before. They collectively incorporated the well-established preventative healthcare principles of non-natural medicine and neurological explanations of sleep.

Knowledge of how sleep worked within the body was widely revised from the late seventeenth century yet a great deal of continuity characterised its day-to-day management, which remained heavily shaped by a preventative culture of healthcare. Long-term health preservation was the chief aim of non-natural health regimens, the principles of which were fused with neurological explanations of sleep, rather than replaced by them. It remained within the reach of most households to procure healthy slumber through a combination of self-discipline, rigorous cleansing and the preparation of medicaments to treat periods of sleep loss when they occurred. The motivations to keep these routines of sleep hygiene were strengthened by sleep's growing association with the health of the mind. Diary entries and letters show that episodes of broken sleep were occasional rather than endemic features of daily life for most people. Those who suffered from broken sleep turned first to familiar household remedies for relief but they could also consult the advice of medical practitioners or turn to more commercial remedies if it proved necessary.

For the vast majority of men and women the means to achieve healthy sleep could be found at home but new methods and technologies to achieve it were more readily available for purchase than ever before. Despite the continuity that characterised sleep management within the home, there were visible shifts in daily practice, not least the growing desire to regulate air quality and temperature at bedtime. This requirement had always been present in non-natural cultures of healthcare but it was strengthened by neurological explanations of sleep, which sparked a series of measures designed to preserve the vitality of the mind and nerves. The increase and diversification of advice and remedies to procure restful sleep in these years reflected the growing importance that was attached to it. The alignment of peaceful sleep with the health of body, brain and nerves thus provides the critical explanation for these subtle yet significant transformations.

CHAPTER 3

Faithful Slumber

SLEEP WAS UNDERSTOOD to be replete with earthly and spiritual dangers. It was 'in our Beds & sleepe' that the diarist, bibliophile and keen gardener John Evelyn feared that Christians could 'take least care of ourselves'. Evelyn here paraphrased Psalm 8:4 on the duty of thankfulness to Almighty God after he had heard a sermon preached on this passage that afternoon in church. He entered it into his diary to remind him that it was only by trusting in God's providential care that his nocturnal 'rest & safty' might be assured.[1] 'Safty' applied here to body and soul, both of which required protection during the defenceless hours of sleep.

Sleep was not just something that people did but also something about which they thought deeply, pondering its meanings, purpose and effects. Sleeping habits were moulded in part by seasonal and environmental rhythms, but its daily practice was embedded within a complex network of Christian beliefs that encouraged people to shape their bedtimes, sleep routines and sleeping environments in distinctive ways. How people practised their sleep in their own homes, and indeed in the homes of others, was central to their lived experience of religion and a core feature of what it meant to be a devoted Christian. The influence of religious beliefs on household sleeping practices was especially potent in the decades after 1660, when incentives to practise 'sleep-piety' within the home were in abundance. I define 'sleep-piety' here as any sleep-related practice or ritual that was inspired, at least in part, by religious beliefs and that formed part of Christians' daily efforts to fit their bodies, minds and souls to receive God's favour. Sleep-piety is here placed at the heart of the household's spiritual life by revealing how and why sleep's spiritual meanings shaped its daily practice and its material environments. Early modern sleep-piety was distinguished by its fervency and by its depth of submission to God's protection during the night, as Christians anticipated the dangers that they might be exposed to as they lay helpless in their beds. They begged for divine protection by repenting of their sins at bedtime, by offering prayers in and around their bedsteads, and by filling their minds with holy thoughts – often with the aid of devotional texts, images and other meaningful objects that surrounded the bedside. By these varied means, men and women recommended their souls into the watchful care of the Lord and his ministering angels. These pious routines were specifically designed to safeguard their physical, psychological and emotional well-being and to offset the feelings of vulnerability that haunted the mind at bedtime, which helped to ease their passage into sleep.

The ideal of a 'spiritualised' household occupied a central place within Reformed Protestant culture and within Catholic devotional culture across the British Isles.[2] Living in a spiritualised household was recognised as an effective vehicle of religious instruction to consolidate religious reform, and as a site of opposition to the established Church. Household devotions were especially appealing to dissenting Protestants and to English Catholics after 1660 because their opportunities to practise public worship were either prohibited or seriously curtailed.[3] It was thus in the decades after 1660 that sleep-piety became most firmly embedded within daily life, and within sleeping chambers, which contained an array of textual, visual and material supports to devotion. The intensification of sleep-piety within the home was in part due to the exclusionary terms of the 1662 Act of Uniformity, which led to the ejection of 2,000 clergymen from the Church of England who refused to conform. This legislation sparked a series of pastoral reform initiatives that encouraged practical forms of household piety both within and beyond the recently restored Church of England. Advice on how to pursue a holy life at home formed an essential part of new visions of worship that were preached from the pulpit and laid out in print by Protestants and Catholics alike. A flourishing genre of devotional handbooks, collections of prayers and forms of service designed for household use were published on an unprecedented scale in these years. These texts offered cheap and accessible advice about how to live in harmony with God, and they helped both to structure daily devotions within the home and to bind together cultures of public and household worship.[4] Sleep-piety was a central ingredient within these works that invited faithful Christians to understand their sleeping habits and bedtime routines as practical methods of devotion. These guides also highlight a set of shared understandings and practices relating to sleep that cut across different confessional groups.

Protestants of many different shades as well as English Catholics shared a belief in the spiritual benefits and moral virtue of early rising, regular bedtimes, clean and sanctified sleeping environments and heartfelt bedtime prayers. This consensus was shaped by a shared appreciation of sleep's links with death and the Christian resurrection, by a common belief in the soul's immortality, and by an acceptance of the combined physical and spiritual benefits of regular and refreshing sleep. In spite of these shared understandings, subtle distinctions of perception and practice were apparent amongst different types of Christians. These contrasts were most visible in the fervency and frequency with which sleep-piety was carried out, and in differences of opinion about the spiritual consequences of its performance and neglect.

Sleep's careful regulation and the devotional rituals that surrounded it were judged a vital defence for those men and women who feared the Devil's attack during the night. The letters and diaries of early Methodists in particular show the persistent vitality of supernatural encounters in sleep and dream reports throughout the eighteenth century. Their accounts reveal that it was on, beneath and around the bedstead that fears of diabolical attack clustered within the household. The Devil's threat reached its peak during the night and it could never be entirely discounted. Many people continued to believe that poor-quality sleep, or sleep that was indulged without bedside devotions, weakened the Christian's defences against the Devil. Even for those Christians who were less perturbed by the prospect of diabolical attack, sleep-piety remained crucial for shaping the quality of their relations with God. Episodes of disturbed sleep were routinely interpreted as the result of physical and spiritual malaise and they continued to prompt vows to repent of sins and to reform daily habits, whether that meant spending less time in the alehouse or performing bedtime prayers in a more heartfelt fashion. The kind of sleep that proved less remarkable, and less noteworthy, was undoubtedly the norm and this sleep was still safeguarded by spiritual meditations, prayers and by objects and materials that were invested with protective qualities. The unique feelings of vulnerability created by sleep's bodily effects explain this persistent need for preservation, and it was to God that people turned to provide it. The Lord remained the chief governor of people's sleep routines even if his protection was issued in different ways and from a greater distance than in previous years. Christians entrusted their bodies and souls into the Lord's care each night and they turned to the natural world that He had created when sleep had forsaken them – it was here that they found the tools they needed to safeguard their bodies and souls whilst they slept.

Sleep in Christian Culture

Sleep was ordained by God as a precious gift of refreshment for his children in return for their daily labour and faithful obedience. Peaceful sleep was part of God's creation, a positive reward for good Christian behaviour and an essential support to human life and spiritual purification. Sleep was also valued as a pathway to divine communication and Holy Scripture is replete with accounts of spiritual forces invading sleeping bodies and minds to deliver revelations, prophecies and warnings. Whilst peaceful sleep was a treasured gift, the very need for such a period of restoration also signalled human weakness, especially in relation to God who required no such refreshment; that God never sleeps is confirmed by the words of Psalm 121: 'Behold, he that keepeth Israel shall neither slumber nor sleep'.[5] Sleepers depended on an ever-wakeful God to make their slumber sound and to guard their bodies and souls against danger whilst their strength was restored. John Milton's God in *Paradise Lost* appoints his angels to march, armed with shields and spears, 'in warlike parade' around the slumberous figures of Adam and Eve as darkness falls in the Garden of Eden to protect them from the rebellious and malevolent spirits that have escaped their chains in Hell.[6]

This figurative yet highly visceral promise of protection offered a powerful sense of reassurance to those that lay on the verge of sleep and anticipated the perils that they might encounter there. Whilst restful slumber was tentatively interpreted as a sign of divine favour, persistent wakefulness – when it was not obviously the result of illness or voluntary sleep deprivation – could signal a soul in need of purification. The physical and spiritual dimensions of sleep were here intertwined and this mixture explains the routine treatment of sleeping problems with a combination of natural medicaments and with prayer. Holy Scripture and an array of classical texts thus ensured that sleep was widely understood as an ongoing process of physical and spiritual nourishment, transformation, or corruption. Sleepers were understood to travel between consciousness and unconsciousness, between the earthly and supernatural realms, and between life and death on a nightly basis.

Day-to-day sleeping practices and bedtime routines were infused with less dramatic but equally important spiritual meanings. Diaries, letters and household inventories show that sleep-piety was a central feature of household devotions between 1660 and 1760. Its daily practice expressed Christian hopes for salvation and a persistent drive to secure physical and spiritual well-being, which was a behavioural ideal rooted in Holy Scripture.

Psalm 127 declared that sound sleep was a divine gift conferred upon wise and dutiful Christians. Those people who understood sleep quality as a measure of their soul's health took up this principle. Presbyterian minister Henry Newcome was ordained in 1648 and ministered to parishioners in Cheshire and Manchester before he was ejected from his post in 1662. Newcome methodically recorded the seemingly mundane events of his daily life in his diary, which he interpreted as evidence of God's favour or disfavour towards himself and his family. Newcome explained the varying quality of his family's sleep within a framework of providential belief in which God worked through nature to deliver rewards and punishments to guide his children towards the path of righteousness. Newcome believed that the Lord showed his 'favour' to the family when he allowed them to rest peacefully in their beds.[7]

The practice of sleep-piety was also motivated by the changing relationship between the Church of England and dissenting groups before and after the formal consolidation of religious divisions. The fragmented religious culture of the late seventeenth century led Anglican churchmen and dissenting ministers alike to prioritise household worship. Sleep-piety was strongly promoted by Church of England ministers and Anglican writers who published practical guides to holy living to secure the loyalties of their parishioners and to enrich Anglican devotional culture. These practical guides were intended to bind together public worship, family prayer and private household devotions, and thereby enhance Christian knowledge and practice. The guides were an essential feature of pastoral reform initiatives that aimed to instil the laity with sufficient zeal, advice and material supports to perform regular and fruitful household devotions, which helped to prepare them for public worship.[8]

For dissenting Protestants, the heightened significance of household devotions was closely linked to the curtailment of public worship. The Conventicle Acts of 1664 and 1670 outlawed unauthorised public gatherings of more than five people who did not belong to the same household. It was not until 1689 that the Act of Toleration permitted limited freedom of worship for those Protestants that remained outside of the Church of England and who agreed to swear particular oaths of allegiance. For English Catholics the value of household worship also grew in direct response to the prohibition of public worship, which continued throughout this period. The household was here understood as a place of resistance to religious persecution and as a fertile ground in which to cultivate Reformed Catholic sensibilities; Alexandra Walsham has thus aptly described the relationship between English Catholics and their households as 'a marriage of convenience'.[9] A varied cross section of ministers and religious writers negotiated these tricky obstacles by producing devotional guides that offered practical timetables of when spiritual exercises should be performed and set forms of prayer to use at home; sleep-piety was a central feature within these influential publications.

Similarities of approach towards sleep's day-to-day management characterised these devotional guides, even though authors differed markedly in their reasons for producing them. They show a high degree of consistency in the kinds of preparations, prayers and pious routines that were recommended to support sleep's daily practice. This overlap is partly explained by the design of these handbooks, which deliberately set out to complement the rhythms of household life and to offer spiritual support in times of trouble, which eased their practical application. Set prayers were devised for each day of the week and for specific times of day and night. Extended bedtime prayers were accompanied by shorter versions that could be used interchangeably as time and circumstance allowed. Bedtime devotions were likewise tailored to particular social groups and to individual members of the household.[10] In 1720 Robert Warren, rector of Charlton in Kent, placed the ideal of sound sleep at the heart of his guide to holy living. Warren composed *The Daily Self-Examinant* to support his parishioners' devotions and to promote 'the Good and Welfare' of their immortal souls. He composed individual prayers for key moments at the bedside; the first was designed for 'When you enter your Bed, or compose your self to sleep', which encouraged veneration of the Holy Trinity. This was followed by a prayer to be recited 'If at any Time in the Night you happen to awake', which urged faithful Christians to contemplate the Lord from their beds.[11] This level of instruction may well have satisfied those Christians that lacked the time and expertise, rather than the inclination, to compose prayers of their own as well as those men and women who wished to vary their diet of personal meditations.

The New Practice of Piety updated the spiritual advice of Lewis Bayly, bishop of Bangor, for a new audience in 1749, and it insisted that physical and spiritual preparations for sleep were inseparable. This collection included set prayers for distinct phases of the night: for undressing, lying down in bed, settling to prayer, waking between the first and second sleep, and for accidental waking, which might be due, for example, to the noise of a striking clock.[12] The usability of these guides was revealed in the 1726 collection *Crumbs of Comfort and Godly Prayers*, which offered separate evening prayers for individual Christians and for families, children and servants. Servants' prayers expressed the hope that restful slumber would

enable them to perform their household and Christian duties more efficiently.[13] *The Pious Country Parishioner*, which was printed in no less than
fifteen editions between 1731 and 1799, also tried to reconcile the practical
problem of balancing the demands of 'covetous Masters' with the servant's
due observance of prayer. Whilst not an ideal solution, its author advised
servants to 'redeem Time enough from his Sleep to enlarge his Devotions'
rather than forego them altogether.[14] The sleep-piety that these guides
encouraged was clearly designed to blend with the practical rhythms of the
household and to negotiate a place for divine worship amidst the hubbub of
daily life.

The opportunity to follow this advice did of course vary according to
occupation, leisure time, available space and personal character. Those men
and women who were most diligent in performing their devotions were
also the most likely to record this good behaviour and to reprove themselves when they failed to keep a strict regimen of sleep-piety. Farmer
William Coe was a dedicated Anglican and sometime churchwarden of
West Row in the parish of Mildenhall in Suffolk. Coe used his diary as a
spiritual account book and he most often recorded those occasions when
he failed to observe his bedtime devotions, which was usually due to the
practical difficulties he faced in balancing his schedule of meditation and
prayer with his professional duties and social engagements. Between 1696
and 1716 Coe rued the neglect of his evening devotions on twelve separate
occasions after he had dined out with friends or entertained them by
playing cards at home. At these times Coe's bedtimes extended from
midnight to two, three or four o'clock in the morning. He regretted
misspending this time and vowed to discontinue these worldly pursuits by
nine o'clock each evening. Coe expressed acute regret when his errant
bedtimes took a physical toll and made him 'listless', 'heavy' or 'drowsy' in
his devotions. He was convinced that such lethargy damaged the quality of
his prayers. Coe was also convinced that these lapses required God's forgiveness and so he resolved to police his sleeping habits more strictly. His deter-
mination to reform was especially strong just before and just after he
received the Holy Sacrament in church, which shows that he clearly understood his personal and public devotions as two sides of the same coin.[15]

The religious beliefs of Manchester barber, wigmaker and bookseller
Edmund Harrold might be best described as High Church Anglican, but his
diary reveals similar preoccupations to William Coe. Harrold clearly understood that disciplined bedtimes formed part of a successful strategy for
preserving the health of his soul and his marriage. Harrold believed that
living 'by rule' gave him good health, tranquillity of mind and 'a good

conscience', which taken together assured sound slumber.[16] Henry Newcome may have hoped for similar refreshment when he had a passage from the first epistle to the Corinthians read to him in his bed, which explained that self-discipline was a holy duty.[17] A clash between domestic and spiritual priorities divided Richard Burdsall and his wife Mary as the couple quarrelled over the frequency of their household prayers. Richard was an early Methodist convert and he wanted Mary to join him in prayer 'every Wednesday, Friday, and Lord's Day evening'. She agreed to his request but resisted her husband's subsequent plea to pray 'every night and morning'. Mary was anxious to complete her household tasks in a timely fashion and she scolded her husband who 'wouldst do nothing but pray' whilst she was overwhelmed with more practical duties that were themselves widely understood as markers of female piety.[18] It was not always easy to reconcile household and spiritual duties, or indeed to reconcile the different religious beliefs that caused conflict between some couples. The regular confession of devotional lapses nonetheless suggests that sleep-piety was a routine part of daily life.

The spiritual benefits associated with well-regulated sleep went hand in hand with principles of good health. Peaceful sleep offered unrivalled refreshment for body and mind and its diligent preservation was conceived as a holy duty. The urge to preserve healthy sleep cut across religious differences but the spiritual consequences of sleep's daily practice varied in important ways. Many Protestants and Catholics kept regular bedtimes and moderated their sleeping hours as part of their Christian duties, but they had different views of how far these practical steps could take them on their path towards heaven. Protestant dissenter and author of popular lifestyle guides Thomas Tryon, who we met in the previous chapter, valued a disciplined schedule of sleep-piety for its combined physical and spiritual benefits. He explained this dual purpose in his *Wisdom's Dictates: or, Aphorisms and Rules Physical, Moral, and Divine, For Preserving the Health of the Body, and the Peace of the Mind* (1696). In this small pocket-sized guide for everyday use Tryon declared that 'Temperance is endued with Divine Power, it fits the Mind for the Worship of God, their Beds are easie, their sleep sound, not subject to Indispositions'.[19] Tryon understood the lively culture of health preservation traced in the previous chapter as a form of sleep-piety. He was convinced of the spiritual value of apparently mundane sleep routines, which was made clearest in his call for the moderation of such daily habits that Tryon considered to be 'the True way, or Royal Road to Peace and Happiness, both in this World and the World to come'.[20]

Yorkshire antiquarian Ralph Thoresby put Tryon's ideas into practice, as did the nonconforming ministers Henry Newcome and Richard Baxter, who each adopted a strict sleep regimen. Thoresby, who occasionally attended the services offered by the Church of England, went to great lengths to regulate his bedtimes to maintain a regular schedule of prayer both at home and on his travels. When Thoresby slept away from home in 1680 he adapted a mechanised clock and set it beside his bed to keep to his vow of rising at five in the morning. He devised this solution after the local church bells had failed to wake him and he had missed morning prayers in Kensington and at St Paul's. His declared purpose was to devote his mornings 'to the *service of God,* by reading and prayer', which he understood to have a beneficial effect on his spiritual health.[21] Henry Newcome's regular hour of rising was around six o'clock each morning. He had a well-developed sense of when he woke 'too soone' or had slept 'too long', both of which might have negative physical and spiritual consequences.[22] Richard Baxter, a Presbyterian minister and prolific author of devotional guides, drew a very strong connection between sleep-piety and spiritual health. The performance of what he termed 'seasonable sleep' was key to the pattern of holy living that he practised and promoted through his pastoral writing. 'Seasonable sleep' was sleep that was indulged at approved times, in appropriate places, and that was sanctified by prayer. This discipline was crucial since Baxter was convinced that the human need for sleep was in itself a symptom of their weakness and liability to corruption.[23] Even though sleep was a daily reminder of human frailty, and of God's omnipotence, it nonetheless had to be safeguarded because its power to refresh Christian bodies and minds allowed them to do God's work in the world.

Richard Baxter justified his own sleep regimen on the basis of this higher spiritual purpose and he sought, above all else, to balance his efforts to redeem as much time as possible for Christian duties and pious devotions, with his need for physical refreshment. To this end Baxter cautioned against the practice of segmented sleep and shunned the advice offered in Psalm 129 that encouraged the faithful to rise from bed at midnight to give thanks to God. In so doing, he rejected the idea that there was more to be gained from midnight devotions than from those undertaken at other times of the day and night.[24] Baxter outlined four main reasons for his objection, which was based on a mixture of spiritual and healthcare concerns:

> It is a foppery and abuse of God and ourselves to think that the breaking of our sleep is a thing that of it self pleaseth God: or that rising to pray at midnight is more acceptable to God than at another hour: usually such rising to pray is sinful, 1. Because it is done in an erroneous conceit that God accepts it better than in the day time. 2. Because they waste

time in dressing and undressing. 3. Or else hurt their health by cold in
the Winter, and so lose more time than they redeem by shortning their
lives. 4. And usually they are more drousie and unfit.[25]

Baxter advised his readers to remain in bed throughout the night and to
take around six hours of sleep each night, which was enough to refresh the
'ordinary sort of healthful persons'. Five hours might suffice however for
those bodies fortified by divine favour, at whatever time of night they chose
to take it. There was then a clear link drawn between people's sleeping hours
and the strength of their individual faith.

Sleep's timing and duration was a matter of spiritual anxiety for Catholics
and for a wide variety of Protestants. Fifteen-year-old Elizabeth Livingston
was a noblewoman and a recently appointed maid in Queen Catherine of
Braganza's privy chamber. She may have been given this prestigious role at
the royal court as a reward to her family, who had fought for the martyred
King Charles I during the civil wars, before they had been forced into exile
in 1649. Elizabeth's religious beliefs are difficult to categorise. Later, she may
have become a Jacobite agent after the death of her husband, the
Northumbrian nobleman Robert Delaval, and she fled into exile in Rouen
to evade capture after a warrant was issued for her arrest. She had, it seems,
been accused of being a co-conspirator in the so-called Pewter Pot Plot.
This now infamous – and perhaps fictitious – episode centred on the
controversial birth of James Francis Edward Stuart, son of King James II
and his queen, Mary of Modena. In the summer of 1688 rumours abounded
that a healthy baby had been smuggled into the royal birthing chamber
inside a warming pan and passed off as a royal baby and the only male heir
of the unpopular Catholic monarch. If Elizabeth did turn to Catholicism in
later life, the fact remains that she was drawn to High Church Anglicanism
in her youth. It was during these early years that she composed a series of
'meditations', which reflected on the Passion of Christ and on Elizabeth's
own failings as a Christian. She often recorded the sinfulness of her erratic
bedtimes, which reduced the quality and frequency of her worship:

> The early lark wellcomes the breake of day,
> But I (alass) drouse many hour's away.
> She to my God praises dos dayly sing
> Reproaching thus my slothfull idle sin;
> Whilest I do still neglect to worshipe him
> Till all the golden houer's of morning light
> Past a recall are vanish'd out of sight.

Elizabeth reproached herself for her habit of 'staying in bed until noon' by calling herself 'Solomans slugard' – a label that clearly identified her sleeping patterns as a source of spiritual anxiety. She feared that her lazy behaviour was caused by a combination of the Devil's temptations and 'an acustomed lasynesse', which led her to neglect her devotions. By her seventeenth year Elizabeth vowed to reform and boldly declared that 'nothing but want of health shall . . . keep me in my bed when I shou'd be praiseing God'.[26]

Elizabeth understood the spiritual pitfalls of her irregular bedtimes and she feared that her behaviour might deliver her into the Devil's clutches. Her anxieties nonetheless paled in comparison to those of Richard Baxter who was gravely concerned when his own ill health disrupted his sleep. He was convinced that a weak and drowsy constitution might forebode or lead to a lack of spiritual fortitude. Worse still, his torpor might be judged a form of self-love that stemmed from 'a sensual unsanctified state of soul'.[27] Sleeping to excess signalled a lack of God's favour and Baxter feared that it might damage his chances of reaching heaven. Henry Newcome expressed similar anxieties when he experienced 'uncomfortable' or 'indifferent' nights of sleep. He interpreted them as a sign of his distance from God, which he sought to address by stricter control of his bedtimes.[28] Newcome was particularly concerned when he rested badly on a Sabbath night in December 1661 and the following morning he humbled himself before God. That evening he catechized his children after supper, led family prayers at bedtime, and thanked the Lord for delivering 'comfort & ease before wee slept', which he accepted as a reward for his acts of atonement.[29] Despite subtle differences in emphasis, Elizabeth Livingston, Richard Baxter and Henry Newcome all connected their sleeping habits with their hopes of salvation. Their fate in the next life ultimately lay in God's hands but managing their nocturnal habits was one important way of sustaining a close and healthy relationship with the Lord. The writings of Baxter and Newcome bore strong traces of older Puritan influences within English religious culture that prized self-discipline as an essential method of worship. These influences began to dilute by the late seventeenth century yet the value of seasonable sleep within the daily diet of faithful Christians was constantly reaffirmed. Richard Allestree's best-selling devotional guide *The Whole Duty of Man* was extensively reprinted and by the mid-eighteenth century it had been renamed *The New Whole Duty of Man*. The Christian's duty to manage their sleep routines and the practical advice about how to do so retained a central place within this later edition.

Some of the most vocal advocates of sleep-piety were, perhaps predictably, clergymen, and their advice about how and why bedtimes should be managed showed a firm understanding of sleep's effects on the brain and nerves. Taking too much sleep reduced the time available for work and worship, damaged the vigour of mind and body, and was injurious to the soul, according to John Wesley. Wesley's sermon on *The Duty and Advantage of Early Rising* declared that the observation of moderate and regular bedtimes was 'an important branch of *Christian Temperance*'.[30] Six hours' sleep was sufficient for most constitutions yet Methodists were also invited to admire Wesley's superior physical fortitude in rising at four o'clock each morning to attend prayer meetings.[31] Getting up at the crack of dawn served Wesley's spiritual purposes but he was also convinced of its physical benefits. Too much sleep was, he believed 'the chief, real, though unsuspected cause of all nervous diseases'.[32] Wesley here echoed a common refrain amongst medical practitioners like George Cheyne, Samuel Tissot, Francis de Valangin and James Makittrick Adair by claiming that nervous disorders had increased exponentially in his lifetime, especially amongst the wealthy and dissolute whose sins were compounded by lying too long in bed. He judged that the health of mind, body and soul depended on the smooth functioning of the brain and nerves. A disturbed mind damaged physical and emotional health: something that Wesley's sleep regimen was designed to eradicate. In his much-published *Plain Account of Christian Perfection* Wesley advised that good Christians should 'constantly go to bed and rise early, and at a fixt hour'.[33] Wesley and many early Methodist converts believed that poor-quality sleep damaged spiritual well-being since it dulled the senses and rendered Christians less receptive to the call of the Lord.[34] A calm mind that was in full control of bodily functions was thus an essential tool of spiritual improvement. Erratic sleeping patterns were, by contrast, an abuse of the body's health and a sin against God. Excessive sleep moreover indulged carnal appetites that prepared the soul 'for every other kind of intemperance' and made Christians unable to practise the kind of self-denial that was essential for spiritual purification. There was thus a fine balance to be struck between the preservation of physical and mental health for the optimum performance of worship and overindulgence in sensual bodily pleasures that could erode 'the spirit of religion' itself.[35]

Christians thus had a key role to play in regulating their nocturnal habits yet John Wesley was eager to stress that the resolve to maintain this kind of self-discipline came only from God. This mixture of active asceticism and submission to God's will was typical of evangelical religious cultures in these years.[36] Wesley advised his followers,

If you desire to rise early, sleep early: secure this point at all events, in spite of the most dear and agreeable companions – in spite of their most earnest solicitations – in spite of entreaties, railleries or reproaches, rigorously keep your hour. Rise up precisely at your time, and retire without ceremony. Keep your hour, notwithstanding pressing business: lay all things by till the morning; be it ever so great a cross, ever so great a self-denial, keep your hour or all is over.[37]

Wesley's writings circulated widely and they were clearly influential. A sermon delivered by Mrs Alexander Mather repeated verbatim Wesley's encouragement to 'Keep your hour of rising, without intermission. Do not rise two mornings, and lie in bed the third'. Her words were heard and subsequently written down by fellow Methodist Frances Pawson in an effort to commit them to memory.[38] Some Methodists such as John Henderson nevertheless found it almost impossible to follow Wesley's strict prescriptions on a regular basis.[39] Henderson's tireless efforts to stick to a regular sleeping pattern nevertheless show that sleep-piety was a central strand of the practical spirituality that shaped Methodist devotional culture. There were then important shades of opinion on the spiritual consequences of sleep-piety and its neglect. Some directly aligned good habits with heavenly reward whilst others interpreted them as part of a practical set of daily behaviours that made them good Christians. Despite these subtle differences of emphasis, sleep's critical importance to body, mind and soul was universally acknowledged.

Sleep and Death

Sleep's association with death and the resurrection proved a powerful motive for the regular and heartfelt practice of bedtime devotions. Christians routinely prepared for sleep as if they were approaching the grave. The vocabulary used to describe sleep reflected the sense of danger and oblivion that this state produced. John Evelyn feared the 'dead time of sleepe', or deep coma-like state, from which his daughter had nearly failed to wake when a fire had spread through her bedchamber in 1697.[40] Comparisons between the physical states of sleep and death found deep roots in scripture and classical literature. The gods of sleep (Hypnos) and of death (Thanatos) are represented as twin brothers in early Greek mythology. The two gods are intertwined in Hesiod's poem *Theogony* (c. 750–c. 650 BC), which narrates the origins of the Greek gods and the cosmos, and in Homer's epic poem the *Iliad*, which had a powerful influence on Renaissance literature. Scriptural texts similarly characterised sleep as a state of acute vulnerability when souls might be plucked suddenly from life and cast unprepared to confront their postmortem fate. In the Old Testament, Ish-bosheth, king of Israel, is beheaded by two of his own captains, Rechab and Baanah, as he sleeps on his bed. Sisera, commander of the Canaanite army, meets a similar fate when Jael, wife of Heber the Kenite, gives him a milky drink to put him to sleep and then drives a tent peg through his head. Her act is celebrated for liberating Israel from the oppression of King Jabin.[41] This analogous relationship between sleep and death also permeated concepts of the resurrection among a broad spectrum of English Christians. The apocalyptic Book of Daniel in the Old Testament and Christ's resurrection in the New Testament promise that the faithful dead will be restored to life on the Day of Judgment. They will wake as if from a blessed sleep to receive their reward on the morning of the last day. Church of England clergyman and antiquarian John Brand traced the root of the analogy between the early-morning dawn and the morning of the resurrection to the time of Christ's birth, which he surmised was 'about the Time of Cock-crowing'.[42]

The prospect of death subtly coloured bedtime routines within daily life, where habits of early rising were symbolically aligned with hopes of an early blessing on the day of resurrection.[43] Wealthy widow Elizabeth Chaddocke kept a copy of Richard Allestree's *Whole Duty of Man* in her Stoke Newington home according to an inventory of her goods taken in 1747. She may have been familiar with one of its special prayers entitled 'Directions for Night' that encouraged Christians to pray and confess their sins before they lay down to sleep. Allestree, and perhaps Elizabeth Chaddocke, were convinced that wise Christians 'shouldest no more venture to sleep unreconciled to God, than thou would'st dare to die so'.[44] The devout Anglican gentlewoman Alice Thornton identified the bed as a physical and symbolic bridge between sleep and death when she described the final moments of her brother's life in her autobiography. As Alice's sibling approached his end he knelt in his bed 'and most devoutly and seriously praied to his God, and heartily recomended his soule to his Creator, and soe laied himselfe quietly downe'.[45] Alice singled out the bed as the most meaningful and convenient place in which to prepare body and soul for the afterlife. She understood her own night-time devotions, which took place in and around her cherished scarlet bed, as nightly protection for body and soul and as a precious rung on the ladder towards heaven.

Securing safe passage through the night preoccupied men and women as they gradually slipped from consciousness. Their sense of anxiety may have been guided by a passage from the Book of Job that warns 'Desire not the night, when people are cut off in their place'.[46] Church ministers issued similar warnings and urged their flocks to prepare their bodies and souls for just such eventualities. Thomas Wilson, bishop of Sodor and Man, insisted that faithful souls were duty-bound to repent of sin before lying down to sleep lest they died unprepared in the night.[47] Wilson was a member of the Society for the Propagation of the Gospel who filled his practical advice about household worship with lessons and prayers from the Book of Common Prayer. The author of *Christian Prudence* likewise cautioned readers that 'When we are in bed, and just going to resign ourselves to *sleep* ... it will be highly proper to think seriously of the end of all living; and to renew those actings of faith and repentance, which we should judge necessary, if we were to awake no more in this world.' The author appended a simple prayer precisely for this purpose, entitled 'A short view of death to be taken just before we sleep'.[48] Thomas Seaton, vicar of Ravenstone in Buckinghamshire, similarly urged the laity to reflect on the precarious state that they were about to enter. He composed the following verse that could have easily functioned as a bedtime mnemonic and as a spur to repentance, 'Nor always for my Rest shall I / A Bed and Blankets have. / Soon shall the Moulds for Blankets serve, / And for my Bed the Grave'.[49] The sermons of Derbyshire Presbyterian minister William Bagshawe proved popular across Derbyshire and the Pennines in the late seventeenth century and were published posthumously for a new audience after his death in 1702. Bagshawe likened the grave to 'a Bed of Rest' that offered the promise of resurrection to faithful Christians. He may have intended these words of comfort to relieve common anxieties surrounding sleep's onset. He assured his listeners and readers that none 'save weak Children' should be afraid to go to bed at night if they had performed their prayers in the proper manner.[50]

The elision of sleep and death thus informed the content of bedtime prayers and also shaped people's interactions with their sleeping environments. *The New Practice of Piety* directed its readers to consider 'the bed-cloaths the mould, that shall one day cover your breathless carcass'.[51] For many Christians this parallel took material form. The devotional uses of linen touched on in the previous chapter extended to the widespread use of linen winding sheets, which were often taken from the bed of the deceased before their bodies were washed and encased in the material before burial. Few have survived for obvious reasons. There was a strong likeness, however, between ordinary household bedsheets and the sheets that were used to cover the bodies of the recently deceased before burial when they lay in their homes to be 'watched' and visited by family and friends who wished to pay their respects.[52] Figure 6 shows a hand-woven linen sheet whose bright white appearance and elaborate stitching lend it a distinct air of sanctity. The central seam of decorative bobbin lace and the sets of embroidered initials that appear on the sheet are remarkably similar to surviving household bedsheets discussed in Chapter 4.

The sheet is in pristine condition despite dating to *c.* 1575–*c.* 1625, and being in use until *c.* 1900, when it was believed to have covered the body of one Sarah Blunt, née Staffurth, who lived at Whittlesey on the Isle of Ely. Light and occasional use is likely given the sheet's age and its lack of visible wear and repair work. The five knotted tassels that are attached to the sheet's central panel and to each of its corners were probably designed to weight it down as it was draped over a dead body, rather than being tucked into a bed. The embroidered initials in pink silk thread provide the final clue to the sheet's mortuary function. There are six sets of initials and four sets of accompanying dates that range from 1786 to 1900. The initials very likely referred to members of the family who had been laid out beneath the sheet across many generations with the dates marking their year of death.

If this sheet lay on top of a dead body, then it may well have been accompanied by the kind of thick plaited carex mattress discussed and depicted in the previous chapter, which could be used during childbirth or for laying

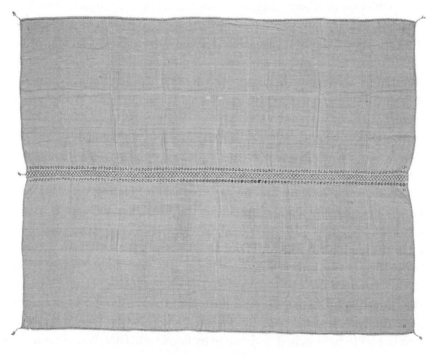

6. Sheet, England, *c.* 1575–*c.* 1625.

out the dead at home. This object combined a practical and symbolic purpose, which is illustrated by its widespread representation on funeral monuments. Figure 7 depicts one of many representations of such mattresses on English funeral monuments beneath the recumbent figures of Sir William Petre (1505/6–1572), who served as royal secretary, and his wife in the church of St Edmund and St Mary, Ingatestone, Essex.[53]

The most remarkable monumental evidence of the links between sleep and death nonetheless appeared on the stone tomb of the Haddon and Makepeace family in St Mary's churchyard in Heworth near Gateshead. The tomb was crafted *c.* 1721 by the local mason Joseph Haddon, who dedicated it to the memory of his three children, William and George and their unnamed sister, who all died within the space of six years. The children lie side by side in a four-poster bedstead and they are covered with a decorative whole-cloth quilt, which was an expensive and fashionable textile at the time of the tomb's creation. The eldest son clutches an open book to his chest, which bears the inscription 'LORD Recive Our Souls'.[54] Joseph Haddon expressed the depth of his paternal grief by depicting his beloved children sleeping peacefully within this safe and comfortable bedstead. He may also have imagined that this serene repose reflected his children's happy fate in the next life as he tried to come to terms with his loss. The rare survival of these kinds of objects and monuments reveals the intimate

7. Petre monument, St Mary's, Ingatestone.

connections between the physical and spiritual states of sleep and death within early modern culture.

Bedtime Prayer

A rich variety of prayers and rituals of preservation were undertaken at bedtime. Some derived from devotional literature, some from the Book of Common Prayer, and others from sermons. They were unified by the hope that God's mercy, if granted, would allow Christians to wake and feel refreshed the following morning. The Book of Psalms confirmed that only God's love provided an impenetrable shield to secure vulnerable sleeping bodies. Many Christians nevertheless believed that the Lord might look favourably on those that invested time and effort in their bedtime prayers. Itinerant Methodist preacher John Valton saw a pressing need to sanctify his sleep with regular bedtime prayer. In 1765 he confessed that 'I have had lately thought, of the Devil's appearing when I have been at prayer, just before going to bed'.[55] Valton later crossed out this passage, which may suggest that he feared this admission uncovered a weakness of faith in the Lord's protection. Valton drew on John Wesley's advice when he felt the need 'to compose myself in bed' to fit his mind to repel the diabolical forces that might assault him during sleep. Valton took physical and spiritual action when he was awoken in the night by terrifying visions of devils; he turned his body from back to front, said a few words in prayer, and was pleased to note that he 'slept undisturbed till morning'.[56]

The language of bedtime prayer further emphasised the overwhelming sense of frailty that sleepers felt at bedtime, which enhanced their need for protection. Morning and evening prayers were the central focus of public worship and of individual and familial devotions at home. These prayers bookended the hours of sleep and they took centre stage within published devotional guides and in household routines of sleep-piety. Thomas Seaton's *Devotional Life Render'd Familiar, Easy, and Pleasant* (1734) included 'An Ejaculation at Night' and a short hymn to be recited 'When about to lie down to sleep'.[57] Seaton dedicated this work to his parishioners and he offered his advice in the lively form of hymns to infuse daily habits with spiritual purpose. When William Pulteney, earl of Bath, was too ill to attend his local parish church he stayed in his bedchamber and read a version of the church service.[58] John Evelyn was similarly diligent in his daily devotions. Evelyn was convinced of the need 'never to omitt our Evening devotion, when we betake our selves to rest, nor our Morning adoration & prayer'.[59] William Coe recorded a prayer in his diary 'to be said at the bed side just before you stepp into bedd' to beg forgiveness for sin, and 'Another prayer to be sayd just att getting out of bedd' that offered thanks for God's protection during the night: 'To thee, my most adorable preserver, I humbly offer up my preserved self: my body, my soul, my members, my senses, my faculties, my thoughts, my words, my desires, my inclinations, my affections, my actions to be governed, guided and sanctifyed by thee and to be made conformable to thy holy will this day and alwaies. Amen.'[60] Coe's words expose the sense of oblivion that sleep imposed upon his body and mind, as well as the reassurance that he sought from the Lord's watchful protection. The gratitude that William Coe expressed to God for his safe-keeping was echoed by Elizabeth Johnson from Bristol who wrote in 1760, 'Lord I adore thee for standing by me in a violent temptation in the night.'[61] It was only with the Lord's assistance that faithful Christians could resist diabolical enticements and their ability to do so was severely compromised when they lay unconscious in their beds.

The form and content of bedtime prayers reveal some of the anxieties that accompanied bedtime as well as the ways that men and women tried to defend themselves and their loved ones from danger. Thomas Ken, nonjuring bishop of Bath and Wells, composed bedtime prayers for his parishioners in which heavenly protection was sought: 'O may my Guardian while I sleep, / Close to my Bed his vigils keep, / His Love Angelical instill, / Stop all the Avenues of ill.'[62] This 'White Paternoster', a lyrical prayer typically sung by children as they went to bed, was adapted from an earlier Catholic version and it carefully avoided the invocation of saints and instead expressed faith in God's saving grace.[63] The relevance of Ken's words in the later eighteenth century led John Wesley to adapt them for his sermons in which he made explicit reference to the protection of guardian angels at the bedside,

O may thine angels while I sleep
Around my bed their vigils keep!
Their love angelical instil
Stop all the consequence of ill:
May they celestial joys rehearse,
And thought to thought with me converse;
Or in my stead the whole night long
Sing to my God a grateful song.[64]

Wesley, and many of his contemporaries, was drawn to the idea that God's angels could shield sleepers from danger during the night.[65] This comforting thought was seconded by Bishop Thomas Wilson in his devotional guide for young Christians; the evening prayer confirmed that God had 'given his Angels Charge concerning his Elect, to preserve them from the Powers of Darkness, from the Dangers of the Night, and from all sad Accidents'.[66] Images of angels surrounding the deathbed was a familiar visual motif in the *Ars moriendi* tradition, which was a body of literature and visual images that gave practical and spiritual advice to Christians about how to die well. Angels typically appeared at the bedside to battle demons for the soul of the dying person, or to encourage him or her to direct their thoughts and prayers to God as they passed from life to death. Protestants fiercely debated the existence and activities of angels in the immediate aftermath of the European Reformations, but their protective function at the deathbed, and indeed during sleep, continued to appeal to ordinary Christians who were keenly aware of the dangers that might befall them in the night. The well-established role of angels in offering solace to the living in times of peril thus remained a comforting balm that could ease an anxious mind at bedtime.[67]

Bedtime prayer gave Christians the chance to make peace with God, to strengthen their faith by cultivating warm spiritual affections, and to recommend their souls to the Lord's watchful care.[68] Meditative bedtime prayer had the added benefit of relieving the mind of the day's anxieties, which helped to bridge the gap between waking and sleeping. Begging forgiveness for the sins of the day and putting aside worldly cares in peaceful spiritual contemplation encouraged physical and psychological sensations that were associated with the approach of restful sleep. Deep breathing and quiet, focused thoughts helped to compose minds and bodies into a state of relaxation that allowed sleep to take hold of them more easily. These habits also chimed with medical advice that encouraged men and women to set aside worldly concerns and calm their passions as bedtime approached; a peaceful mind and tranquil nerves were, after all, the best preparation for a good night's sleep.

These devotional habits also helped to alleviate the stresses of work and family life that often weighed heavily on the mind at night and that could easily delay sleep's onset. The calming effect that spiritual contemplation could provide was recognised by devotional writers who recommended bedtime prayer as a combined source of spiritual, physical and psychological comfort. Thomas Seaton's bedtime hymn urged faithful Christians to empty their minds of all worldly distractions before attempting to sleep: 'All pure and all devout shall be / The Thoughts upon my bed / No low, and no inglorious Theme / Shall exercise my Mind.' Seaton adapted his advice on bedtime worship to blend with the sleeping habits of his readers. If they awoke in the night he recommended that 'your Meditations be ever pure and holy, and the Subject of 'em profitable'. In these moments of wakefulness, Christians should beg the Lord to keep their minds free from 'vile Fancy' and 'impure Desire' that might trigger unclean sexual acts.[69] When Henry Newcome woke unexpectedly in the night he 'endeavoured to meditate of God on my bed accord: to Ps. Lxiii, 6, and had some profit yre from'. Psalm 63, line 6 went as follows: 'On my bed I remember you; I think of you through the watches of the night'.[70] In 1761 Richard Burdsall was unable to sleep as he was tormented by thoughts of his brother's spiritual fate soon after his death. As he lay alone and awake in his bed, Richard sought solace in prayer to calm his fears that his brother was now being tormented by the Devil in hellish 'globes of fire'.[71] In 1745 Moravian convert William Hammond likewise addressed the 'Tumults' of mind occasioned by 'vain Delights' and 'Carnal Thoughts' at bedtime and he turned to prayer, begging Christ to help him raise his thoughts above such base concerns.[72] Ralph Josselin similarly understood the need to fit his mind for holy worship and for sleep. In February 1680 he chided himself that his head was 'full of vain thoughts and on my bed'.[73] Josselin believed that his bed was a particularly inappropriate place to entertain worldly thoughts, especially when prayer and meditation had helped to sanctify it.

The way that bedtime prayer affected the body and mind was just as important as its content in securing good health and longevity. A tension existed nonetheless between the desire to perform heartfelt bedside devotions, the soporific effects of prayer, and the physical exhaustion associated with this time of night. The sister-in-law of politician John Perceval, Lord Egmont, reproved herself when fatigue led her to pray one night 'as she lay in bed' rather than on her knees at the bedside. She may have feared that the comfort and warmth of her bed would lure her to sleep before her devotions were complete.[74] Henry Newcome expressed similar anxiety about the sinfulness of feeling sleepy during bedtime prayer, which could impede its quality and cut short its duration. In December 1662 he included the following reproof in his diary: 'I would have meditated at night & did but little, onely family dutys were somewh: more lively yn somet: they have beene. I am much out of order, very unworthy of any favor.'[75]

For Henry Newcome, and for many of his contemporaries, bedtime prayer was a vital ingredient within household schedules of piety. Anticipation of its soothing effects must also be acknowledged as a compelling reason for its routine practice since it eased the passage into restful slumber. These calming effects could also help to ease the tensions of family life. It was in bed that husbands and wives shared their innermost thoughts and emotions and experiences of the day, which sometimes led to conflict. Yorkshire farmer Adam Eyre rose from his bed to pray in the middle of the night after he had quarrelled with his wife. Upon rising he turned to the advice 'of Lawrence concerning the assistance of Angells ... [and] I prayed God again to direct mee, ans [sic] so slept til morne quietly, praysed be God'. Eyre likely took his solace from Chapter 6 of Henry Lawrence's work *Of Our Communion and Warre with Angels*, a commentary on the New Testament's Ephesians, which encourages Christians to battle spiritual wickedness.[76] When Samuel Pepys confessed to cheating on his wife in 1668 he wrote in his diary that 'I did this night promise to my wife never to go to bed without calling upon God upon my knees by prayer, and I begun this night, and hope I shall never forget to do the like all my life; for I do find that it is much the best for my soul and body to live pleasing to God and my poor wife, and will ease me of much care as much expense.'[77] Elizabeth's demand may not have been motivated by a care for her husband's soul but the couple nevertheless valued bedtime prayer as a means of resolving marital discord and calming their passions before sleep. Bedtime prayers could thus combine emotional and spiritual consolation during moments of personal crisis that cemented their place at the heart of household life.

Bedtime Reading

Bedtime prayer was often preceded, accompanied or followed by bedtime reading. Its content, as far as is recoverable, was usually of a spiritual nature and it was typically undertaken in sleeping chambers, adjoining closets or in bed where readers could benefit from the light of fires, bedside candles or moonlight that shone in through the chamber window, or even through a small 'moon-hole' cut into the wooden window shutters, an example of which survives in a bedchamber at Hanbury Hall that was built at the turn of the eighteenth century for the chancery lawyer and Whig politician Thomas Vernon.[78] The quality of light available through a window waxed and waned in line with prevailing weather conditions, and depending on the house's location and arrangement; some may have benefited from the dim light of oil lamps on urban streets whilst those that lacked any kind of window would have relied entirely on internal illumination. Candlelight was difficult – and often expensive – to obtain, with few households able to afford a plentiful supply of good wax candles that gave off a more consistent light (and a less disagreeable odour) than the cheap tallow candles and rushlights that were made from, or coated in, animal fats.[79] Glimpses of how people negotiated these obstacles nevertheless surface in letter and diary entries and they illuminate what must have been habitual reading practices. In his youth Henry Newcome fashioned a rudimentary candle-stick holder made of vellum that he nailed to his bedhead so that he could read before going to sleep. Newcome fell asleep whilst reading one night and awoke the next morning to find that the candle had entirely burned away but had not fallen into his bed and set light to his covers – a mercy for which he thanked God. In spite of this scare, Newcome could not be deterred from his bedtime reading but he did become accustomed to placing his candle in the chamber window, rather than over his bed in future years.[80] When Henry Newcome later formed his own household, he may have had more privileged access to candlelight than the other members of his household as he guided his children to bed and secured the doors. It was usually the father's role, as head of the household, to secure its boun-daries at night, although this was not always the case. Clergyman Samuel Wesley kept one candle burning at bedtime in his family home, which he used to guide himself to bed and perhaps to aid his reading, before it was collected by his daughter Molly, who was responsible for 'shutting in'.[81]

The practical difficulties of reading at night were offset by the psycho-logical benefits that it offered, which was comparable to saying a prayer. Henry Newcome read one of Bishop Ussher's sermons before retiring and noted that he was 'a little better disposed before I went to bed' as a result. Newcome kept psalmbooks and other 'good' books close at hand during the night to 'keepe the heart company' just in case he woke unex-pectedly. He may have hoped that these works would keep his mind fixed on spiritual matters and defend him against the assaults of Satan, about which he wrote in his diary.[82] Alice Thornton read devotional works to her husband William whilst they lay together in bed at night. The strength that William drew from this material fortified him to rise early each morning to perform his Christian duties. Alice may have learned this pious habit from her father, Christopher Wandesford, who engaged one of his servants to read to him from some 'good booke' until he was overcome with sleep.[83] Samuel Pepys sometimes read himself to sleep, whilst Edmund Harrold's bedtime reading included William Sherlock's *Practical Discourse concerning Death* and sermons by John Norris. The first was carefully selected to support Harrold's meditations on death whilst the second offered him 'a great deal of comforts to my soul' after he had squabbled with his wife about his excessive drinking. After being ejected from the marital bed, Harrold lay down on a couch chair to read and then slept quietly there for three hours.[84] The calming effect that bedtime reading was expected to produce may have been one important reason for widespread disapproval of novel reading at bedtime, which encouraged readers to dwell on worldly concerns, overexcited their nerves and passions, or invited lascivious thoughts.[85] Bedtime reading could help prepare people for sleep's approach by comforting their bodies and minds, and by putting them in the right frame of mind to contemplate the Christian afterlife. After reading the letters of Roman lawyer and magistrate Pliny the Younger that described the eruption of Mount Vesuvius in AD 79, the young tailor's daughter Sarah Hurst was prompted to reflect on the fragility of human life and the 'Instability of all earthly things'. The tone of Sarah's reflections suggests that these thoughts were also strengthened by the solemn associations that sleep's onset often brought with it.[86]

The sobering and soporific effects of bedtime reading inspired devout Anglican and countess of Pembroke, Dorset and Montgomery, Lady Anne Clifford, to have scriptural passages read to her whilst she lay in bed. This may have been her regular practice but she noted down its beneficial effects in her diary at times of crisis and transition in her life. When Anne was in her final year of life she directed George Goodgion to purchase no less than twenty-eight 'bookes of Devotion' at Penrith, which he delivered to her bedchamber. The countess gave six to her domestic servants and the rest to her family and friends for their edification.[87] The urge to seek spiritual consolation and relaxation from bedtime reading was likely to have been instilled from an early age. Children were educated in the basics of literacy and Christianity each night.[88] The Bible was the staple source of bedtime instruction for children but James Janeway's austere *A Token for Children* (1676) was also specially designed for bedtime use. Janeway was licensed as a Presbyterian minister in London in 1672 and his work may have had a distinct appeal amongst Nonconformist communities in the capital, being composed of a series of sober and exemplary narratives of the holy lives and peaceful deaths of Christian children.[89]

The content and effects of devotional literature offered natural supports for bedside prayer. As darkness fell, Edmund Harrold read from Thomas Comber's weighty volume *A Companion to the Temple and Closet: or, a Help to Publick and Private Devotion* (1672).[90] Comber was dean of Durham and a prolific writer whose guide offered a close commentary on the Book of Common Prayer that was intended to promote its daily use. The first part of the guide was dedicated to morning and evening prayer, which was designed to lift the mind upwards from worldly oppression to divine contemplation. Similar works were listed in principal sleeping chambers or in adjacent closets in the household inventory sample. In September 1755 wealthy London widow Martha Dodson paid one shilling for a copy of Thomas Ken's *Manual of Prayers for the Use of the Scholars of Winchester Colledge*. This popular devotional guide spawned twenty-one editions between 1674 and 1728. The *Manual* included morning, evening and midnight hymns that drew parallels between the human need for sleep and spiritual weakness. This frailty made pleas for divine protection during the night even more pressing.[91] Thomas Ken died in 1711 but a devotional guide of 1725 that bore his name urged Christians to kneel and pray before getting into bed to invite peaceful rest.[92] When the Westminster home of widow Mary Martin was appraised in January 1669 '2 bibles &c.' were listed. Both were located in Mary's sleeping chamber, which also contained the most expensive and well-appointed bedstead in the house. The 1737 inventory of Essex spinster Elizabeth Beacon listed 'A large book of martyrs, one large Bible, 33 small old books, poems & plays' amidst a pile of bedsheets and pillowcases.[93] Rebecca Weekes's home had just two sleeping chambers, the principal of which was simply yet comfortably furnished with a bedstead, clock, a chest of drawers and two bibles. The 1738 inventory of Richard Burford's substantial Wapping residence listed one bedstead and its trappings alongside 'three bibles & a prayer book' in one of the upstairs chambers. If these books were largely reserved for the bedtime devotions of a particular individual, the 'two old Bibles' and 'nine Books of Divinity' on the kitchen bookcase may have offered a shared resource for other members of the household.[94] In the 1750s Benjamin Coster's appraisers listed 'one volume Follio of Burket on the New Testament' and 'a common prayer book' on his parlour staircase. The former text was most likely authored by Church of England minister William Burkitt, whose folio *Expository Notes, with Practical Observations, on the New Testament*, first published in 1700, had reached its twenty-second edition by 1736.[95] Householders, children or servants who progressed up the staircase at night could have easily accessed these texts. The staircase also housed a 'hand lanthorn' to light the way upstairs to bed and perhaps a light by which to read.[96] Inventories list these texts but they do not detail who read them, or how often. There is nonetheless widespread evidence that morning and evening prayers, the collects and the Psalms were learned by rote and committed to memory.[97] Anglican churchgoers could moreover have heard the collect read, and perhaps sung, on a regular basis.[98] If members of Benjamin Coster's household had read the appropriate section of the 1662 Book of Common Prayer they would have been familiar with the third collect at evening prayer that beseeches the Lord 'by thy great mercy defend us from all perils and dangers of this night'.[99] The specific content of some bedtime reading confirmed sleep's spiritual meanings and on occasions this habitual practice offered a practical method of inducing sleep.

Sanctifying the Bedchamber

Having sufficient time, space and the necessary materials to perform bedtime devotions was just as important as having the motivation to undertake them. Chapter 4 charts the relative degrees of seclusion that men and women enjoyed at bedtime within their homes. Whilst this varied widely, the desirability of an enclosed personal space was no doubt enhanced by the opportunity it afforded for Christians to perform their prayers and meditations in peace and quiet. Even those who did not enjoy this luxury might seek out a quiet time and a secret place for prayer when the rest of the household was busy, or had already retired to bed.[100] For many Christians, however, 'secret' prayer was a relative term that sometimes referred to quiet prayer in a pair, or in a small group, rather than in isolation. The key for all of these varieties of worship was to find a time and place that allowed calm clarity of thought.[101]

William Best was minister of the guild church of St Lawrence Jewry and St Mary Magdalen, which had been rebuilt by 1687 after the original medieval church was destroyed in London's Great Fire of 1666. Best was also rector of Keston in Kent and he composed an 'EVENING PRAYER, for a Person in private' for his parishioners' use. The prayer was later published for a broader audience when it featured in the collection of Church of England devotions that Best compiled for the Society for Promoting Christian Knowledge, first published in 1746. Best's prayer included a confession, petitions for repentance and a request for divine protection during the night. He incorporated a recommendation from Independent minister Isaac Watts,

> that PARENTS and MASTERS, who take due Care of the Souls of their Children and Servants, should not only admonish and encourage them to pray to God in secret, Morning and Evening, but should point out a proper Place for their Retirement. This is easily done in small Families; and they should inquire whether their Children, or Servants, observe the Seasons of secret Prayer, or not.[102]

Watts and Best recognised that some degree of seclusion for bedtime devotions was not always available to everybody. They nonetheless encouraged householders to temporarily reserve a space for these essential devotions.

These routine practices were rarely recorded in textual form except on those occasions when the time and space to undertake them was not available. Ralph Thoresby lamented frequent interruptions to his prayer schedule during his tour of the British Isles. In 1703 he rued the lack of 'conveniency of retirement to prayer', which related to a shortage of time and to the necessity of sharing a chamber, and even a bed, with his fellow travellers. Thoresby was fond of secret prayer at his home in Leeds, where he could perform it in his own bedchamber or adjoining closet.[103] In 1708 Thoresby's lodgings in the Yorkshire village of Bishopthorpe were so overcrowded that there were three to a bed; his main concern, however, was that he 'could have no opportunity of private prayer'. Some months later Thoresby devised a tactic to deal with these circumstances by rising two hours earlier than usual 'Being afraid of omitting secret prayer, (if I should lie till my chamber-fellow got up)'. Pleased with his success, Thoresby noted the very next evening that he 'got an opportunity in secret to bless God for mercies vouchsafed, and implore further protection, though had a Scotch physician for my chamber-fellow'. The greatest inconvenience, however, came in 1712 when Thoresby undertook a journey with four gentlemen acquaintances. The pleasure he gained from his companions was offset by the fact 'that all four gentlemen being in one chamber, I was in a manner prevented of private prayer, both evening and morning. The Lord pity and pardon!' It was only when Thoresby parted from his friends that he was able to speak to his God secretly and directly; being unable to do so even for short periods of time was a cause of anxiety for which faithful Christians like Ralph Thoresby begged forgiveness.[104]

Once again the perceived vulnerability of the sleep state framed these practices. Scripture taught that earthly and spiritual enemies could assault sleepers in their beds and practical experience confirmed that sleeping chambers were uniquely dangerous places. These rooms relied heavily on candlelight, warming pans and fires for light and warmth, especially in the cold winter months. The unpredictable stirrings of sleepers frequently resulted in fires and other accidents. Ralph Josselin was thankful for his deliverance after his 'maides sleepiness or carelesnes' allowed a candle to set light to a wooden bowl in her chamber.[105] Josselin drew a stark contrast between the mercy that his own household had been shown on this occasion and the judgment passed on one of his wayward parishioners who was 'burnt in his bed' after lying down drunk in 1677.[106] Alice Thornton thanked the Lord for preserving the life of her child Naly who fell into the fire in her bedchamber after stumbling on the hearth. Alice's household was again threatened by fire in 1661 when her maidservant Nan Wellburne 'carlesly struck the candle at her bed head, and fell asleepe, soe it fell downe on the pillow and her head, and burned her clothes'. Nan woke to extinguish the flames when smoke began to fill her lungs, for which Alice praised God's mercy.[107] Both Ralph and Alice interpreted the physical dangers they encountered in their sleeping chambers within a providential system of judgments and mercies, which likely had their roots in deep-seated perceptions of beds as sites of transition between the earthly and spiritual realms.

Sleeping chambers assumed acute spiritual significance precisely because they hosted vulnerable sleepers who were transported between different states of consciousness each night. The transformative quality associated with sleep also extended to sleeping chambers and their material trappings. As Tara Hamling has shown, the walls, ceilings and moveable goods of many sixteenth- and seventeenth-century Protestant homes were adorned with biblical scenes and lessons from devotional guides that were intended to support household worship and to provide didactic instruction to their inhabitants at all times of the day and night. The spiritualised household that Hamling describes was heavily composed of visual and material objects and this was nowhere more visible than in sleeping environments, whose physical make-up and management marked them out as thresholds between the natural and supernatural worlds.[108] These meanings were partially signalled by the visual cues that surrounded the bedside, by the devotional practices that took place within them, and by commonplace beliefs that divine and diabolical spirits might visit sleepers during the night. A dramatic encounter of this kind features in the popular ballad 'Young Bateman's ghost, or, a godly warning to all maidens', which was published in eight separate editions between 1658 and 1760.

8. 'Young Bateman's ghost, or, a godly warning to all maidens', London, 1760.

Here God punishes a young woman for breaking a secret vow to marry her first love – a young man from Nottingham named Bateman, whom she forsakes to wed a richer man. Bateman hangs himself before the bride's door on the day of her wedding and his miserable ghost, aided by the Devil, is later permitted to carry away his beloved as she sleeps in her husband's arms. The young woman anticipates her fate and tries to prevent it by staying awake, and by begging her friends (in vain) to keep vigil over her during the night:

O! watch with me this night I pray
and see you do not sleep;
No longer then you do not wake,
My body can you keep:
All promised to do their best,
Yet nothing could suffice,
In middle of the night to keep
Sad slumber from their eyes.
So being all full fast asleep,
To them unknown which way,
The child bed woman that woeful night
From thence was born away;

This morality tale shows in dramatic form that it was during sleep, and in their bedsteads, that humans felt most vulnerable to diabolical attack, especially if they had committed some offence against God, who might withdraw his protection from them whilst they rested.[109]

The need for protection during the night shaped the decoration of sleeping chambers, which was a common and meaningful pursuit. Objects, images, inscriptions, texts and textiles provided physical comfort and convenience but they also conveyed important religious and psychological meanings. These factors converged in the home of Lincolnshire physician and antiquarian William Stukeley. In 1727 Stukeley wrote to his friend and fellow antiquarian Samuel Gale to tell him that he had 'adorned my study with heads, bas reliefs, bustos, urns, & drawings of Roman antiquitys, as my bedchamber adjoining with Aegyptian, which become prophylactic, & drive off all evil'.[110] Stukeley redecorated his bedchamber after he moved from London to establish a new household and a medical practice in Grantham. Here he indulged his interest in religious antiquities, which was encouraged by his friendship with fellow physician Sir Hans Sloane. Stukeley's interest in antiquities was underpinned by his medical training and by his Christian faith, and he was ordained in the Church of England in 1729.

William Stukeley's efforts to protect himself from danger signalled his belief that his bedchamber was a place of particular weakness, especially during sleep when body and soul were open to attack. His impression was echoed by popular ballads, poems and plays which dramatised the ability of supernatural agents to prey on sleepers. The perils to which sleeping children were exposed during the night were depicted by English playwright Ben Jonson, whose *Masque of Queens*, performed at the court of King James I on 2 February 1609, describes a hag-witch that creeps beneath the cradles of babies and young children to suck out their breath. Placing protective charms and objects in and around cradles at night appears to have been a common practice within many households and this may well have helped to ease fears of destruction during the night. It would appear that the power of these objects was thought to be especially strong when they were made of coral. Medical practitioner John Pechey noted the widespread parental habit of hanging coral amulets around children's necks at bedtime. Henry Bourne, an antiquarian and curate of All Hallows' Church in Newcastle upon Tyne, surveyed the customs and beliefs of rural communities in northeast England in the early eighteenth century. Bourne's research was republished in 1777 by John Brand, a fellow antiquarian and curate of Cramlington near Newcastle, who noted coral's popularity for making 'that well-known Toy, with Bells &c. and *Coral* at the end, which is generally suspended from their [children's] Necks'. Two decorative children's rattles from the eighteenth century neatly fit this description and both feature coral teething sticks, bells and a whistle.[111] These toys promised both entertainment and protection to their young owners. Coral, when ingested, was commonly thought to ward off childhood ailments such as epilepsy and tooth and gum problems.

Coral's protective qualities combined natural and spiritual elements that rested on the transformative capacity of this organic material and on its symbolic significance within early modern religious culture. This was based in part on the myth of coral's origin, which dated back to antiquity. Ovid describes in his *Metamorphoses* how coral was born from the dwindling power of the snake-haired gorgon Medusa, whose gaze had the power to turn people into stone. After the Greek hero Perseus chops off Medusa's head whilst she sleeps, the plants onto which it falls harden and turn the colour of blood. This story, and the deep pink and red shades of many coral pieces, eased their application within Christian culture, where the material was associated with death, with Christ's passion and with resurrection. The infant Jesus was often depicted wearing a coral necklace in Italian and Dutch paintings from the twelfth century onwards and coral was also a popular material from which devotional objects like rosaries were crafted. Indeed, the demand for coral boomed in the early modern period when it supported vibrant centres of coral fishing and manufacture in Trapani, Sicily, in Marseilles, in the Caribbean, and close to St Michael's Mount off the Cornish coast.[112] Different philosophers and physicians variously classified coral as a marine plant and as an animal in the course of the early modern period. Coral's ability to live underwater and on land complemented its use both as a cool medicinal treatment for sleeping problems and as a spiritual talisman to wear to bed. Here was a substance that, just like sleep, was able to traverse different environments and states of being. It was perhaps for this reason that coral amulets were believed especially effective for protecting young people from physical ailments and from ghosts, demons and nightmares, since they could accompany the sleeper as he or she passed from the waking world into the realm of sleep.[113]

Alongside coral, the precious stone known as chrysolite, or topaz, shared a potent affinity with sleep and was widely credited with the power to ease the mind of sadness and drive off nocturnal fears. Like coral, this stone's healing reputation combined its mineral properties with its sacred history. In the Book of Exodus, chrysolite is one of twelve carefully chosen jewels placed on the sacred breastplate worn by the High Priest of the Israelites, with each stone engraved with the name of one of Israel's twelve tribes. The relative softness of chrysolite and its translucent appearance may well have affirmed its reputation as an organic healing material. Similar qualities were attributed to the oily-black stone known as gagate, stone-coal or jet. This light, glistening and malleable carbon fossil was widely used to make amulets and medicinal talismans as well as to craft rosary beads and sacred images of the saints in ancient times. Gagate's protective qualities still resonated in seventeenth-century England. Thomas Nicols of Jesus College, Cambridge reported in 1652 that wearing the stone upon the body was commonly believed to prevent nightmares and the visit of evil spirits, especially the incubus.[114] Protection of a more visceral kind may have been sought from hanging wolves' teeth around a child's neck, or from the suspension of carving knives over the cradles of unbaptized children. This practice was described as customary in eighteenth-century Northumberland and in the West Riding of Yorkshire, where unbaptised children were judged to be at the mercy of fairies during the night because they had not received God's protection through the baptismal ceremony.[115]

Children were deemed especially vulnerable to supernatural incursions during sleep but adults also tried to protect themselves by surrounding the bedstead with comforting visual and material supports. Anne Clifford was in the habit of noting down '*things new and old*, Sentences, or Sayings of remark, which she had read or learned out of Authors' onto small pieces of paper with the help of her servants. These pieces were then pinned onto the countess's walls, bed and hangings so that she, or her servants, could 'make their descants on them'.[116] These scraps of paper served an important mnemonic function for Anne and her household staff and she hoped that they might trigger earnest prayers that begged for the Lord's protection during the night.[117] Edward Rainbowe, bishop of Carlisle, warmly approved of Anne's practice, and he recommended it to others when he delivered her funeral sermon in 1676. In his oration, Rainbowe compared Anne's bedchamber to 'a Temple' and a fit place 'where God was daily, nay, thrice a day, worshipped'.[118]

The ceilings of sleeping chambers were also the most common place to find candle marks, which were distinctive marks made by wax and black carbon that were deliberately made above the bedstead by specialist practitioners of 'candle magic', probably at the commission of anxious householders. Architectural historian Timothy Easton has traced sixteen marked ceilings of this kind from the early modern period across the counties of Suffolk, Norfolk, Essex, Kent and Derbyshire. They illustrate a complex mixture of symbols, motifs and letters. The vast majority of candle marks survive in the principal sleeping chambers of gentry households and the protective powers associated with these marks appear to have been purposefully designed to protect the bodies and souls of sleepers during the night. Candle magic was a form of natural magic but it was blended with Christian symbols through the drawing of crosses and gridirons, which pointed to the divine source of the sleeper's protection and may have encouraged them to offer prayers to God in return as they glanced upwards from the bed. Gridirons were cooking utensils used to cook meat or fish over a fire, but they also doubled as musical instruments on special occasions. Gridirons were played and crosses were marked on the ceilings of many households during festive Twelfth Night celebrations and during Carnival as ritual methods of securing its boundaries from the attack of evil spirits. When placed above the bedstead, these protective marks very likely offered a feeling of reassurance and safety to those on the verge of sleep. Protection of a very specific kind is associated with an intriguing set of candle marks from a house in the village of Great Barton in Suffolk, which are shown in Figure 9.

9. Candle-marked ceiling from Great Barton, Suffolk,
c. 1660–*c.* 1700.

These candle marks decorated the ceiling of the sleeping chamber above the kitchen, which was marked several times with the name 'Sarah Sugate', who was the daughter of Robert and Mary Sugate who moved to Great Barton in the 1650s.[119] Timothy Easton has persuasively argued that Sarah may well have been a sleepwalker because the candle marks in the chamber in which she most likely slept, were placed above the bedstead and they continued on the ceiling of the neighbouring stairwell that led from the chamber down to the kitchen. The candle marks may have been intended to protect Sarah from diabolical forces in this disturbed state or simply to protect her from falling down the stairs. Either way, Sarah's parents were anxious to shield their daughter, and perhaps the rest of their household, from harm during the night.[120]

The use of candle marks and habitual routines of morning, evening and midnight prayer expressed potent feelings of insecurity and an accompanying desire for magical or supernatural protection during sleep. The bedtime prayers traced previously helped to prepare people physically and mentally for the transition between waking and sleeping and they also established the overlapping functions of bedsteads as places of sexual activity, illness and recuperation, and as sites of worship. The prominence of bedsteads during major life-cycle events such as childbirth and death reinforced their sanctified meanings at certain times. On Christmas Day, 1668, Alice Thornton was delighted to receive the Holy Sacrament as she sat in bed, recuperating her strength and her spirits following her husband's death.[121] In the last months of Anne Clifford's life, her local parson, Mr Grasty, read from the Book of Common Prayer and sang Psalms to those gathered around Anne's bedstead on Wednesdays and Sundays. Her bedstead doubled as a place of physical relief and as her principal place of worship as she prepared her soul for the next life. In 1763 clergyman James Woodforde performed a private baptism on the newborn son of a parish-ioner, which took place 'in Mrs. Cross's bedroom' after he had finished afternoon service at church.[122]

The sleeping chambers of English Catholics similarly doubled as spaces for sleep and as sites of sacramental worship, containing a variety of litur-gical objects that ranged from portable altars to images of the cross. Holy relics were also present on some occasions. Staffordshire yeoman Henry Hodgetts wrapped some relics of St Chad, which had been preserved from Lichfield Cathedral, in a piece of buckram and placed them on the tester at the top of his bedstead. Henry's choice of location offered a safe place of concealment for these illicit and precious remains and it may also have intensified the sanctity of his sleeping hours by drawing his eyes and his mind upwards towards the heavens when he lay down at night.[123] Catholic services held within the household were prized substitutes for public worship and they boosted the sanctity of sleeping chambers at certain times.[124] Queen Catherine of Braganza did not need to restrict her devo-tions in quite the same way as ordinary Catholics, yet the make-up of her bedchamber at Whitehall was clearly designed with one eye on her spiritual well-being. When Samuel Pepys visited Whitehall in the summer of 1664 he described a chamber that contained 'nothing but some pretty pious pictures and books of devotion. And her holy water at her head as she sleeps, with a clock by her bed-side wherein a lamp burns that tells her the time of night at any time'.[125] The night-clock and holy water were carefully positioned next to her bedstead to regulate the Queen's schedule of prayer and to sanc-tify her sleep should she wake unexpectedly in the night. The books and pictures may have offered visual cues to confession and repentance and supports to divine meditation at bedtime. Conventions on the display of religious art also marked out sleeping chambers as the most suitable places in which to hang sacred images. Italian physician Giulio Mancini insisted on a clear division between profane artwork that he placed in sociable spaces of his own household, and images of Christ, the Virgin and scriptural allegories that were better suited to the bedchamber to signal that it was a sanctified space. Frances Gage's insightful analysis of Mancini's *Considerazioni sulla pittura* shows that his guidelines were heavily influenced by the social function of particular images and their anticipated effects on the body, mind and passions of the viewer.[126] Mancini's habits of display suggest that he believed in the power of devotional images to enclose sleepers within a holy place of safety during the night. Catherine of Braganza may well have shared Mancini's view and perhaps drew solace from the pictures in her bedchamber that offered her spiritual protection as she slept.

Catherine of Braganza's sensibilities about the use and meaning of religious art may have differed markedly from those of many English Protestants who were warned of the dangerous seductive qualities that could emanate from sacred imagery. They nevertheless continued to fill their homes, and especially their sleeping chambers, with devotional pictures and objects that functioned as supports to prayer and meditation.[127] The pictures and prints that were displayed in sleeping chambers within the household inventory sample may well have reinforced connections between sleep and death, which complemented the routines of repentance and prayer that preceded sleep. Coventry widow Elizabeth Dugdale kept 'Three pictures of Death in black frames' and a picture of Saul, first king of Israel, and his successor, David, in a black frame.[128] The image of Saul, whose weak faith and disobedience to God ultimately led to his spiritual ruin, may have reminded Elizabeth just how important it was to commend her soul to the Lord's protection before she lay down each night. More black-framed images were listed in sleeping chambers than in any other household chamber in the inventory sample and this choice of edging may well have signalled the sombre nature of the images they surrounded.

Alongside framed pictures, surviving architectural evidence reveals the variety of materials and rituals that were used to invoke protection against physical and spiritual dangers during sleep. The half-ceiling of a bedchamber in the village of Woolpit, Suffolk, still bears the marks of seventeenth-century candle magic. The central zone of the half-ceiling that once sat above the bedstead features a blank square space framed at each corner by two ladder symbols and two representations of early Christian crosses.[129] These markings, and the images or text that they once surrounded, very likely offered reassurance to the bed's occupant by inviting thoughts of a divine protector who could keep dark spiritual forces at bay as they slept. Christian devotions thus shaped how sleeping chambers looked, and they

also influenced customs surrounding the bedstead's position and orienta-
tion. Care was taken to position bedsteads in a north–south direction and
to prevent the sleeper's feet from pointing towards the door. The latter was
described as a 'funeral superstition' because it was the position in which
corpses were laid out before being carried from the house for burial.[130]
Householders in Shropshire, Somerset, Wiltshire, Devon and Cornwall
were similarly vigilant not to locate the bedstead across the natural line of
the floorboards or beneath a crossbeam in the ceiling. Transgressing these
rules was believed to herald the early death of a sleeper, to impede the soul's
journey to the afterlife, or to invite the Devil to take hold of the sleeper in
the night. Turning the sheets at the wrong time of day or turning the
mattress on the Sabbath-day was believed to invite evil spirits to reside
there in parts of Sussex.[131] These beliefs and rituals marked out sleep's material surroundings as plausible sites of physical and spiritual destruction that
demanded special forms of protection.

Sleeping bodies and uncleansed souls were secured each night by the
warmth of familiar sheets, blankets and quilts that were often invested with
spiritual and health-giving properties. Some of these textiles were made
from the best-quality fibres and were often ornately decorated. Yet, even if
these coverings were luxurious and pleasing to the eye, they still blended
with religious sensibilities by enveloping bodies and souls within a protective textile shield. Some religious and moral commentators perceived a
tension between Christian culture and the acquisition of luxury goods, but
this was probably offset by the practical uses that bedsteads and their
textiles served – not least in providing a safe and clean environment in
which bodies and minds could be refreshed. Thomas Tryon believed that
these goods, which had a clear spiritual purpose, could be counted as 'great
friends unto Mens Souls' rather than enemies.[132] Ornate bedsteads and
sumptuous bedding textiles that inspired spiritual thoughts could be easily
absorbed within routines of sleep-piety.[133] The set of wool, linen and cotton-
fibre bed-curtains dating from *c.* 1676 to *c.* 1725 shown in Figure 10 may
well have served such a purpose. The joints and stitching on the curtains
suggest that they were adapted from another part of the house before being
transported to the bedstead. Here, their decoration may have brought to
mind the perils that might be met during sleep, thus reinforcing the need to
rein in impious thoughts, to avoid spiritual complacency, and to perform
heartfelt prayer. The curtains are ornately embroidered in polychrome
worsted thread with biblical imagery of trees, flowers, birds, insects and
serpents, which may have evoked thoughts of the fall of humankind in the
Garden of Eden.

10. Bed-curtain, *c.* 1676–*c.* 1725.

Depictions of Adam, Eve and the Fall often featured as wall paintings in sleeping chambers and on bedsteads and their textiles.[134] Whilst these images may have signalled an inherent tension between the spiritual and sexual activities that bedsteads hosted, they may have also cautioned the viewer about the unparalleled dangers that could be met in sleep. It was, after all, in the idyllic landscape of Eden that the slumbering Eve had first been tempted by Satan to disobey God's orders and eat from the Tree of Knowledge. The furnishing of William Cole's sleeping chambers very likely conjured similar thoughts. Cole was pleased to note that one of his chambers had 'much the Appearance of a Chapel'. To complement this design, he converted an old bedstead 'into a neat arched Bed' and dressed it with 'neat' red and white linen that he judged 'very much suited to the Room it occupies'.[135] The arched bed satisfied religious and aesthetic sensibilities that enhanced the feeling of sanctity that William Cole associated with sleeping chambers. His choice to dress the bed with linen sheets probably combined a concern for physical and spiritual purification. The previous chapter described the liturgical uses of linen and the sensations of cleanliness and purity that this fabric could trigger. The robust fibres of some linen sheets, which could be stiffened further by starching, may have been prized as a resilient shield to defend sleepers against nocturnal threats of all kinds.[136]

The spiritual meanings invested in bedding materials could run very deep. When the Methodist Richard Burdsall was just ten years old he prayed for God's forgiveness after wasting the Sabbath-day playing football. He confessed that he was 'greatly afraid the devil would fetch me away that very night' in punishment. His youthful mind infused the warm layers of comfort provided by his bedcovers with a powerful sensation of spiritual protection and Richard remembered that he had 'crept entirely under the bed-clothes, thinking by this means to save myself'.[137] As a child John Valton also hoped that his bedcovers might save him from the diabolical spirits that he feared would seize him whilst he slept. The reassurance that a warm and familiar bedstead offered at times of spiritual crisis was dramatically revealed in a series of family letters that documented a haunting at Epworth rectory in Lincolnshire in the winter of 1716–17. This was the home of the Reverend Samuel Wesley, his wife Susanna and their ten surviving children. Samuel was a Church of England minister, a poet and one of the editors of the early periodical the *Athenian Mercury*, which was published in the 1690s, but he is more famous as the father of John Wesley, who went on to establish the Methodist Church. The Wesley's visitor, who was known as 'Old Jeffrey', appeared in a variety of animal forms, resembling a badger, a turkey and a white rabbit, but he was more often to be heard knocking on the wooden bedheads in the nursery or in the children's bedchambers at night-time. When Samuel's daughter Molly heard the latch of her chamber door rattling one night, followed by the noisy clatter of the warming-pan lid that lay at her bedside, 'She started up, leaped into the bed without undressing, pulled the bed-clothes over her head, and never ventured to look up till next morning.' As Molly's sister Emily was undressing for bed, she also dived under the covers for protection when she heard a noise that resembled bottles smashing under the best staircase. Her sister Suky also 'leaped into bed with all my cloathes on' when she heard knocking in the locked chamber beneath her feet. Whilst the Wesley daughters took solace beneath their bedding, Samuel Wesley's manservant Robin Brown took a large mastiff dog to his bedside for protection against the malevolent spirit.[138] Although their methods of preservation differed, the Wesley family and servants all understood the need to defend themselves during sleep. Sleep's status as a perilous process of physical and spiritual transformation coloured the ways in which people shaped, managed and interacted with their beds and sleeping environments – especially during moments of crisis. The objects and materials that surrounded sleepers as they drifted from consciousness reflected and strengthened complex understandings of sleep as a precious state of nourishment and as a time of acute physical and spiritual vulnerability.

Sleep's Christian meanings were vital to its physical practice and psychological associations. The widespread understanding of sleep as a fragile state of bodily transformation and as a conduit between the natural and supernatural realms ensured that its daily performance was an inseparable part of Christian identity and practice. Body and soul were in jeopardy as people were exposed to an array of divine and diabolical influences and to physical threats whilst they slept. This sense of powerlessness intensified the value of sleep management, bedtime devotions and rituals of protection as the chief line of defence against physical and spiritual ruin. The physical and psychological effects of bedtime prayers and meditations also had an important affinity with sleep's onset, as they helped to calm the body's passions and empty the mind of worldly preoccupations that had the potential to delay or disrupt sleep. These practices assumed unprecedented importance after 1660 as sleep-piety became ever more firmly entrenched within the daily lives of English Protestants and Catholics. The arrangement of sleeping chambers and the spiritual meanings invested in bedding textiles and bedside objects testify to this development and to the ongoing need for protection during sleep. Bedsheets, covers and sleep-related objects offered practical supports to prayer and meditation, and they also demarcated the boundaries between the natural physical world and the invisible realm that lay in store when they were invested with life- and soul-preserving powers. The material composition and use of sleeping chambers thus reveal a great deal about what it meant to be a Christian and about how religious beliefs pervaded the most intimate settings of everyday life.

English Protestants prized well-ordered sleeping habits as part of a practical set of Christian behaviours and as part of their pursuit of a heavenly reward. A flourishing body of devotional guides that explained how to infuse bedside habits with Christian meaning supported them in this endeavour. Well-regulated sleep was judged to be an effective method of devotion when it was indulged in moderation, at appropriate times, in suitable locations and when appropriate reading or prayers accompanied it. Individual men and women nevertheless understood the link between their sleeping habits and their spiritual fortunes in different ways. Temporary lapses in bedtimes, or periods of broken sleep, triggered resolutions to reform but in some extreme cases they were judged to forebode physical and spiritual ruin. Sleep was thus not simply an end in itself but an important barometer of a Christian's spiritual health.

CHAPTER 4

Sleeping at Home

O N SUNDAY 7 January 1666 Samuel and Elizabeth Pepys returned to their home in Seething Lane near Tower Hill after a lengthy stay at Mrs Clerke's lodging house in Greenwich. The couple had retreated there in October 1665 to escape the plague outbreak of that year. As the New Year dawned, Samuel was anxious to return home to resume his work and to plan for the future after his patron and benefactor, Lord Sandwich, had run into difficulties. When the couple arrived home, Samuel made the following entry in his diary: 'Being come home, my wife and I to look over our house and consider of laying out a little money to hang our bedchamber better than it is, and so resolved to go and buy something to-morrow, and so after supper, with great joy in my heart for my coming once again hither, to bed.'[1]

Samuel's words expressed a palpable tone of relief, happiness and ease as he imagined the satisfaction that would come from lying down in the familiar and comfortable bed that he shared with his wife. Samuel and Elizabeth's immediate desire to refresh their sleeping chamber after a lengthy absence revealed its value as a safeguard of health, and as the physical and symbolic heart of their home and marriage. Samuel's contentment combined the emotional joy of returning home with the anticipation of familiar sensations of relaxation, security and belonging that his bed offered. As he recalled the sight, smell and warmth of its carefully chosen layers, Samuel looked forward to a deep and nourishing sleep. These thoughts comforted his body and mind and prepared them to rest peacefully. It was during these hours of repose that Samuel could escape the tribulations of his waking life and look forward to refreshment the next morning. For him, and for many early modern men and women, the sensory pleasures of sleeping in a familiar bed each night epitomised the physical and psychological satisfactions of home.[2]

Sound slumber satisfied a biological need for refreshment but the settings in which it took place shaped its rhythms, routines and quality. Men and women exerted control over their sleep by carefully arranging and tending their sleeping environments in very distinctive ways. The location, organisation and content of these spaces reveal the values and expectations that structured sleep's daily practice. Sleep represented a period of contented refreshment and a time of physical and spiritual vulnerability; feelings of uncertainty thus typically preceded sleep's onset. The make-up of sleeping environments helped to offset these anxieties by offering physical and emotional reassurance to their occupants. Solace was sought in stable, familiar and secure environments that satisfied personal sensibilities and that procured ease and relaxation at bedtime. This could be achieved by sleeping in an enclosed bedstead or secluded chamber, by resting in a clean and comfortable bed, or through the habitual use of familiar, trusted and meaningful bedding textiles and objects that clustered around the bedside. Carving out a personal place of refuge within the household, however small, imperfect or temporary it may have been, was a widespread practice. The desire to retreat into a comforting place of safety reached its peak at bedtime when the defences of body and soul were most likely to be breached during sleep.[3]

Early modern sleeping chambers, bedsteads and bedding textiles formed the building blocks of household life. This period saw the spatial relocation of bedsteads, which migrated from multifunctional ground-floor parlour chambers to the upper floors of many middling- and upper-sort households. Sleeping chambers were gradually singled out as special-status rooms through their location, decorative schemes, material enhancement, and through the labels given to them: all of which revealed degrees of personal attachment and specialisation of function. In these households, which feature heavily in what follows, sleep's daily practice became more tightly defined in spatial, material and linguistic terms. Its environments were personalised to structure feelings of relaxation, security and belonging, which coincided with lively debates about sleep's purpose and value that were taking place in pulpit and in print. There were of course vast numbers of men, women and children who did not benefit so clearly from these changes. Those people who lived and slept under other people's roofs, in homes with fixed leases, in rented lodgings, or even in the makeshift huts, sheds and stables that were used as dwelling places in the City of London and its suburbs after the Great Fire of 1666, were faced with the challenge of living in structurally and temporally unstable homes.[4] They may not have enjoyed a chamber, or even a bedstead, of their own, yet they were still able to exert limited control over their sleeping environments, which they tried to fashion as personal places of safety and refreshment.

The gradual expansion and material enhancement of early modern households has been well documented by historians. Maxine Berg, John Crowley, Tara Hamling, Carole Shammas, John Styles, Amanda Vickery, Lorna Weatherill and others have shown how people's homes and tastes were transformed by the availability of new goods that were purchased, consumed and sought after by men and women from all social back-grounds.[5] The use and meanings ascribed to the parlour, and to other rooms intended for display and sociability, have been prioritised because these were the chambers where new goods were most heavily used and displayed. Sleeping chambers have been neglected by comparison even though bedsteads and their furnishings were ubiquitous features of the household that often accounted for at least one third of the total value of its goods.[6] A handful of recent studies have focused more intently on the make-up, use and meaning of beds, which have been identified as inimitable stages for marital intimacy, conflict and life-cycle events. The bed has also been marked out as the most important site for the display of textiles that shed light on consumption patterns, social, economic and gender relationships, and on aesthetic, religious and emotional sensibilities.[7] These studies have firmly located bedsteads at the heart of daily life yet principally in relation to conscious waking activities. Bedsteads and sleeping environments are assessed here in relation to their primary function – as places for sleep. In so doing, this chapter reveals how the creation, use and management of bedsteads, bedding textiles and sleep-related objects shaped physical prac-tices and psychological understandings of slumber. Sleep's complex cultural meanings are also interwoven in the following pages, which uncover the mixture of biological and cultural incentives that shaped financial and emotional investments in sleep's everyday settings.

Relocating Sleep

The gradual acceleration of room specialisation in early modern house-holds played an essential role in moulding perceptions and practices of sleep. In light of existing studies it might be assumed that bedsteads, which were once a staple feature of multifunctional parlours, were relocated above stairs largely as a by-product of the attention lavished on living spaces as they were transformed into spaces of display and sociability. Sleeping cham-bers, however, had a unique and highly personal significance of their own.

These were the spaces that gave rhythm and structure to slumberous routines and their location and content was strongly shaped by changing understandings of sleep's value and practice, which have been traced in previous chapters.

The years 1500 to 1800 saw dramatic improvements in the size, quality and comfort of housing across early modern Europe. The pace of change varied in different states and regions but a common trend for households to become 'larger, more solid and healthier to live in' clearly emerged.[8] In England the most rapid phase of change occurred from the mid-seventeenth to the mid-eighteenth century and centred mainly on southern and eastern counties, which predominate in the inventory sample used in this chapter from the Prerogative Court of Canterbury. The City of London in particular sat at the heart of changes in the size and arrangement of household space. Architectural surveys show that the one- and two-room dwellings that were characteristic of post-medieval London housing became less and less common during the seventeenth century.[9] One- or two-room dwellings were, by necessity, made up of multifunctional living spaces. A single room was often used for cooking, for day-to-day social interactions, and for sleeping. These modest dwellings were gradually supplanted by more extensive homes that usually included a minimum of three rooms, which most commonly comprised a kitchen, hall and parlour. Political economist Gregory King noted further expansion within the homes of England's middling sorts in the 1670s, whilst Lorna Weatherill calculated an average of between three and six rooms in a sample of 3,000 middling-sort households across eight English regions between 1675 and 1725.[10] This compares with an average of 3.2 rooms per household based on Peter King's sample of 51 pauper inventories from eighteenth-century Essex.[11] An expansion of living space across all categories of housing thus had important implications for the structure, timing and experience of all household activities, including sleep.

The status of the hall as the chief living and sleeping space fell into sharp decline from the mid-seventeenth century. In 1668 the contents of John Ellis's hall, which contained a small number of chairs and stools, show that this trend had spread beyond London to Ely in Cambridgeshire. This sparse furnishing was typical of halls elsewhere, which show that these transitional spaces were no longer centres of sociability; nor were they the spaces in which people typically slept.[12] Those instances where the hall still overlapped as a sleeping area were usually because of lack of space, which was not unusual further down the social scale. The hall had, however, slipped down the hierarchy of preferred places in which to sleep for many people as the eighteenth century dawned.

The same was true of kitchens, which began to feature as more distinct parts of the household's main structure.[13] Kitchen contents in the PCC inventories strongly suggest that most were used almost exclusively for the preparation and serving of food, drink and medicines, and for household storage. Chairs and stools were common but bedsteads and related furnishings were rarely listed here or in ancillary chambers; this was true even of the most modest households. In 1688 Samuel Dennett's home was described as having only a 'Lower Roome' and an upstairs 'Chamber'. His lower room included all of his cooking equipment, a table, some chairs and a bible, whilst his upper chamber contained a bedstead, bed sack, a bolster, rugs and a pillow. Dennett's example was far from unique. Only four households in the inventory sample listed bedsteads, beds or any other bedding materials in the kitchen and only two of those bedsteads appear to have been in regular use with one most likely to have been used for an ageing member of the household who was no longer able to climb the stairs to bed. The bedstead in Job Orchard's Exeter kitchen was, by contrast, a child's cradle. It was likely stored there because it was no longer in use when the inventory was taken in 1678 and where it was listed alongside a pile of pewter and other household utensils.[14] Court records show that maidservants occasionally bedded down for the night in the kitchen, close to the tools of their trade, but these chambers were more likely to serve the needs of sleepers in less direct ways by housing stores of bedpans, warming pans to heat the covers, and equipment for preparing sleep medicaments.[15]

If sleep was less likely to take place in halls and kitchens then the same was true of parlours, which were increasingly marked out as the centre of the household's social life. The parlour's most characteristic features were seats of different sizes and types, ceramic tea sets, storage chests and punchbowls that were designed to impress visitors and to ease social interactions with family, friends and neighbours.[16] Bedsteads had once featured prominently in these chambers but this began to change as the size and complexity of households increased. By the late seventeenth century the main parlour rarely contained the best bedstead or bed furnishings.[17] Most middling-sort homes had an average of two or three ground-floor rooms with the same number arranged above them on the first floor.[18] Even small and relatively modest dwellings had rooms on the first or second floors by the mid-eighteenth century and their contents suggest that they were primarily used as sleeping chambers at night-time, even if they hosted a range of daytime activities.[19] In the PCC inventory sample, approximately 73 per cent of the total number of rooms that contained at least one bedstead were located on the upper floors of the household by the 1660s. From

1728 to 1758 this figure rose substantially and never dipped below 90 per cent.[20] The removal of bedsteads from parlours was not a sudden or complete development, and indeed its roots have been traced to the late sixteenth century. It varied according to the size and complexity of each household, according to financial resources, occupation and age. Legal records also show that temporary and overcrowded sleeping environments remained characteristic for many people and could have damaging consequences.[21] Yet by 1760 it was the exception, rather than the rule, for sleep to take place in the main living spaces of the household, or in their ground-floor chambers.

Sleeping upstairs became increasingly commonplace as bedsteads and bed furnishings were vertically relocated. Bedsteads located above stairs were almost always contained within specific chambers although they were occasionally present in open, transitional parts of the household. The PCC inventories contain two references to bedsteads in parts of the house that might be described as points of access. Richard Burford's Wapping residence had a cheap turn-up bedstead, a quilt and three blankets 'in the passage'. This was the only one of the nine bedsteads in Burford's house that was located in a thoroughfare rather than a self-contained chamber.[22] This turn-up bedstead could be easily folded up to save space during the daytime but the accompanying bedding materials suggest that it may have been in regular use, perhaps by one of the household servants. Whoever slept here was perhaps the only member of the household that did not enjoy an enclosed sleeping space. The bedstead in the second-floor passage of spinster Elizabeth Neale's home in Kent may have afforded a greater degree of seclusion. Neale's bedstead appeared to be a semi-permanent fixture since a chair and 'four prints' accompanied it. The inventory nevertheless suggests that this bedstead may have been tucked away into a niche of some kind, thus providing a treasured degree of enclosure.[23] This niche may have been akin to the small partitioned spaces known as 'bed enclosures' or 'bed alcoves' that featured in a row of houses on Black Raven Alley near London Bridge in the early eighteenth century. A bedstead could be squeezed into these compact spaces, which were notable features of the one-room-plan brick-built houses that were built in the capital after the Great Fire. These homes, which often housed skilled tradespeople, artisans and sometimes their tenants, typically had one large room on each of their three storeys, in addition to commercial premises on the ground floor.[24]

John Peach's home in Ludlow, Shropshire, inventoried in 1738, was more typical of the layout of homes in the PCC inventory sample. It had a separate kitchen, parlour and storage rooms but the space simply labelled

'Above Stairs' contained the only three bedsteads, mattresses and bolsters in the house.[25] The chamber directly above the best parlour (after which many such chambers were named 'parlour chamber' or 'chamber over the parlour') was usually the main sleeping space and contained the most expensive bedstead and bed furnishings. The labels 'parlour chamber' or 'chamber over the parlour' were used directly in 26 per cent of the inventories but this is undoubtedly an underestimate of the number of principal sleeping chambers that were located above the parlour, which are obscured by labels such as 'room over', 'chamber over' or simply 'upper room'. All of the upstairs rooms that were linguistically associated with the main parlour contained at least one, and usually only one, bedstead. The contents of parlour chambers show a tendency amongst householders to dedicate these chambers to sleep where circumstance allowed. Of those rooms that can be reliably identified as the main sleeping chambers, 88 per cent listed one bedstead. There was thus an important correlation between the special status of the downstairs parlour and the corresponding chamber above stairs – both contained the highest-value possessions in the home, which signalled the essential activities that they hosted.

Alongside the parlour chamber the next most common upstairs room associated with sleep was the 'kitchen chamber' or 'chamber over the kitchen'. Kitchen chambers contained at least one bedstead in 23 per cent of the inventories. There was at least one bedstead present in upstairs chambers with the functional labels of 'room over', 'chamber over' or 'upper room' in 65 per cent of the households examined. Other rooms that frequently listed bedsteads, beds and bed furnishings included garret chambers, cocklofts, which were often located beneath the roof's ridge and accessed by a ladder, and rooms that were functionally identified by their position within the house such as '2 pair of stairs forwards'. The inventories do not, however, record how many people slept in each of the bedsteads, nor are the sizes of bedsteads recorded in any detail, although the dimensions of extant bedsheets give an approximate guide to their proportions.[26] Bed sharing is difficult to quantify in any meaningful way but the following chapter suggests that this practice was commonplace, often pleasurable, and could offer a reassuring sense of security at bedtime.

The most expensive bedstead and bed furnishings in the Essex home of husbandman William Peacocke were listed in his parlour chamber.[27] This pattern was widely replicated. In 1708 the parlour chamber of yeoman William Beeching contained a single bedstead surrounded by 'cornish curtaines'. This room also contained the only clock in the house, which was probably a prized possession and useful for regulating Beeching's sleeping hours. The special status of Beeching's parlour chamber was underlined by the fact that the neighbouring chambers over the kitchen and buttery each contained two bedsteads.[28] Those who slept in the main sleeping chamber thus benefited from a greater degree of enclosure and comfort. Thomas Dullison's home in Coventry contained a 'best room', which suggests its distinctiveness within the household. The bedstead within was enclosed by flowered curtains, a valance, quilt, bolster and pillows, and by no fewer than four blankets.[29] Men and women of more modest means were nonetheless able to restrict the use of upstairs chambers in some instances. Saddler John Barrow had just two upstairs chambers in his Sittingbourne home in 1738 and their contents indicate that they were used exclusively for sleeping during the night.[30] John Ellis of Ely, however, was less fortunate. His parlour chamber contained a well-appointed feather bed and associated furnishings. Three trundle beds and a cradle nevertheless accompanied the main bedstead, which suggests that a large number of sleepers were squeezed into this space. Ellis's bed-curtains and rods may have provided partial seclusion and extra warmth to the occupants of the main bedstead.[31] It nevertheless remains clear from the contents of parlour chambers, and from surviving diaries and letters, that concerted efforts were made to separate sleep from other household activities at night. The items most frequently listed in parlour chambers were strongly linked to the bedstead and its furnishings.

There was great variety in the labels given to those parts of the house containing bedsteads, which tentatively signals the type and range of activities that took place within them. The term 'bedroom' to denote a space primarily associated with sleep was not in widespread use until the nineteenth century. The PCC inventories nevertheless document greater specificity in the labelling of sleeping chambers as distinct from other parts of the household. The first direct reference to a 'Bed Chamber' appeared in the 1718 inventory of London coachmaker Henry Clack. The label most likely signalled that this first-floor chamber was his principal sleeping space. This was one of just three chambers that contained a bedstead. The others were well appointed with feather beds and bolsters but were simply labelled 'Back Garrett' and 'Fore Garrett'. The latter chamber contained two bedsteads and its bed furnishings sat alongside some 'lumber', which signalled its joint use as a storage space. The furnishings of Clack's 'Bed Chamber' suggest that it was primarily envisaged as a space for rest, unlike other parts of his dwelling that were more strongly linked to his trade. Two comfortable 'beds' were listed alongside a quilt, blankets and one 'small carpet', whilst the walls were decorated with prints.[32] Two further references to a 'bed chamber' surface in inventories from the 1720s and 1750s. Spinster Elizabeth Cooper had a 'Bed Chamber' on the first floor of her Peckham home. The room was comfortably and expensively furnished with a four-post mahogany bedstead, a feather bed, calico quilt, a dressing table and 'two wilton bedside carpets'.[33] The importance of this room stood out in Cooper's otherwise simply furnished home and it was clearly devoted to sleep, being the only room in the house that contained a bedstead or bedding. Explicit references to bedchambers in the inventories are patchy, but the 'best chamber' – a label that was used regularly from the 1670s – very likely paralleled the role of these rooms. References to 'best chambers' are most densely concentrated in the years after 1718 and they were almost exclusively located over the parlour and on the first floor. John Lichford's 'best chamber' contained one of fifteen bedsteads spread across thirteen rooms in his large Lincolnshire home. The chamber name, and the range and cost of its bedding, show that it exceeded the value of the neighbouring 'hall chamber' and 'chamber over the kitchen' and was dedicated to the pursuit of a sound night's rest.[34]

Comparisons must of course be made with more modest households and with those residences that included co-residents or multiple occupants from different families. Church court records, the proceedings of the Old Bailey, London's central criminal court, and visual sources show that some servants, apprentices, lodgers and children slept in many different parts of the household, often in shared or multifunctional chambers, and some-times with a variety of bedfellows. These arrangements were especially pronounced in the growing metropolis of London. The length of individual service contracts, which varied from a matter of months to many decades, also affected the relative instability of servant's sleeping arrangements. Lodgers could enjoy limited seclusion during sleep if they were able to lock their own chamber doors, or if their landlords and landladies locked them in during the night, but not everyone was so lucky. These sources offer brief snapshots of daily life for certain individuals at very specific (and often chaotic) moments in their lives. Ordinary or 'typical' experiences of sleep are therefore difficult to extract from these sources. Rather than being regarded as 'typical', they should instead be acknowledged as important pieces of a more complex jigsaw of sleeping experiences, which varied according to wealth, status, gender, location, occupation, age and household circumstance. A partial degree of enclosure during sleep, however it was achieved, may not have been such a rare luxury.[35] The 'Best Chamber' of widow Maria Barrett from Hook Norton in Oxfordshire clearly served a dual function as a place for sleep and as a general storage space for her household goods. It was nevertheless distinguished as an identifiable living space as opposed to a place of work. This contrasted with Barrett's 'garrett chamber' that contained a rudimentary bedstead, an old flock mattress and a spinning wheel.[36] William Lewis's home contained only one bedstead in 'the Best Room', alongside a table, a small mirror and a few chairs. The value of its contents was nevertheless more than double that of all the other listed chambers in his home.[37] The 'best chamber' in the Kent home of former clerk John Darlinge contained a corded bedstead, worked curtains, a variety of seating and some small cups, bowls and 'a parcel of toyes' that suggests a range of activities took place there during daytime hours. Darlinge's own room, which was clearly labelled by the appraisers, was simpler in form and perhaps in function. The appraisers valued its contents at less than half of those contained in the 'best chamber'; they included a 'corded bedstead', feather bed, bolster, bed-curtains, a quilt, two blankets and 'two old window curtains' to keep out the light.[38] The specialisation of parlour chambers as sleeping chambers is similarly evident in the household inventories of Norwich artisans and tradesmen in this period.[39]

The spatial and linguistic demarcation of sleeping environments was not restricted to householders. The sleeping chambers of many servants were relocated and partially specialised over the course of the early modern period. The PCC inventories show a pronounced desire to separate and distinguish the sleeping environments of householders and servants where possible. This arrangement was a marked feature of houses that were newly built. Designated servants' bedchambers were constructed on the upper floors of Dunham Massey in Cheshire in the 1720s.[40] The location of servants' bedsteads nevertheless varied according to gender and their place within the service hierarchy. Some servants had sleeping chambers of their own, which were often labelled according to their occupant's status. At Ham House in Richmond, home of the duke and duchess of Lauderdale from 1672, the servants that enjoyed this privilege included the steward, house-keeper, cook, clerk of the kitchen, chaplain and the gentleman of the horse. The most extensive inventory in the PCC sample, taken from the house-hold of Sir Philip Harcourt in 1688, indicates that servants' sleeping cham-bers were separated by rank and gender with a separate 'Maids' Chamber' and 'Men's Chamber'. More than one servant shared these chambers but they afforded a relative degree of comfort and security even though they lacked any additional furniture apart from the bedsteads.[41] Temporary dividers, which ranged from wooden screens to simple textiles, also offered limited forms of enclosure in shared chambers.[42]

The sleeping conditions of indoor servants contrasted sharply with those servants whose duties required them to work and sleep outside of the main house. The 1654 inventory of Ham House listed 'Six flok-beds, 6 bolsters 6 white rugges and 6 coloured rugges' in the stables and outhouses. Woollen 'flock' beds were considerably cheaper than the feather beds provided for the indoor servants at Ham who slept in the garrets. Flock beds were nevertheless warm and easy to clean. Outdoor servants were more likely to share their sleeping quarters with 'lumber', or with animals, than with fellow servants. The sleeping environments of servants thus varied enormously. The location and make-up of their bedsteads was largely determined by their employers, as was the length of time they were able to spend in them. Many servants slept in close proximity to their employers, or to other servants in modest households with limited space. There is nevertheless evidence that fixed and permanent bedsteads for servants were becoming more commonplace in these years.

Many servants may not have benefited from a room of their own but bedsteads that were specifically listed in servants' chambers were usually concentrated in upstairs garret chambers in the PCC inventories, which had certain advantages. John Fransham described his garret chamber as 'the quietest room in the house' and Robin Brown, the manservant of clergyman and poet Samuel Wesley, had a chamber and a bedstead of his own in the garret of Epworth rectory in rural Lincolnshire.[43] Brown's chamber and the garret chambers at Ham House were each accessed by a separate staircase, which limited potential disturbances from other members of the household. This peacefulness may, however, have offered little compensation for the general lack of light and heating in these spaces on dark wintry nights, or from the suffocating heat of the summer months. The location of these bedsteads may however have offered some protection against the danger that befell Mary Prigg from Colchester in 1668.[44] Mary was sexually assaulted in her bed, which was located in a ground-floor hall that functioned as 'a thoroughfayre from the streetdore into the rest of the said house'.[45] Servants' chambers, or personalised sleeping enclosures, may not have been elaborately decorated or furnished but some certainly benefited from a greater degree of seclusion than in previous decades.

Caution must be exercised before interpreting these shifts as an advancing threshold of sleep-privacy.[46] Sharing a sleeping chamber with an employer or with a temporary visitor could not always be avoided and the sexual exploitation that sometimes ensued was a persistent concern for the Church courts, which heard presentments for sexual offences committed in shared sleeping chambers.[47] Securing the relative enclosure of servants' sleeping arrangements was also a cause of concern for householders by the mid-eighteenth century and it clearly signalled a token of decency amongst their acquaintance. In 1745 Horace Walpole's letter to his friend Sir Charles Hanbury Williams, an MP, diplomat and poet, reported that Lord and Lady Bath's maidservants 'go to bed publicly every night, because the Peer and Peeress will not allow shutters, window- or bed-curtains'.[48] It was a sign of impropriety that this most basic of expectations had not been met, and it allowed Walpole to draw attention to the avarice and neglect for which Lord and Lady Bath had become notorious in high society.

As this example suggests, the sleeping environments of servants were heavily influenced by the wishes of their employers and by considerations of practical economy. The need to secure the household from intruders in the night led to further variation in the places where servants slept. The porter at Ham House slept in a press bed in the great hall. This bed had a walnut veneer and resembled a handsome chest when folded up so that it could remain in the hall during the daytime to resemble similar furniture in this central reception area. Ham's 1683 inventory listed a feather bed, bolster, blanket and rug that may have been stored in the nearby cupboard under the stairs to bring out at night. The two iron rods that accompanied the press bed and bedding show that it had a tester, or overhead canopy, and it was probably enclosed by curtains to provide a degree of enclosure, comfort and warmth. This design was particularly important when bedsteads occupied thoroughfares that could be accessed from different parts of the house. The bed's location also under-lines the perceived vulnerability of sleepers whilst they lay unconscious in their beds, which was the main reason that it was placed in this part of the house. The porter had a range of weapons at his disposal in the great hall with which he could defend the threshold from unwanted intruders. The doorman may also have assisted him in defending the house as the inventories list an additional bedroll that was stored behind the main door during the daytime. A feather bed and bedding were kept 'in *the hole* under the stairs' in the inner hall, which may have been used by the doorman or by another servant who slept at the foot of the stairs to protect those above.[49]

Children, rather than servants, may in fact have had the least stable sleeping arrangements of all – especially in large families with limited space. Rare insights into how these arrangements were managed are provided by the haunting of the Wesley family, mentioned in the previous chapter, at Epworth rectory. The location of the family's bedsteads, and their occupants, can be pieced together from a series of letters that were exchanged between the family concerning the movements of the malevolent spirit that they had nicknamed 'Old Jeffrey'. Samuel and his wife Susanna had ten surviving children, of which seven girls – Susanna (Suky), Mary (Molly), Emily, Anne (Nancy), Mehetabel (Hetty), Kezia and Patty – were living at the rectory at the time of the haunting in 1716–17. The boys – Samuel, John and Charles – were all studying or working away from home. As the family swapped notes about where Old Jeffrey had been heard, felt and seen, they revealed that Samuel and Susanna slept together in the 'best chamber', whilst manservant Robin Brown slept alone in the garret. The two eldest sisters, Suky and Molly, who were around twenty years old, slept together in the 'Paper Chamber'. Emily and Nancy, who were around fifteen years of age, also shared a room and a bedstead, whilst the younger sisters Hetty, Kezia and Patty slept together in the nursery, also known as the 'Green Chamber'. When Old Jeffrey made a noise there much like a rocking cradle, the family was also reminded that the nursery had once contained a baby's cradle, which had long since been relegated to storage or disposed of. These shared bedsteads and chambers were most likely organised according to age, character and sibling friendships and they must have changed as babies grew into infants, as infants grew into young adults, and as children left home to study, to take up apprenticeships, or to marry. The Wesleys, although cramped, were perhaps fortunate that they did not have to find separate chambers for their three sons at this time but this difficulty must have befallen many other families.[50]

The location of bedsteads alone thus does not tell us everything we need to know about the significance of the person or people that slept in them since this was often dictated by the practical needs of the household, by specific anxieties relating to sleep, and by changes in the family life cycle. Bearing in mind these variations, it remains clear that the principal bedsteads of many households were gradually relocated from multifunctional ground-floor chambers to largely self-contained sleeping chambers on the upper floors. This movement was a gradual and long-term development across the early modern period and it spread beyond London to encompass a variety of urban and rural areas. The urge to enclose sleep within a safe and secure physical space was powerful, even if the means of achieving it were limited for some men and women. For those who could afford to demarcate this essential habit, their bedsteads were gradually being contained within a narrower range of rooms with a degree of enclosure that were simply equipped to support peaceful repose and to defend vulnerable bodies.[51] One consequence of this development was less variation in the type of chamber that was deemed appropriate for sleep, and rising expectations of it.

A Good Bed

On a visit to Salisbury the Reverend James Woodforde was pleased to note that he slept 'exceeding well last night having a very good bed'.[52] He was only too aware that a 'good bed' was essential to secure peaceful sleep, good health and happiness. Woodforde invested a great deal of time, money and thought when he furnished his own bedchamber at Weston Longville parsonage near Norfolk and he carefully managed its daily use. Like many of his contemporaries, James Woodforde anticipated restless nights when he slept away from home, which explains why he tried to replicate the familiar sensations of his own bedchamber when he was removed from it, and why he commented, perhaps with surprise, on the pleasant night he had enjoyed at Salisbury. Continuity of material environment was highly prized in early modern sleep culture and at the centre of this complex matrix of perceptions, sensations and materials was a 'good bed'. A 'good bed' was in part an ideal construct, and it meant different things to different people. A shared understanding of a 'good bed' can nevertheless be reconstructed; it was a site where individual bodily needs, material layers and personal meanings converged to provide physical and psychological ease. Close examination of the PCC inventories reveals consistent patterns in the preferred composition of beds that cut across individual eccentricities. Their make-up was shaped by cost, by health concerns, and by a powerful desire to rest in enclosed and familiar surroundings.

Feelings of safety, status and contentment could all be obtained by possession of a familiar bedstead, over which some control of its furnishing, cleanliness and use could be exercised. There was a distinct rise in the number of bedsteads listed per household in England from the mid-sixteenth to the mid-eighteenth centuries. The PCC inventories show a rise from 3.5 bedsteads per household in the 1660s to 4.92 by the 1750s. Across the hundred years from 1660 to 1760 the mean number of bedsteads per household was 4.34.[53] In Kent the mean number increased from 3.67 per household in 1600–1629 to 4.28 in 1690–1729. This increase may be explained by a growing number of household servants, or as evidence of the general expansion of households.[54] However many bedsteads each household may have contained, they were invariably made of wood. Mahogany and ash were two of the materials specifically identified by the PCC appraisers, whilst stained or painted beech offered cheaper alternatives. Important exceptions to the use of wood were the wickerwork bassinettes and cradles made for babies and very young children, as shown below. This hooded cradle from the village of Boxford in Berkshire, which dates to *c.* 1770, is approximately 3 feet in length and was probably hand-crafted, perhaps by its owners, with straw and briar before being lined with some kind of linen to protect the infant that lay inside. Its rounded ends allowed for gentle movement and the worn edge at the cradle's bottom corner may be the wear marks of a hand or foot that habitually rocked a child to sleep.[55]

For older children and adults, the frames of their wooden bedsteads were typically held together at the base by bed-ropes or by cords that were knotted at the end. Beds and mattresses were usually placed on top of this system of ropes, and their knots could be easily tightened to prevent the bed from sagging.[56] This practice is probably the root of the phrase 'sleep tight', which suggests that this adjustment in tension had a beneficial effect on sleep quality. Ropes and cords were a more expensive, and probably a more comfortable way of supporting sleepers than simple sacking-bottom bedsteads. John Ashton ranked such loose bedsteads at the bottom of his self-constructed bed hierarchy in the early eighteenth century. He described these beds as being cheaply woven, often from hemp.[57] The flat wooden boards of pallet or truckle beds must surely have ranked even lower than this.

11. Hooded lipwork cradle, *c.* 1770.

As Chapter 2 revealed, the health dangers posed by wooden bedsteads were widely noted in recipe books and books of household management, which offered practical advice on how to clean them. Details of the size, age and condition of bedsteads, which were often passed down as family legacies, were occasionally given in the household inventories, which noted when bedsteads were 'large', 'small', 'old', 'very old' or simply broken.[58] The advanced age of many bedsteads was in fact the most common description given. Bedsteads were not simply places of rest; they were prominent symbols of status and carriers of family history. The carved images, inscriptions or initials displayed on some bedsteads tied many generations of a single family together and they expressed a powerful desire for future prosperity by offering a secure place for the family's restoration and reproduction. The bedstead's essential procreative function was reflected in and encouraged by decorative iconography on the bedstead itself or by the objects that surrounded it.[59] These meanings combined with the high economic value of bedsteads to guarantee that they had a longer lifespan than most items of household furniture. Their cost and personal associations also ensured that they featured strongly in the list of personal bequests in wills that were gifted to family members and other loved ones.

The longevity of wooden bedsteads was also supported by a lively second-hand trade, which allowed those with a limited budget to acquire a good plain bedstead to sleep on, or to buy something more ornate as an expression of their social and economic aspirations. For those who didn't inherit a bedstead, personal meanings could still be created by the motivation for a bedstead's purchase, which was typically due to marriage or a significant change in personal circumstance. This certainly appears to be the case with the oak box bedstead shown in Figure 12, which was owned by yeoman Henry Hutchinson from the valley of Baldersdale in the North Riding of Yorkshire. The two wooden doors that enclosed the bed carry the initials 'H.H.' and 'D.H.', for Henry and his wife Dority, alongside the date of their marriage – '1712'.[60]

Beds represented the practical and symbolic heart of the household and indeed of marriage.[61] The cost of a brand new bedstead could nevertheless be prohibitive. Lancashire farmer Richard Latham purchased a feather bed and bolster weighing 61 lbs with bolster-ticking and bed-cords following his marriage to Ann or 'Nany' Barton in August 1723. At £2 3s, the bed and bolster was the single most expensive financial outlay of the Latham household in 1724. Latham's account book shows that he spread the purchase of bed furnishings over several years: the material for the bed-curtains was bought in 1725 and the iron rods on which to suspend them in 1726.[62] The

12. Box bedstead, *c.* 1712.

Lathams saved money by growing and spinning flax to make their own sheets, and by bleaching their own linens in the summer months. There was a notable upsurge in Nany's spinning output in the years immediately after her marriage. Some of the material that she produced would surely have been intended to furnish her marital bed whilst some may well have been sold to help pay for the couple's heavy financial expenditure at this formative stage in their family life cycle.[63] Given this degree of monetary and personal investment it is no surprise that many bedsteads were of advanced age and appraised at high prices since they were likely to be hard-won and cherished possessions. Levels of personal attachment to these unique pieces of furniture are also hinted at by the hoarding of bedsteads that were no longer fit for purpose. The appraisers of Anne Blackburn's London home listed 'part of an old press bed . . . part of an old bedstead and some other lumber' and 'part of a press bedsted' in 1718. These items had not been discarded but instead relegated to storage spaces in Anne's home, since she seemed unable, or unwilling, to part with them.[64]

On top of the sacking, ropes, cords, mats and hard wooden frame of the bedstead was a blanket and at least one 'bed' or 'mattrass', the most common terms used to refer to a soft stuffed pad of some kind that lay on top of the bedstead. Samuel Johnson defined a 'Ma'ttress' as 'A kind of quilt made to lie upon' in his *Dictionary of the English Language*.[65] An 'under quilt' could serve a similar purpose and Lancashire gentleman Nicholas Blundell recorded his purchase of one at a cost of three shillings from a Liverpool house sale in June 1717.[66]

The mean number of beds or mattresses per household was 4.82 across the period 1660–1760.[67] The presence of an average of one bed or mattress per bedstead is largely supported by analysis of individual households. This mean number nonetheless disguises incidences of bedsteads that had multiple beds stacked on top of one another for superior comfort. It may have been fairly typical in some wealthy households to have three beds or mattresses on each bedstead, each with a distinct purpose and arranged in a deliberate hierarchy. The bottom bed or mattress was usually made of a hard-wearing and stiff material like straw; the second bed or mattress was made of wool or horsehair for warmth, whilst the third and top bed or mattress was stuffed with a softer, cooler and more expensive material such as linen or cotton ticking.[68] Relative degrees of physical comfort and warmth undoubtedly depended on the type of stuffing used and on the number of beds or mattresses present. The PCC appraisers did not always note the type of stuffing used in each bed unless it was expensive.[69] Feather beds were often given independent valuations, unlike cheaper flock beds whose cost was usually estimated in combination with related bedding textiles. Flock beds were typically found on the bedsteads of children and servants, which had a shorter lifespan within the household. Children's beds were also more likely to be stuffed with cheap and absorbent materials like chaff, seaweed or beech leaves that could better withstand bed-wetting. Flock beds must have been preferable to the basic 'bead sack' found in Samuel Dennett's home, and this was preferable still to the straw-filled beds that were often listed amongst the possessions of defendants at London's Old Bailey.[70]

The mean number of beds is probably a significant underestimate of the number regularly in use within many homes. Beds were valuable household furnishings and they were portable. Many were removed, sold or gifted to friends, relatives and servants before the testator died and before probate inventories were compiled. In the 1660s Edward Simpson was in possession of one feather and one flock bed at his home in Battersea, but these goods were reclaimed after his death by his daughter-in-law Joyce Howard, who owned them.[71] London widow Margaretta Douglas bequeathed a feather bed and related items in her will, which do not appear in her inventory. London widow Elizabeth Allen similarly gifted a range of luxury bed furnishings to her sister before her inventory was taken.[72] Beds and their textiles also featured strongly in the lists of goods stolen from London's lodging houses in the eighteenth century. Their resale value was undoubtedly one motivation for their theft but familiar beds, even if landlords had initially provided them, very likely accumulated personal meanings over time for those that slept in them on a regular basis. John Styles has described these items as 'an intimate part' of the material world of lodgers who actively sought to take possession of them.[73] The pleasing sensory associations of a familiar mattress may well have reinforced these feelings of ownership. Taking these exceptions into account, most members of the households examined could typically expect to rest on a fixed bedstead that was topped by a bed or beds filled with feathers or flock.

Variations in the physical make-up of bedsteads and beds conveyed differences of status and of comfort. The kind of comfort that was on offer combined physical and psychological satisfaction, which is revealed by the meanings attached to the height of individual bedsteads. The total height of a good bed comprised the wooden frame of the bedstead from foot to canopy and the layers of beds, mattresses and bedding that accompanied it. In general, the more bedding layers to be counted, the higher the cost. Multiple layers of mattresses offered more protection from the hard wooden slats, or from the cords and ropes at the base of the bedstead. Bed height was rarely recorded in the PCC inventories. There is only one reference to a 'raised bed' in one of Thomas Johnson's upstairs chambers in 1708, which may have been an indication of the elevated status of its occupant. The contents of this chamber were valued at one-third higher than Johnson's next best sleeping chamber, which contained a 'sacking bedstead' and more modest furnishings.[74]

The importance of height is better illustrated by the inventories from Ham House. In 1654, the four-poster bedstead of Elizabeth Tollemache, later duchess of Lauderdale, had three quilts, which probably served as mattresses, three woollen blankets, two fustian coverlets, four pillows and a bolster stuffed with down feathers. By 1677 the bedstead had acquired an additional feather bed and a silk blanket. The bed hangings were made of silk damask and the maximum number of six curtains surrounded the bedstead so that it could be fully enclosed when required. These ornate materials were a sign of status whilst also satisfying demands for warmth, seclusion and security. The duchess may have appreciated partial enclosure from the female servant who shared her bedchamber and whose bedstead and bedding are listed in the inventories, whilst remaining comforted by the presence of a trusted sleeping companion.[75] The duchess's raised bedstead was modelled on the state bedsteads of the royal court whose grandeur was marked by their physical proportions, decoration, textiles, and by the distance of the sleeper from the floor. The importance of elevating the sleeper was similarly reflected in the use of raised platforms on which bedsteads were positioned: this was the case in the state bedchamber at Ham House, which was planned for the visit of Queen Catherine of Braganza.

In stark contrast, many household servants slept on low truckle beds or on low fixed bedsteads with only one layer of padding. The reduced height of these bedsteads distinguished levels of physical comfort, but they also carried important social connotations. The *Oxford English Dictionary* defines 'truckling' as the act of taking 'a subordinate or inferior position; to be subservient, to submit, to give precedence'.[76] Samuel Pepys seemed acutely aware of these meanings and he was disgruntled when he was occasionally forced to sleep in a truckle bed. His frustration probably combined a sense of disappointment at sleeping on a bedstead that did not reflect his status with a more general concern for the quality of his sleep given the bed's lack of padding and its proximity to the cold and damp floor.[77] As Chapter 2 explained, medical writers warned of the damaging effects of sleeping in truckle beds and recommended that flat solid boards were placed at the base of the bedstead, instead of cords, to stop drafts and the toxic night air from penetrating them too easily.[78] The unfamiliar sensations that the truckle bed produced for Samuel Pepys may have stirred anxieties about his status and his well-being as he approached bedtime in an alien environment.

The association of truckle beds with economic dependency, modest social position or deliberate degradation was more broadly inscribed in early modern culture. John Dryden's comedy *The Wild Gallant*, which was first performed at London's Vere Street Theatre in Lincoln's Inn Fields in 1663, features a gentleman who has been robbed. He is offered a truckle bed on which to sleep for the night because he has no money to pay for even the poorest of lodgings.[79] A 1653 account of a bewitched maidservant described her tormented fits whilst she lay in her 'truckle bed', or 'low bed' – terms that were used interchangeably – whilst a gentleman observer lay nearby 'on the high bed'.[80] The same binary distinction between high and low featured in *Satan's Invisible World Discovered* (1685), which was a compilation of reports of diabolical spirits, witches and apparitions produced by the Scottish engineer, natural philosopher and schoolmaster George Sinclair. Nurses, maidservants and children occupied truckle beds in the homes depicted by Sinclair as he described the incursions of supernatural agents.[81]

The mock-heroic poem *Hudibras* was written by poet and satirist Samuel Butler and first published in 1663. The poem shows that the term 'truckle bed' could double as a metaphor for powerlessness, passivity or ignominy: 'If he that in the field is slain, / Be in the *Bed of Honor* lain: / He that is beaten may be sed / To lye in Honor's *Truckle-bed*.'[82] The poor survival of truckle beds underline their negative associations and suggest that they were made from cheap materials with a limited shelf life. Simple 'beds' or cloth sacks stuffed with straw or flock nevertheless occupied an even lower rung on the material hierarchy of beds. This flimsy layer of protection between the sleeper and the floor signified the most reduced of circumstances. Quaker leader George Fox considered it the basest of insults that the cruel jailors of his fellow evangelist and Quaker martyr James Parnel 'would not let him have so much as a Truckle-bed' to sleep on, which some Friends had tried to deliver to him at Colchester Castle.[83] This was seemingly just one step away from the cold wet stones on which Parnel was instead forced to lay his head.

The most common accompaniment to the bedstead and bed was a bolster, which was used to support the sleeper's head or body. Bedsteads and bolsters were usually listed in combination in inventories and the total number of bolsters was almost identical to the total number of bedsteads in each household. In the 1740s these figures were an exact match. It was rare for individual bedsteads of any value to have more than one bolster, which points to some degree of shared physical experience, perhaps underpinned by the medical advice about sleep posture traced in Chapter 2, which urged sleepers to rest with their heads slightly raised during the night. Rather than being distinguished by number, bolsters more often varied by the quality of their stuffing and textile covering. Feather bolsters were frequently listed – occasionally in servants' sleeping chambers – and their stuffing usually matched the beds on which they sat.

Bedsheets were universal accompaniments to bedsteads and beds. Their quality and value varied from room to room although separate valuations for individual sheets were rarely provided in probate inventories. The increasing volume of bedsheets in early modern households, and variations in cost and quality, can nevertheless be traced in household account books, from the locations in which sheets were stored, and from surviving sheets, which sometimes featured laundry marks that were numbered sequentially. In the PCC inventories storage locations ranged from prime indoor sites such as the stairhead to an outdoor shed in Christopher Wilson's Southwark home. Ornate linen chests also offered an alternative storage option that combined practical function with symbolic value.[84]

Bedsheets were the most heavily used, laundered and replaced bed furnishings within the household since they lay in closest proximity to the body. Household account books show that bedsheets and pillowcases were amongst the cheapest and most frequently purchased textiles, with two pairs of sheets generally recommended for each bed to allow for regular laundering.[85] This functional purpose did not prevent sheets from taking on very personal meanings however. The provenance, decoration and use of linen sheets within many families ensured that they were regularly bequeathed, especially by female testators, to cherished servants and family members, whose stocks of textiles represented a form of capital that they used to define their social networks and emotional relationships.[86] There was wide variation in the quality, value and texture of bedsheets. Good-quality 'holland sheets' were regularly listed in the inventory sample, albeit in small quantities. Holland sheets were made from a fine linen cloth that originated in the Low Countries. They were used sparingly in many households due to their cost, and owning such sheets was a sign of luxury and status whose use extended as far as the royal household of King William and Queen Mary. In 1715, the enterprising Scottish businesswoman Lady Grisell Baillie, who managed a large household almost single-handedly, paid nearly £3 for the material to make just two sheets of holland. She described one of these textiles as an 'upper' sheet, which may suggest that she tried to prolong its life by using an additional under sheet of inferior quality that would perish more quickly.[87]

London painter William Brewer had at least twenty-six pairs of bedsheets in his home that ranged from holland and calico through to 'coarse flaxen', whilst Philip Harcourt's inventory listed four pairs of holland sheets, three dimity sheets, flaxen sheets and eleven pairs of 'coarse' sheets.[88] As well as distinguishing sheets by the quality of their textile, the PCC appraisers also separated 'old' and 'ordinary' sheets from 'new', 'good' and 'fine' sheets. In the 1690s Oxfordshire widow Elizabeth Mayne kept eight pairs of 'ordinary' sheets as compared with just one pair of 'fine' sheets in her Woodstock home. Mary Griffin's modest Kent home, which contained just one sleeping chamber, similarly combined eleven pairs of ordinary sheets with just one pair of 'fine sheets'.[89] The gradations between 'coarse', 'good' and 'ordinary' most likely distinguished different types of textile but they may have also signalled variations of linen sheets according to their thread counts, drape and texture. A comparison of eight surviving linen bedsheets dating from this period shows great diversity in the quality and density of these textiles. A smooth and even finish distinguished the finest linen sheets from cheaper varieties alongside a high thread count.[90]

One pair of good-quality sheets was not therefore inaccessible to many households. The beds on which different sheets were placed could also signal the status of the sleeper who lived in the household, or the affection with which a guest was regarded, with holland or cambric sheets usually reserved for the most esteemed visitors. Laundry marks also suggest a close link between the quality of sheets and their users: 'B' often indicated 'best' sheets; 'F' denoted sheets for the use of the family, and 'S' referred to sheets used by servants that were usually made of coarser linens.[91] The power of these different textiles to create pleasant or disagreeable sensations at bedtime should not be underestimated. As Chapter 2 explained, the cool and smooth sensations of linen sheets were aligned with preferences for airy and clean sleeping environments and this material predominated in the manufacture of bedclothes, sheets and nightcaps. The growing pre-eminence of the nerves in medical understandings of sleep also drew greater attention to the sensations produced by different bedding textiles. Different levels of sensibility thus shaped individual preferences for bedding textiles, which were closely allied with sleep's physical sensations.

A blanket usually lay on top of the bedsheets. Each household in the inventory sample had a mean number of 7.83 blankets. The mean number of blankets per bedstead was approximately 1.8 but this figure is likely to be an underestimate, whilst seasonal variations in the use of bed coverings must also be taken into account.[92] The regularity and manner in which blankets were listed nonetheless makes clear that they were key ingredients of a good bed. Where more detailed descriptions exist, even the most rudimentary bedstead had at least one blanket. This number predictably rose for servants who slept in cold outbuildings; two blankets were relatively easy to procure since they were usually sold in pairs, or with two blankets woven together that could be cut and separated or doubled up for greater warmth. Blankets were occasionally distinguished by colour, age, size, condition and fabric. Thomas Alstone's lumber chamber in Bedfordshire had a 'kidderminster' blanket to accompany the bedsteads housed inside. This thick two-ply material was probably intended to give an extra layer of protection against the cold surroundings of this outlying chamber.[93] Lady Grisell Baillie also made important distinctions between blankets in her account book. She paid fourteen shillings 'For ane fine blanket to my own bed' and this single item cost more than the combined price of twelve blankets that she had purchased earlier that year.[94] There may well have been a functional overlap between blankets and 'rugs' that were frequently listed alongside other bedding materials in the inventories and that Samuel Johnson defined as 'A coarse, nappy coverlet, used for mean beds'.[95] A blanket was also the type of bedding textile that was most commonly lent to the poor. Their owners took care to air the blankets when they were returned to them and even to bake them in an oven to kill any bedbugs before they were recycled.[96]

The next most frequently cited categories of bed coverings were quilts, coverlets and counterpanes. Quilts were made by stitching together two pieces of cloth that were separated in the middle by some kind of filling to give an extra layer of softness and warmth.[97] Quilts were listed in 52 per cent of the PCC households and most of them typically had just one or two of these items. Significantly fewer quilts were listed in the early part of the period but by 1760 it was the exception rather than the rule to be without one. The growing appeal of cotton or calico quilts lay partly in changes in global manufacture, trade and fashion.[98] Concerns to secure peaceful sleep may also have informed these purchases since these quilts shared similar health-giving associations to the bedsheets already explored. Cotton counterpanes grew in popularity and affordability in the second half of the eighteenth century with specialist manufacturing centres popping up in Lancashire in the 1760s and later in the northeast of England.[99] White crisp cotton counterpanes promised a healthy and a comfortable night's sleep through their fresh look and smooth sensations.[100] Cottons and linens were also more easily laundered than other bedding textiles and their perceived effects on sleep quality encouraged medical practitioners to recommend their use. Changing ownership patterns of quilts and counterpanes were probably influenced by practices and perceptions relating to sleep as well as revealing broader shifts in the production and consumption of global textiles. Finally, watch pockets may have also become a staple part of the bedstead's textiles by the end of the eighteenth century. Watch pockets were small pouches made of linen, cotton or silk that could be made at home and tied or sewn to the bed where they were used to hold watches, smelling salts or handkerchiefs, which all serviced practical bodily needs.[101] A 'good bed' thus comprised an array of materials that was influenced by cost and cleanliness, by considerations of social status, and by different expectations of warmth, sensation and comfort. Individual expectations about sleep's sensory environments were vital in determining the make-up of beds and the personal associations of these materials enhanced them still further.

Personalising Sleep

The desire to sleep peacefully in a 'good bed', however it was made up and wherever it was located, influenced the acquisition and use of bedding textiles. Sleeping chambers, bedsteads and bedding textiles were highly personalised and their meanings, colours and fabrics conjured feelings of security, familiarity and comfort that helped to procure relaxation at bedtime. Sleeping in particular bedsteads helped to satisfy social expectations about the most appropriate sleeping environments to suit the status of particular individuals, but even more important was how they satisfied physical and psychological expectations of sleep. Here, personal memories played a vital role.

Cambridgeshire clergyman and antiquary William Cole prized the comforting familiarity offered by his old but treasured tent bed. Tent beds were typically small and low to the ground and they could be folded up and easily moved. They were widely used during military campaigns and in schools and other institutional settings where sleeping quarters were shared by large numbers of people. Many tent beds had curved canopies and covered sides that enclosed the sleeper's head and offered a degree of seclusion. William Cole chose to sleep in his tent bed, rather than in the 'best' bedstead in his home, because it reminded him of how he had slept in the long chamber at Eton College when he was a schoolboy there in the 1720s and 1730s.[102] Eton had made William Cole miserable. He suffered regular beatings and tried to run away several times but his bed very likely offered a safe retreat from this unhappiness and a comfortable place of solace to soothe the pains of the day. In later life, Cole refreshed this bed by replacing its hangings with newer and richly decorated cotton curtains operated by pulleys, yet he chose never to draw them and to keep his door open because he had become accustomed to sleeping in this manner since childhood. Age-old habits, familiar beds, bodily sensations and powerful memories all combined to shape people's interactions with sleep's material apparatus. Falling asleep was an intensely personal feeling that was sensed, learned and absorbed within memories and daily routines. It was also a feeling that was materialised through regular interactions with particular textiles and objects that sparked thoughts and feelings of security, familiarity and belonging.[103] Replicating these feelings of ease and relaxation on a nightly basis required consistency in the sensory cues that preceded sleep. Lying down in stable and recognisable surroundings helped to relax bodies and minds to a state where sleep could more easily take possession of them, and it reassured people that they would wake safely the following morning as they had in the days, weeks and months preceding.

The process of making, using and mending bedding textiles helped to create these feelings of stability at bedtime and these practices are vital in reconstructing the lost sensory world of early modern sleep. The creation and adaptation of textiles for bed hangings, covers, quilts and sheets was commonplace, partly due to the practical economy of making furnishings and recycling good-quality materials. The PCC inventories show the near-constant presence of 'wrought' bed furnishings, a term that usually indicated that they had been worked at home. The 'Workt Chamber' in the Reverend William Byatt's Essex home suggests that it may have contained a good proportion of handcrafted objects and textiles, and its decorative scheme was clearly distinguished from Byatt's other sleeping chambers that were more functionally titled 'middle chamber', 'middle garrett' and 'apple garrett'.[104] William Brewer's home contained a 'piece of wrought dymotye for a bed'.[105] Dimity, a thick cotton fabric, was widely used to make bed hangings and bedcovers. The base, usually undyed material, could be embellished with personal decorations whilst still remaining affordable. The cream linen-and-cotton bed-curtain shown in Figure 13, dating from c. 1691–c. 1720, is also likely to have been embroidered at home and adapted for use in a sleeping chamber. The bold tree pattern is sewn in crewel embroidery in dark teal-green wool and the curtain's edges are crudely hemmed, suggesting non-professional manufacture.[106]

13. Bed hanging, c. 1691–c. 1720.

In the late seventeenth century Abigail Pett embroidered her own linen-and-cotton bed-curtains and valances using crewel wool embroidery with restful images of trees, foliage and animals; this design was heavily influenced by the import of Indian bedding textiles into Britain and it also had strong associations with themes of immortality and restoration.[107] Some men and women commissioned local artists to incorporate familiar images from the local landscape onto their bedding textiles for a small fee.[108] Designs for crewel embroideries were widely available and they could be taken from hand-drawn, copied or purchased templates and laid onto the textiles. Some linen bedcovers still bear the pencil marks where their embroidery patterns were traced onto the fabric.[109] These kinds of details were frequently added to bedding textiles to enhance their visual appeal and to personalise them. Crewel embroidery was particularly popular for the domestic production of bedding because the wool stitching produced a thick, raised and robust design that could withstand frequent use and washing. The wool's texture also complemented thicker, warmer woollen textiles that were commonly found in sleeping chambers at this time.[110]

Motivations for making bedding textiles combined practicality and personality. Their creation was a common pursuit for women for whom needlework provided an outlet for self-expression, for making money, and for developing and advertising domestic virtue, artistry and piety. Plain bedsheets could be enlivened and personalised by the insertion of a bobbin-lace centre panel, which fixed the two loom-widths of fabric together, or by decorative needle weaving around their borders. Adding a centre panel to the sheet was pleasing to the eye but it also allowed the two linen widths to be unstitched and turned to ensure that the sheet was evenly worn and that its life could be extended for as long as possible. Similar decorations were sometimes added to pillowcase borders, especially if they matched the sheets that accompanied them. This was the case with the woven linen pillowcase shown in Figure 14, which belonged to a set of seventeenth-century English bedding textiles that comprised two sheets and three pillowcases decorated with delicate whitework stitching and bobbin-lace embroidery. This pillowcase bears the initials 'I.W', which probably referred to its first owner. The quality and aesthetic appeal of this set ensured that it passed through successive generations of one family as a treasured heirloom. It is perhaps for these very reasons that this ornate set of textiles is unlikely to resemble the coarser, plain and mismatched materials used on a regular basis and in the homes of less wealthy people. The addition of simple initials or decorations to bedding textiles was not, however, out of reach for many people.[111]

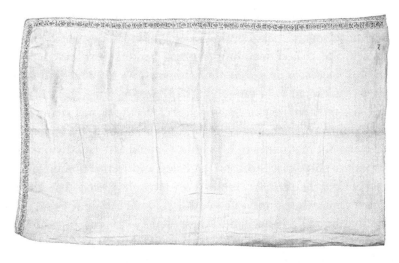

14. Pillowcase, England, seventeenth century.

The physical process of making these textiles involved purposeful medita-tion on the task in hand, which sparked moments of quiet thoughtfulness and probably heightened the maker's emotional attachment to their work. The meditative process associated with needlework also had an affinity with the peaceful moments that preceded sleep and unfinished textiles sometimes offered solace to women during unexpected periods of wakeful-ness. They picked up their work and resummoned sleep through the repeti-tive and relaxing movement of their needles, which calmed the mind and nerves.[112] The handmade finished products were undoubtedly sources of pride and admiration. Birmingham-born novelist and letter-writer Catherine Hutton was mightily pleased with the quilted counterpanes that she adorned with 'various patterns of my own invention'.[113] Creations of the needle were thus akin to creations of the pen in expressing the hopes, expectations and feelings of their producers, who invested time, labour and imagination in personalising the materials that were to keep them and their loved ones safe, warm and secure from harm during the night.[114]

Alongside handmade objects, professionally manufactured bedding textiles were readily available and affordable. Individuality could still be expressed through careful commissioning and selection of fabrics, colours and designs. In the early eighteenth century professional patchwork and quilt manufacturers were concentrated in vibrant urban centres like London, Canterbury and Exeter, where customers could choose from a variety of quilt patterns, textiles and stitching techniques. Customers could be precise and demanding in their requirements and they often wished to incorporate personal details. Local seamstresses and tradespeople were also trusted with the task of mending favoured bedding textiles, completing half-finished pieces, or providing them complete. In 1752 Richard Latham paid a local tradesman 3s 7d 'for quilting bed covering' and in 1759 Margaret Blundell received a shilling for making part of a quilt for the Latham household.[115] Confirmed bachelor William Cole used local tradespeople to recover worn-out mattresses in his home. He paid Mrs Goodwin to make six new calico pillowcases whilst Tom Allen and Henry Stubbings spent four days at Cole's house in November 1767 recovering two old bedquilts.[116] Cole's outlay may simply indicate good household economy but it is also possible that he was as attached to these quilts as he was to his old tent bedstead and sought to extend their life for as long as he could.

Feelings of ownership and sensory familiarity were enhanced by investments of time, thought and effort and this process was particularly compelling in the making and mending of quilts. The very act of creating these coverings merged practical function with personal meanings. These feelings were then reinforced by the reassurance, warmth and protection offered by the finished product. Quilts could be purchased ready-made in a range of materials but lively household gatherings of family and friends, known as 'quiltings' in eighteenth-century Europe and America, also fostered collective manufacture at home. This mode of production offered opportunities for pleasant sociability, especially for women, as well as enabling the creation of a snug and satisfying bed.[117] Patchwork quilts, whose top layers usually combined small and distinct scraps of material, varied greatly in the cost and quality of their textiles. They could be made of expensive silks, cheaper printed cottons that had been carefully collected over time, and recycled scraps of material that had been used elsewhere in the house or in items of clothing.[118] They could be expensive or economical to produce but the process of making them blended into the rhythms of household life. Squares of quilting could be easily transported between different rooms with sewing implements and scissors carried in the dress pockets of their creators that allowed them to be worked on in short bursts in between other tasks.[119] Patchwork was a desirable skill that symbolised household economy and fashion by the mid-eighteenth century and this appeal may partly explain why patchwork bedcovers were so frequently stolen in these years.[120] The charm of patchwork quilts undoubtedly also lay in their high levels of personalisation and practicality since they allowed for the integration of different materials. They sometimes had life stories sewn into them as well as offering a warm

and inviting layer of protection for sleepers. James Woodforde was especially proud of the patchwork quilt created by his niece Nancy that was
'very much admired' amongst their acquaintance. Woodforde helped Nancy
by purchasing scraps of cotton and linen from a salesman who called at the
parsonage.[121] Patchwork quilts, like many other bedcovers, carried intensely
personal meanings due to the labour and imagination expended on them.
They helped to forge strong bonds with their creators which structured
sleep's sensory dimensions.

Bedquilts often drew detailed descriptions from the PCC appraisers,
who distinguished them by design, colour, quality and value. Quilts were
also valued by the quality of their stuffing, which ranged from cheap flock
to wool or even otter's down.[122] Those households with a modest number of
quilts generally concentrated them in the best sleeping chambers over the
parlour, hall or kitchen. The only quilt in John Riddiough's Lambeth home
was located in his 'Best Chamber'.[123] In Richmond, Richard Edward-
Holmwood kept a calico quilt in his hall chamber, whilst his principal
sleeping room over the parlour contained a quilt made of yellow silk.[124]
Philip Harcourt's sumptuous balcony chamber contained a silk quilt valued
at £2 10s. A prominent member of his household staff had a less expensive
quilt of 'saten' and two blankets to keep her warm at night, whilst one of
Harcourt's female servants slept beneath a flock quilt. Servants' quilts may
have also been distinguished by colour, with dark brown, grey and violet
favoured in some households.[125] Coventry widow Elizabeth Dugdale owned
six quilts of varying quality that ranged from two calico quilts to the most
expensive 'green silk quilt lined with white', whilst at the other end of the
scale, widow Anne Blackburn had a 'striped dimity quilt' to accompany a
sacking bottom bedstead that she favoured over the 'old ragged white quilt'
kept in a store cupboard at the top of the staircase.[126] One quilt of green
damask and one of chintz were listed in the 1740s and the lone reference to
an 'old Holland quilt' in the home of Kent clerk John Darlinge may well
have been useful in the summer months since it was made of a breathable
linen fabric, as was one of Richard Smith's quilts that was stored in his back
garret.[127] The vast majority of quilts listed were made of calico, which
afforded feelings of freshness and breathability. A rich variety of homemade, semi-finished or purchased bed coverings thus kept sleepers warm
and comfortable at night. These textiles were made, updated and adapted to
suit many different tastes, pockets and bodily preferences and they all
helped to create familiar sensations of ease and relaxation.

The way that sleeping chambers looked may have been equally important to the tactile sensations created by their textiles in helping to calm the

body and soothe the passions at bedtime. This could be achieved through the use of particular colour schemes, decorative features and other visual stimuli that were prized for their protective and healing qualities. Many physicians believed that restful vistas of the natural world gave balance and harmony to the viewer. These scenes were believed to temper the passions and to ease troubled minds and they may even have prompted thoughts of God's creation, which made them effective precursors to a peaceful night's sleep.[128] Red, blue and green were the most common colour schemes for sleeping chambers in the inventory sample, followed by white and shades of brown.[129] The colours described in the inventories only give partial insights into the spectrum of colours that may have made up these rooms when the decoration of walls and the colour of textiles are considered alongside movable goods. The bodily effects of certain colours are difficult to trace yet they were likely to promote particular moods, thoughts and sensations that blended with sleep's approach and with its cultural meanings. Shades of blue had strong associations with feelings of purity, sincerity, love and temperance. These meanings may have spoken loudly to Protestants who prized the Christian virtue of temperance particularly highly and displayed their powers of self-discipline by moderating their sleeping hours. The colour blue may have also complemented the use of sleeping chambers for meditation, spiritual devotion and marital intimacy.[130]

Green was also a popular choice and its use ranged from modest dwellings to more extensive residences. Reverend Benjamin Carter hung his green sleeping chamber with 'green china' that matched his fashionable 'china bed'; this design was no doubt inspired by European tastes for exotic Eastern textiles and furniture designs.[131] Widow Mary Martin may not have been able to afford to replace the 'old stript hangings' in her sleeping chamber but she was able to surround her bedstead with 'greene perpet-uana curtaines' that matched the single green chair at its side.[132] Perpetuana was a hard-wearing woollen fabric that no doubt had practical appeal and Mary's partially matching decor might have produced feelings of satisfaction for the widow who probably worked hard to make or to buy them.[133] The desirability of green traversed social ranks: it was one of the few colours mentioned in Old Bailey indictments for textile theft.[134] The appeal of green sleeping chambers and bedding textiles may have also been linked to fashion and to production. The two-stage process for making green dye probably heightened its cost and prestige for discerning consumers. Passages from classical texts may have also enhanced its popularity since they linked green to the Roman goddess Venus, who exerted power over love and sleep. More recently Bruce Smith has explained the desire for green furnishings within Renaissance culture as preferences for visual representations of the natural world. Early modern bedding textiles were indeed covered with landscape images.[135] The landscape painting that hung over the chimney in Richard Edward-Holmwood's parlour chamber may have triggered calm feelings of restfulness as Richard and his family gazed upon the fresh verdant countryside before them.

'Sad-colour' furnishings in shades of purple and grey were popular in Baroque interiors but they featured in declining numbers in the inventory sample.[136] In 1666 Samuel Pepys hesitated over decorating his closet with purple serge, a durable twilled woollen or silk textile, because he feared that the colour would prove 'too sad for that melancholy room'.[137] Closets, like sleeping chambers, were routinely used as places of religious devotion at bedtime. Pepys was mindful of the sombre mood that these activities produced in him and he tried to offset it with a carefully chosen colour scheme. The relationship between image and viewer described here was one that encompassed mind and body with particular colours evoking distinctive thoughts and feelings.[138] Widespread use of the term 'sad' to denote sombre shades reinforces this important point: 'sad' is not a description of a colour but a description of a human feeling triggered by a colour. The feelings that 'sad' colours produced may have influenced declining preferences for this colour scheme if they stirred anxieties at bedtime. When Samuel and Elizabeth redecorated their sleeping chamber in 1666 they opted instead for a blue colour scheme, which perhaps conjured more pleasing associations of devotion and marital intimacy (with which they perpetually struggled), or thoughts of the sea that reminded Samuel of his beloved role as a naval administrator.[139] The colour scheme would have been carefully selected as the couple invested a great deal of imagination and effort in this redecoration project. Samuel noted that his wife worked 'all day at home like a horse at the making of her hanging for our chamber and the bed', so this was clearly a place of great emotional significance for both of them. Yellow was similarly recommended for offsetting gloominess at night and for summoning 'chearfulness', and this colour had growing appeal as a decorative scheme for sleeping chambers by the late eighteenth century.[140] Yellow was closely linked to Hymen, the Greek god of marriage, in classical mythology. The sexual and procreative meanings of yellow may have been particularly suitable for sleeping chambers given their practical and symbolic links with marriage and childbirth.[141]

If different colours created links between sleeping chambers and the feelings associated with sleep then the same was true of meaningful images that were kept at the bedside, which had the power to personalise these environments and to offer comforting reminders of absent loved ones whose virtual presence conjured feelings of contentedness and safety. Paintings and prints were increasingly displayed in the sleeping chambers of London freemen during the eighteenth century, whose homes have been examined by David Mitchell.[142] John Lichford had seven pictures in his Lincolnshire sleeping chamber whilst Anne Blackburn kept 'four painted pictures and thirteen prints' at her bedside. The subject of these images is unrecoverable yet their concentration around the bedstead suggests that they had significant meanings for their owners. Family pictures had the power to reassure and to create feelings of belonging at bedtime. The presence of trusted loved ones at night was, and still is, believed to have a beneficial effect on sleep quality by producing a calm and relaxed state of mind. Loved ones might not be physically present, or even alive, but thoughts and sensations associated with them could be aroused through images and objects. The sleeping chamber of London widow Mary Evans contained just one 'family picture' whilst George Ashbey's main sleeping chamber in Leicestershire and the 'Widow's Room' in Benjamin Coster's home contained no less than three each. The widow in question was perhaps Coster's mother, or an elderly female relative, who drifted off to sleep at night accompanied by thoughts of her dearest loved ones with whom she may have wished to be reunited after her own death.[143] Whatever the bodily effects of such images may have been, it is clear that a complex web of negotiations was involved in the visual composition of sleeping environments. Men and women took great care when shaping these vistas, which combined practical and personal motivations for making, displaying and interacting with particular images and objects around the bedside.

The presence of family prints at the bedside was one way that sleeping environments could take on deep personal meanings. Spending time with loved ones at bedtime was also recognised as an effective relaxation technique. The textiles and objects created by them, or associated with them, could produce similar effects by triggering comforting memories and sensations that compensated for their temporary or permanent absence. These objects tended to cluster around bedsteads and on bedding textiles, which were complex sites of emotional meaning that seamlessly blended old and new materials with personal histories. The regard that Yorkshire widow Alice Thornton had for her scarlet bedstead and furnishings reveals the heady mixture of physical and psychological ease that lay at the heart of sleep's successful practice. Alice ran into financial trouble following her husband William's death in 1668. When her household goods were valued to clear the debt she fought a desperate battle to retain possession of these treasured objects that her mother had gifted to her upon marriage. Alice had no documents to establish her ownership of these goods so she relied instead on the testimony of her mother's faithful servant Dafeny Lightfoot, who told the appraisers that Alice's mother had gifted the bedstead and its textiles to her daughter 'to use, but not pay debts, but out of kindness to assist them in theire house'. Dafeny was able to identify the textiles by the laundry marks that appeared on them, most of which she had made herself.[144] A struggle ensued in which Alice protested against the high valuation of £40 that the appraisers placed on these goods because she could not afford the cost of repurchase.

Retaining possession of a seemly and handsome bed was at once a token of self-sufficiency, decency and household reputation, but Alice's attachment went much deeper than this. As she feared the loss of this bed, Alice recalled the soft warmth of its materials, which had provided a place of refuge and solace at traumatic moments in her life. She described it as her 'sorrowfull bed' in 1668 when she grieved beneath its covers as she anticipated the imminent death of her beloved husband William. The scarlet bed had fortified her spirits as she prayed there when she feared that God had forsaken her. This was the bed where she had recruited physical strength following the birth of her nine children and it was the bed beside which her daughter, also named Alice, had been secretly married to local clergyman Thomas Comber in 1668. The scarlet bed also triggered sensations and memories of maternal affection as Alice remembered the times when her own mother had laid her down there to recover from childhood accidents. It was here that Alice had retreated when her children fell ill and here that she felt confident of slipping into the restorative sleep that she so desperately needed to care for them.[145] The scarlet bed was a valued possession in much more than monetary terms: it offered sensory and emotional connections to Alice's mother and family and to embodied memories of her own life. Tactile interaction with the bedstead produced familiar sensations of sleep's relief, which had eased Alice's mind and body at difficult times in her life. Little wonder then that she was so fearful of its loss.

Alice's scarlet bed was, in many ways, an extension of her own body and of the bodies of her loved ones who had interacted with it over generations.[146] It served a physical and psychological purpose by recalling feelings of safety, homeliness and regeneration. Such detailed insights into the personal and sensory meanings of beds are rare. Few people chose to write down how sleep felt and how their beds helped to structure those feelings.

Sleep was so deeply engrained in daily life that its experience was rarely articulated in ways that are easily recoverable. Rich insights nevertheless surface when people were jolted out of their habitual sleep routines and environments, whether due to personal crisis, financial ruin, widowhood, moving house, travel or sociability. It is therefore unlikely that the connections that Alice Thornton made between her scarlet bed, her sleep and her sense of comfort in the world were unique. Beds were after all a pivotal focus for the making and gifting of textiles across the British Isles, Europe and America. They were often deliberately crafted to forge personal relationships and to narrate a family's history by marking significant moments in the life cycle such as courtship, marriage, childbirth and death.[147] Each of these life stages was linked to unique physical sensations and emotions, which beds, mattresses and textiles helped to create and allay. The look and feel of bedding textiles were likely to have sparked thoughts, feelings and memories of happiness, love, loss and belonging that helped bodies and minds to negotiate transitions between pleasure and pain and between different states of consciousness.

The expressive capacity of bedding textiles reached a peak in those materials that were created to mark important family events such as the cot quilt that Nany Latham made in 1753 for one of her children.[148] The only reference to a homemade textile in George Ashbey's household inventory referred to a coverlet listed in the nursery.[149] A small patchwork quilt was created to mark the birth of Susanna Redding in 1693. The quilt was passed on to Susanna in 1713 when her first child James was born.[150] Figure 15 shows the surviving central patchwork panel of a cotton bedcover that celebrates the birth or christening of 'Henry Iane Haines' in 1786. These biographical details are embroidered in cross-stitch, and the use of cheap fragments of material and black wool stitching suggests that it may have been relatively inexpensive to make. The preservation of the central panel, which was later framed behind glass for display by its owner, suggests that the cover was in regular use with the rest of the textile having disintegrated or been discarded.

The careful preservation of such textiles underlines their combined practical and personal meanings. Bedding textiles were regularly gifted as treasured keepsakes through many generations, which connected each generation to one another. Stroud widow Dorothy Punnett bequeathed her 'second best quilt' that had lain on her own bed to her son Augustine in 1718, whilst Catherine Hutton inherited a calico bedquilt that her Aunt Perkins had made out of an old gown and petticoat that Catherine's grandmother used to wear.[151] Two well-worn and heavily repaired linen sheets,

15. Bedcover, England, *c.* 1786.

which originally belonged to a family in Somerset, reveal the habitual movement of bedding textiles between family generations. The outer edge of the sheet in Figure 16 features two sets of initials in blue cross-stitch, 'E.B.' and 'B.H.', which may have been the initials of a mother and daughter, or of a husband and wife, who used the sheet on a regular basis. Initials were frequently marked in ink or sewn onto bedsheets to identify their owners, to prevent loss or theft whilst travelling with them, and to ensure that they returned to the correct bedsteads after being laundered.

The second – much coarser and hand-woven – linen sheet in Figure 17 dates to 1757. An ink inscription in the top corner nevertheless reveals that 'This sheet is 115 years old 10 February 1873'. The remarkable durability of this kind of sheet is partly due to the robust quality of its linen fibres but the survival of some sheets must also be linked to their status as cherished personal objects that created stable sleeping environments for their owners. These layers perhaps conveyed sensations of security and warmth by evoking the bonds of love and safety between parents and children as they lay down to sleep each night. The hoarding of valuables, secret objects and love letters within and beneath bedsteads, or underneath pillows and mattresses, similarly suggests that they were viewed as highly personalised places of safety and individuality.[152]

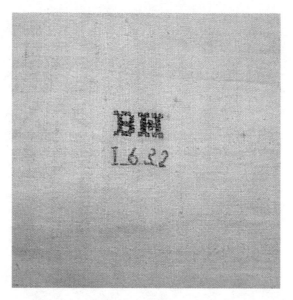

16. Sheet, *c.* 1600–*c.* 1632.

17. Hand-woven linen sheet, late eighteenth century.

Marriage was another important milestone that triggered the creation and personalisation of bedding textiles. Figures 18 and 19 show the quilted bedcover and set of pillows embroidered by the young gentlewoman Ann Breton between 1725 and 1750. The large linen bedcover, which was worked in cream silk flat quilting, provided Ann with the ideal canvas on which to display her taste, education and needlework skills. The decorative motif at the centre of the cover is ornately embroidered with a roundel of roses, tulips and carnations that are flanked by her initials 'A.B.' Each of the four corners features a plant motif and the rest of the sheet is embroidered with colourful Chinese figures holding parasols, and with birds, dragons, goats and mythical creatures. The cover's size and the intricacy of its silk and gilt thread embroidery show that its creation was a long-term and important project. The cover's incomplete embroidery shows that the project was time-consuming for Ann, who may have squeezed in time to work on it between her other household responsibilities.

18. Bedcover, *c.* 1725–*c.* 1750.

19. Pillow cover, *c.* 1725–*c.* 1750.

Ann Breton's bedcover was intended to grace her future marriage bed and the hours she spent working on it very likely afforded her time to imagine the pleasures and sensations that married life might bring.[153] Ann died before she finished her masterpiece, which she appears to have made in anticipation of an engagement that was never realised. These textiles were stored away by Ann's family after her death and passed down through multiple generations. This is one reason that the textiles have survived in such pristine condition: they were never used for their original purpose. This bedding became a repository of personal memories for the Breton family rather than being absorbed into the ordinary rhythms of household life.

The surviving fragment of a hand-woven white linen bedsheet shown below suggests a similar motivation for its creation but a much heavier use than Ann Breton's bedding. The initials 'M.M.M.' are cross-stitched onto the sheet in white thread above the date '1702' to mark the significance and date of its creation.

The fragment is marked with a brief note, which indicates that the complete sheet was once part of a bride's plenishing, a stock of household goods brought by the bride to her marital home, and that the initials stand for 'Martha and Matthew Moss'. These initials probably referred to the newly married couple, or to the bride's parents, who perhaps gifted the sheet to their daughter to mark the year of her marriage and to help

20. Sheet (part), England, c. 1700.

establish her new household. The sheet's high thread count and its silk embroidery very likely pushed up its cost and its importance within the household linen stock. The remaining fragment, which measures just 80cm by 71cm, contains numerous holes, and the disintegration of the complete sheet suggests that it was heavily used. The sheet is believed to have connections to the Wyman family of Stonebury in Hertfordshire, who appear to have preserved its most meaningful section as part of their ancestral history. The Breton and Moss textiles uncover the poignant affections that bedding materials could possess and transmit. If Alice Thornton's scarlet bed conjured reassuring memories then these collections expressed optimistic hopes of future longevity, decency and happiness. Bedding textiles thus formed a tactile bridge between the waking and sleeping worlds and they eased people's journeys into restful slumber by evoking thoughts and sensations of loved ones.

Laying down to sleep in a secure, enclosed and familiar bedstead was an ideal to which almost everyone aspired in early modern England. Safety and protection were the principal watchwords that shaped this ideal, but its achievability was of course determined by a person's age, occupation, status and gender and by the practical needs of the household they inhabited. For many middle and upper-sort householders and their families, sleep became ever more closely associated with chambers on the upper floors, which were partially specialised in function and that were carefully decorated and arranged to comfort weary bodies and minds. The will, and indeed the means, to secure some kind of partial enclosure during sleep nevertheless spread more widely and is revealed by the design, make-up and location of beds throughout the early modern period, as well as by evolving patterns of room usage. Widespread use of bed-curtains, box beds and tent beds offered some semblance of seclusion to sleepers at particular times of day and night and the bedside space that was surrounded by curtains was termed a 'room' in contemporary vocabularies.[154] These arrangements reveal deeply held desires for security during sleep and preferences for resting in quiet, clean and familiar environments. Lying down in meaningful and comfortable surroundings was arguably even more important to early modern men and women than the precise location of their bedsteads. Sleeping environments were dramatically enhanced in their look, decoration and feel by the mid-eighteenth century. High, roped and well-padded bedsteads with multiple layers of luxurious textiles could enhance levels of comfort for those who could afford to pay for them. Satisfaction of a different kind could nevertheless be secured more cheaply as personalised objects, images and textiles that offered cosiness, pleasure and reassurance to their owners clustered

around the bedside. These carefully chosen or handmade materials structured the physical sensations and thoughts that eased sleep's passage.
Achieving a good night's sleep thus involved meeting individual expectations of 'comfort' that combined physical and psychological dimensions.
The familiar fabrics, images and objects that surrounded the bedside both
reflected and sustained the physical and emotional life of the household,
forging feelings of homeliness, intimacy and safety. They helped both to
stage sleep and to invite its approach by evoking the same sensations,
thoughts and feelings night after night. These objects, and the care and
attention lavished on them, show just how important it was to get a good
night's sleep.

CHAPTER 5

Sleep and Sociability

O N MONDAY, 26 January 1756, shopkeeper Thomas Turner made the following entry in his diary:

> My wife went down to Mr. Porter's about 4 o'clock. I went down to her
> about 7 and found Wm. Piper, his wife and brother there, as also Tho.
> Fuller, Mr. and Mrs. Hutson and Dame Durrant. We supped there and
> stayed until 5 o'clock in the morning and I may I think justly say there
> was not one sober man in the company. I am sure I was not, for, finding
> myself in liquor I came home 1 hour or more before the rest.[1]

At the time of writing Turner was in his mid-twenties, recently married, and
a relative newcomer to the village of East Hoathly in Sussex. The Turners
socialised with their new neighbours in order to make friends and professional contacts, and to establish their good character to cement their place,
and their business, in this close-knit community. Business and pleasure
combined again two years later when Thomas and his wife met Mr Elless to
agree a rental price for a warehouse above the local school. They sealed the
transaction by playing whist together from seven at night until seven in the
morning.[2] The Turners' motivation for keeping late hours is obvious enough
but Thomas's diary recorded the damaging effects that these social interactions had on the couple's sleep. Thomas was convinced that these late nights
were worthy of note and in need of careful justification. His reflections
underline two important themes that form the subject of this chapter.
Firstly, unusual bedtimes and sleeping environments occasioned remark
because they interrupted habitual routines and bodily sensations that were
essential for a good night's sleep. They disrupted a deeply held yet rarely

articulated desire for continuity and security at bedtime that was touched on in the previous chapter. This chapter forms a natural partnership with its predecessor by revealing those moments when sleep's habitual boundaries were transgressed. These moments of rupture help to uncover the ordinary expectations of sleep that marked its mundane daily practice.

The second crucial implication of Thomas Turner's diary, and of others like it, is that these transgressions grew increasingly familiar, worthy of comment and of action. Turner's reflections signal a critical phase of change in perceptions and practices of sleep that was triggered by wider socio-cultural developments – namely the pursuit of public and household forms of sociability, which disrupted sleeping hours and sleeping environments on a hitherto unprecedented scale. Diaries, letters and a wide variety of printed texts show that men and women of different ranks and stations of life retired to bed at ever-later hours, slept outside of their own beds and homes, and lay down with a range of companions in the pursuit of new forms of sociability that grew in strength from the late seventeenth century.

Erratic bedtimes and sleeping environments sparked lively debates at the same time as they diversified. Enlightenment philosophers and Christian moral commentators explained the religious, medical and civic value of restorative sleep but they often disagreed about the appropriate times and places in which it could be safely indulged. The shifting cultural influences that shaped understandings of sleep are thereby revealed alongside the ways in which they transformed sleep's daily practice. By focusing on migratory sleeping habits this chapter charts the impact of public modes of sociability, including visits to the theatre, playhouse, opera, pleasure garden, spa resort and to continental Europe, which reshaped sleep's daily rhythms and prompted debate about the social value of erratic sleeping habits.

The gentry, the 'beau monde' and wealthy ladies and gentlemen who travelled frequently in the British Isles and Europe, or who resided for part of the year in London, were most regularly engaged in public sociability.[3] A much broader range of people who resided in or travelled to London and other provincial centres were, however, eager participants in the whirlwind of nocturnal entertainments that appeared in the decades after 1660, albeit on a more occasional basis. These travellers often went to great lengths to offset the potential dangers that might befall them in alien sleeping environments and to replicate the familiar sensory cues of home. The second part of the chapter examines the more thoroughgoing impact of household sociability on sleep's daily practice, which shaped the material infrastructure and management of households and the social codes that informed the treatment of overnight guests. Household sociability encompassed a broader range of participants, from the aristocratic residents of Bedford Square to provincial householders attempting to live politely, and people whose profession or trade simply required the cultivation of patrons and personal networks. The sleep routines of household servants are traced through the accounts of their employers, to whose habits they were often required to attune themselves. I examine how, why and with what success householders tried to accommodate their overnight guests in decent, clean and comfortable surroundings. The physical arrangement, contents and management of households suggest that many of them became increasingly well equipped to accommodate a steady flow of overnight guests, and indeed of daytime nappers, by the mid-eighteenth century. Finally, the chapter reveals the emergence of a unique code of sleep-civility that accompanied these changing habits, which intertwined sleep's physical, psychological and cultural dimensions. These measures taken together offered support and consistency to seemingly transgressive sleeping habits that reinforced the desirability of sleeping at home, whilst also recognising the increasingly fragmented nature of sleep's daily practice.

The Battle Over Bedtime

In 1680 Leeds merchant Ralph Thoresby wrote down some salient words in his diary that he had heard during a sermon. Dr Sharp had cautioned his congregation to refrain from the pernicious habit of current times to 'outstare the sun'.[4] Sharp's wisdom may have helped Thoresby to resist the nocturnal pleasures of London society when he visited the capital some years later and was awed by the brightly lit streets and the hustle and bustle of the metropolis at night. Sharp was not alone in voicing his disapproval of the late bedtimes and erratic sleeping habits that seemed to be subverting the hours of darkness that God and Nature had safeguarded for rest. By 1754 Edward Moore, editor of weekly periodical *The World*, declared that a new species of human had emerged that he labelled 'children of the night'.[5] The unprecedented expansion of evening leisure activities across London and in other provincial centres was identified as the principal cause of receding bedtimes.

Historian Craig Koslofsky confirmed the impressions of Edward Moore and defined this early modern development as an emerging culture of nocturnalisation that involved the extension and legitimisation of social, religious and political activities deep into the night.[6] European sovereigns engaged in theatrical displays of political strength by sponsoring court masquerades, operas, ballets and elaborate firework shows. Public assemblies, trips to the theatre, playhouse, opera and pleasure garden became evening habits for those ladies and gentlemen that could afford to sustain them on a regular or occasional basis. All of these activities involved the annexation of the night for waking activities, in pursuit of pleasure and to create and maintain social and political networks. These entertainments gained practical support from important changes in urban infrastructure. London acquired its first public streetlights between 1684 and 1694 and by 1700 it had become the most populous city in Europe. A further 5,000 oil lamps had been installed by 1736 through a combination of Parliamentary and private acts that had the common aim of 'better Cleansing and Enlightening the streets'.[7] Staging or participating in late-night sociability in the high-profile venues of the capital was an expression of power, wealth and status but it also had demonstrable effects on bedtimes and sleeping habits.[8]

The hours that sleep consumed and the time at which sleep was taken were heavily influenced by the duties and pleasures of social interaction. The fashionable periodical *Tatler* noted this trend in 1710 by publishing an anecdotal observation about the disruption of well-established sleeping hours. An article entitled 'The Britons, satisfied with little night' identified the growing tendency of London's fashionable ladies and gentlemen to postpone their bedtimes in favour of personal and professional pursuits:

> the Night was much longer formerly in this Island than it is at present. By the Night, I mean that Portion of Time which Nature has thrown into Darkness, and which the Wisdom of Mankind had formerly dedicated to Rest and Silence. This used to begin at Eight a Clock in the Evening, and conclude at Six in the Morning. The Curfeu, or Eight a Clock Bell, was the Signal throughout the Nation for putting out their Candles and going to Bed.[9]

The author blamed these unnatural rhythms on late-night card games and in-depth political and business discussions indulged by gentlemen 'at the Time when their Fore-Fathers were laid down quietly to Rest'.[10] The author's estimation that eight o'clock marked the end of ordinary waking hours does not of course reflect the seasonal, regional, professional and social variations that determined daytime schedules and bedtimes. Similar social critiques about receding bedtimes nonetheless reverberated elsewhere. William Ellis, author of household guide *The Country Housewife's Family Companion* (1750), counted seasonable bedtimes as an essential duty of female householders. Ellis's model of the good country housewife who turned in when the sun set was constructed in direct opposition to the 'Dames of our Days, who pass all the Morning in sleeping and dressing, the rest of the Day to receive and pay Visits, and all the Night at Play, at Ball, at Comedy, at Feasts, and all other Diversions that they can invent'.[11] A similar satire of female bedtimes claimed that it was now the fashion to 'lie in Bed till Noon, dress all the Afternoon, Dine in the Evening, and play at Cards till Midnight'.[12] The women in question were most likely part of the beau monde and affiliated to prominent men at the royal court or in Parliament. The seemingly frivolous lifestyles of these women were frequently derided in print, yet they clearly invested great care, diligence and time moulding their personal networks through tiring social interactions.[13] A measure of the scale and vitality that the grandest gatherings could attain was given in accounts of the opening of Norfolk House, home of the duke and duchess of Norfolk, in St James's Square in 1756. Horace Walpole was amongst the invitees and he wrote to his friend Henry Seymour Conway in February of that year to describe the event: 'All the earth was there last Tuesday. You would have thought there had been a comet, everybody was gaping in the air and treading on one another's toes'.[14] Poet and essayist Richard Owen Cambridge was inspired to write a parody of the gathering through the eyes of Lady Townsend who was left off the guest list. His *Elegy written in an Empty Assembly-Room* expressed the sense of shame and distress that she may have suffered by this social snub. The elegy nevertheless concluded with the consolatory thought that 'N * * [Norfolk] *has murder'd Sleep*': exhaustion was the price of attendance at this illustrious assembly.[15]

It became a common refrain in parodies, moral commentaries and novels to suggest that nature was being overturned by the artificial pleasures of nocturnal sociability. Tobias Smollett's *Expedition of Humphry Clinker* underlines the seemingly unnatural bedtimes kept by London's fashionable elite. The idealised seasonal rhythms of the countryside are sharply contrasted with metropolitan habits, with the beau monde routinely going to bed after midnight. *The World*, which was supported by Lord Lyttleton and Horace Walpole, quoted the complaint of a lady of quality regarding the 'unseasonable hours' kept by her fellow Londoners. The late-night revelry of her neighbours meant that the lady's sleep was 'constantly broke by the noise of cars, drays and hackney-coaches'.[16] This hyperbole was probably directed at the excessive revelry that surrounded court and Parliament, which would satisfy the sensibilities of polite middling-sort readers for whom seasonable bedtimes represented the esteemed virtues of piety and self-discipline with which they liked to be associated. This convergence of complaints signalled the fact that a battle over the timing and meanings of bedtimes had begun.

Diaries and letters teem with chaotic timetables of nightly entertainments and they expose the practical relationship that existed between receding bedtimes and cultures of public sociability. Nocturnal sociability was at its most visible in London. This was partly due to the density of wealthy families that spent a large part of the year in the capital to participate in political life and in the highly ritualised leisure events that filled the autumn and spring months. This political elite congregated in 'the town' or West End, which underwent a dramatic physical expansion in the early eighteenth century and which offered easy access to court, Parliament and an ever-expanding range of entertainment venues.[17] The daily timetable of the Hill family was not perhaps untypical. In an account of 1715 they were reputed to 'lie in bed every day till twelve, go to dinner at six, to supper at twelve, and go on and make great entertainment' thereafter.[18] Engagement diaries and memorandum books show the regularity with which people frequented Drury Lane, the King's Theatre, the opera and the pleasure gardens at Vauxhall and Ranelagh. Receding bedtimes were rarely noted in these records yet they were a natural consequence of the fast-paced round of sociable interactions that had become a mundane reality for people of fashion – sociability was both expensive and exhausting.

Visits to the theatre, assembly rooms and concerts offered pleasant evening diversions and a chance to secure a place in the best company in provincial towns and cities further afield.[19] Lancashire recusant Nicholas Blundell of Little Crosby Hall regularly joined with neighbours, friends and acquaintances in evening entertainments. He visited Liverpool, Preston, York and Harrogate to meet friends and family and to buy new goods, including a bed for his mother on one occasion.[20] Blundell often concluded these trips by eating and drinking with friends late into the night, which in turn demanded overnight lodgings.[21] In January 1706 he took supper at the Talbot Inn in Liverpool with a group of male companions who were due to sail for Ireland. Blundell recorded in his diary that the cheerful company 'set up drinking till Morning'.[22] Circles of male sociability shaped Blundell's bedtimes but he and his wife Fanny also shared many late nights in the company of mutual friends. In 1706 the couple attended a performance of the tragedy *The unhappy favourite, or, The Earl of Essex,* which arrived in Liverpool after being staged at the Theatre Royal in London. Here the Blundells bumped into friends Mr Norris and Mr and Mrs Plumb and arrived home at two o'clock the next morning. When the couple returned to see the same play with new companions in 1712 they stayed out until 'between 4 and 5 next Morning'.[23] Young female companions Sarah Hurst and Miss Pigott had a similarly late night when they travelled from Horsham to London in the summer of 1759 to see the play *Hamlet & Lethe.* The two women outlasted their male companions who went home to bed rather than accompanying them on the adventure.[24] Motivations for recording these instances in diaries and correspondence are complex yet insightful. Entries sometimes emphasised the unusual and ad hoc nature of late-night entertainments that may have been a more common experience for those with a smaller purse who lived further away from a large urban centre. An element of self-fashioning naturally shaped these reflections since the ability to engage in such activities required a decent income, independent leisure time and well-developed social networks. These habits nevertheless drew censure if there was no discernible purpose for them beyond the naked pursuit of pleasure. Diarists and correspondents were alive to these accusations and took care to emphasise the professional obligations and neighbourly duties that kept them from their beds. Others, like Thomas Turner, reproached themselves when they overstepped the acceptable boundaries of sociability. Building strong social networks through face-to-face encounters was, however, essential for those wishing to secure a place in good company.

City entertainments were supplemented in the summer months by spa bathing, one of the fastest-growing leisure activities in eighteenth-century England. Spa resorts became important stages for ritualised courtship and socialising, with the added draw of health restoration on offer.[25] These visits furnished opportunities to develop personal and professional networks that were equal to, and sometimes more important than, the anticipated medicinal relief to be found. In 1712 Ralph Thoresby set out for Hampstead, which was noted 'for its mineral waters and confluence of gentry'.[26] Spending time in Bath, Epsom, Harrogate, Margate, Southampton and Tunbridge indicated a healthy income and a surfeit of leisure time akin to the pleasures of the city. Visitors to these destinations nonetheless sought fresh air and an escape from the fast-paced urban life that might relieve the array of nervous complaints that preoccupied medical practitioners and patients in these years. As Chapter 1 explained, disturbed sleep was now defined as a nervous disorder and it acquired modish overtones as physicians, philosophers and writers linked it ever more closely to fashionable lifestyles, luxurious diets and to intellectual exertion, which is explored at length in the following chapter. It was something of a paradox then that the intensive schedule of social gatherings and poor-quality lodgings to be found at spa resorts made sleeping problems even worse.

Anne Dormer, whose sleep loss was described in Chapter 2, paid regular visits to spa towns to improve her failing health. During a visit to Tunbridge in 1690 she complained about the intensive round of social obligations that she was expected to fulfil that prevented her from getting enough sleep.[27] The relief that Anne gained from bathing was counteracted by her social commitments at Tunbridge that could include between eight and ten visits each day. She described the pains of being 'always carried aboute to visit or at home to sitt entertaining visitors, and when I have wanted sleepe never to be able to get half an houre . . . [or] be by my self'. When she tried to decline invitations after a bad night's rest she claimed that her efforts were met with 'nothing but angry expressions'.[28] The highly ritualised forms of sociability that were characteristic of spa resorts may well have intensified the degree of offence that could be taken from declined invitations. Anne Dormer was in an unenviable position since attending and hosting social gatherings in such resorts was considered to be a form of social currency. Anne's social interactions were most successful after a sound night's sleep yet her chances of enjoying it were thwarted by the exhausting demands of sociability. The rest and relief that she anticipated at Tunbridge proved frustratingly elusive since Anne's preferred hours of rising, napping and retiring to bed conflicted with the social engagements in which she was required to participate.

Anne Dormer's chronic sleeplessness was unusual but her vexation at the interruption to her rest was echoed more widely by men and women who viewed such visits, at least in part, as periods of recovery from the heavy social schedule of their daily lives. The quality and location of Nicholas and Fanny Blundell's sleep was frequently disrupted when they took the waters at Liverpool and Harrogate due to a combination of social commitments and poor-quality lodgings.[29] Experienced traveller Celia Fiennes, a gentlewoman from Salisbury, encountered similar difficulties on a prolonged tour of the British Isles that was designed to restore her health 'by variety and change of aire and exercise'.[30] In 1697 she visited the bath and well at Buxton Hall in Derbyshire, where her ordinarily peaceful sleep was disturbed by over-crowded and unhealthy lodgings. At Buxton she observed that there were:

> 2 beds in a room some 3 beds and some 4 in one roome, so that if you have not Company enough of your own to fill a room they will be ready to put others into the same chamber, and sometimes they are so crowded that three must lye in a bed; few people stay above two or three nights its so inconvenient: we staid two nights by reason one of our Company was ill but it was sore against our wills, for there is no peace and quiet with one Company and another going into the Bath or coming out.[31]

Exploratory travel was becoming fashionable in the 1690s but the infra-structure to support heavy flows of visitors was often lacking. The degree of commercial development of resorts and spa towns had a strong influence on the quality of visitors' sleep. Diaries, letters and travel journals abound with pained reports of discomfort, overcrowding, filth and noise at inns and lodging houses. The lack of seclusion and security available at bedtime was a recurrent complaint and this may have contrasted starkly with the sleeping environments to which people had become accustomed at home. Celia Fiennes anticipated such difficulties and tried to offset them by travelling with her own 'nightcloths and little things'. She may have placed these cherished objects within a linen nightgown bag that was expressly designed for travelling. These bags could be made at home, embroidered with the owner's initials, and filled with a nightgown, cap, dressing gown and a change of linen.[32] These items were easily transported and they no doubt helped Celia to cope with a series of unfamiliar sleeping environments by reminding her of the smells and sensations that accompanied bedtime at home. She used her own sheets to shield herself from the 'dirty blanckets' under which she lay at a cottage in Haltwhistle, Northumberland. However, the familiar touch of these sheets was not enough to secure a peaceful night's sleep as the peat smoke from the cottage's open chimneys filled Celia's lungs and kept her awake.[33] Anne Dormer and Celia Fiennes highlight the damage that public sociability, wherever it took place, could have on sleep quality. It disturbed the natural rhythms created by regular bedtimes and threatened to destroy physical and mental health. These effects were especially damaging for women like Anne Dormer whose fragile complexions were easily hurt by prolonged periods of sleep loss. These uncomfortable experiences certainly debunked the complaints of moral commentators who described nocturnal leisure pursuits and spa visits as a nonstop whirlwind of hedonistic delight.[34]

Further afield still were the celebrated elite venues of sociability of continental Europe. By the mid-eighteenth century growing numbers of men and women ventured to destinations like Paris, Rome and Venice hungry for education, culture, social connections and precious antiquities to display in their homes. Receding bedtimes, lost mornings and unpleasant sleeping environments were necessary consequences of participating in these activities. The degree of enthusiasm with which sociability was embraced differed according to the make-up of particular companies and the strength of individual constitutions. On a visit to Paris in 1769 Horace Walpole wrote to his friend George Montagu after he arrived home at eleven o'clock one Sunday evening. Walpole confessed that he was 'heartily tired' yet believed that it was 'too early to go to bed' and so stayed up to pen a vivid description of his recent visit to the coastal resort of Saint-Cyr in southeast France.[35] Walpole may well have fitted the description of a 'lychnobite'. This word entered the English language in the early eighteenth century, being taken from the

Greek 'lukhnobios' meaning 'lamp-life'. The influential folio *Dictionarium Britannicum* (1730) written by schoolmaster and lexicographer Nathan Bailey, defined a lychnobite as someone who pursued business or pleasure by night: a lychnobite had become a distinctive type of person in need of categorisation.[36] Former ambassador's wife, traveller and writer Lady Mary Wortley Montagu was a reluctant lychnobite at best. In 1758 she described how Venetian society had altered her sleeping habits. She rose late in the morning after visits to the theatre and opera and it was not unusual for some assemblies to break up at five o'clock in the morning. Mixing with influential ladies and gentlemen was undoubtedly appealing but Lady Mary's enthusiasm was diluted by the physical burdens it imposed: 'As for those who have money to throw away, they may do it here more agreeably than in any town I know; strangers being received with great civility, and admitted into all their parties of pleasure. But it requires a good estate and good constitution to play deep, and pass so many sleepless nights, as is customary in the best company.'[37] Lady Mary's forbearance is partly explained by the shifting moral implications that surrounded bedtimes since nocturnal recreations were increasingly advertised as a way to affirm or claim status. Lady Mary sacrificed sleep and altered her hours of rising and retiring to carve out a place in the 'best company'. She described these habits as 'customary' in Venetian society yet her late nights evidently took a heavy toll on her ageing body as she approached her seventieth year.[38]

Sleep loss was a necessary evil that had to be endured if people were to profit from sociability. Travellers understood this dilemma and they tried to cushion its negative effects by replicating the familiar comforts of home when they were on the road. It was a routine precaution to carry personal bedding on long journeys. Celia Fiennes and Elizabeth Pepys shared the desire to sleep in fresh and clean linen as they elected to take personal bedclothes with them on their respective journeys.[39] When Lady Grisell Baillie journeyed to Naples and Frankfurt in 1732 she also went well prepared. Her account book for that year lists payments for bed-cords and sheets, onboard bedding, down pillows, pillowcases and for the transportation of a complete bed.[40] London merchant Robert Udney took similar precautions by carrying sheets, pillows and pillowcases with him in anticipation of the 'terrible accommodation' that he later met with in Rome whilst Horace Walpole described the inns of Dover as a 'paradise' when compared to those that he met with on his travels to Italy.[41]

Essex clergyman and economist John Howlett suffered when he failed to predict the squalid nature of his Paris lodgings, where he complained that his sheets were 'not clean or well aired'. He tried to protect himself instead by sleeping in his clothes.[42] It was Warwickshire gentleman George Lucy, however, who gave the fullest account of the health hazards with which the traveller might meet when he travelled to Italy in search of health restoration in the 1740s. George travelled with a personal set of flaxen sheets but they could not protect him from the bugs that invaded the bedsteads and mattresses on which he was forced to sleep. He described in painful detail how these invasions marred his trip and made him pine for the comfort, cleanliness and security of his own bed. He wrote to his house-keeper Mrs Hayes to ask that she 'would have my bed altered . . . instead of the feather bed order another mattress; and instead of the cords of the bedstead, lay some flat boards the breadth of the bedstead, no matter what sort, provided they are clean and free from insects.'[43] These requests show that George valued his health more highly than his creature comforts. His pained letters reveal just how important a good night's sleep was to strengthen his fragile constitution, whether at home or on the road.

The importance of physical security during sleep was particularly acute during periods of travel, as people had limited control over the cleanliness of their accommodation. Lodging-house beds had a notorious reputation as harbingers of filth and disease. This was confirmed in 1715 by sometime excise officer and schoolmaster John Cannon from the village of West Lydford in Somerset, who described how he and his wife Susanna 'contracted a disorder with breakings out like the itch' after they slept in the lodging-house bed of one Mrs Evans that was 'damp like dung'. John later discovered that the bed had not been aired since Evans's husband had died in it.[44] He carefully recorded this encounter, perhaps as a reminder never to lie there again or to caution friends against its dangers. It became a token of civility amongst friends to exchange warnings about unacceptable inns and lodging houses and to recommend those that were healthy, secure and elegant in handwritten letters.[45] The cleanliness of temporary beds often superseded demands for good-quality private lodgings amongst travellers. Nicholas Blundell commented on the variable quality of lodgings that he met with on his travels; cleanliness was held in the highest esteem, followed by reasonable cost and the hospitality of staff.[46] Steps were taken to safeguard bodily health and to secure peace of mind when sleeping away from home. Thomas Tryon believed that it was 'a general Custom, when Men go abroad or travel, to desire clean Sheets' yet he doubted if this precaution was sufficient to prevent the spread of disease from the harmful vapours of 'old stale Beds'.[47] Joseph Price, social climber and vicar of Brabourne in Kent, was one of many who took such precautions when he journeyed to Margate in search of social prefer-ment. Securing a good night's sleep weighed heavily on his mind and he took the advice of a friend by taking his bed linen and even his own bed with him.[48] The feeling of safety conferred by familiar and clean sleeping environments was clearly revealed by Catherine Hutton. Catherine was hungry for travel and regularly noted the conditions of the inns and lodging houses in which she stayed. When she was shown to her room on a visit to Shrewsbury, Catherine noted with pleasure that 'the landlady assured me that it was her own, that she was clean and wholesome, and her parents were just and true and upright, and I might with safety lie down on her bed'.[49] Catherine offset the sense of unease created by this strange and unknown environment by vetting the history of her bed, the reputation of its owner, and by dressing it with familiar textiles. Catherine imagined these tactile layers as a protective shield that would defend her from harm whilst she slept.

Personal textiles had a trusted provenance and they recreated the comforting sensations of sleeping at home. Obtaining continuity and security was a persistent undercurrent in reflections on sleep, wherever it took place. This could be achieved with customary bedtime routines, by replicating the familiar sights, smells and sensations of home, or by sleeping in the same beds and chambers on return visits to the homes of friends or lodging houses. Samuel Pepys was certainly grateful when he was allowed to sleep 'in the same bed I did before' at a lodging house in 1665.[50] James Woodforde inserted marks of approval in his diary after he stayed at pleasant lodgings. He was fond of the King's Head, which he affectionately termed his 'old Inn' due to his regular visits and the preferential treatment that he received there. He and his party were permitted to sleep 'in our own Beds' when they lodged there, which probably meant a recognisable set of beds, chambers and textiles to which they had become accustomed. Woodforde prized the continuity offered by these familiar beds and he seems to have regarded the inn as a home away from home. His attachment was underlined on a rare occasion when he discovered that the inn was 'quite full of Company', which obliged him and his companion Mr Du Quesne to sleep in an unfamiliar room down the yard.[51] Regular contact with particular beds and chambers fostered feelings of relaxation that facilitated sleep. The routine precautions that sociable sleepers took to procure sound and safe rest underlined the increasing mobility of sleepers in these years as well as their deep-seated attachments to their own beds. Sociability thus had disruptive and painful consequences particularly in relation to sleep. A workable compromise had to be reached between successful participation in cultures of sociability and securing sufficient sleep on a daily basis. This was a practical and a philosophical problem that prompted widespread comment and discussion.

Variations in bedtimes and sleeping locations sparked lively debates about the moral legitimacy and public utility of these habits. Supporters and critics of erratic bedtimes were generally the advocates or censors of elite society. Many enlightenment philosophers argued that broken or lost sleep was a small price to pay for the civic, commercial and intellectual benefits that accrued from regular meetings of the great and good. Scottish moral philosopher and political economist Adam Smith declared in his *Theory of Moral Sentiments* (1759) that the health of individuals, and of the social organism, depended on the 'happy commerce' of friendship that comprised the 'social passions'.[52] The public value of sociability was prioritised by Smith and by political philosopher Bernard Mandeville who agreed that shorter sleeping hours could have beneficial civic outcomes if the extra waking hours were efficiently utilised. In 1704 Mandeville, who had emigrated from Rotterdam to London, published an English translation of Jean de La Fontaine's *Fables Choisies* (1668), which had been adapted from classical Greek, Roman and Persian fables. 'The Owl and the Nightingale' was the longest fable in the collection, which was designed for the lively moral instruction of children, and it praised the self-sacrifice of the faithful owl, who surrendered its sleep to attend to the needs of king and court.[53] The owl was here akin to the faithful servant who sacrificed their sleep in service of their employer. In Mandeville's more famous work *The Fable of the Bees, or, Private Vices, Publick Benefits* (1714) he addressed the question of sleep in starkly functional terms. He criticised the religious man who diligently 'leaves his bed for his devotion' because he discerned no public benefit in this individual act of piety. Scottish philosopher and historian David Hume framed the real value of human sleep as a practical support for commercial activities and for the advancement of knowledge in the arts and sciences. Sound sleep provided essential refreshment for bodies and minds engaged in these pursuits that 'cannot support an uninterrupted course of business or pleasure'. Hume conceded that the 'quick march of the spirits' produced by social interactions 'does in the end exhaust the mind, and requires some intervals of repose'. Refreshing sleep, whenever it was taken, was an implicit part of Hume's pragmatic vision of continued enlightenment because it allowed the mind to increase its capabilities. Flexible bedtimes were essential to the practical realisation of Hume's philosophical ambitions, which demanded lively participation in sociability:

> The more these refined arts advance, the more sociable do men become
> ... They flock into cities; love to receive and communicate knowledge;
> to show their wit or their breeding ... Both sexes meet in an easy and

sociable manner; and the tempers of men, as well as their behaviour, refine apace. So that, beside the improvements which they receive from knowledge and the liberal arts, 'tis impossible but they must feel an increase of humanity, from the very habit of conversing together, and contributing to each other's pleasure and entertainment. Thus *industry, knowledge,* and *humanity,* are linked together by an indissoluble chain, and are found, from experience as well as reason, to be peculiar to the more polished and luxurious ages.[54]

David Hume and his fellow philosophers agreed on sleep's critical importance to mind and body but they also understood that flexible bedtimes enhanced sleep's beneficial social consequences. The acceptability of erratic sleeping habits thus drew support from new social and economic philosophies, which blended with neurological models of sleep traced in earlier chapters. Late hours and disturbed sleep had been associated with studious and educated people for centuries but these habits were now confidently described as the corollary of worldly success, lively sensibility and creative genius that had clear social benefits.

Swiss physician and neurologist Samuel Tissot was one of many eighteenth-century physicians who promoted public health and who attributed broken sleep to the late-night sociability of successful ladies and gentlemen whose delicate nerves were easily disturbed. Tissot practised medicine in Lausanne but his patients, networks of medical correspondents, and best-selling publications stretched across Europe. Tissot diagnosed disturbed sleep as endemic amongst 'the rich and brilliant inhabitants of cities' whose sleep was 'short' and 'uneasy' because their ordinary slumber was disturbed 'by business, projects' and 'pleasures'.[55] Tissot may well have exaggerated the severity of these disturbances to maximise sales of his *Essay on the Disorders of People of Fashion* but his comments still resonated with fellow physicians like Francis de Valangin who blamed sleep loss on a combination of rich diets and late-night sociability. Valangin, like Tissot, was Swiss-born but he dispensed his medical advice to the fashionable citizens of the metropolis from his practices in Soho and Cripplegate. His *A treatise on diet* included a chapter entitled 'Of the proper Time for SLEEP' that was addressed to people whose habit of turning 'Night into Day' had become 'second Nature'. Valangin cautioned his readers about the damaging long-term effects of these habits with the salutary example of 'Mrs. M.', a rich London widow who was unable to give up her addiction to late-night sociability. Mrs M.'s irregular bedtimes and daytime sleeping ruined her health and that of her servants who had 'fallen a Sacrifice to the Want of Rest at Night, their Health having been totally ruined and destroyed'. Even if sociable sleepers took the recommended number of six to eight hours' sleep during the daytime, Valangin was convinced that its benefit was dramatically reduced and created citizens who were 'wan, pale, and always ailing'.[56] Valangin's treatise signalled the customary nature of daytime sleeping and he joined a chorus of medical practitioners who tailored their healthcare advice to suit the changed schedules of late-night revellers.

Household Sociability

Spending time with friends and acquaintances in public venues went hand in hand with socialising at home. The household in fact became the nucleus of sociability for many householders who visited and hosted friends, family and neighbours on a near-daily basis across eighteenth-century England.[57] Social interactions within the home encouraged pleasurable conversation and thickened the web of social, professional and political relations that bound individuals and communities together. The intimacy of the household setting also allowed deeper bonds of friendship to be forged. These habits were not restricted to urban areas and they could be easily tailored to suit different budgets, which made the household a more inclusive venue for the practice of sociability. Despite these important differences between public and household sociability, the disruption of sleeping hours and environments was just as visible in domestic settings. Catering for overnight guests in a polite and seemly fashion became an integral part of household management in these years that revealed an emerging culture of sleep-civility and a unique set of sleeping practices that supported the spread and success of sociability.

Visiting friends, neighbours and acquaintances was a defining feature of household sociability in town and country. Nicholas and Fanny Blundell took pleasure in many 'Merry Night's playing at cards' at their home in rural Lancashire, on one occasion until after nine o'clock in the morning. In 1709 Nicholas called on one of his neighbours and discovered a company that had been playing cards all night until noon the following day. For Nicholas and Fanny the local celebrations with neighbours ensured that communal bonding and sleep loss went hand in hand.[58] The diary of young gentlewoman Sarah Hurst similarly teems with descriptions of evenings spent in the company of young female friends. If women were less likely to feature in clubs, coffee houses and taverns, they compensated for this with dance assemblies, card games and conversational gatherings at home. Hurst played at piquet and had 'very agreeable conversation' about forthcoming marriages and local assemblies with Betsy and Sally Sheppard, Miss Piggott and Miss Kitty Mortimer amongst others. These gatherings could last all night with the young women sometimes remaining together until six o'clock in the morning.[59]

The frequency of social calls varied according to status, location and the density of personal social networks. The household account book of Benjamin Rogers, rector of Carlton in Bedfordshire, contained regular entries for expenses accrued on visits to nearby relatives as well as friends and acquaintances in local market towns. These visits were reciprocal and Benjamin and his wife Jane ensured that their home was well set up for overnight visitors. Benjamin made a note of when they stayed and the length of their visits and he took particular pride when esteemed guests passed several nights under his roof. Accommodating guests was a routine part of Benjamin's lifestyle that helped to create and sustain bonds of friendship and neighbourliness, which was essential to his success as a country clergyman.[60] In 1675 the Buckinghamshire landowner and politician Sir Ralph Verney undertook such a punishing schedule of social visits with his son that he complained of being 'so, so weary and sleepy'.[61] Verney was fond of country hospitality but his experience was perhaps not untypical for a man of his status and occupation. Multiple daytime visits often led to drowsiness whilst long-distance journeys usually required overnight lodgings. The ageing rector William Cole had a busy round of social visits to manage that induced enjoyment and exhaustion in equal measure. When he received an invitation to dine with friends in January 1766 he confessed that he 'was glad to excuse myself laying out of my Bed' after one of the guests fell ill and the gathering was cancelled.[62] It is particularly revealing that Cole's main satisfaction in this cancellation lay in his wish to stay in his own warm and comfortable bed. Cole's desire to sleep at home, and according to his own timetable, may have also been shaped by his knowledge of the extremely late bedtimes that could ensue from these gatherings, which were nevertheless required for clergymen in need of patronage.

William Cole's attachment to his own bed most likely grew as his ageing body became less able to withstand late-night entertainments. As a clergyman he may also have been alive to the censure that could ensue from overindulgence in such occasions if they had no direct connection to his work. Cole's professional obligations nevertheless demanded that he sacrificed the comforts of home on occasion to engage in the culture of politeness. He justified staying up after midnight and sleeping away from home when he was called to dine with the chancellor of his diocese in

Ely. Cole's financial dependence similarly obliged him to cultivate the favour of his hedonistic patron Henry Bromley, who drank through the night and once opened a 'Bottle of Burgundy' at breakfast-time before retiring to bed.[63] Cole was careful, however, to locate his own receding bedtimes within the boundaries of respectable, polite company and in fulfilment of his clerical duties, which stood in stark contrast to Bromley's unrestrained excesses that appeared to have no end except pleasure. Ralph Thoresby chided himself in similar fashion when his evenings were dominated by purely pleasurable gatherings but he did not apply the same moral censure to engagements with professional acquaintances. In 1702 Thoresby proudly reported that he accompanied several prominent magistrates to see the posture master at Preston – a professional contortionist who could shape his limbs in seemingly impossible ways. This eccentric show could hardly fail to entertain yet Thoresby justified retiring to bed at three o'clock in the morning on the basis that he was cultivating important professional contacts.[64] This distinction was critical to deflect potential censure.

The legitimacy of late bedtimes was measured on a case-by-case basis and it varied according to religious and moral sensibilities. Presbyterian minister Henry Newcome's attachment to Puritan values of temperance and time management may have made him more sensitive to the fluctuations of his bedtimes, of which he kept an almost daily record in the surviving volume of his diary. Newcome tried hard to rise before eight each morning and to retire to bed by ten at night. Late nights were, however, par for the course when Henry was called on to attend his ill or dying parishioners. On more sociable occasions, the quality of the company on offer was crucial to the way that Henry judged its value. He was most disgruntled when he and his wife were forced to retire late after 'beinge kept up by ye unseasonable company of J. Johnson'.[65] 'Unseasonable' may have referred to the late hour of Johnson's visit or to its unsolicited nature. By contrast Newcome reproached himself when more pleasurable company disrupted his preparations for service or his evening schedule of private and family prayers. When Henry's son was struck by illness in 1662 he interpreted this as a punishment for his habit of 'needlessly goeinge out'. He tried to atone for his sociable excesses by denying himself a Saturday evening's entertainment with friends on the grounds that 'I have noth[ing]: by goeinge onely a pleasure in suitable company'.[66] Henry was concerned that his erratic sleeping habits might invite physical and spiritual punishments and he took careful steps to regulate his bedtimes accordingly. Suffolk farmer and churchwarden William Coe likewise distinguished between late nights that resulted from personal or professional obligations and those that were spent 'idley', 'in vain and fruitless discourse', or most commonly 'att play' with friends and neighbours playing cards at home, or drinking and playing games of chance like 'rattlecap' and 'shacklefarthing' at the Cock or the White Hart. Particularly late nights were kept at home where Coe dined and played cards with his guests until four and five o'clock in the morning. He was sensible of the need to repent for these lost hours that usually meant that he had failed to lead evening prayers in his household.[67] Regulating evening entertainments emerged as a distinct concern in these years due to the detrimental effect that they could have on sleep quality. People were concerned to secure their physical and spiritual well-being by sleeping at familiar times and in familiar places: these temperate routines were being increasingly threatened by the spread of sociability.

The expansion and reorganisation of households charted in the previous chapter ensured that they were capable of hosting overnight guests in clean and comfortable surroundings. These changes also shaped expectations about the kind of sleeping accommodation that might be encountered away from home. Those that could afford it converted or installed permanent chambers expressly for the use of guests. In 1668 John Vaux installed a 'New Building Chamber' in his Bedfordshire home that he converted to his main sleeping chamber, which freed up space elsewhere in the house to lodge guests. Catherine Hutton's family home had acquired 'a handsome chamber' over the parlour by the mid-eighteenth century, which was explicitly designated to accommodate visitors.[68] Horace Walpole had sufficient means to promise his friend and politician George Selwyn that 'Bed or beds will be ready as they are commanded' in anticipation of his visit to Walpole's new home at Strawberry Hill in 1762. The reputedly fine beds and bedchambers provided an added incentive for illustrious guests to socialise at Walpole's recently renovated home.[69] Samuel Pepys did not have the means to build new rooms for his guests but he declared himself 'mighty proud' in 1666 when he was able to afford 'a spare bed for my friends', which was an emblem of worldly success and a guarantor of civility.[70] Walpole and Pepys were acutely aware that the sleep quality of their visitors could make or break their friendships with them.

Most of the households in the PCC inventory sample were equipped to receive a small number of overnight guests. This is revealed by the number and variety of bed-types, their specific location and a surplus of bed linen that could cater for the cleaning regimes of the household and for the needs of guests. There were considerable improvements in the quality and quantity of bedding in homes and lodging houses from the sixteenth to the eighteenth centuries.[71] The inventory sample shows a significant rise in the number of bedsheets and pillowcases owned per household by the mid-eighteenth century. In addition to the bedding that was listed alongside, and usually in the same room, as individual fixed bedsteads, 66 per cent of households had a surplus of bedding that was listed and valued separately by the appraisers. The uses that this bedding served are difficult to gauge but the appraisers noted important variations in the quality, age, condition and fabric that indicated flexibility of use. These growing stocks also sparked the purchase of new furniture in which to carefully store these essential items.[72] The locations in which the bedding was stored likewise distinguished better-quality materials that may have been reserved for the use of cherished guests. In 1711 Elizabeth Freke compiled an inventory of her household goods and listed a pair of fine holland linen sheets that she kept expressly 'for strangers' in a portmanteau in her upstairs closet.[73] Enclosing guests within the right kind of bedding was an unspoken token of esteem and friendship that showed a concern to satisfy their most intimate bodily needs.

The inventory sample shows the persistent presence of temporary and space-saving bedsteads alongside a surplus of bedding textiles, which occurred in spite of the growing preference to accommodate servants in fixed permanent bedsteads. Such bedsteads diversified in form and design and they may well have been used on an ad hoc basis when visitors came to stay. Alongside truckle bedsteads, the inventories show the presence of 'buroe bedsteads', 'turn up bedsteads', 'desk beds' and a 'chest of drawers bedstead', each of which was designed to satisfy functional needs and aesthetic sensibilities.[74] London-born chimney sweep turned architect Isaac Ware observed in his *Complete Body of Architecture* (1756) that it was both convenient and practical for the capital's dwellings to contain temporary bedsteads that could be assembled or let down when circumstance demanded.[75] In 1668 the Cambridgeshire home of John Ellis contained three trundle bedsteads that supplemented more luxurious fixed bedsteads with feather beds in his parlour and parlour chamber. Elizabeth Freke's spacious country dwelling contained a trundle bedstead in the west garret as well as fixed bedsteads for servants in designated chambers elsewhere in the house.[76] Norfolk merchant Richard Langricke housed a 'close bed' in his 'little parlour' that could be easily folded into a box-like shape to maximise space during the daytime, whilst Henry Mosse of West Ham stored a 'settle bedd' in his coach house alongside a cart and lumber.[77] Mosse's house was otherwise amply furnished with bedsteads and beds of varying quality and value on the upper floors of his house. Settle beds were multifunctional pieces of furniture that could be used for sitting or for sleeping. Richard Holmwood's house in Richmond and Thomas Johnson's London home listed settle beds in the garret chambers alongside large numbers of fixed bedsteads. The location of these bedsteads suggests their occasional use to cater for an overspill of guests since the houses contained designated servants' chambers with modest fixed bedsteads.[78]

Thomas Tryon also hinted at the widespread use of press bedsteads for overnight visitors in his *A treatise on cleanness* in 1682. Press bedsteads were useful for accommodating guests in small spaces since they could be closed up to resemble a neat chest or toilet table when not in use. They were not, however, considered 'wholesome' for extended use because they were 'confined', low to the ground and exposed to dampness from standing in the corners of many chambers.[79] Tryon was concerned that these overflow beds were likely to spread contagion since they hosted multiple bodies on a regular basis, which was a concern that was widely shared.[80] The sleeping arrangements in Samuel Pepys's ten-room house were quite well defined. His great chamber nevertheless contained a bed for occasional use either for guests or for Samuel to sleep in when his wife Elizabeth fell ill.[81] Such items of furniture were no doubt invaluable given the congestion of sleeping bodies that Pepys sometimes accommodated and he went the extra mile for his most treasured guests. When his brother John came for an extended stay Samuel purchased and put up an extra bedstead to ensure the comfort of his close family member.[82] The household of Lady Grisell Baillie was even better stocked with bedchambers. Her 1715 account book nonetheless recorded the purchase of '2 folding beds' and 'a table bed with canves Bottem'.[83] The latter was housed in the laundry and it may have been called into use when there was an overflow of guests to accommodate. Truckle beds were particularly well suited to these purposes. They were constructed low to the ground and set on castors so they could be easily manoeuvred between rooms and stored under higher fixed beds when not in use. Despite the negative associations of truckle beds, people of many different backgrounds slept in them when necessary – usually following social gatherings. Samuel Pepys complained that he 'lay in some disquiet all night' after he was relegated to a truckle bed when he returned home in the early hours of the morning after staying out hunting treasure with friends. In his absence his wife had taken their female servant to her bed for warmth and security.[84] No complaints were voiced, however, when Samuel shared a 'neat and handsome' press bed with the judge advocate John Flower, with whom he had dined one evening. Pepys and Flower were still able to distinguish their sleeping arrangements, and their status, from Samuel's young servant boy who slept in the same room 'upon a bench'.[85] Samuel's expectations of his sleeping arrangements were much more flexible when he slept away from home and sacrificed the anticipated comforts of his own bed. Truckle bedsteads and other space-saving bedsteads were in regular use by the mid-eighteenth century and their flexibility was essential in the practical management of sociability.

Sociability's influence on sleeping habits extended beyond sleeping chambers into more porous parts of the household, which began to house new items of furniture designed to facilitate short naps during the daytime. In the 1690s an upholstered daybed was installed in the home of Thomas Osborne, 1st duke of Leeds and earl of Danby, at Kiveton Hall in South Yorkshire. The bed imitated court fashion and was specifically designed to aid leisurely repose: its occupants could rest for short periods of time with feet outstretched and head resting on a cushioned arm. Henry, 7th Viscount Irwin remodelled the long gallery at Temple Newsam House near Leeds between 1738 and 1745. The gallery was the main entertaining space and it included a suite of twenty reposing chairs, four settees and a couch. The suite was upholstered in original petit point embroidery and designed by London carver and gilder James Pascall.[86] This furniture was intended to impress visitors with its intricate decoration and to support their tired limbs as they were entertained late into the night. They may have taken a break to 'soss' – a movement that Samuel Johnson defined as 'To fall at once into a chair'.[87]

The first edition of furniture designer Thomas Chippendale's pattern book *The Gentleman and Cabinet-Maker's Director* (1754) laid out 'Elegant and Useful Designs of Household Furniture'. The book incorporated a design for a canopied sofa in Chippendale's celebrated Chinese style that was particularly suitable for short naps, whether in sleeping chambers or in more porous parts of the house. Chippendale's sofa could be 'converted into a bed, by having the Sopha so made as to come forward, the curtains to draw to the front of the Sopha, and hang sloping, which will form a sort of tent, and look very grand'.[88] The sofa thus imitated the design of fixed, permanent tester bedsteads and thereby revealed its purpose. Similar reposing chairs and sofas were found in rooms for receiving company at Ham House in Richmond, as well as in more secluded chambers following extensive alterations by the duke and duchess of Lauderdale. In 1677 the duke's closet, listed as the 'Reposing Closset' in the 1683 inventory, included a single-ended cane-bottomed couch complete with quilt, bolster and tester. Two years later the couch had been replaced by a 'sleeping chayre', shown in Figure 21, with adjustable side and back panels. The chair was one of a pair, with the second initially installed in the queen's closet alongside a double-ended cedarwood couch. This chair was later moved to the duchess's chambers where she may have used it for short naps during the day to relieve her infirmities.[89] The 4th earl of Lauderdale redecorated Ham House in the 1730s and 1740s when additional furniture purchases included a pair of winged easy chairs with 'enormous duck-filled cushions', six armchairs and a sofa.[90] These comfortable chairs were heavily padded and their side panels could easily support drowsy heads during short naps that precluded the more formal and time-consuming rituals of extended night-time rest.

Easy chairs were developed in the 1670s and their design and location within many households signalled a close relationship with flexible sleeping habits.[91] The inventory sample shows that easy chairs were almost exclusively found in sleeping chambers where they were used for sitting and sleeping.[92] Sir Horace Mann's letter from Florence to Horace Walpole signals the occasional use of these chairs for sleeping. Mann wrote affectionately of the corpulent Lord Plymouth whose indulgent lifestyle had rendered his body 'immovable' by the age of thirty. Mann declared that he

21. Sleeping chair, attributed to Jean Poictevin,
c. 1677.

now preferred 'a bed and an elbow chair to all other amusements'.[93] Wing chairs were natural successors to easy chairs and they blended elegantly into comfortable downstairs chambers for receiving guests. Wing chairs offered flexible resting places for the weary frames of late-night socialisers, for those who suffered from broken sleep, and for those who simply wished for a short nap.[94] Some went so far as to equate 'comfort' with 'a heavy, well-stuffed arm-chair in which the master of the house goes to sleep after dinner'.[95] In 1751 Northamptonshire maidservant and budding poet Mary Leapor made specific reference to these habits in her verse *Crumble Hall*, 'the soft Stools / and eke the lazy Chair / To Sleep invite the Weary / and the Fair'.[96] Mary's reflections were probably inspired by scenes that she witnessed at Edgcote House near Banbury, where she was in service in the 1740s. A similar state of repose is illustrated in a 1714 portrait of the sleep-deprived poet Alexander Pope, shown below. The Irish-born artist Charles Jervas, who was later appointed as king's painter to George I and George II, depicts Pope's attempts to secure rest in a wing chair.

22. *Alexander Pope*, attributed to Charles
Jervas, *c*. 1713–*c*. 1715.

Alexander Pope's ill health, late-night intellectual pursuits and caffeine addiction led to frequent episodes of broken sleep for which he tried to compensate with daytime naps.[97] His erratic sleeping habits were revealed in 1711 when he wrote of the need to keep 'a sober dish of coffee, and a solitary candle at your side, to write an epistle *lucubratory* to your friend'.[98] A 'lucubratory' referred to a place of midnight study, or to a work composed by artificial light during the hours of darkness. Sheffield-based physician Thomas Short recommended tea drinking for the benefit of 'lucubratory' students in 1730 and passed no negative moral judgment on this habit.[99] The dictionaries of Samuel Johnson and Thomas Sheridan also signalled the widespread currency of this term and practice by the mid-eighteenth century.[100]

These publications and portraits conferred an air of distinction upon erratic bedtimes if they improved knowledge and inspired creativity. In so doing they signalled a growing acceptance of daytime napping – if undertaken in moderation and for justifiable reasons. It was imperative that daytime sleep was of short duration, which was best managed by taking 'a nod sitting in a chair' or by leaning against a cupboard.[101] The upright position of chairs was critical for moderating the length of the nap and medical practitioners made it clear that lying prostrate on a bed was not to be ventured under any circumstances lest it invited long periods of sleep. Subtle shifts in the perception of daytime naps, which had once been condemned as signs of sloth, paralleled the commonplace use of comfortable chairs and daybeds that were specifically fashioned for daytime rest. English habits may also have been influenced by Italian customs where daytime naps were supported by similar kinds of furniture and by health regimens.[102] In 1678, naturalist and theologian John Ray hinted at this European influence in his *Collection of English Proverbs* relating to 'health, diet and physick', which included the allowance: 'When the Fern is as high as a spoon / You may sleep an hour at noon'.[103] Ray's advice acknowledged the influence of Italian physicians, whom he had encountered on a botanical tour of southern Europe. The changing material infrastructure of many households thus highlights subtle variations in the hours and locations of sleep, which had begun to fragment due to the practice of sociability. New furniture and furnishings were an essential support to these habits, which also produced a unique set of social conventions and a vocabulary of sleep-civility that were designed to relax the bodies and minds of those that slept away from home on a regular basis.

Ensuring the comfort and satisfaction of overnight guests was a vital mechanism by which relationships of status, duty and affection were negotiated. Fondness could be powerfully conveyed by the quality and cleanliness of bedding textiles reserved for particular guests and by the type and location of the bedsteads they were given. Careful attention to these seemingly trivial details was expected and appreciated. Henry Newcome spent all day 'getinge ye roome ready' for his cousin when he and his wife came to visit in 1663.[104] George Hardinge was so pleased with the 'sweet little bed' with which he was greeted at Horace Walpole's home that he requested the same accommodation on a return visit with his new fiancée.[105] The 'sweet' bed may have evoked the fresh, clean smell of his bedding textiles, which promised to secure his health and ease him into peaceful and restorative sleep. Samuel Pepys appreciated being lodged 'very civilly' at Commissioner Willoughby's house on his way to the Navy Office in July 1660, which resulted in a good night's sleep.[106] On a visit to Impington in Cambridgeshire in 1661 he was lodged 'with great respect' in 'the best chamber in the house' and in 1665 he considered himself 'mighty highly treated' when his host gave him a 'noble chamber' in which to rest.[107] These favours show that sleeping practices were bound by codes of civility that helped to broker bonds of sociability and friendship.

Large social gatherings could present difficulties for lodging guests comfortably in households with limited space yet this was often overcome by careful rearrangement of space. James Woodforde hosted a large party of visitors from London at his Norfolk parsonage, which included Mr and Mrs Howes, Mr Bodham, Mrs Davy and her children Betsy and Nunn, and Mr and Miss Donne and their cousin Charles Donne. The assembly dined together and played cards into the early hours of the morning. Woodforde, Mr Bodham and Mr Donne played through the night. The host favoured Mr and Mrs Howes by willingly giving up his own bed to them when they decided to retire at two o'clock in the morning. Miss Donne and Mrs Davy's children lay together in Woodforde's guest room whilst Mr Donne's cousin was squeezed into the servant's chamber with Donne's manservant. The modest size of the parsonage meant that Woodforde's own servants had to give up their beds and sit up through the night.[108]

Aside from the logistics of space, James Woodforde organised the sleeping arrangements of his visitors according to a set of conventions that linked particular beds and chambers with degrees of status and affection. The codes of civility that informed these arrangements were comparable to the gradations of status and conduct observed in more public forms of company. The specific chamber in which guests were lodged and the level of comfort they were afforded was a means of cementing and of weakening social bonds. Interpersonal dynamics between guest and host played a critical role in this process. When James Woodforde hosted Mr Hall from Andover in Hampshire, he offered up his bed to this unexpected guest since he had no other available space. Mr Hall refused to accept this generous offer, however, and instead obliged his host 'to sit up with him all Night'. Woodforde grumbled that this lack of rest, which resulted directly from the uncertain bonds of friendship between the two men, had made him 'quite ill'. Woodforde was again disgruntled after a visit from a fellow clergyman named Campbell with whom he had studied at university. Despite this early acquaintance Woodforde considered that their connection 'was not so intimate as to expect that he would have taken such freedom especially as he never made me a Visit before'. He therefore housed Campbell 'in the Attic Story' since Woodforde judged that he might 'be too free if treated too kindly'.[109] Woodforde was sensitive to the effect that his decision might have, having experienced similar disgruntlement himself on a visit to Mr Priest's house, where he slept 'if I can call it so ... very uncomfortably indeed'.[110] Woodforde's conduct was specifically tailored to each of his guests and his actions show that bonds of familiarity, friendship and trust guided his treatment of them. Guests were likewise sensible of the social meanings of sleeping arrangements and sought to align them with levels of acquaintance. In 1776 Lady Powis made plans to visit Horace Walpole en route to Hampton Court with a party of friends. She judged that her own friendship with Walpole was not close enough to accept his invitation to sleep at Strawberry Hill but she allowed him to arrange nearby lodgings at the George Inn in Twickenham.[111] Poorer-quality beds and chambers did not necessarily preclude sound slumber but they could easily offend the sensibilities of those forced to sleep in them.

Ensuring the safety and comfort of valued guests at bedtime was a microcosm of the wider culture of politeness and civility that ordered social relations. The fact that sleep was involved intensified the significance of these exchanges. Overnight guests and lodgers delivered their bodies and souls to their hosts for safekeeping during this most vulnerable and intimate time. Hosts understood the anxieties created by sleeping in unfamiliar environments, which they tried to offset by securing the physical and psychological ease of their guests. When the diarist Maria Nugent (née Skinner) and her children went to stay with her friend Lady Buckingham, her host went to extraordinary lengths to ensure Maria's comfort by replicating the familiar vistas and associations of her domestic sleeping environment. Maria was so struck by this kindness that she carefully recorded it in her journal:

> In the evening, Lady B. said she was sure we all wanted exercise, and should walk over the house, and see my apartment in particular, as she

had contrived so nicely for the little ones. Judge of my surprise, upon entering my own room, when she drew aside a curtain, and shewed me the bust of my dear Nugent, placed on a little cabinet, close behind the bed. It is an excellent likeness, and invaluable to me, and I could not help jumping up, and kissing her most heartily for her kindness, and all the party seemed to share in my pleasure and satisfaction. – The rest of the evening as usual, but many jokes, by Lord Temple, on their givinge me a husband of marble, &c.[112]

Maria's husband, her 'dear Nugent', was working in Jamaica at this time and so Lady Buckingham tried to make up for this physical separation by offering a reminder of him in the hope that it might secure Maria's happiness at bedtime and cement their bond of friendship.

Lady Buckingham's act of kindness may not have been widely replicated but providing clean, neat and appropriate bedding was a habitual way of showing affection to overnight guests. Providing fresh white bed linen was a symbolic marker of household reputation and respectability, which was particularly important when guests came to stay. Visitors were often treated to the best-quality sheets and their pillows might be covered with linen or with calico slips beneath the ordinary cases to brighten their clean, white appearance.[113] These favours may have helped to procure relaxation at bedtime as guests associated the fresh bedding with health-giving properties that might protect them from disease and bedbugs. Hosts were especially careful to ensure that beds were well aired before guests arrived. The health concerns that surrounded well-ventilated chambers were explored in Chapter 2 but this routine precaution also represented a token of esteem. Horace Walpole was eager to inform George Montagu that his bed, and that of his servant, would be aired ahead of his visit to Walpole's home in Arlington Street. Walpole himself noted the courtesy of being offered 'a nice bed' by his friend Mrs Hancock should he pay her a visit. William Cole, who had forged a strong rapport with Walpole during their school days at Eton, tried to lure his friend to visit his humble home with the promise of a clean, warm and well-aired bed.[114] It was important to inform guests that they were worthy of this kindness, which was judged both a favour and a preservative of good health.[115] Ensuring that visitors had a good night's rest was not simply a show of wealth, it was a measure of household respectability and symbolic of the depth of friendship that existed between host and guest. These arrangements were also heavily bound up with cultural understandings of sleep as a time of unique vulnerability that required extra special care and trust – little wonder that friendships could be won and lost according to the manner in which sleep was managed.

Bedfellowship

Spatial constraints could present problems for housing guests in suitable comfort, as shown by James Woodforde's complicated rearrangement of his household. Sharing a bed was a pragmatic solution to nocturnal over-crowding and it had the added benefit of ensuring that co-sleepers felt warm and secure.[116] Sleeping companions were usually of the same sex, of similar age, comparable social status and preferably had some level of acquaintance. Brothers and sisters, and children of a similar age routinely shared a bed at home and on their travels.[117] A common religious affiliation could also prove helpful if bedfellows had complementary routines of bedtime prayer.[118] The prescribed rules of bedfellowship were thus cali-brated to reflect values of decency and civility and they were followed as and when circumstance allowed.

Sharing a bed with a stranger was an unpleasant and potentially dangerous prospect, but sleeping beside the right kind of person could affirm or enhance a friendship by sharing close physical contact, an inti-mate conversation and a bond of trust.[119] Shopkeeper Thomas Turner shared his bed with John Long on several occasions; he chose to affirm Long's credentials for this role in terms of his career progression from local writing master to trainee excise officer.[120] Samuel Pepys expressed clear preferences in his choice of bedfellows whom he ranked by the quality of their conversation and by their behaviour in bed. Pepys expressed 'great satisfaction' when he shared a bed with merchant Thomas Hill. The two men exchanged views about 'Berchenshaws music rules' whilst lying together and they conversed more philosophically about 'most things of a man's life' in the moments before sleep took hold of them.[121] John Brisbane, judge advocate of the Fleet and later secretary to the Admiralty, was also a favourite bedfellow for Pepys because he was 'a good scholar and sober man' who was eager to share stories of his journeys to Rome.[122] Pepys's friend Mr Creed similarly provided 'merry' and 'excellent company' between the sheets.[123]

Pillow talk could bring ease and contentment but compatible bedfellows had to know when to stop. During an overnight stay at the home of his patron, the 1st earl of Sandwich, Samuel Pepys had intended to lie with William Howe, Sandwich's household servant and deputy-treasurer of the Fleet. The amity between the two men spilled over, however, when they 'fell to play with one another', which prevented both of them from securing sufficient rest. Samuel ordered William to lie instead with the household steward Edward Shipley although he noted in a regretful tone that he 'lay alone all night' as a result.[124] When the young Elizabeth Raper shared a bed with her aunt she claimed she was 'almost stifled' by disagreeable conversation and 'had rather sat up' than lose her sleep.[125] In 1739 John Cannon described his cousin-in-law and regular bedfellow Stephen Knowles, rector of Meare in Somerset, as 'troublesome in the night' after a round of heavy drinking with his parishioners caused him 'to snoar & make a hideous noise, which I was not pleased with'. John compared his bedfellow to a pig but he might also have labelled him a 'bed-faggot' – a scornful term for an unruly bedfellow that was popular in East Anglia.[126] Securing peaceful rest was thus a primary consideration in ordering the behavioural codes that surrounded sociable sleeping practices.

Female bedfellows similarly prized agreeable conversation, felicity and friendship as sleep approached. After an evening of card playing with friends at Eastbourne, Sarah Hurst felt pleased to be able to lie with Kitty Mortimer 'with whom I have a great deal of chat & am very merry'.[127] In November 1759 Hurst testified to the depth of affection that could develop between bedfellows when she composed a poem lamenting the loss of her regular bedfellow Sally Sheppard. The poem, entitled 'The Consolation', praised the comfort that could be found in sharing a deep physical and emotional bond of this kind. Sarah's words conveyed the tangible physical and psychological balm offered by an agreeable bedfellow:

> A friend sincere, will kindly treat
> Each woe that racks the mind;
> The sympathetic heart will beat,
> Where Friendship's band's conjoin'd,
> Dividing thus the load of grief,
> Life's ceaseless care is less;
> Her soothing converse yields relief;
> Her pity can redress.[128]

The treasured interval of time as bedfellows lay together before sleep allowed friends and acquaintances to share each other's concerns, unburden their minds and ease one another into peaceful and restorative sleep.[129]

Bedfellowship could be both functional and desirable, especially in the context of sociability where it presented unique opportunities to deepen friendships and strengthen professional networks. Sleeping peacefully was nevertheless uppermost in the minds of those selecting an appropriate bedfellow. The choice was guided only in part by social status and much more frequently by the depth of acquaintance, trust and affability that existed between them. Bedfellows within marriage and in same-sex friend-ships could create deep bonds of intimacy by sharing their sleeping spaces. The physical proximity implicit in bed sharing and the defencelessness imposed by sleep called for a deeper level of familiarity than fleeting inter-actions in assembly rooms, theatres or playhouses.[130] Historian Alan Bray compared sharing a bed in the early modern period to 'the symbolic gift of a friend's body', which signalled a commonality of interest, mutual affection and, above all else, trust.[131] The trust implicit in bedfellowship was reflected in courtly practices and in humbler households. The sovereign's bedfellows were invested with the most profound confidences in the hours between retiring to bed and falling asleep. Kings and queens unburdened their most secret thoughts and fears to trusted bedfellows who were charged with providing physical security and emotional felicity as darkness fell.

The most highly prized bedfellows were believed to bring peace, ease and reconciliation to their companions – qualities that cut across social divisions.[132] Physical security and emotional contentment was paramount when men and women selected companions to lie with as those on the verge of sleep sought feelings of ease and safety. These could be realised through a familiar and comfortable bed, or through the performance of customary rituals, from hair combing to solemn prayer. A trusted and pleasant bedfellow offered another way of securing a relaxed frame of mind, especially in times of emotional distress. Fanny Lynes lodged with her fiancé William Kent in the house of Methodist minister Richard Parsons in London's Cock Lane in the 1760s. When William left the capital on business for a few days, Fanny expressly requested that Parsons's eldest daughter, Elizabeth, slept beside her. Elizabeth's presence may have provided Fanny with warmth, comfort or pleasant conversation, but Fanny may have also been anxious to safeguard her health, as she was heavily pregnant at this time.[133] Thomas Turner shared his bed with his friend Sam Jenner on a regular basis in the months following his wife's death. His diary records an uneasiness of mind and a lack of a confidante at this time, which may have been relieved by Jenner's company.[134] An amiable bedfellow conferred happiness whilst an unfamiliar companion could prove to be a source of anxiety. This was unsurprising given the number of physical attacks, robberies and even murders that befell sleepers in temporary lodgings who were forced to share a bed with a stranger. The need for physical security was at its most acute during sleep when people were least able to defend themselves from danger. When Nunn Davy paid a visit to James Woodforde's home, his host noted that Nunn 'slept by choice with my Servt Willm'.[135] Nunn's preference was worth recording since it excused any incivility on Woodforde's part for allowing social divides to be traversed in this manner. Nunn's decision underlined the unique bonds of familiarity and trust that underpinned habits of bedfellowship. The need for reassurance at bedtime was marked within the familiar confines of home but it was even more pressing when men and women slept away from home. Bedfellows played a crucial role in filling this gap and in helping to create feelings of ease and relaxation.

Cultures of sociability ensured that men and women of different ranks continued to share beds with a variety of companions, often by deliberate choice and careful planning. This evidence provides an important counter-weight to historical accounts based largely on conduct literature that describe bedfellowship as exceptional or undesirable for those that had the means to sleep independently.[136] There was no straightforward march of sleep-privacy, nor was there a discernible decline of bedfellowship despite the progressive specialisation of sleeping chambers. Sleeping away from home on a regular basis differentiated experiences of sleep in distinctive and important ways. The heightened anxiety that it caused made the need to sleep in close proximity to a trusted friend more, rather than less, pressing. Bedfellowship was not simply an ad hoc solution to a practical problem but a deliberate choice that offered time and space for cementing personal bonds and for easing companions into slumber.

The practical pursuit of sociability had tangible physical and psycho-logical consequences that altered perceptions and practices of sleep in short- and long-term trajectories. Engaging in public and household socia-bility was a powerful imperative that led to periodic episodes of broken sleep, sleep loss or even to sustained periods of sleep deprivation. The spread of new hybrid forms of furniture to allow short seated daytime naps is particularly suggestive of the close links that were forged between socia-bility and increasingly flexible sleeping patterns. The physical effects that sociability had on sleep were widely documented in personal testimonies and in print, where they were censured and celebrated in equal measure as a battle was fought over the moral implications of sleeping habits. These practices were lent coherence and support by Enlightenment philosophies, which challenged the concerns of religious commentators and medical practitioners. The imperative to be sociable was not new but it intensified as philosophers and social reformers prioritised the creation of socialised citizens whose collective efforts, based on amity and affection, promised to transform knowledge and society. Irregular bedtimes, sleeping out of one's own bed and sharing a bed with a variety of companions were increasingly justifiable acts if they advanced civic virtues and were contained within the bounds of politeness. The material supports and social codes that emerged around these mobile sleeping practices were judged essential to this new vision of society, which was championed by the likes of David Hume. The body's sensible feelings were central to Hume's model of amicable sociability and they proved central to the way that sleeping arrangements were ordered for friends, family and esteemed guests. This unique set of sleeping practices was thus forged by the convergence of specific social mores and the sensibilities of individual bodies and minds.

Socialising undoubtedly conferred pleasure and preferment but this should not obscure the pains and inconveniences that it sometimes produced. Sleeping away from home disrupted the physical and mental ease afforded by the sensations of a familiar bed and chamber. Comforting the bodies and minds of overnight visitors at bedtime was thus critical to the maintenance of affectionate relationships – this was understood by guests and by their hosts. Anxieties could be offset by carefully selected bedsteads, clean and good-quality bedding, and by well-chosen bedfellows as many households became better equipped to accommodate guests on a regular basis. By the mid-eighteenth century, the demands of sociability had reshaped the acceptable times and places for sleep, as well as its moral boundaries; but these factors had to be carefully balanced with deeply held desires for security, familiarity and trust during the shadowy hours of slumber.

CHAPTER 6

Sleep, Sensibility and Identity

'MARIANNE WOULD HAVE thought herself very inexcusable had she been able to sleep at all the first night after parting from Willoughby. She would have been ashamed to look her family in the face the next morning, had she not risen from her bed in more need of repose than when she lay down in it.'[1] Marianne Dashwood's romantic state of agitation is artfully described in Jane Austen's account of her wakeful night in *Sense and Sensibility*. Austen's novel, set in the southwest of England in the 1790s, narrates the emotional dramas of the teenage Marianne during her fateful love affair with the charming rogue John Willoughby. She is a young woman ruled by her feelings and her potent sensibility finds physical expression in her sleep loss. Austen's protagonist represents a microcosm of transformed attitudes towards nervous debilities, and indeed towards sleep, whose origins were readily traced to refined sensibilities in eighteenth-century culture.

In 1797 the *Encyclopaedia Britannica* defined sensibility not simply as a fictional construct, but as

> a nice and delicate perception of pleasure or pain, beauty or deformity. It is very nearly allied to taste: and as far as it is natural, seems to depend upon the organization of the nervous system. It is capable, however, of cultivation, and is experienced in a much higher degree in civilized than in savage nations, and among persons liberally educated than among boors and illiterate mechanics.[2]

The entry testified to the pervasive influence of sensibility within English culture, which aligned nervous constitutions with fashionable concepts of selfhood.[3] Marianne Dashwood is an archetypal woman of feeling whose capacity for emotional expression marked her out as a natural and elegant victim of her age. These qualities were highly prized by men and women who claimed that their delicate nerves made them oversensitive to their physical and social environments. Sensibility, as a concept, and as a way of representing the self, gathered strength from the 1740s, peaked in the 1760s and 1770s, and helped to reconfigure the relationship between sleeping patterns and personal identity.[4]

The concept of sensibility fused physiology and psychology on a linked spectrum: both relied on the understanding that moral sentiments and feelings were expressed through physical discomfort and emotional crisis. As John Mullan puts it: 'With feelings come pain and illness'.[5] Compensation for such torments came in the knowledge that these symptoms conferred social exclusivity on the sufferer because sensibility could not be easily acquired. And so it was with sleep loss and sleep disorders. The language of sensibility combined with neurological models of sleep to transform sleep states of all kinds into powerful vehicles of self-expression, self-knowledge and social distinction. Observing the sleeping patterns of others also allowed judgements to be made about individual constitutions and characters. Sleep states were thus widely figured as external signs of the internal composition of the nerves, degrees of mental agility, and of emotional and moral depth. It was in this context that sleep's bodily effects, whether pleasant or painful, became a notable preoccupation for artists and writers, and for men and women whose letters and diaries chronicled their nocturnal habits. They recorded their sleeping patterns, speculated about their origins, and used them to construct a sense of personal identity that shifted in tone across this period.

The intimate connections that were drawn between sleep states and personal identity were built on sleep's neurological foundations, which established the inseparability of bodies, brains and feelings. Unprecedented attention was paid to the role of non-conscious states of mind in the formation of identity in a period that has long been singled out for innovative explorations of selfhood.[6] Reflections on the nature, quality and meaning of sleep, played a crucial part in this voyage of self-discovery. These reflections were influenced by medical philosophies that subtly reshaped understandings of sleep and sleeplessness, by representations of sleep states that circulated in print and visual culture, and by bodily experiences of sleep in daily life. These overlapping layers uncover the ways in which sleeping patterns, and their interpretation, open a new window onto changing historical understandings of self and society.

This chapter begins by examining the ideal of a rational healthy mind, or the 'managed self', which could be secured by peaceful sleep. This was forged on the growing web of connections between body and mind that made sleep quality essential for physical and mental well-being. The role that restorative sleep played in preserving physical and mental acuity was widely promoted in the first half of the eighteenth century. John Locke's identification of the sensible origins of ideas was an important milestone in establishing a natural foundation for enquiries into states of consciousness and models of personal identity. Locke spoke for many of his fellow physicians and philosophers when he distanced uncontrolled visions and non-conscious thoughts from the rational waking self. The second section of this chapter traces an important shift of opinion from the rational 'managed self' to an emerging ideal of a 'sensible self' in which conscious and non-conscious mental states were fused in expressions of personal identity. Growing preoccupations with sleep states, and especially with sleep disorders, accompanied this shift within print, drama, opera and visual culture. Interim or imperfect sleep states such as sleepwalking provoked particular fascination in natural philosophers, Romantic poets and artists. The letters and poems of Samuel Taylor Coleridge offer persuasive evidence that sleeping patterns had become an intrinsic part of psychological understandings of selfhood by the close of the eighteenth century. The chapter concludes by examining how ordinary men and women drew on these interpretative models to reflect on their own sleep states and identities in daily life.

Sleep and the Managed Self

In February 1756 country shopkeeper Thomas Turner considered the damaging effects of the drunken late nights he spent with his friends. Thomas wished to remedy his wayward behaviour after hearing a Sunday sermon at his local church. Thomas was a faithful member of the Church of England and a parish officer; as such his motivation to reform was rooted in his quest for salvation. He nonetheless reflected on the importance of sound and well-regulated sleep for maintaining his emotional balance: 'I by experience find how much more conducive it is to my health, as well as pleasantness and serenity to my mind ... to rise as early as I possibly can; that is, always to allow myself between 7 and 8 hours' sleep, unless prevented on any particular or emergent occasion'. Thomas vowed to retire to bed 'before ten o'clock when it can be done' as part of his new regimen.[7]

Thomas Turner, along with many of his contemporaries, was well aware that the quality of his sleep had a dramatic effect on his state of mind. Chapters 1 and 2 explained how and why sleeping soundly was believed to maintain bodies and minds in good working order. This principle was a foundation stone of the sleep regimens of early modern Europe that prescribed moderate habits of sleeping and waking as part of the healthcare system of the six non-naturals. The self-discipline that this moderation required also made sound sleep a central feature of Christian piety and identity. As the ideal of moderate sleep moved into the eighteenth century, it was increasingly prized as a guardian of the mind's rational faculties. Policing sleeping habits was strongly encouraged to preserve healthy, rational minds and a healthy body politic from decay and disorder.[8] This attitude was typified by a verse on the title page of *A Treatise of Diseases of the Head, Brain & Nerves*, first published in 1711. Its anonymous author, identified only as a 'Physician', declared that '*Man's Health more on his Head depends / Than Child on Parents, or a Poor Man, Friends*'.[9] This text was available to purchase stitched for 1s 6d, or bound for 2s, and it was published in no less than seven editions between 1711 and 1741. Achieving perfect sleep and securing the mind's health formed part of the self-conscious promotion of intellectual, social and cultural development. Unprecedented optimism about the human capacity to exploit nature and transform society was a hallmark of many Enlightenment philosophies whose ambitions relied on the maintenance of finely tuned bodies and brains. Healthy sleeping habits were critical to these objectives: they held the key to the health and longevity of individuals and to the progress of civil society.

Philosopher and physician David Hartley noted in his *Observations on Man, his Frame, his Duty, and his Expectations* (1749) that there were 'many Advantages to Body and Mind, which result from rising early'.[10] Hartley's interest in psychology drew heavily on the neurological discussions of body and mind described in Chapter 1. Hartley gave careful consideration to sleep because of its potential to nurture and to damage the mind's capabilities. Hartley's concern was not unique, nor was it restricted to a small coterie of philosophers. Best-selling writer and long-suffering melancholic Samuel Johnson tried hard to remedy his frequent bouts of sleep loss since he was acutely aware of the benefits that restorative sleep would bring to his fragile body and anxious mind. Johnson limited his intake of rich food and alcohol before retiring to bed and he took care to have a lamp burning at his bedside throughout the night so that if he awoke he could lull himself back to sleep by reading. 'To have the management of the mind', he believed, was 'a great art', of which sound sleep formed an intrinsic part.[11]

Johnson's reflections, and those of his friend and collaborator William Gerard Hamilton, were influenced by the shifting focus of medical attention on sleep's connections with the brain and nerves. In his 1750 ode *On Sleep*, Hamilton mused on the power of restful sleep to soothe the mind and promote creative thought.[12] Laments on sleep loss feature strongly in the opera *Semele*, composed by George Frideric Handel, which was first performed on 10 February 1744 at the Theatre Royal in London's Covent Garden as part of the annual Lenten concert series. The opera is based on classical Greek mythology and narrates the fateful death of Semele who is betrayed by her love rival Juno with the magical assistance of Somnus, the god of sleep.[13] Ovid's *Metamorphoses* cast a long shadow in highlighting the perilous nature of sleep, and similar reflections on its dangers surfaced in periodical literature. In February 1737 the *Gentleman's Magazine* and the *Universal Spectator* published an essay entitled 'Meditations on a Bed' that expressed concern about the power of unruly sleep to disorder the senses. In 1763 the *Gentleman's Magazine* cited extracts from Alexander Sutherland's *Attempts to Revive Antient Medical Doctrines*, which confirmed that unnatural sleeping patterns damaged the mind's health.[14] Reverend Samuel Perrott also praised the virtues of sound sleep that 'proves a most happy restorative to the mind, and gives it self-possession'. He dedicated a large part of his *Sermons on Practical Subjects* to the unique restorative power of sleep to fit minds for purposeful activity. For Perrott, the ultimate objective of careful sleep management was to support individual and collective 'improvement in knowledge', for which a lively mind was indispensable. Thanks were naturally due to God, who Perrott believed had created sleep to render humans fit for 'the careful and diligent exercise of their rational powers'.[15]

Synergies of opinion on this subject surfaced in medical treatises, in personal correspondence and in didactic literature. George Wright, author of *The Young Moralist* (1782), was determined to promote the government of the mind as an essential part of the training of young ladies and gentlemen. Wright gently cautioned his pupils against overindulgence in sleep because this was a sure means by which to 'stupify' them and to dilute their rational powers. He was convinced that careful sleep management held the key to emotional balance and observed that 'Our passions are excellent guides, whilst reason holds the rein; but; if we let them loose, they will hurry us with unbridled fury into destruction'.[16] Wright thus praised sound, moderate sleep as part of his instructions on the duties and comportment of good citizens, which was an essential accompaniment to physical, mental and emotional well-being. The dangers presented by immoderate sleep were expressed with equal force. Buckinghamshire clergyman Thomas Seaton described a mind disturbed by immoderate sleep as 'unpinion'd' and unable to perform its necessary functions.[17]

These explanations were translated into daily life by a variety of men and women who understood the value of managing the mind through careful regulation of their sleeping patterns. Samuel Taylor Coleridge wrote to his friend Thomas Poole to reassure him that his mind was 'more in my *own power*' thanks to careful governance of his sleeping hours. In a second letter to Poole a few months later, Coleridge described the pleasure he derived from his 'light & lively' faculties and compared this sensation to the feeling of having 'risen from healthy sleep on a fine spring morning'.[18] The value of restorative sleep was idealised to an unprecedented degree in these years thanks to its links with the health of the mind.

The attention lavished on healthy sleep also sparked lively debates about the causes and consequences of imperfect sleep states, which had equally important repercussions for individual and social health. In 1709 the Whig politician and outspoken Nonconformist John Trenchard defined perfect sleep as sleep 'without any Dreams at all'. Trenchard believed firmly in sleep's natural physiology and the mental states that it produced. 'Who is there', he asked, 'that does not perceive that in Dreams, our Thoughts and Desires are the natural and necessary productions of the affections of our Bodies?' Trenchard did not require an answer to his question as he identified sound sleep as the corollary of a healthy body and mind. Imperfect sleep, and the visions and dreams that attended it, were judged by contrast to be perversions of the mind's 'noble faculties'.[19] Trenchard described the ideas and images met in these interim states of consciousness as a species of mental disorder that predisposed people to fanciful illusions and superstition.[20] The limits of personal identity had been reached, Trenchard believed, when people were deprived of full consciousness and thus of the ability to distinguish between reality and fantasy.

Trenchard's voice resonated loudly with a number of writers who were set on removing any trace of religious enthusiasm from medical philosophies in the early decades of the eighteenth century.[21] They forged and defended the ideal of the natural conscious mind in direct opposition to radical millenarian groups, such as the French Prophets, who claimed a divine origin for the revelatory visions they met with in their sleep and dream states. Trenchard firmly rejected the influence of external spiritual forces on the mind but his view represented one extreme within a diverse spectrum of opinion on this subject. The origins of imperfect sleep and dream states and their relationship to personal identity were keenly contested in print and visual culture throughout this period. These conflicting viewpoints nevertheless shared a common interest in sleep's neurological origins, which explained non-conscious thoughts as the exclusive products of natural bodily processes.

The naturalisation of sleep and dream states was especially marked in explanations of nightmares and of the distinctive dream state in which the chest and stomach felt stifled by a heavy weight. As Chapter 1 revealed, this state of oppression was sometimes explained by the intervention of a demonic spirit known as the 'incubus', which was believed to visit sleepers during the night and sit on their chests. Supernatural explanations of the incubus were keenly contested in medieval medical scholarship, but the incubus spirit was recognised for a time in medieval civil and ecclesiastical law. The description of a similar state of oppression resulting from demonic attacks during sleep also appeared periodically in medieval and early modern witchcraft depositions, in healthcare guides, and in folkloric collections in many parts of Europe.[22] It was in the years after 1660, however, that supernatural explanations of disturbed sleep and dream states were more systematically challenged in print. Thomas Tryon presented a hierarchy of dream causes in his *Treatise of Dreams & Visions* (1695) that prioritised constitution, occupation and diet whilst admitting the possibility that supernatural beings, including the souls of the dead, might communicate with the living through dreams in exceptional circumstances.[23] He outlined the natural causes of the 'incubus' dream and dismissed the idea that a malicious 'Ghost' or 'Hob-goblin' was to blame since this disorder could be easily explained by the stagnation of ill humours within the body that might stem from disease, an irregular diet or from poor sleep posture.[24] Physician John Bond offered an even more comprehensive account based on hydraulic principles. In his *Essay on the Incubus, or Night-Mare* (1753) Bond explained that this state was triggered by the stagnation of blood at the base of the brain.[25] Physicians and medical practitioners increasingly attributed the incubus, and more mundane nightmares, to undue pressure on the brain and nerves and offered practical advice about how to prevent them.[26] Predominantly supernatural explanations of sleep and dream states were thus deprioritised within the hierarchy of likely causes of dreams by medical authors, natural philosophers and religious writers.

John Locke set the terms of debate surrounding states of consciousness in the early eighteenth century in his best-selling *Essay Concerning Humane Understanding*. The *Essay* went through four editions in Locke's lifetime and additional full and abridged editions of the text were published in each decade of the eighteenth century throughout the British Isles. In the *Essay* Locke equated personal identity with the rational waking mind. He did not entirely dismiss the possibility that waking identity might persist in non-conscious mental states but he cast serious doubt on its likelihood since it had a fragile empirical basis. In an adaptation of Aristotelian thought, Locke instead proposed a radical division of identity between the conscious and non-conscious mind. '*Socrates* asleep and *Socrates* awake, is not the same Person; but his Soul when he sleeps, and *Socrates* the Man consisting of Body and Soul when he is waking, are two Persons'. Locke denied the intervention of external spiritual forces and he also cast doubt on the special insights that non-conscious thoughts were thought to offer since he believed they were 'all made up of the waking man's ideas, though for the most part oddly put together'.[27] Locke's account of sleep and dreams prompted critical questions about the relationship between different degrees of consciousness, personal identity and the operations of mind and body. Legal writer Thomas Branch was similarly sceptical about the persistence of identity in sleep and dreams and he questioned the reliability and reality of the ideas met in these states. Branch proposed a natural physiology of dreams and other non-conscious states in his *Thoughts on Dreaming* (1738). He judged these mental states to be deceptively mundane because they were triggered by the inconsequential events of daily life. Branch was certain that they formed no part of waking identity: 'As *Consciousness identifies*, or makes us be *ourselves*; and that it does so, is on all Hands agreed; the want of it would certainly divest us of that Identity'.[28] To be asleep was thus to be transformed into an entirely different person.

Sleep and the Sensible Self

Interpretations of sleep states were transformed from the mid-eighteenth century as the culture of sensibility took hold of English imaginations. Non-conscious states of mind were detached from critiques of religious enthusiasm as dissenting groups weakened, were defeated, or became more quiescent to civil authority. The development of what G.J. Barker-Benfield termed 'sensational psychology' also spawned a revaluation of imperfect sleep states. These conditions were now routinely fashioned as symptoms of social capital, moral virtue and intellectual distinction rather than as evidence of mental derangement or corruption, when they were understood as symptoms of excessive sensibility.[29] It was in this context that imperfect sleep states began to attract ever-greater curiosity. Since sleep's neurological origins were firmly located within the brain, sleep states promised to reveal unique information about psychological depth and character. Unpeeling hidden layers of consciousness now offered a path to self-knowledge rather than distancing people from the thoughts and deeds they met in their sleep and dreams. This motivation triggered wide-ranging efforts to record and to explain these seemingly invisible cognitive processes in relation to personal identity.[30]

Sleep disorders became intrinsic features of personal identity in eighteenth-century England thanks in large part to the spread of neurological explanations of sleep. Thomas Tryon described the localisation of the brain's faculties of memory, imagination and judgement, which occupied 'distinct Seats, or Cells in the Brain'. They sat in close proximity to the nerves that controlled sleep and to the nerves that enervated the body's muscles that formed the 'Instruments of *Motion*'.[31] His explanation of sleepwalking, or somnambulism as it was now commonly termed, was not untypical. The term 'somnambulism' combined the Latin terms *somnus* and *ambulare*. Its widespread use from the late seventeenth century coincided with the circulation of neurological models of sleep and sleep disorders. The term 'somnambulism' was used extensively from the mid-eighteenth century to describe the movements of unquiet sleepers that filled the pages of periodicals, scientific magazines, novels, poems and print miscellanies on an extraordinary scale.[32] The 1756 edition of the miscellany *Every Man Entertained* applied a fashionable interpretation to a collection of sleepwalking reports gathered from across the British Isles and Europe. These episodes were explained by 'certain Motions of the Fibres of the Brain', which unsettled the nerves. Recommended treatments included the ingestion of soporific liquids, immersion in cold baths and the application of other cooling agents.[33] Sufferers might also turn to Dr John Scot's pills for relief, which were regularly advertised for sale in *The Times* newspaper and priced at 10s 6d per box. Scot wrote a number of medical treatises on nervous conditions and his pills were advertised to potential customers as an 'elegant Medicine' that was effective against 'obstinate Watchings' and 'disturbed sleep', amongst other things.[34] In each of these cases, direct links were drawn between the physical condition of somnambulism and the virtues of those who suffered from it.

There was cultural caché attached to a diagnosis of somnambulism by the mid-eighteenth century. The newfound appeal of this condition was enhanced by its unique pathology that distinguished it from other nervous disorders. The symptoms of somnambulism were visually dramatic and the uncertain state of consciousness inhabited by the sufferer promised to uncover valuable evidence of the mind's hidden activities. The fascination that somnambulism inspired is well attested by a case history published in the *Weekly Entertainer* (1783–1814), in the *Aberdeen Magazine* (1789), and in the *Scientific Magazine, and Freemasons' Repository* (1798).[35] These reports narrated the somnambulism of a thirteen-year old Swiss boy named Sieur Devaud, whose case was investigated by a learned committee of gentlemen on the commission of the Société des Sciences Physiques de

Lausanne. The committee carried out a series of experiments that were designed to manipulate Devaud's senses and movements to test the degree of volition that he retained in this state. His lip was tickled with a feather and his sense of smell stimulated with the aroma of burning cedarwood and with wormwood wine, a pungent ingredient used in brewing. Devaud reportedly imitated the sound of a cuckoo during these experiments that was a familiar noise made by the public clock in his hometown of Vevey on the shores of Lake Geneva. His movements remained purposeful and closely tied to his waking activities. He ate, drank and dressed himself without the aid of light and he composed a piece of prose with great precision. Devaud's performance led the committee to conclude that his somnambulism was a partial state of consciousness that sat between full sleep and waking. This allowed Devaud to be influenced by the 'small circle of objects, that relate to the few ideas, with which, at his age, his mind is furnished; such as his lessons, the church, the bells, and especially tales of ghosts'.[36] No spiritual force was responsible for Devaud's mental processes, however: instead his condition was attributed to the refined state of his nerves, which were acutely tuned to his social environment. Devaud's nerves were declared to be 'organized with peculiar delicacy, and to discover marks of the greatest sensibility and irritability: His senses of smell, taste, and touch, are exquisite; he is subject to fits of immoderate and involuntary laughter, and he sometimes weeps without any apparent cause'.[37] Here then was a confident statement that Devaud's somnambulism had a natural, neurological basis that marked this young man out as a sensitive and sensible individual of distinction.

The Lausanne committee's report prompted a series of responses from the British press, each of which described Devaud's condition as an enhancement of his ordinary capabilities. His disorder seemed to betray marks of genius because he was able to refine his physical and intellectual powers when he was partially separated from the mundane distractions of the waking world.[38] According to the *Scientific Magazine*, Devaud the somnambulist perfected his Latin phrases and arithmetic and displayed 'a deal of vivacity in all his words, notions, and actions'.[39] This report drew on fashionable descriptions of other nervous disorders, including melancholy and gout, which depicted sufferers as victims of social ills. George Cheyne and Samuel Tissot were just two of the medical practitioners who linked physical and psychological disorders with particular lifestyles, occupations and intellectual endeavours. Cheyne was convinced that the nervous diseases he identified 'never happens or can happen, to any but those of the liveliest and quickest natural Parts, whose Faculties are the brightest and most spiritual, and whose Genius is most keen and penetrating'.[40] This successful marketing strategy was adopted by Tissot, whose *Essay on Diseases Incidental to Literary and Sedentary Persons* (1771) identified sleep disturbances as the bugbear of 'sensible' ladies and gentlemen whose nerves were frayed by overstimulation of the mind and by the acute sensitivity of their passions. The physical and emotional debilities associated with somnambulists could thus enhance the reputation of individual sufferers. These case histories also appealed to a wider audience of non-sufferers because they were used to pioneer explorations of personal identity. Devaud's somnambulism offered food for thought to those people who favoured a model of personal identity that was largely forged by environmental stimuli and to those who preferred to emphasise an autonomous inner self that was unique to each man, woman and child.

The original Swiss report of Devaud's condition was translated into English and published in William Smellie's *Philosophy of Natural History*. William Smellie was a printer, editor and independent author of some distinction who had a strong interest in the relationship between body and mind. Smellie's early medical training influenced his printing and editorial projects. He was an early member of the Philosophical Society of Edinburgh, the forerunner of the Royal Society of Edinburgh, and he published ground-breaking texts in medicine and natural history that included the works of Scottish physician William Cullen, whose influence was explored in Chapter 1. Smellie dedicated a whole chapter of his book to sleep and dreams and his interest in somnambulism underlined the unique potential of this disorder to reveal the concealed operations of the human mind. In 1764 Smellie presented his own reports of somnambulists to members of the Newtonian Club – a gathering of intellectuals that included leading thinkers in Scotland's Enlightenment. Smellie's reason for sharing these cases with a crowd of illustrious scholars was their shared ambition to better understand the 'powers and operations of the human mind'. When Smellie declared that non-conscious states of mind were 'as characteristic of the genius or disposi-tions of any individual as his waking thoughts', his words fell on sympathetic ears amongst the Newtonians. Observing somnambulists allowed Smellie to bridge the divide between conscious and non-conscious thoughts and thereby improve knowledge of the mind's operations and its role in the formation of personal identity. William Smellie was convinced that 'to know one's self is the most important of all knowledge, and, at the same time, the most difficult to attain'.[41] Somnambulists appeared to offer a live simulation of the mind's actions when it was freed from reason and waking prudence: something that was imperceptible in ordinary waking states.

Like so many of his fellow physicians, William Smellie identified the origin of somnambulism in the sensibility of individual nervous systems. The cultural milieu in which these reports were embedded was evident in Smellie's work, which credited reports of somnambulism when they were supported by trustworthy sources, and when the social profile of the sufferer fitted the conventions of the typical victim. It was on this basis that Smellie recommended a number of cases that circulated in European networks of natural philosophers and that seeped into the pages of British periodicals. One of the most notable cases that Smellie reported was that of a somnambulistic student of divinity at the University of Bordeaux. The archbishop of Bordeaux was listed as an eyewitness to the case, whose protagonist composed sermons and musical compositions with a precision and elegance that eluded him whilst awake. The report was adapted for the entry for 'Noctambule' in the French *Encyclopédie* that combined the latest knowledge from the arts and sciences and that was co-edited and published by Denis Diderot and Jean-Baptiste le Rond d'Alembert between 1751 and 1780. The circulatory paths of these volumes ensured that the case was scrutinised across Europe. In Britain the account first featured in 1779 in the six-volume *Antient Metaphysics* of Scottish judge and philosopher James Burnett, Lord Monboddo. Burnett was a founder member in 1754 of the literary club the Select Society. He hosted Edinburgh's leading intellectuals for supper at his residence in St John Street, Canongate. Burnett may have recommended this particular case to his guests, who included William Smellie and the diarist and biographer James Boswell. Boswell published a version of the report in the *Scots Magazine* in October 1789 and one year later the case became part of the standard entry for 'SLEEP-*Walker*' in the *Encyclopaedia Britannica*, which occupied no less than four pages in this prestigious compendium of knowledge.[42]

The curiosity that somnambulists provoked drew practical support from interactive print forums that created a virtual community of sufferers, physicians, philosophers and interested observers. Through the pages of these publications somnambulists became subjects of enquiry for those eager to trace the contours of interior mental processes. The *New Magazine of Knowledge* included a 'Remarkable Instance of Somnambulism' that had been sent in by one of its readers. The report described the musical and intellectual accomplishments of an educated gentleman and somnambulist whose disorder was characterised as the mark of a superior mind.[43] Nathaniel Wanley, a vicar from Coventry, approved of the abilities of a young poet and somnambulist who composed elegant verse and he sent his reflections to be published in *The Wonders of the Little World: or, A*

General History of Man in 1774.[44] In 1788 a contributor from Leeds, identi-fied only by the initials 'D.D.', recommended an effective cure for somnam-bulism to readers of the *Aberdeen Magazine*. If a tub of cold water was placed near the bed of a somnambulist, he or she would fall into it and be so startled by the cold liquid that their disordered nerves would be instantly realigned. The contributor claimed that this remedy had been tried and tested by family members and that he himself had been cured of his youthful somnambulism when his mother adopted the method. He had been prompted to share this advice moreover after reading an article about a gentleman somnambulist in the widely circulating Methodist publication the *Arminian Magazine*.[45] D.D. may have offered this instruction out of civic benevolence or as a way of affirming his own intellectual and emotional capacities.

Those who observed somnambulists in full flow were fascinated by the penetrating powers of perception they displayed. Botanist and physician Erasmus Darwin used contemporary reports of somnambulism to distin-guish human cognitive functions in his influential medical work *Zoonomia; or, The Laws of Organic Life* (1794), which includes chapters on sleeping and dreaming. Darwin believed that nervous sensibility increased during sleep when the nerves were endowed with a unique 'vivacity'. He explained that 'somnambulation' could be distinguished from perfect sleep because the somnambulist retains a degree of volition that is absent in more complete sleep states in which mental operations seemed to be suspended. This was by no means a bad thing, however, since somnambulism produced a more lively imagination, which appeared to be 'whetted, and rendered more active'. Darwin compared this state to a 'waking dream' – a mental state that seemed to breach the boundary between conscious and non-conscious perception.[46]

Erasmus Darwin and William Smellie were convinced that somnambu-lists had to be carefully observed because they physically acted out the ideas that were ordinarily confined to the non-conscious mind. There were important parameters within which these observations operated, however, which revealed distinctions of social status and gender. In the early 1760s William Smellie investigated reports that a young maidservant named Sarah was walking and talking in her sleep. Sarah lived and worked in Smellie's lodgings near Edinburgh and his diagnosis of her behaviour differed markedly from his conclusions about Devaud's delicate nervous sensibilities. Smellie was persuaded that it was Sarah's tempestuous char-acter that disturbed her passions and made her rise from her bed to walk in nearby fields. Her behaviour in this state was described as brutish rather than elegant. On one occasion Smellie discovered Sarah wandering around her bedchamber in a state of undress. He pretended to be Sarah's lover, fellow servant John Porteous, which led her to reprimand him for numerous breaches of promise. During this outburst Sarah revealed the intimate details of her romance to Smellie and to her employers. In William Smellie's case report he chose to underline Sarah's fits of temper. She labelled her mistress 'suspicious, cruel and narrow-minded' before defending herself against allegations that she had stolen alcohol from the house. Sarah tried to jump out of a window and had a violent dream that an angry bull was chasing her. When Smellie tested Sarah's sensory responses by pricking her arm with a sharp instrument, she did not flinch, which provided yet further evidence of the stolid quality of her nerves.[47] William Smellie was unwilling to explain Sarah's condition as the product of a refined nervous sensibility and concluded instead that its cause was her base passions and illicit romantic affairs. Claiming the status of a delicate and sensible being was not open to just anybody. Peering into the hidden workings of the mind could reveal marks of sordidness as well as refinement: either way the thoughts and actions of somnambulists were ever more closely aligned with personal character.

French naturalist Georges-Louis Leclerc, comte de Buffon, similarly identified a range of different sleep and dream states in the human and animal economy in his multi-volume *Histoire Naturelle*. He separated humans from 'brutes' and 'ideots' because only humans possessed the ability to reflect on their own non-conscious experiences. Despite this superiority, de Buffon also distinguished two different types of human dreams. Those produced internally by the mind were rare and valued more highly than the animalistic dreams produced by external vibrations on the body or by the motions of the body's lower organs.[48] De Buffon's work proved influential amongst British physicians and philosophers and it may well have shaped William Smellie's diagnoses of somnambulism, which varied according to social status and occupation; Smellie translated de Buffon's *Histoire Naturelle* into English in 1780.

William Smellie was not alone in prioritising the status of the sufferer in his diagnoses of somnambulism. A young French maid was the central character in a case investigated by the Royal Societies of Montpellier and Paris and published in the *Gentleman's Magazine* in 1747. The physicians who attended the young woman noted that she conversed with an unchar-acteristic liveliness and eloquence, yet on other occasions she betrayed her indelicate nature by openly insulting members of her household.[49] When the young woman was slapped in the face, had tobacco stuffed up her

nostrils, her skin pierced with sharp needles, and her fingers bent back-
wards, she showed no signs of sensible feeling – much like the Scottish
maidservant Sarah. The attending physicians appeared unwilling to explain
this episode as a delicate imbalance of the nerves and they appealed instead
to the Royal Society for guidance. Diagnoses also varied according to age
and gender. Erasmus Darwin described the sufferings of an 'ingenious and
elegant young lady' who sleepwalked on a daily basis for six months. This
young woman held elegant conversations, sang to music and recited complicated verses of poetry whilst in this state. Her behaviour suggested a degree
of learning and sophistication yet Darwin qualified his diagnosis by
suggesting that her condition may have been triggered by her menstrual
cycles. Her cognitive functions, Darwin suggested, were most likely upset
by the biological rhythms of her body rather than by any innate genius.[50]

Many observers thus distinguished different types of somnambulism
based on the symptoms displayed by the sufferer and according to their
occupation, age and gender. These distinctions meant that many cases were
probably never investigated because they were considered unremarkable,
or they went unobserved, or because the somnambulists in question were
labourers, servants or women of marginal interest. In 1779 James
Woodforde's niece Nancy was discovered naked in the kitchen whilst
walking in her asleep. When Woodforde described the episode in his diary
he was concerned that Nancy's nudity had broken the boundaries of household decency but he did not attempt to discern any peculiar marks of
refinement in her.[51] In 1782 the *Gentleman's Magazine* published a report of
a somnambulist apprentice bricklayer from Maidstone in Kent. He rose
from his bed and climbed out of the chamber window onto the rooftops of
his neighbours' houses. The editors of the magazine never probed the origin
of the young man's malady. The correspondent merely noted that the man
had been lucky to escape death after one of his neighbours suspected him
of housebreaking.[52] It is impossible to quantify the number of people that
suffered from somnambulism, or to identify what kinds of people actually
suffered from this condition. It is nevertheless possible to trace the cultural
conventions that surrounded this increasingly fashionable disorder, as well
as the backgrounds of those people who were more likely to seek and to
attract deeper interest in their cases. The social aesthetic that framed
somnambulism, which rested on sleep's neurological foundations, thus
helped to create a hierarchy of worthy and unworthy sufferers.[53] Those
somnambulists who merited further investigation offered a precious
resource for those eager to discern the inner workings of the mind and to
tap the roots of personal identity.

Sleep, Dreams and the Romantic Imagination

Contentious debates about the interactions of body and mind in sleep and dream states helped to transform understandings of personal identity. This process reached its peak in the late eighteenth century when they became a prime focus of artistic inspiration, creativity and self-knowledge for leading figures in the Romantic movement. Samuel Taylor Coleridge's literary works reflected the growing interest in the relationship between body and mind in these years. Coleridge, like many of his contemporaries, was convinced that the mind's creative potential reached its peak when it was not fully conscious. In somnambulism, for example, the imagination seemed to have free rein over words and deeds. The somnambulists' actions were understood as a live demonstration of the unfettered imagination whose power was unobstructed by the mundane waking world. Romantic poets and artists immersed themselves in the study and experience of different sleep and dream states to tap the deepest recesses of their own creative powers.

Coleridge, William Blake, Lord Byron, George Crabbe, Henry Fuseli, William Hazlitt, Leigh Hunt, John Keats, Percy Bysshe Shelley, Robert Southey and William Wordsworth were just some of the poets, artists and novelists who probed the creative potential of the non-conscious mind and its relationship to personal identity. William Blake developed a unique psychology of interiority through his art and poetry, whilst Coleridge, Shelley and Southey each kept a record of their dreams and non-conscious visions, which they used as inspiration for their poetry.[54] Shelley used dream visions to bridge the waking natural world and a transcendent supernatural realm in his poem *Alastor; or the Spirit of Solitude* (1816). A variety of supernatural spirits also animate the human mind in his lyrical poem *Prometheus Unbound* (1820) in which sleep and dream states feature heavily.[55] Shelley's interest in alternate states of consciousness may have been shaped by his own experiences since he had suffered from acute bouts of sleepwalking since childhood. Instead of seeking a cure for this ailment, Shelley tried to multiply it by allowing himself to be induced into artificial states of magnetical somnambulism by his wife and by his cousin Thomas Medwin. It was in this state that he was apparently able to recite poems in flawless Italian.

Explorations of disturbed sleep and dream states appeared in a range of textual and pictorial forms. Zürich-born painter Henry Fuseli, who went on to become professor of painting and keeper at London's Royal Academy, presented the most iconic image of this kind in his oil painting *The Nightmare* (1781). The portrait features a recumbent female body, possibly that of Fuseli's lover Anna Landolt, in the throes of disturbed sleep. Fuseli signals her distress by placing an incubus spirit upon her chest, and by including a horse's – or mare's – head that gazes on the sleeper through the curtain. The inclusion of supernatural and folkloric motifs is striking and it allows Fuseli to signal the nightmare's occurrence to the viewer. This masterpiece was central to Fuseli's artistic production since he explained in his *Aphorisms on Art* that dreams were 'One of the most unexplored regions of art'.[56] His choice drew criticism from the *Morning Chronicle, and London Advertiser*, which complained that the depiction of 'hag-riding' was 'too unpleasant a thought to be agreeable to any one, and is unfit for furniture or reflection'.[57] Whilst the painting's supernatural overtones smacked of erroneous superstition to some, a more palatable explanation for the sleeper's distress could be drawn from the position of the subject's body, which was recumbent on its back and in direct contravention of accepted medical wisdom on sleep posture. Indeed, a surviving letter to the artist dated 1794 made direct reference to the instructional use of *The Nightmare* that might teach infants 'how to lie in their beds' and, more particularly, not to lie on their backs to avoid troubling dreams.[58] The medicine bottle at the young woman's feet also signals the influence of a nervous disorder: she is surely the victim of a refined and delicate sensibility. Criticism of *The Nightmare* did not dampen Fuseli's fascination with sleep and dream states, which he indulged in many of his other works including *Joseph Interpreting the Dreams of the Butler and Baker of Pharaoh* (1768), *Lady Macbeth Sleepwalking* (1783), *The Shepherd's Dream* (1798), *An Incubus Leaving Two Sleeping Women* (1810) and *Julia appearing to Pompey in a Dream* (1741–1825).

Fuseli's *Nightmare* was first exhibited at London's Royal Academy on 29 April 1782 and its display fed speculations about the connections between sleep's physiology and the stirrings of the non-conscious mind. The image sparked numerous imitations and satirical adaptations. London-based engraver Thomas Burke produced the official stipple-engraved reproduction of the work in 1783, depicted in Figure 23.

The engraving was published by printmaker and fellow engraver John Raphael Smith and it went on to become a bestseller across Europe – Smith claimed to have made more than £500 from sales of the work. Erasmus Darwin's 'Night-mare', a short poem that appeared in his 1789 work *The Loves of the Plants*, also accompanied Burke's engraving. The poem pondered the presence of human will in alternate states of consciousness and it invited sympathy with Fuseli's sleeper who was surely a victim of her unruly nerves.[59] One version of *The Nightmare* hung in the home of

23. Thomas Burke, *The Nightmare*, London, 1783.

bookseller and publisher Joseph Johnson, who was Fuseli's friend and former landlord. The image prompted discussions amongst the 'Johnson circle' – the name given to the weekly dinners that Johnson hosted in St Paul's Churchyard in London for leading intellectuals, who included William Godwin and Mary Wollstonecraft.

Another adaptation of Fuseli's painting surfaced in 1784 with Thomas Rowlandson's *The Covent Garden Night Mare*, which invites revulsion rather than sympathy with its subject. Rowlandson was an artist, print-maker and political cartoonist who trained at the Royal Academy. He piggybacked on the popularity of Fuseli's portrait to launch a satirical attack on Whig politician Charles James Fox, who was embroiled in polit-ical crisis as the coalition government that he had formed with Lord Frederick North in 1783 was dramatically dissolved by King George III in March 1784.[60]

Rowlandson's image displays the natural causes of his subject's disturbed sleep and grounds them in a well-established literature that credits such disturbances to shameless excess. Fox's notoriously luxurious lifestyle is represented by his corpulent naked body, which lies flat on its back. A set of gaming dice and a dice box are visible on his bedside table in place of the medicine bottle used by Fuseli, which gives a clear steer to the viewer about

24. Thomas Rowlandson, *The Covent Garden Night Mare* (print),
London, 1784.

how to interpret his condition. Fox had accumulated vast gambling debts in
the 1770s and 1780s and had twice faced bankruptcy. This ignominy is
signalled by the figure of the incubus, which Rowlandson transforms into a
demon of gambling to tarnish Fox's reputation still further.

Political caricaturist James Gillray was a good friend of Thomas
Rowlandson and he adopted similar visual motifs in his hand-coloured
satirical etching *Duke William's Ghost* (1799), shown in Figure 25. Thomas
Rowlandson's critique of Charles James Fox is tame in comparison to
Gillray's depiction of the red-faced, drunken and oversized body of George,
prince of Wales, who lies on his back in the same pose as Fuseli's sleeper
and in the midst of a troublesome sleep. Empty and broken wine bottles
litter the floor next to the prince's bed, and a half-drunk bottle slips from
his greedy fingers as he loses consciousness. Critics reviled the prince of
Wales for his flagrant adultery and for his indulgent lifestyle. James Gillray's
damning diagnosis of sloth and greed is delivered by the ghostly figure
of the prince's great uncle, William Augustus, duke of Cumberland. The
duke looms over the sleeping prince with an hourglass in hand to presage
the fatal consequences of George's wanton behaviour. The print is one
of a series of four satires in which the duke's ghost appears to urge his
great nephew to mend his ways before it is too late.[61] Rowlandson and
Gillray's interventions in the political dramas of the early 1780s show that

25. James Gillray, *Duke William's Ghost* (King George IV; William Augustus,
duke of Cumberland), 7 May 1799.

the mind's agility, along with its debilities, were inseparable from the physical condition of the bodies to which they were attached.[62] Mental processes
were thus constantly changing, whether swayed by bodily ailments for
which sympathy might be given, or by self-inflicted lifestyle excesses that
invited censure. Either way, sleep and dream states were understood to be
born of individual bodies and to be powerful ciphers of personal character
and moral fibre.

Samuel Taylor Coleridge was captivated by the effect that sleep had on
the mind and his work encapsulated the transformed status of the non-
conscious mind in medical philosophy, art and literature by the close of the
eighteenth century. Coleridge frequently reflected on the relationship
between the quality of his own sleep and his creative imagination. Two
things are particularly evident from his work: Coleridge believed that
bodily processes drove the operations of the waking and non-conscious
mind, and he was similarly convinced that his non-conscious thoughts
were extensions of his personality. He explored his own sleep and dream
states at length in his correspondence and poetry.

Coleridge's interest in different mental states began at an early age. In a
letter to his friend Thomas Poole, he recalled having run away from home
after a childhood fight with his brother. He fell asleep in the fields on a

stormy October night and remembered how his waking sensations and sleeping thoughts merged as he slipped from consciousness:

> I felt the cold in my sleep, and dreamt that I was pulling the blanket over me, & actually pulled over me a dry thorn bush, which lay on the hill – in my sleep I had rolled from the top of the hill to within three yards of the River, which flowed by the unfenced edge of the bottom. – I awoke several times, and finding myself wet & stiff, and cold, closed my eyes again that I might forget it.[63]

His letters reveal an obsession with his nervous debilities whose origin was located 'in *mental* causes' by a medical practitioner that visited the poet.[64] Coleridge complained to his friends that he suffered from regular bouts of sleeplessness due to persistent rheumatic pain in his head and shoulders.[65] These aches sometimes kept him awake until five o'clock in the morning. On one such occasion Coleridge explained to his friend and fellow poet Robert Southey that his sufferings were caused by his 'overworked' brain, which meant that he could only 'doze troublously' rather than enjoying a full and restorative sleep.[66] Coleridge described the effect that his sleeping problems could have on his artistry in a letter to the chemist and inventor Sir Humphry Davy: 'My eyes have been inflamed to a degree, that rendered reading & writing scarcely possible; and strange as it seems, the art of poetic composition, as I lay in bed, perceptibly affected them, and my voluntary ideas were every minute passing, more or less transformed into vivid spectra.'[67] These reflections probably met with a receptive audience in Davy, who shared his friend's passion for poetry and for the chemical experiments at Dr Thomas Beddoes' Pneumatic Institution, which opened in Dowry Square, Bristol, in 1798. Coleridge was an enthusiastic participant at the Institution, whose establishment was part-funded by his patron, the master potter Josiah Wedgwood, before his death in 1795, and thereafter by his son Tom Wedgwood. Here, chemical gases were used to induce patients into different states of consciousness, which Beddoes hoped would extend human knowledge of the mind's complex operations.[68]

Coleridge's explorations of his own mental states revealed both positive and negative dimensions to his character but he clearly understood his bed, and his half-dozing states, as sites of inspiration. The sensibility of Coleridge's feelings was particularly acute at bedtime, partly due to the exertions of the day and partly due to the emotional associations that his bed produced. He wrote impassioned letters to his wife from his bed when he was away from home. These verses expressed a yearning for reconciliation upon which he reflected during the peaceful moments when he was alone with his thoughts and lying in anticipation of sleep. Coleridge partly framed his understanding of lost sleep as romantic expressions of longing for his wife.[69] He believed that a half-sleeping state was an especially productive time to excite the imagination. This was underlined in one of his lectures where he explained how the body's sleeping posture could stir the brain into action.[70] The images that populated Coleridge's semiconscious states sometimes entered his dreams and consolidated the links between his waking and sleeping thoughts.[71] He read and wrote into the early hours of the morning during his years as a journalist, not simply for convenience, but to improve his receptivity to the latest publications. He described the frightened and agitated state produced by reading Friedrich Schiller's play *The Robbers* (1781) after midnight. Coleridge may have anticipated a particularly lively set of thoughts that night, if he managed to sleep at all.[72]

The fullest statement of the connections that Coleridge drew between his sleep and dream states and his own identity came in his poem *The Pains of Sleep*, written in 1803. The verses describe how his physical ailments affect the quality of his slumber and reveal glimpses of the dark and shameful thoughts that pulsed through his semi-conscious mind:

> And shame and terror over all!
> Deeds to be hid which were not hid,
> Which all confused I could not know
> Whether I suffered, or I did:
> For all seemed guilt, remorse or woe,
> My own or others still the same
> Life-stifling fear, soul-stifling shame.

These nocturnal torments made Coleridge afraid to fall asleep for fear of what might be revealed about his own psyche.[73] The unstable and fragmented nature of his mind, and of his character, was laid bare by his reflections on his own sleep states. He struggled to reconcile the sinister implications of these experiences with the creative fervour that they produced. Coleridge, and many of his contemporaries, thus understood the relationship between sleep states and personal identity as paradoxical. They might reveal untapped depths of creative genius yet they might equally uncover the shameful recesses of the human mind. Either way, sleep states had become an intimate part of individual psychology by the close of the eighteenth century.

Sleep, Dreams and Daily Life

Psychological interpretations of sleep were routinely expressed in everyday contexts. Sleeping patterns were interpreted in relation to the trials and tribulations of daily life and especially during the emotional crises that marked different life stages. The relationship between sleep and sensibility heavily shaped these understandings. In diaries and correspondence poor sleepers fashioned themselves as delicate emotional beings whose disrupted sleep and troubled dreams signalled their acute sensitivity to their physical environments. Sleep quality was used to convey a range of personal anxieties and emotional states, both as an expression of genuine physical and psychological suffering, and as a means of self-fashioning.

Physician Samuel Tissot observed in 1771 that business concerns and financial transactions were common causes of sleep loss: 'The man of fashion, disturbed by business, projects, pleasures, disappointments, and the regrets of the day, heated by food and drinks, goes to bed with trembled nerves . . . and for a long time keeps him waking.'[74] The faculties of reason and judgement could easily be impaired by 'an incapacity of thinking or application' induced by poor sleep.[75] Tissot's medical treatises traded on the social aesthetic associated with disturbed sleep and he offered practical advice to his readers about how to prevent these disruptions, which were framed as by-products of worldly success. Tissot had a ready market to tap into as sleep quality became an important preoccupation in letters and diaries. Somerset parson William Holland was in the habit of using the medicine known as 'Dover's powder' to relieve his sleepless nights. Holland's sleep was sometimes disturbed by untimely bell-ringing at his local church, and on one occasion by the noise of 'a disagreeable cow', but it was more often the result of family troubles and professional anxieties.[76] The same was true of Ralph Thoresby, whose sleep was disturbed on a Sunday in September 1712 by an impending change of employment. His diary extract from that day read: 'Morning, could not sleep; was much concerned at what Mr. Milner told me last night, about the Corporation's design to elect me to supply a late job vacancy, which I earnestly and heartily desired his assistance to prevent.'[77] Financial troubles caused isolated episodes of sleeplessness for Peregrine Bertie, brother of the earl of Lindsey, who was struggling to secure his family's estate at Grimsthorpe, Lincolnshire in the 1690s.[78] On New Year's Day 1713 Edmund Harrold entered the year with 'a troubled mind' and a body that 'sleeps ill' due to a scarcity of money and his struggle with alcoholism.[79] Disturbed sleep was thus understood as an extreme symptom of psychological distress, which was consistently prompted by professional and financial troubles. The cause of this sleep loss is hardly surprising but the ways in which its effects were linked to personal character, and the methods used to offset it, show the degree to which psychological understandings of sleep pervaded daily life.

Business, work and financial troubles featured more prominently amongst the triggers of sleep loss in the diaries and letters of men, but they were not exclusive to them. Concerned wives recorded their own episodes of sleep loss as a consequence of their husbands' affairs, to which they were highly attuned as sensible beings and dutiful wives. Some women also described the effects of sleep loss as a way of protesting against marital abuse and unhappiness, as was the case with writer Eliza Fay (née Clement). Eliza and her husband Anthony had set out for India in 1779 so that he could practise his trade as a barrister at the Calcutta Supreme Court. The couple were imprisoned for three and a half months on the orders of the governor of Calicut as they travelled overland to their destination. Eliza described the pains caused by her sleep loss to convey the traumatic experience of captivity. In February 1780 she wrote 'such is the harassing confusion of my mind, and the weakness of my nerves, that I can merely offer you a simple statement of facts, and even that must necessarily be incorrect; for incessant anxiety and constant anticipation of more intolerable evils, have totally unhinged my faculties'.[80] Eliza's wakefulness was brought on by her 'fretting' and by the agitated state of her mind, which continued for some time after this period of imprisonment. She recorded that 'I went to bed, but in spite of every endeavour to calm the agitation of my mind, passed a *sleepless* night'.[81] Eliza's domestic circumstances at this time were far from tranquil. Her husband had fathered an illegitimate child soon after their arrival in India and the couple formally separated on 11 August 1781. Eliza's sleeplessness may have been genuine, but the recording of its physical and mental effects also offered a way of expressing the distress caused by her troubled marriage.

Maria Nugent reflected on her own sleeplessness to articulate the daily pressures of family life with which she struggled. Maria married English army officer and MP George Nugent, who was posted to Jamaica and India, from where his wife recorded her daily activities. Maria took an active interest in Jamaica's political affairs, a country where her husband had been appointed lieutenant governor and then commander-in-chief. It was in the guise of dutiful wife that she recorded her sensitivity to the local environment by describing her sleep quality. On 6 July 1803 she rose at four thirty in the morning after passing 'an almost sleepless night, thinking of the state of this wretched country'. Just one week later she described how she and George were 'overpowered with all sorts of business' and were unable to secure sound rest.[82] Maria understood that her state of mind at bedtime was key to her sleep quality and she frequently reflected on it. She prefaced accounts of restless nights with concerns about her children's health, or about local affairs. Maria did not involve herself directly in politics but they indirectly affected her mood, and her sleep, through concern for her husband's well-being. After the Nugents had returned to England in 1805 Maria observed that she rose early 'after a sleepless night, from the excitement and anxiety of my mind'. This had seemingly been triggered by her involvement in affairs at court surrounding the bestowment of a baronetage. That night she retired to bed at midnight but wrote in her diary that her mind was 'too anxious, and too much occupied with my dear N.'s vexation about the baronetage, and his affairs'.[83] By recording these interruptions to her rest, Maria marked herself out as a delicate emotional being and as a loving wife who shared the burden of her husband's anxieties.

Women's sleep may have been less frequently disturbed by business and financial troubles but concern for the health and well-being of loved ones provided a consistent cause for disturbed periods of rest. Childcare, unsurprisingly, figured strongly in the sleep reports of married women who drew heavily on the language of sensibility to express the physical and emotional stresses of motherhood. Maria Nugent's sleep was routinely disturbed by the illnesses of her young children George and Louisa, which ranged from simple toothaches to dangerous fevers. As a dutiful mother Maria sacrificed her own rest to sit up and watch her children as they slept. She linked her own emotional health to her children's fluctuating spirits and she was careful to note in her diary that her mind was 'constantly anxious for those I love'. When the children were healthy and cheerful, Maria rested well.[84] She conveyed the delicacy of her maternal sensibilities by showing concern for George and Louisa's tormented dreams, which led to extended periods of broken sleep. When Maria sat up through the night to tend to her infants, she compensated by lying in in bed the following morning. She surmised that her nerves had become disordered from prolonged sleep loss and declared herself 'unfit' for society on such occasions.[85]

Sarah Fox (née Champion) also recorded how the trials of caring for her young children resulted in a series of bad nights.[86] Sleep loss in these contexts was gender-related but it was not gender-specific. When Edmund Harrold's daughter lay ill in bed, both he and his wife suffered interrupted nights as they watched over her. Edmund wrote that he 'was very thoughtfull' and 'lay much awake' as he fretted that her disease might end her life. In

January 1713 Harrold was preoccupied by the well-being of his wife and children as he lay in bed unable to sleep. These reflections provoked 'very strange dreams' that prompted him to pray to God for his family's safe-keeping.[87] Harrold actively sought to connect his sleep and dream states to the concerns of his daily life despite the demands of philosophers like John Locke to do just the opposite.

Maria Nugent used the term 'comfort' to describe the beneficial state of mind that preceded a peaceful night's sleep. This was comfort of a psychological kind, and, on the rare occasions that Maria enjoyed it, she was thankful that her 'state of nervousness and weakness' was temporarily subdued. Maria's habitual commentaries on her state of mind at bedtime reveal the value that she attached to sleep, which could support or disrupt her physical, mental and emotional well-being at any time. Maria tried a variety of methods to calm her nerves and procure 'comfort' at bedtime. Pleasant sociability seemed to help as conversing with close female friends in the evenings ensured that Maria went to bed 'much comforted'.[88] She may have been aware of medical advice that recommended agreeable conversation as a way of soothing a troubled mind. The inseparability of physical and psychological comfort was continually evident in Maria's reflections on her evening routines. In November 1803 she bathed and spent a 'merry' evening playing with her children and wrote that 'I went to bed almost happy'.[89] On another occasion, a tranquil day spent with her young children allowed Maria to retire 'more at ease in my mind than usual'.[90] She may well have recorded those occasions when she retired to bed in good spirits to call upon when sleep eluded her. Whatever her motivation she clearly linked the quality of her slumber to her delicate psychological state.

The psychological effects of sleep also figured strongly in personal reflections on ill health, death and mourning. The way that men and women responded to the traumatic loss of a close family member or friend reveals a great deal about emerging psychological ideas of sleep and sleeplessness. In 1729 Penelope Herne wrote to her mother Lady Mordaunt from Winchester following the death of her husband: she was haunted by constant thoughts of her dead spouse that made it impossible for her to sleep.[91] A love affair of a different kind disturbed the rest of the noblewoman and letter writer Lady Mary Coke. Mary described periods of sleep loss to convey her grief at the 1767 death of Edward Augustus, duke of York and Albany, with whom she had a long-standing obsession. Her descriptions of sleep loss were interspersed with lucid accounts of disturbed dreams that she identified as the product of her disordered mind and nerves:

I have passed a terrible night; cou'd not sleep any time together; yet four times I dreamed the same dream. I thought I was in Westminster Abbey, & the Funeral service was performing for the poor Duke, that I had not resolution to go into the Chapel, but sat down on a Tomb in another part of the Abbey, where I thought the figures on the Monuments moved. I then seemed to be left alone, & fancy'd I was shut up, but on walking down one of the great Isles I saw a door open, which I went out at, & was then perplex'd walking about the streets. My mind was so disturb'd that I rose early.[92]

On Sunday 25 October she again passed a sleepless night: 'Was up a little after seven, & went to the Closet at eight; luckily nobody was there, for I was so shock'd, that I cou'd not help crying, having constantly seen him there ... In the Evening I was worse then Usual; I went early to Bed'. Mary styled herself as a delicate female who suffered from nervous melancholy in earlier passages of her journal, which corresponded neatly to her periods of sleeplessness.[93]

The grief occasioned by a family death was a common trigger for sleep loss, which was explicitly linked to psychological turmoil. Impending deaths had a similar effect. Alice Thornton was tormented by 'somme little slumbers, but very unquiet and full of feares, tremblings, and sad apprehensions' as she lay alone at night, awaiting news of her husband's death.[94] Tending to a dying loved one kept sleepers from their beds for practical reasons, which aggravated their feelings of distress. Buckinghamshire gentleman Roger Hill complained in a letter to a friend that he 'had not 36 hours sleep in 12 days' following the death of his cousin Richard South in 1692.[95] When the Reverend George Woodward's stepmother lay dying in November 1761 the duty of care fell on his sisters, who he noted 'had a vast fatigue of late, poor girls! For they were not in bed for ten nights together, I wish it may not make them ill.'[96] Samuel Taylor Coleridge's sleep was also disturbed by the practical burden of caring for his sick friend and fellow poet Charles Lloyd. He wrote to his friend, Bristol bookseller Joseph Cottle,

under great anguish of mind, Charles Lloyd being very ill. He has been seized with his fits three times in the space of seven days; and just as I was in bed, last night, I was called up again – and from 12 o clock at night to *five* this morning he remained in one *continued* state of *agoniz'd Delirium*. What with the bodily toil exerted in repressing his frantic struggles, and what with the feelings of anguish for his agonies, you may suppose that I have forced myself from bed with aching temples & a feeble frame. I was not in bed till after five.

Just a few days later Coleridge penned a similar account for Josiah Wade in which he self-diagnosed the cause of his sleep loss as his nervous constitution and delicate sensibilities.[97]

The half-conscious moments immediately before and after sleep were particularly evocative of loved ones both living and dead. Quiet contemplation time was more readily available during these moments and the deep-seated associations between sleep and death traced in Chapter 3 may also have encouraged these reflections. Sarah Fox wrote in her diary that she lay awake in her bed and felt very close to her nephew John Prideaux, who had recently passed away. Her thoughts were provoked by partial memories of her dream the preceding night; Sarah could not recall its precise details but she described its comforting effect in bringing 'a sense of sweetness' to her mind.[98] Sarah drew a close link between her state of mind, nerves and the quality of her sleep. When her sister was ill she noted that she 'slept little . . . from the extreme delicacy of both her mind & body' and she described herself at this time as 'tremblingly alive' to her sister's sufferings. She was similarly deprived of sleep after the sudden death of her cousin, which triggered thoughts of the transience of human life.[99] Sarah's fragile sensibility and emotional depth was clearly signalled by the poor sleep quality that she described.

Edmund Harrold's grief at the death of his wife was a major cause of sleep loss and disturbed dreams. On 18 June 1713 he 'Dream'd of death and other things this night thro' over tho[ugh]tfullnes on ye loss of my wife ½ year ago, and other changes and chances [tha]t does dayly befall me'. Edmund again lost sleep and suffered disturbed dreams at the one-year anniversary of his wife's death: 'This day twelve months [ago] I buried my wife Sarah, and I dream'd on her last night'. He begged God to be spared an early and unprepared death.[100] The rest of tailor's daughter Sarah Hurst was interrupted by extreme anxiety about her father's health. Her diary entry for 12 November 1760 reads: 'Sleep badly, extreamly restless, my mind foreboded my father's illness, sure this portends no new misfortune, but let me not anticipate, I already experience evils enough without dreading those to come'.[101] Lost sleep was understood as an intimate expression of feeling and it played a central role in conveying the physical and psychological torments brought on by grief.

The explanations that men and women offered for sleep loss framed their day-to-day preoccupations. Affairs of the heart were especially prominent amongst the causes of sleep loss in the letters and diaries of young unmarried women. Sarah Hurst expressed her romantic attachment to soldier Henry Smith by describing her inability to sleep soundly. Sarah was in the midst of a turbulent and long-distance love affair with Henry. Her fervent passions found physical expression in nocturnal restlessness that she believed was caused by her disturbed mind and frayed nerves. Her diary shows that broken and lost sleep were symptomatic of her self-diagnosed weak nerves and lively sensibility; in this, Sarah presaged Marianne Dashwood's expressions of romantic sensibility. Sarah frequently reflected on the ills of a disorderly mind that prevented her from sleeping peacefully and that 'discomposes our whole frame & renders us incapable of acting like rational creatures'. She resorted to cold baths and sea bathing to 'attain an even disposition of mind'; this was a psychological state to which she seemingly aspired at the same time as she revelled in the painful effects of her romantic affairs.[102]

Sarah spent many hours before bedtime writing love letters to Henry Smith, or sitting up with female companions hoping to receive a letter from her beloved. She declared in her diary that 'This solemn time of night suits a love sick Mind & soothes its Melancholy' in an overt attempt to draw attention to her sufferings.[103] When she failed to receive a letter from Henry in April 1759 she noted waking very early the next day and reflected that 'when the Mind is agitated how impossible it is for the Body to have any rest'.[104] As Sarah waited impatiently for news of Henry's fate when he was away on military service she considered the effect that her overactive mind had on her sleep. In March 1760 she read in a local newspaper of the bloody military battles in which Henry was caught up. That night she wrote in her diary that 'My unhappy heart, in painfull throbings, sighs for my dearest Harry & is a stranger to repose'.[105] Her fears for Henry's well-being also shaped the interpretation of her dreams, which were especially lucid at this time. On Sunday 6 April 1760 she dreamt that Henry had been wounded in battle and begged 'Heaven forbid an Illusion of this shocking sort shou'd ever be realis'd.'[106] The physical sensations caused by this fragile courtship are laid bare when Sarah describes being plunged into 'the deepest distress, my appetite & sleep forsakes me' having failed to receive the anticipated correspondence from her sweetheart.

Henry Smith's frequent absences led Sarah to question the strength of his feelings for her, which led to yet more restless nights. When Sarah was able to sleep her turbulent love life was matched by a series of 'Troublesome dreams' in which she imagined herself reunited with Henry. On Sunday 4 March 1759 she wrote, 'fancy I am a Pilgrim in great danger from Wild Beast. Imagine I see my Smith, embrace & part from him, ah where is he now, on the Wide Ocean but there is the same divine power presides by Water as by land, in that I trust'.[107] One month later Sarah dreamt 'that I am shipwreck'd & then made a Slave, but escape after great danger & difficulty'. The bizarre content of these dreams does not confuse their origin: Sarah was certain that 'thoughts of my dear Smith occasions these strange Ideas. He has this day been gone 4 months.'[108] A few months later Sarah once again constructed her romantic persona through her half-remembered dreams: 'Dream my dear dear Harry is here. I hear him talk & feel his caresses, sweet delusion, but I wake & it fleets away.'[109] When Sarah recalled her dreams in the mornings she struggled to pinpoint a clear dividing line between her conscious and non-conscious thoughts. Instead she plotted her waking and dreaming thoughts on a continuum that informed her sense of identity as a young woman in love.[110] Sarah's diary exposes intimate details of her love life but it also connects her to broader cultural debates about the origins of sleep states and their effects upon body and mind. She developed her own philosophy about the uncertain relationship between her body, mind and passions and reflected on her own character by pondering the causes and effects of her lost sleep.[111]

Sleep states of many different kinds had become key to understandings of human psychology, character and emotional depth by the close of the eighteenth century. This period saw the brain firmly established as the seat of reason, creativity and personal identity. Widespread acknowledgement of sleep's neurological origins was crucial to this process. Sleep states were used to structure debates about the mind's inner life and capabilities, its relationship to the body, and the organic nature of personal identity.[112] The relationship between sleep, mind and character assumed critical significance in medicine, philosophy, art and literature, whilst also offering a vivid way of expressing the trials and tribulations of daily life.

The conclusions that were drawn from sleeping patterns shifted in line with religious, political and cultural life. It was the culture of sensibility that allowed individuals to take full possession of their own sleep experiences and to relate them to their inner thoughts, sensations and feelings. Men and women who speculated about the origins of their restless nights were at the same time speculating about the origins of feelings of happiness, pain, anxiety and distress. Reflections on sleep thus reveal insights into the triggers of emotional unease and the physical sensations that they produced in daily life. This voyage of discovery reached its peak in the work of Samuel Taylor Coleridge who recognised, for better or for worse, that sleep states offered a unique pathway to self-knowledge and self-expression. This journey of exploration was one in which ordinary men and women participated with enthusiasm, offering up evidence of their own sleeping lives, and of their own characters, to be discussed and dissected.

CONCLUSION

GETTING A GOOD night's sleep held the key to good health and to personal and spiritual fulfilment in early modern England. The quest to secure it structured the rhythms of household life and the lifestyles and imaginations of men, women and children. There was widespread acknowledgment throughout this period that peaceful sleep was a gift of both God and Nature, yet the sense of human powerlessness that this produced spurred people to take ownership of those aspects of their sleeping lives that lay within their grasp. Early modern people attended carefully to sleep's three distinct phases – its approach, its cessation, and the dormant hours of rest in between. They tried to influence each one of them, and the transitions between them, to secure their health, happiness and heavenly reward. They prepared their homes, bodies, minds and souls for sleep's onset, and they reflected on their sleeping patterns as facets of their own identities as Christians, citizens, wives, parents and intelligent and sensible human beings. The household was the principal arena in which these daily practices and reflections took place and close study of them has revealed how and why sleep's successful pursuit dominated the lives of early modern people.

The heavy investments of time, labour and imagination that surrounded sleep's daily practice underline the unique cultural value that sleep states of different kinds had in the late seventeenth and eighteenth centuries. The rules and rituals that clustered around the bedside demarcated sleep's unrivalled importance in daily life. They were directly shaped by knowledge of sleep's physical and psychological benefits, which in turn drew on the distinct cultural understandings of sleep that characterised this period. New motivations emerged for taking possession of sleep's timing and environments, alongside new methods and technologies for achieving this ambition. People were acutely conscious of the benefits and dangers that sleep presented and that could stem from its successful practice or misman-agement. The value of refreshing sleep intensified, as did anxieties about the potential damage that sleep loss might cause, both in this world and the next.

The perceived benefits of restorative sleep to the health of body and mind were unrivalled. Peaceful sleep was an essential support to human life – as revealed by daily experience, by classical literature and by the words of Holy Scripture. Its life-sustaining qualities nevertheless took on even greater significance as sleep's operations became more closely aligned with the health of the brain and nerves. Widespread acceptance of sleep's neuro-logical foundations, a development pioneered by the work of English physi-cian Dr Thomas Willis, played a central role in its cultural revaluation by heightening its perceived benefits and dangers. These years witnessed a flood of investigations into sleep's properties and effects upon body and mind across the British Isles, alongside enquiries into related sleep and dream states, with sleep disorders being widely recognised and classified as independent categories of neurological disorder. Optimising sleep quality had always been important within the context of non-natural healthcare but sleep's demonstrable effects on the sensibilities of bodies, brains and nerves enhanced it yet further. These developments subtly strengthened the impulse to cleanse household sleeping chambers and to prepare and purchase soporific medicaments to deal swiftly with sleep loss when it occurred. These transformations constitute an early and important phase of sleep's medicalisation, if that is understood to mean the widespread recognition of sleep quality as a critical health issue for individuals and for wider society.[1]

Another major shift that gradually took place within English society across the early modern period was the reorganisation of many households and the relocation of bedsteads to the upper floors of many homes into semi-specialised sleeping chambers. Sleeping environments became more firmly aligned with their principal purpose and these highly meaningful spaces were personalised by investments of time and money in furnishing, arranging and cleaning them. People sought, wherever possible, to satisfy a powerful impulse to enclose their bodies within safe and familiar surround-ings that they hoped would secure them from earthly and spiritual dangers. This tactic, when successful, had the added benefit of providing physical and psychological ease that helped to relax bodies and minds in anticipa-tion of restful sleep. Privacy in the bedchamber was not desirable in and of itself but some degree of enclosure at night allowed men and women to control their immediate environment and to limit potential dangers and disturbances. This was achieved by the use of familiar sleep-related objects and textiles, by careful cleansing of the bedstead and its furnishings, by the careful selection of trusted bedfellows, and by securing a quiet space for prayer and spiritual contemplation where Christians could renew their relationship with God and put the day to rest. These rituals marked out sleep's special status within daily life as its loci became more strictly proscribed. Creating a physical and psychological distance between bedsteads and the distracting sights, smells and sounds from other parts of the house must then be understood, at least in part, as an attempt to optimise sleep quality. These at least were the priorities of daily life as revealed by the words and deeds of the people studied here. They created comfortable and familiar sleeping environments in many different ways to satisfy their own bodily and mental needs. The evidence presented here suggests a strong psychological and emotional investment in sleep's material apparatus, which must have been encouraged by sleep's emblematic status as the guardian of personal, social and spiritual life.

As sleep's material world was transformed, its timing and duration also attracted scrutiny as bedtimes were delayed and sleep loss accepted as the cost of late-night sociability. Much evidence does exist to support the widespread practice of biphasic sleep but such routines were not uniformly characteristic of early modern habits. Widespread variations in people's bedtimes became a prominent cause of comment and complaint within households and in wider society and these habits were not always vilified if their civic benefits could be justified. The moral boundaries that surrounded sleep's daily practice – and particularly its timing – thus began to shift as sleep's social benefits, and its worthy sacrifice for the greater good, were widely debated and sometimes admired. Instead of defining a 'typical' set of bedtimes, this book has instead emphasised the wide range of influences that shaped sleep's timing and length, which included the practical demands of daily life, the changing life cycles of individuals and households, and the prospect of the Christian afterlife. These layers intertwined to create a complicated jigsaw of bedtimes that differed between individuals and throughout the course of life.

The shifting balance between internal bodily causes of sleep and its external agents allowed sleep quality to be more closely connected to personal identity. Experiences of sleep, as well as dreams, were increasingly valued for revealing insights into psychological and emotional states of body and mind.[2] This internalisation of sleep's meanings laid the groundwork for a revaluation of different states of consciousness in the late eighteenth century. Sleeping experiences were absorbed into narratives of self-fashioning, being alternatively presented as signs of physical health, emotional sensitivity, intellectual depth and Christian piety. Sleep's history – its perception and its practice – thus contributes an important new dimension to understandings of psychological identity. Acknowledged links between sleep, dream states and psychology emerged strongly from the late seventeenth century and they anticipate the later institutionalisation of non-conscious mental states by professional psychologists in the nineteenth century. New anatomical knowledge of sleep's relationship with the mind and debates about the natural pathology of body and soul framed sleep states as unique pathways to self-knowledge by the close of the eighteenth century.

The internal psychological meanings given to sleep experiences did not obscure its spiritual significance, which continued to be an important dimension of Christian identity. Medical and spiritual motivations for pursuing restful sleep complemented each other, and the methods used to secure it also fused together in important ways. The day-to-day measures employed to prevent sleep loss were motivated by principles of healthcare and by deeply held religious beliefs amongst an increasingly diverse population of Protestants and Catholics within England's borders. These interweaving bodies of knowledge also shared the objective of securing long-term physical health, and the health of the soul, which assured sleep's importance throughout the human life cycle and into the life beyond. There were nevertheless important long-term changes in the relationship between sleep and devotional culture. Intermittent periods of sleep loss were less often interpreted as signs of impending damnation but the growing importance of household devotions intensified the daily regulation of bedtimes and sleeping environments. Healthy sleep was prized not just for functional ends but also as a sign of piety, morality and faithfulness for a wide spectrum of Christians.

This book has uncovered a transformative phase of change in sleep's rich history and it has furnished invaluable new information about the single most time-consuming feature of early modern life. Sleep's daily management reveals the deep-seated anxieties, preoccupations and beliefs of early modern people as they approached the vulnerable hours of sleep and tried to set their earthly and spiritual affairs in order. The fusion of embodied practice and culture was nowhere more evident than in the careful regulation of slumber and in the make-up and use of sleeping chambers. Sleeping practices uncover distinct preferences for stable, familiar and secure sleeping environments that invited ease and relaxation to mind and body. Indeed, this book has exposed a distinct understanding of 'sleep comfort' that combined tactile sensations and mental relief. Enclosing sleeping bodies in clean, familiar and personalised materials and surrounding the bedstead with meaningful objects offered a way to ease anxieties at bedtime. Keeping a loved one's picture close by, or a bible at the bedside, were understood as material and spiritual safeguards that offered reassurance at this critical time of night. The embodied sensations associated with sleep's onset merged with the deep-seated cultural anxieties that pervaded bedtime to shape desires for comfortable sleeping environments of a very specific kind. The objects and textiles that enclosed sleepers at night were undoubtedly considered decencies and necessities, but above all else they were understood as safeguards of life and limb.

Sleep: Past, Present and Future

Sleep's knowledge economy in the modern world is firmly focused on the biological sciences, neurosciences and pharmaceutical industries as the key agents of sleep management. This study offers a radically different context in which to contrast past and present sleeping practices and it suggests that the presumed relationship between biology, culture and environment should be recalibrated. Studying the interactions of embodiment and culture in specific historical contexts help to establish which characteristics of sleep are shared across time and space and which are not. Early modern people expressed strong and familiar desires for protection, enclosure and comfort during sleep – of both physical and psychological kinds. Similar wishes have been echoed in different periods and places, which suggest that they are heavily shaped by sleep's unique physical effects. Descending into a non-conscious state of body and mind triggers anxieties of potential dangers that in turn prompt precautionary measures. This sensation also renders people acutely sensitive to the sleeping environments upon which they rely for protection in the hope that they will wake safely the next morning. It is hardly surprising that so many communities have sought to sleep, where possible, in stable and familiar settings to which their bodies and senses have become attuned. The routines and reflections of early modern men and women offer a particularly rich case study of the importance of sleep's material habitats, and of the emotional states they triggered, which they went to extraordinary lengths to control. The modern sleep industry, encouraged by public health authorities and scientific research, has transformed sleep's material technologies by inventing orthopaedic pillows and mattresses, new bedding materials and devices to regulate air quality, body temperature and light infiltration. Much less attention has been paid, however, to the personal and cultural associations of these commodities that shape incentives for their purchase and daily use. Further comparative study of historical sleeping practices, and their associated emotions, should enrich the work of sleep researchers by prioritising sleep's environmental cues in tandem with its internal biological triggers and the medicines that help to shape sleeping and waking cycles.

The importance of sleep's material world has also revealed the widespread understanding of sleep as a three-stage process. People paid equal attention to the period of sleep's onset, to the hours of slumber, and to those moments that immediately follow waking. The conscious thoughts and practices that bookended the hours of sleep recognised these distinct phases and catered for the sensations, thoughts and emotions to which they were linked. These habits highlight the critical degree of agency that early modern people exerted over their sleeping and waking habits. The people studied here were intimately engaged with their nocturnal experiences, which they managed locally and with great diligence. The methods they used to optimise sleep quality, and to prevent and prepare for periods of sleep loss, may offer productive points of comparison for modern sleep researchers and medical practitioners. They might also promote a wider range of responses to sleep loss beyond professional medical intervention and commercialised therapies to encourage proactive care of sleep within the home and to promote a long-term preventative culture of sleep management. Early modern sleeping practices lend support to recent work that encourages individual sleep management through the regulation of lifestyle choice, through the design, layout and content of sleeping environments and through the implementation of restful bedtime routines. These measures appear to have been crucial in securing a peaceful state of mind at night in different periods and places.[3]

The final lesson to be drawn from this study is the correlation between sleep's fluctuating cultural value and the degree of time and care invested in its practice. I have argued here that the heightened cultural value of sleep between c. 1660 and c. 1800 directly influenced its daily practice. Early modern people placed sleep management at the heart of household life, not at its margins, because they believed in its fundamental importance to their physical, mental, emotional and spiritual well-being. The early phase of sleep's medicalisation traced here played a central role in moulding these perceptions and practices. The location of sleep's medicalisation in the late nineteenth and twentieth centuries should thus be more carefully nuanced, as should any assumption of a progressive improvement in medical knowledge about sleep's causes and practice. The nineteenth and twentieth centuries certainly witnessed the widespread institutionalisation of sleep by public health authorities but it did not see the first wave of its medicalisation. It may be more productive to recognise distinct phases of sleep's medicalisation and investigate their independent paths of development.[4] It may also turn out that early modern English households were better equipped to procure healthy sleep precisely because they were more acutely attuned to its benefits and to the dangers of its loss. The cultural value of sleep assured it a place at the core of daily life – something that has arguably been sidelined in more recent times. Early modern men and women had countless ways of prompting relaxation as bedtime approached, from sewing to reading, from amicable conversation to heartfelt prayer. These habits helped to ease their bodies and minds into a state of relaxation in which sleep could more easily take hold of them. Comparable techniques for promoting relaxation at bedtime, and for establishing safe environments for sleep, are key to many modern sleep therapies and to commercial advertisements for beds, quilts, pillows and other sleep-related technologies.[5] The distinctive sleep culture traced here may thus be of particular interest to contemporary medical practitioners and especially to those seeking to halt the denigration of sleep's value in contemporary Western cultures. Jonathan Crary, Colin Espie, Russell Foster, Jim Horne, Arianna Huffington, Steven Lockley and Charles Morin are just some of the voices calling for a revaluation of sleep's importance in the modern world, for better education and training about sleep for medical practitioners, medical students and the wider public, and for heightened appreciation of the role that healthy sleep plays in preventing and managing a range of physical and mental health problems.[6] Sleep's history is clearly ripe for deeper exploration and its comparative study can further test the balance between biological, cultural and environmental factors in shaping slumberous practices in different periods and places. Analysing sleep's cultural, chronological and geographical contexts will further complicate the apparently straightforward division between pre- and post-industrial sleeping habits that has been a prominent feature of recent sleep studies. Further historical studies should also question the technology-driven explanations of sleeping patterns that have held sway in recent years and that underestimate the active agency that people play in shaping their own approaches to sleep.[7]

From the viewpoint of early modern history much more remains to be discovered about the sleeping practices of the poorer sorts since they appear only sporadically in this study and usually through the eyes and pens of others. A broader range of sleeping environments would certainly offer important points of comparison to the households examined here. Parallel research into sleep's management within prisons, hospitals and workhouses may also tell a different story to developments within household life. The limited geographical scope of this book would benefit from in-depth regional studies, from a comparative British study and indeed from wider comparisons with European and global sleep cultures, which may have shared important overlaps in medical understandings of sleep and its everyday practice. Further enquiries might also take a cue from sociologists by contrasting approaches to sleep according to life-cycle stages – from childhood to pregnancy and from parenthood into later life. Case studies of early modern insomniacs also offer a fascinating point of entry into the richness of sleep culture. The cultural history of insomnia has been traced in the *longue durée*, and in studies of early modern melancholy, but it deserves independent focus alongside other non-conscious sleep states like sleepwalking. However future studies proceed, I hope that they will be enriched by the actions of early modern men and women who were far from dormant participants in their own sleeping lives. They played a formative role in forging their sleep quality and in interpreting its meanings in relation to their own lives, bodies and preoccupations. The distinctive cultural environment in which they lived, and indeed slept, was essential in moulding these perceptions and practices.

APPENDIX

Table 1: Location of households examined in the Prerogative Court of Canterbury inventory sample

Location	Number of testators
Bedfordshire	2
Berkshire	2
Buckinghamshire	1
Cambridgeshire	4
Cheshire	1
City of London	35
Cornwall	1
Coventry	2
Derbyshire	1
Devon	1
Dorset	1
Essex	5
Glamorgan	1
Gloucestershire	2
Herefordshire	4
Hertfordshire	3
Huntingdon	1
Kent	7
Leicestershire & Rutland	2

Lincolnshire	2
Middlesex	2
Norfolk	1
Oxfordshire	6
Somerset	4
Suffolk	1
Surrey	13
Sussex	3
Warwickshire	1
Wiltshire	1
Worcestershire	2
Location unrecorded	3
Total	**115**

Table 2: Total number of rooms recorded per household in the Prerogative Court of Canterbury inventories

Number of rooms	Number of households	% households
Not specified	27	23
1–3	13	12
4–6	20	17
7–9	23	20
10–14	16	14
15 or more	16	14
Total	**115**	**100**

ENDNOTES

Introduction

1. *Spectator*, ed. Donald F. Bond, vol. 2 (Oxford: Clarendon Press, 1965), iv, 293.
2. Ibid., 224–7. William Hill, *A full account of the life and visions of Nicholas Hart* (London, 1711). William Hill, *The true and wonderful history of Nicholas Hart: or, a faithful account of the sleepy-man's visions* (London, 1711). Anon., *Account of the apprehending and taking six French prophets, near Hog-lane in Soho, who pretended to prophecy that the world should be at an end* (London, 1707). Anon., *An Account of the trial, examination & conviction of the pretended French prophets* (London, 1707).
3. On the location of sleep's medicalisation, commercialisation and the birth of sleep research in the twentieth century see Lodewijk Brunt and Brigitte Steger (eds), *Worlds of Sleep* (Berlin: Frank & Timme, 2008), 10–11.
4. During sleep the brain is believed to progress through four or five stages of sleep that vary in depth, beginning with deeper paradoxical sleep and progressing towards lighter REM phases. These variations ensure that the sleeper's awareness of environmental stimuli oscillates throughout the sleep cycle. Sue Wilson and David Nutt, *Sleep Disorders* (Oxford: Oxford University Press, 2008), 5.
5. Jim Horne argues that human evolution has transformed sleep's principal biological purpose from an energy conserver to a recovery mechanism for the complex human brain. Jim Horne, *Sleepfaring: A Journey Through the Science of Sleep* (Oxford: Oxford University Press, 2006), 18.
6. Andrew Green and Alex Westcombe (eds), *Sleep: Multi-Professional Perspectives* (London and Philadelphia: Jessica Kingsley Publishers, 2012), 19.
7. On the tripartite process of sleep see Susan Venn and Sara Arber, 'Conflicting Sleep Demands: Parents and Young People in UK Households', in *Worlds of Sleep*, ed. Brunt and Steger, 126.
8. For an overview see Green and Westcombe (eds), *Sleep: Multi-Professional Perspectives*, 9–17. Till Roenneberg's model of natural time and social time acknowledges a potential conflict between natural sleep preferences and the artificial demands of social life. Till Roenneberg, *Internal Time: Chronotypes, Social Jet Lag, and Why You're So Tired* (Cambridge, MA: Harvard University Press, 2012).
9. Wilson and Nutt, *Sleep Disorders*, 3.
10. Domien G.M. Beersma, 'Models of Human Sleep Regulation', *Sleep Medicine Reviews* 2 (1998), 31–43. Wilson and Nutt, *Sleep Disorders*, 3–4. A.A. Borbély, 'A Two-process Model of Sleep Regulation', *Human Neurobiology* 1 (1982), 195–204. Louise M. Paterson, David J. Nutt and Sue J. Wilson, 'Sleep and its Disorders in Translational Medicine', *Journal of Psychopharmacology* 25 (2011), 1226–8.

11. Research on the operation of the circadian process in Mediterranean countries takes into account the afternoon siesta in a biphasic sleep pattern. See Wilson and Nutt, *Sleep Disorders*, 4. For definitions of 'monophasic', 'biphasic' and 'polyphasic' sleep cycles see Brigitte Steger, 'Cultures of Sleep', in *Sleep*, ed. Green and Westcombe, 74.

12. Louise M. Paterson, 'The Science of Sleep: What is it, What Makes it Happen and Why Do We Do It?', in *Sleep*, ed. Green and Westcombe, 28–9. C.B. Saper, T.E. Scammell and L. Lu, 'Hypothalamic regulation of sleep and circadian rhythms', *Nature* 437 (2005), 1257–63.

13. For a definition of 'sleep-hopeful bodies' see Paul Ashmore, 'Bedtime Material: Recording Becoming Asleep', *Area* 43 (2010), 211–17.

14. On perception as a holistic experience in phenomenological theory and in Renaissance culture see Maurice Merleau-Ponty, *Phenomenology of Perception* (London: Routledge, 2013), 219, and Bruce R. Smith, *The Key of Green: Passion and Perception in Renaissance Culture* (Chicago: University of Chicago Press, 2008), 3–8.

15. On the importance of bedtime routines see B. Schwartz, 'Notes on the Sociology of Sleep', in *People in Places: The Sociology of the Familiar*, ed. A. Birenbaum and E.E. Sangrin (London: Nelson, 1973). On the interactive sensations and perceptions that emerge at bedtime see Eyal Ben-Ari, ' "It's Bedtime" in the World's Urban Middle Classes: Children, Families and Sleep', in *Worlds of Sleep*, ed. Brunt and Steger, 180.

16. Horne, *Sleepfaring*, 144, 156.

17. Ben-Ari, *Worlds of Sleep*, 180. On sleep's vulnerability see Horne, *Sleepfaring*, 6, 142.

18. Gabriele Klug has outlined a similar combination of physical and spiritual dangers relating to sleep that circulated in medieval German literature. Gabriele Klug, 'Dangerous Doze: Sleep and Vulnerability in Medieval German Literature', in *Worlds of Sleep*, ed. Brunt and Steger, 31–52.

19. On the relative expansion of household comfort in early modern culture see Keith Wrightson, *Earthly Necessities: Economic Lives in Early Modern Britain* (London: Penguin, 2002), 298.

20. On the psychological dimensions of material comfort see Giorgio Riello, 'Fabricating the Domestic: The Material Culture of Textiles and the Social life of the Home in Early Modern Europe', in *The Force of Fashion in Politics and Society: Global Perspectives from Early Modern to Contemporary Times*, ed. Beverly Lemire (Ashgate: Farnham, 2010), 60. John Styles, 'Picturing Domesticity: The Cottage Genre in Late Eighteenth-Century Britain', in *Imagined Interiors: Representing the Domestic Interior since the Renaissance*, ed. Jeremy Aynsley and Charlotte Grant, with assistance from Harriet McKay (London: V&A Publications, 2006), 154. Patrick Griffin, 'The Pursuit of Comfort: The Modern and the Material in the Early Modern British Atlantic World' (Review of *The Invention of Comfort: Sensibilities and Design in Early Modern Britain and Early America* by John E. Crowley), *Reviews in American History* 30 (2002), 365–72.

21. John E. Crowley, 'The Sensibility of Comfort', *American Historical Review* 104 (1999). 749–82.

22. A. Roger Ekirch, 'Sleep We Have Lost: Pre-Industrial Slumber in the British Isles', *American Historical Review* 106 (2001), 343–86. A. Roger Ekirch, *At Day's Close: Night in Times Past* (New York: W.W. Norton & Company Ltd, 2005).

23. A. Roger Ekirch, 'The Modernization of Western Sleep: Or, Does Insomnia Have A History?', *Past and Present* 226 (2015), 170.

24. Gabriele Klug, *'Wol ûf, wir sullen slâfen gan!' Der Schlaf als Alltagserfahrung in der deutsch-sprachigen Dichtung des Hochmittelalters* (Frankfurt: Peter Lang, 2007).

25. Craig Koslofsky, *Evening's Empire: A History of the Night in Early Modern Europe* (Cambridge: Cambridge University Press, 2011).

26. Human geographers have demonstrated the persistent importance of seasonality, light and natural ecology in regulating sleep in different periods and places. See Peter Kraftl and John Horton, 'Spaces of Every-Night Life: For Geographies of Sleep, Sleeping and Sleepiness', *Progress in Human Geography* 32 (2008), 509–24. Barbara Adam, *Timescapes of Modernity: The Environment and Invisible Hazards* (London: Routledge, 1998). P. Macnaghten and

J. Urry (eds), *Bodies of Nature* (London: Sage, 2001). E.R. Power, 'Domestic Temporalities: Nature Times in the House-as-Home', *Geogorum* 40 (2009), 1024–32.

27. Simon Williams, *Sleep and Society: Sociological Ventures into the (Un)known* (London: Routledge, 2005). J. Hislop and S. Arber, 'Understanding Women's Sleep Management: Beyond Medicalization–Healthicization?', *Sociology of Health and Illness* 25 (2003), 815–37. P. Stearns, R. Perrin, and L. Giarnella, 'Children's Sleep: Sketching Historical Change', *Journal of Social History* 30 (1996), 345–66. Steger, 'Cultures of Sleep', 68–85. Caroline H.D. Jones and Helen L. Ball, 'Medical Anthropology and Children's Sleep: The Mismatch Between Western Lifestyles and Sleep Physiology', in *Sleep*, ed. Green and Westcombe, 86–103. Andrew Green, 'A Question of Balance: The Relationship Between Daily Occupation and Sleep', in *Sleep*, ed. Green and Westcombe, 121–48. Stephen Jacobs, 'Ambivalent Attitudes Towards Sleep in World Religions', in *Sleep*, ed. Green and Westcombe, 247–67.

28. On 'dormatology' see Brunt and Steger, *Worlds of Sleep*, 17.

29. Garrett A. Sullivan Jr, 'Romance, Sleep and the Passions in Sir Philip Sidney's "The Old Arcadia"', *ELH* 74 (2007), 735–57. Garrett A. Sullivan Jr, *Sleep, Romance and Human Embodiment: Vitality from Spenser to Milton* (Cambridge: Cambridge University Press, 2012). William MacLehose, 'Fear, Fantasy and Sleep in Medieval Medicine', in *Emotions and Health, 1200–1700*, ed. Elena Carrera (Leiden: Brill, 2013), 67–94. William MacLehose, 'Sleepwalking, Violence and Desire in the Middle Ages', *Culture, Medicine and Psychiatry* 37 (2013), 601–24.

30. Anna Whitelock, *Elizabeth's Bedfellows, An Intimate History of the Queen's Court* (London: Bloomsbury, 2013).

31. The psychological significance of affective objects at the bedside has been considered in cross-cultural contexts in Suimin Bunka Kenkūjo (eds), *Netoko-jutsu* (The Technique of the Sleeping Place) (Tokyo: Popura-sha, 2005) and Shuji Yoshida, *Suimin bunka-ron* (Essays on Sleep Culture) (Tokyo: Heibonsha, 2001). Leora Auslander has highlighted the special properties of objects used in familiar, embodied routines that were conceived as 'expressions of the psyche, or extensions of the body', even if they were not explicitly verbalised. Leora Auslander, 'Beyond Words', *American Historical Review* 110 (2005), 1015–16.

32. On the importance of kitchen physic see Elaine Leong and Sara Pennell, 'Recipe Collections and the Currency of Medical Knowledge in the Early Modern "Medical Marketplace"', in *Medicine and the Market in England and Its Colonies, c. 1450–c. 1650*, ed. Mark S.R. Jenner and Patrick Wallis (Basingstoke: Palgrave Macmillan, 2007). Sandra Cavallo and Tessa Storey, *Healthy Living in Late Renaissance Italy* (Oxford: Oxford University Press, 2013), 113–44.

33. On medical thought about sleep before 1660 see Pedro Gil Sotres, 'The Regimens of Health', in *Western Medical Thought from Antiquity to the Middle Ages*, ed. M.D. Grmek (Cambridge, MA: Harvard University Press, 1998), 291–318. Karl H. Dannenfeldt, 'Sleep: Theory and Practice in the Late Renaissance', *Journal of the History of Medicine* 41 (1986), 415–41.

34. Alec Ryrie, 'Sleeping, Waking and Dreaming in Protestant Piety', in *Private and Domestic Devotion in Early Modern Britain*, ed. Jessica Martin and Alec Ryrie (Farnham: Ashgate, 2012), 73–92. Erin Sullivan, ' "The Watchful Spirit": Religious Anxieties toward Sleep in the Notebooks of Nehemiah Wallington', *Cultural History* 1 (2012), 14–35.

35. Phyllis Mack, *Heart Religion in the British Enlightenment* (Oxford: Oxford University Press, 2008), 174–244.

36. Carole Levin, *Dreaming the English Renaissance: Politics and Desire in Court and Culture* (New York: Palgrave Macmillan, 2008). Lucia Dacome, ' "To What Purpose Does It Think?": Dreams, Sick Bodies, and Confused Minds in the Age of Reason', *History of Psychiatry* 15 (2004), 395–416. Jonathan Andrews and Andrew Scull, *Undertaker of the Mind: John Monro and Mad-Doctoring in Eighteenth-Century England* (Berkeley and Los Angeles: University of California Press, 2001). Daniel Pick and Lyndal Roper (eds), *Dreams and History: The Interpretation of Dreams from Ancient Greece to Modern Psychoanalysis* (London and New York: Routledge, 2004). Ann Marie Plane and Leslie

Tuttle (eds), *Dreams, Dreamers, and Visions: The Early Modern Atlantic World* (Philadelphia: University of Pennsylvania Press, 2013). Alan Richardson, *British Romanticism and the Science of the Mind* (Cambridge: Cambridge University Press, 2001). Alan Richardson, *The Neural Sublime: Cognitive Theories and Romantic Texts* (Baltimore: Johns Hopkins University Press, 2010). Janine Rivière, 'Demons of Desire or Symptoms of Disease? Medical Theories and Popular Experiences of the "Nightmare" in Premodern England', in *Dreams, Dreamers and Visions*, ed. Plane and Tuttle, 49–71.

37. John Styles, 'Lodging at the Old Bailey: Lodgings and their Furnishing in Eighteenth-Century London', in *Gender, Taste and Material Culture in Britain and North America, 1700–1830*, ed. John Styles and Amanda Vickery (New Haven and London: Yale University Press, 2006), 61–80. Lena Cowan Orlin, 'Fictions of the Early Modern Probate Inventory', in *The Culture of Capital: Properties, Cities and Knowledge in Early Modern England*, ed. H.S. Turner (London: Routledge, 2002), 51–83.

38. Riello, 'Fabricating the Domestic', 47, 58.

39. On the prominence of sleep discussions within domestic life see Brigitte Steger and Lodewijk Brunt, 'Introduction: Into the Night and the World of Sleep', in *Night-time and Sleep in Asia and the West*, ed. Brigitte Steger and Lodewijk Brunt (London and New York: RoutledgeCurzon, 2003), 1–23.

40. On the meanings of early modern textiles see Riello, 'Fabricating the Domestic', 44–8, 56–8. On early modern textiles and bodily sensation see Beverly Lemire, 'Draping the Body and Dressing the Home: The Material Culture of Textiles and Clothes in the Atlantic World, c. 1500–1800', in *History and Material Culture: A Student's Guide to Approaching Alternative Sources*, ed. Karen Harvey (Abingdon: Routledge, 2009), 85–91. Margaret Ponsonby, *Stories from Home: English Domestic Interiors 1750–1850* (Aldershot and Burlington: Ashgate, 2007). Clive Edwards, *Turning Houses into Homes: A History of the Retailing and Consumption of Domestic Furnishings* (Aldershot: Ashgate, 2005).

Chapter 1: Sleep, Medicine and the Body

1. Thomas Cogan, *The haven of health chiefly gathered for the comfort of students* (London, 1636), 269.

2. David Raeburn (trans.), *Ovid, Metamorphoses* (London: Penguin Books, 2004), 38–41, 82–8, 445–58.

3. Ulinka Rublack, 'Fluxes: the Early Modern Body and the Emotions', *History Workshop Journal* 53 (2002), 1–2.

4. On the metaphorical use of sleep as a mode of transport between earthly and spiritual realms in William Shakespeare's *The Tempest* see William H. Sherman, 'Shakespearean Somniloquy: Sleep and Transformation in *The Tempest*', in *Renaissance Transformations: The Making of English Writing (1500–1950)*, ed. Margaret Healy and Thomas Healy (Edinburgh: Edinburgh University Press, 2009), 182. The power of metamorphic narratives within early modern culture is elegantly laid out in Marina Warner, *Fantastic Metamorphoses, Other Worlds: Ways of Telling the Self* (Oxford: Oxford University Press, 2002), 1–28.

5. Hannah Newton has described the personification of Nature as a 'benevolent female who inhabited the body' and acted to restore health. Hannah Newton, ' "Nature Concocts & Expels": The Agents and Processes of Recovery from Disease in Early Modern England', *Social History of Medicine* 28 (2015), 466.

6. On the relationship between the elements and planets see Marsilio Ficino, *Three Books on Life: A Critical Edition and Translation with Introduction and Notes by Carol V. Kaske and John R. Clark* (Tempe, Arizona: Arizona Center for Medieval and Renaissance Studies, in conjunction with the Renaissance Society of America, 2002), 4, 31–3.

7. Roy Porter, 'Introduction', in *The Popularization of Medicine 1650–1850*, ed. Roy Porter (London and New York: Routledge, 1992). Andrew Wear, 'The Popularization of Medicine in Early Modern England', in *The Popularization of Medicine*, ed. Porter, 17–36. Mary Fissell, 'Popular Medical Writing', in *The Oxford History of Popular Print Culture*, vol. 1, ed. Joad Raymond (Oxford: Oxford University Press, 2011), 418–31.

8. On medieval physiological explanations of sleep see MacLehose, 'Sleepwalking, Violence and Desire', 604–5.

9. Sir Thomas Elyot, *The Castel of Helthe gathered and made by Syr Thomas Elyot knyghte, out of the chiefe authors of physyke, wherby euery manne may knowe the state of his owne body, the preseruatio[n] of helthe, and how to instructe welle his physytion in syckenes that he be not deceyued* (London, 1539), 47.

10. *The Best and Easiest method of preserving uninterrupted health to extreme old age: established upon the justest laws of the animal oeconomy, and confirmed by the suffrages of the most celebrated practitioners among the ancients and moderns* (London, 1752), 15–16.

11. Elyot, *Castel of Helthe*, 47–8.

12. Mary Fissell estimates that Elyot's guide ran to at least seventeen editions. Mary Fissell, 'Popular Medical Writing', in *The Oxford History of Popular Print Culture*, vol. 1, ed. Joad Raymond, 419.

13. Andrew Boorde, *A Compendyous Regyment or a Dyetary of Healthe made in Mountpyllyer* (London, 1547), fol. Biv.

14. William Bullein, *Bulleins Bulwarke of Defence Againste All Sicknes, Sornes, and Woundes that dooe daily assaulte mankinde* (London, 1562), fol. 17. William Bullein, *The Government of Health* (London, 1558), 59–63.

15. For a comprehensive survey see Dannenfeldt, 'Sleep'.

16. Nicholas Culpeper, *Pharmacopoeia Londinensis: or the London Dispensatory* (London, 1653), 59. Nicholas Culpeper, *A New Method of Physick* (London, 1654), 415.

17. John Pechey, *A General Treatise of the Diseases of Infants and Children* (London, 1697), 69–70. *The Compleat Servant-Maid: or, the Young Maiden's and Family's Daily Companion* (London, 1729), 7–8. John Pechey, *The Compleat Midwife's Practice enlarged in the most weighty and high concernments of the birth of man containing a perfect directory of rules for midwives and nurses* (London, 1698), 247.

18. Harold J. Cook, 'Pechey, John (*bap.* 1654, *d.* 1718)', in *Oxford Dictionary of National Biography*, Oxford University Press, 2004, accessed 4 September 2015, http://www.oxforddnb.com/view/article/21737.

19. John Archer, *Every Man his own Doctor* (London, 1671), A2–3, 99–100. The relationship between sleep and the bowels is also prominent in Thomas Sherley's translation of Theodor Turquet de Mayerne's *Medicinal Councels, or Advices* (London, 1677), 128; John Pechey, *Collection of Chronical Diseases* (London, 1692), 5.

20. John Allen, *Dr Allen's Synopsis Medicinae*, vol. 2 (London, 1730), 136. For similar conclusions see Thomas Stanley, *The History of Philosophy: containing the lives, opinions, actions and discourses of the philosophers of every sect* (London, 1750), 258, 436, 592.

21. Peter Lowe, *The Whole Course of Chirurgerie* (London, 1597), F1–2.

22. Cogan, *The haven of health*, 274.

23. Boorde, *Compendyous Regyment*, Cii. John Trusler, *An Easy Way to Prolong Life, by a little attention to what we eat and drink* (London, 1775), 10.

24. Peter Lowe, *The Whole Course of Chirurgerie* (London, 1597), F2. Bullein, *Government of Health*, 33. Cogan, *The haven of health*, 274.

25. 'English Medical Receipt Book', British Library Western MS 809 (*c.* 1635), fol. 192v.

26. Iona Opie and Moira Tatem (eds), *A Dictionary of Superstitions*, (Oxford: Oxford University Press, 1989), 16. John Gaule, *Pus-mantia the mag-astro-mancer, or, The magicall-astrologicall-diviner posed and puzzled* (London, 1652), 181.

27. Cogan, *The haven of health*, 274. Genesis 3:1–5.

28. Boorde, *Compendyous Regyment*, ix.

29. Anon., *Aristotle's Secret of Secrets contracted; being the sum of his Advice to Alexander the Great, about the preservation of health and government* (London, 1702), 56. Ralph Josselin, *The Diary of Ralph Josselin 1616–1683*, ed. Alan Macfarlane (London: published for the British Academy by Oxford University Press, 1976), 170. Trusler, *An Easy Way to Prolong Life*, 14–15.

30. Nicolas Andry de Bois-Regard, *Orthopaedia: or, the art of correcting and preventing deformities in children*, vol. 1 (London, 1743), 86–7; this was the first English translation of Bois-Regard's work.

31. *The Art of Nursing: or, the method of bringing up young children according to the rules of physick* (London, 1733), 46.
32. John Ray, *A Collection of English Proverbs digested into a convenient method for the speedy finding any one upon occasion* (Cambridge, 1678), 351.
33. Another important exception to this rule was women who had recently given birth. They were advised to sleep on their backs until their womb and stomach had returned to their normal size and strength. John Pechey, *A general treatise of the diseases of maids, bigbellied women, child-bed women, and widows* (London, 1696), 95–107.
34. Cogan, *The haven of health*, 274.
35. Dannenfeldt, 'Sleep', 420.
36. Bullein, *Bulwarke*, verso 22.
37. Cited in John Allen, *Dr Allen's Synopsis Medicinae*, vol. 1 (London, 1730), 202. Thomas Willis, *Two discourses concerning the soul of brutes which is that of the vital and sensitive of man* (London, 1683), 142–4.
38. G. Borsieri de Kanifeld, *The Institutions of the Practice of Medicine; delivered in a course of lectures, by John Baptist Burserius, De Kanifeld. Translated from the Latin by William Cullen Brown*, vol. 4 (Edinburgh, 1800–1803), 106.
39. John Milton, *Paradise Lost* (4.790–884), ed. John Leonard (London: Penguin, 2000), 94–6.
40. *Paradise Lost* proved particularly influential amongst Romantic artists and poets. See for example William Blake, *The Marriage of Heaven and Hell* (London, 1790) and *Milton's Paradise Lost. A new edition. Adorned with plates*, engraved chiefly by F. Bartolozzi from designs by W. Hamilton and H. Fuseli (London, 1802). An engraving by Matthew Urlwin Sears from *c.* 1825 is also based on this scene and entitled 'Millions of spiritual creatures walk the earth'. Its title was taken verbatim from Book 4 of *Paradise Lost*. These words immediately preceded the watchful guard of the angel Gabriel who was charged with protecting the slumbering Adam and Eve from Satan's approach. The heavenly angels in the skies and the swirling diabolical figures and serpent depicted below them were locked in battle to seize control of the sleeping woman's body and soul. The engraving acknowledged the acute vulnerability of sleepers to supernatural powers and their utter dependence on God's favour to preserve them from harm. Matthew Urlwin Sears, 'Millions of spiritual creatures walk the earth: unseen both when we wake and when we sleep', London, *c.* 1825, Lewis Walpole Library, Yale University.
41. *The true relation of two wonderfull sleepers* (London, 1646).
42. Jonathan Bate, *Shakespeare and Ovid* (Oxford: Clarendon Press, 1993), 1–47.
43. William Shakespeare, *Henry IV, Part II*, 3.1.7–16.
44. William Shakespeare, *Richard III*, 1.3.220–30.
45. William Shakespeare, *Macbeth*, 5.1.49–53.
46. On the meanings of disturbed sleep and dream states in Renaissance drama see Sherman, 'Shakespearean Somniloquy', 177–91. Sullivan, *Sleep, Romance and Human Embodiment*.
47. Archer, *Every Man* (London, 1671), 100.
48. Cavallo and Storey, *Healthy Living*, 113–14.
49. Trusler, *An Easy Way to Prolong Life*, 8.
50. Elizabeth Lane Furdell, *Publishing and Medicine in Early Modern England* (Rochester, NY: University of Rochester Press, 2002), 56.
51. Thomas Willis, *Dr. Willis's practice of physick* (London, 1684), epistle dedicatory.
52. Thomas Willis, *The Anatomy of the Brain and Nerves; including facsimile reprint of the translation by Samuel Pordage, from the remaining medical works of Thomas Willis*, ed. William Feindel, vol. 1 (Montreal: University of McGill Press, 1965), i, xi.
53. On debates about the movement of the animal spirits see George S. Rousseau, *Nervous Acts: Essays on Literature, Culture and Sensibility* (Basingstoke: Palgrave Macmillan, 2004) 11–13.
54. MacLehose 'Fear, Fantasy and Sleep', 67–94.
55. Willis, *Dr. Willis's practice of physick*, 75.

56. Herman Boerhaave, *Boerhaave's Institutions in Physick*, trans. J. Browne (London, 1715), M2.
57. William Cullen, *Institutions of Medicine, Part I. Physiology. For the use of the Students in the University of Edinburgh* (Edinburgh, 1785), 23.
58. W.F. Bynum, 'Cullen and the Nervous System', in *William Cullen and the Eighteenth Century Medical World*, ed. A. Doig, J.P.S. Ferguson, I.A. Milne and R. Passmore (Edinburgh: Edinburgh University Press, 1993), 152–3.
59. Cullen, *Institutions*, 96–102, 106–7.
60. William Cullen, *Synopsis Nosologiae Methodicae* (Edinburgh, 1769), 238.
61. Borsieri de Kanifeld, *Institutions*, iv, 69–70.
62. Cullen, *Synopsis Nosologiae Methodicae*.
63. On Cheyne's medical practice at Bath see Anita Guerrini, *Obesity and Depression in the Enlightenment: The Life and Times of George Cheyne* (Norman: University of Oklahoma Press, 2000), 89–117.
64. On Cheyne's education in Newtonian principles see Guerrini, *Obesity and Depression*, 22–45.
65. George Cheyne, *An Essay of Health and Long Life* (London, 1724), 78.
66. George Cheyne, *The English Malady: or, a treatise of nervous diseases of all kinds* (London, 1733), 221, 232.
67. Hugh Smythson, *The Compleat Family Physician; or, Universal Medical Repository* (London, 1781), 105, 301.

Chapter 2: Healthy Sleep and the Household

1. Gervase Markham, *The Dumbe Knight, A Historicall Comedy* (London, 1608), D–D2. Gervase Markham, *Countrey Contentments, or The English Huswife* (London, 1623).
2. Studies of early modern recipe collections reveal the depth and range of preventative healthcare practices carried out at home. Elaine Leong, 'Making Medicines in the Early Modern Household', *Bulletin of the History of Medicine* 82 (2008), 145–6. For recipes prepared in poorer households see Alun Withey, *Physick and the Family: Health, Medicine and Care in Wales, 1600–1750* (Manchester: Manchester University Press, 2011), 99–120.
3. Anthropologists have interpreted strict rules of cleanliness as mechanisms of control that reveal deep-seated cultural and moral values. Mary Douglas, *Purity and Danger: An Analysis of Concepts of Pollution and Taboo* (London: Routledge, 2003).
4. James Makittrick Adair, *Essays on fashionable diseases* (London, 1790), 57–8.
5. William Alexander, *Plain and easy directions for the use of Harrogate waters: adapted to the meanest capacity; and principally intended for the use of all who attend there* (Edinburgh, 1773), 53–4.
6. John Sinclair, *The Code of Health and Longevity or, A General View of the Rules and Principles Calculated for the Preservation of Health, and the Attainment of Long Life* (London, 1818), 317.
7. James C. Riley, *The Eighteenth-Century Campaign to Avoid Disease* (New York: St. Martin's Press, 1987). Mary Lindemann, *Medicine and Society in Early Modern Europe* (Cambridge: Cambridge University Press, 1990), 155–92.
8. Makittrick Adair, *Essays on fashionable diseases*, 56.
9. Adair dedicated an entire chapter to the dangers of 'noxious air', which he tried to quantify. He calculated that one person 'destroys the vivifying principle of a gallon of air in a minute', which reinforced the need for sound ventilation. Makittrick Adair, *Essays on fashionable diseases*, 29.
10. *London Magazine, or, Gentleman's Monthly Intelligencer*, vol. 23 (1754), 126–7. Ventilators were also recommended for use in the lying-in chambers of pregnant women, which were likely to be overheated by the presence of female attendants. Charles White, *A Treatise on the Management of Pregnant and Lying-in Women, and the means of curing, but more especially of preventing the principal disorders to which they are liable* (London, 1772), 169–70.

11. Horace Walpole, *Horace Walpole's Correspondence with Sir Horace Mann*, vol. 22 of *The Yale Edition of Horace Walpole's Correspondence*, ed. W.S. Lewis, Warren Hunting Smith and George L. Lam (London and New Haven: Oxford University Press and Yale University Press, 1960), 203.

12. Francis de Valangin, *A treatise on diet, or the management of human life; by physicians called the six non-naturals* (London, 1768), 285.

13. Cavallo and Storey, *Healthy Living*, 134–6.

14. Thomas Tryon, *A treatise of cleanness in meats and drinks of the preparation of food, the excellency of good airs and the benefits of clean sweet beds also of the generation of bugs and their cure* (London, 1682), 7.

15. Trusler, *An Easy Way to Prolong Life*, 16.

16. 'Francis Elcocke, List of diseases arranged astrologically', MS Sloane 2287, British Library, fol. 21. 'Culinary Receipts', MS Sloane MS 703, British Library, fols 8, 99.

17. *The Art of Nursing*, 46–7. *The workwoman's guide, containing instructions . . . in cutting out and completing those articles of wearing apparel, &c. which are usually made at home* (London: Simpkin, Marshall, & Co., 1838), 42.

18. *The Art of Nursing*, 48. John Locke, *Some thoughts concerning education* (London, 1693), 227.

19. Makittrick Adair, *Essays on fashionable diseases*, 29–53.

20. Robert Boyle, *Essays of the strange subtilty great efficacy determinate nature of effluviums* (London, 1673), 39–40.

21. John Partridge, *The treasurie of commodious conceits, and hidden secrets Commonlie called The good huswiues closet of prouision, for the health of her houshold* (London, 1591), 18.

22. John Wesley, *The Duty and Advantage of Early Rising* (London, 1783), 6–7.

23. Thomas Tryon, *Wisdom's dictates, or, Aphorisms & rules, physical, moral, and divine, for preserving the health of the body, and the peace of the mind* (London, 1693), 106. Emily Cockayne, *Hubbub: Filth, Noise & Stench in England 1600–1770* (New Haven and London: Yale University Press, 2007), 59.

24. Locke, *Some thoughts*, 23–4. *The Workwoman's Guide*, 44.

25. Smythson, *The Compleat Family Physician*, 10.

26. *The Annual Register, or a View of the History, Politics, and Literature for the Year 1777*, vol. 20 (London, 1805), 112–16.

27. Makittrick Adair, *Essays on fashionable diseases*, 30.

28. Tryon, *A treatise of cleanness*, 10.

29. James Makittrick Adair, *An essay on regimen, for the preservation of health, especially of the indolent, studious, delicate and invalid* (Air, 1799), 82.

30. Makittrick Adair, *Essays on fashionable diseases*, 55–6.

31. John E. Crowley, *The Invention of Comfort, Sensibilities & Design in Early Modern Britain and Early America* (Baltimore & London: Johns Hopkins University Press, 2001), 141.

32. James Woodforde, *Diary of a Country Parson, The Reverend James Woodforde*, ed. John Beresford, vol. 1 (Oxford: Oxford University Press, 1981), 165. On the draughty conditions of many early modern bedchambers see Cockayne, *Hubbub*, 139–40.

33. Crowley, *The Invention of Comfort*, 141.

34. On the manufacture, use and smell of tallow and wax candles and rushlights see Cockayne, *Hubbub*, 146–7, 214.

35. 'Culinary Receipts', MS Sloane 703, British Library, fols 8, 99.

36. William Cole, *The Blecheley Diary of the Rev. William Cole, M.A., F.S.A., 1765–67*, ed. Francis Griffin Stokes (London: Constable & Co Ltd, 1931), 324–5.

37. An increase in the number of bedsheets per household has been traced in Mark Overton, Jane Whittle, Darron Dean and Andrew Hann, *Production and Consumption in English Households, 1600–1750* (Abingdon: Routledge, 2004), 110.

38. On the desirability of white textiles see Giorgio Riello, 'Fabricating the Domestic', 60.

39. John Styles explains that it was not until the nineteenth century that cottons began to supplement linens in the market for bedsheets and other plain, utilitarian products.

John Styles, 'What Were Cottons for in the Early Industrial Revolution', in *The Spinning World: A Global History of Cotton Textiles*, ed. Giorgio Riello and Prasannan Parthasarathi (Oxford: Oxford University Press/Pasold Research Fund, 2009), 307–26.

40. I am grateful to Alice Dolan for sharing her extensive knowledge of English linens with me. On the good economy of using and making household linens see Alice Dolan, ' "The Fabric of Life": Time and Textiles in an Eighteenth-Century Plebeian Home', *Home Cultures* 11 (2014), 355.

41. On conceptions and uses of linen in medieval France see Veronica Sekules, 'Spinning Yarns: Clean Linen and Domestic Values in Late Medieval French Culture', in *The Material Culture of Sex, Procreation, and Marriage in Premodern Europe*, ed. Anne L. McClanan and Karen Rosoff Encarnación (New York and Basingstoke: Palgrave, 2002).

42. 'Chalice and paten, *c.* 1630–*c.* 1650', Victoria and Albert Museum, Object No. M.1A-1986.

43. Recipes for bleaching linen sheets and restoring their whiteness can be found in *The Workwoman's Guide*, 218, 221, 223. Strong preferences for white bedcovers were also evident in eighteenth-century Virginia. See Linda Baumgarten and Kimberly Smith Ivey, *Four Centuries of Quilts: The Colonial Williamsburg Collection* (Williamsburg, New Haven and London: The Colonial Williamsburg Foundation, in association with Yale University Press, 2014), 64–5, 74–9.

44. Makittrick Adair, *An essay on regimen*, 11–12.

45. Directions for unpicking and turning sheets can be found in *The Workwoman's Guide*, 181.

46. Vigarello also expanded on the analogous use of linen and bathing. Georges Vigarello, *Concepts of Cleanliness: Changing Attitudes in France since the Middle Ages* trans. Jean Birrell (Cambridge: Cambridge University Press, 1988), 9, 58–61. See also Douglas Biow, *The Culture of Cleanliness in Renaissance Italy* (Ithaca and London: Cornell University Press, 2006).

47. This miniature pocket guide offered a model of female behaviour for the entertainment and instruction of 'Bachelours' and 'Virgins'. Braithwaite's advice proved popular into the eighteenth century; poet and songwriter Henry Carey appended Braithwaite's lectures to an entertaining collection of reports that voyaged 'to the isles of love and matrimony'. Henry Carey, *Cupid and Hymen: or, a voyage to the isles of love and matrimony* (London, 1742). This collection merited further editions in 1745, 1746, 1748 and 1772. Very similar bedclothes, and a scene of spousal conflict, feature in the frontispiece to Thomas Heywood's *A Curtaine Lecture* (London, 1637).

48. For images and descriptions of 'bedgowns' worn by English and Welsh women see John Styles, *The Dress of the People: Everyday Fashion in Eighteenth-Century England* (New Haven and London: Yale University Press, 2007), 22, 38–9, 75, 84, 276.

49. For servants sleeping in 'smocks' see John Cannon, *The Chronicles of John Cannon, Excise Officer and Writing Master, Part 1, 1684–1733*, ed. John Money (Oxford: Oxford University Press and The British Academy, 2010), 159. Styles, *The Dress of the People*, 27–8. Susan F. North, 'Dress and Hygiene in Early Modern England: a study of advice and practice' (PhD diss., Queen Mary, University of London, 2013), 27–8.

50. North, 'Dress and Hygiene', 30–1.

51. *The Workwoman's Guide*, 61.

52. Susan North's research has been instrumental in distinguishing the labels and common usage of these arguments. North, 'Dress and Hygiene', 30–3.

53. Felix Platter, Abdiah Cole and Nicholas Culpeper, *Platerus golden practice of physick* (London, 1664), 7.

54. Makittrick Adair, *Essays on fashionable diseases*, 53–4. Trusler, *An Easy Way to Prolong Life*, 17.

55. 'Linen, silk and silver-gilt thread embroidered nightcap, *c.* 1600–*c.* 1624', Victoria and Albert Museum, Object No. T.258-1926.

56. On night coifs and croscloths see North, 'Dress and Hygiene', 31.

57. *The Workwoman's Guide*, 62–7.

58. 'Linen nightcap *c.* 1680–*c.* 1699', National Trust, Snowshill Wade Costume Collection, 1348925. 'Linen nightcap, *c.* 1700–*c.* 1759', National Trust, Snowshill Wade Costume Collection, 1348924. 'Bleached linen and muslin nightcap *c.* 1700–*c.* 1720', National Trust, Snowshill Wade Costume Collection, 1348928. Clare Rose, 'The Manufacture and Sale of Marseilles quilting in eighteenth-century London', *CIETA Bulletin* 76 (1999), 104–13. For examples of German nightcap patterns from this period see Moira Thunder, 'Deserving Attention: Margaretha Helm's Designs for Embroidery in the Eighteenth Century', *Journal of Design History* 23 (2010), 409–27.

59. North, 'Dress and Hygiene', 32.

60. 'Cap liner, *c.* 1630–*c.* 1650', Victoria and Albert Museum, Object No. T.68-2004.

61. Cavallo and Storey, *Healthy Living*, 65. A knitting pattern for a gentleman's cotton nightcap is detailed in *The Workwoman's Guide*, 269.

62. 'Ledger', Royal London Hospital Archives, LH/F/8/11 (June 1798–December 1807), 156. Anne Brockman's account book listed the cost of laundering nightcaps in 1702. 'Brockman Papers: Household accompts of Anne, wife of Sir William Brockman', vols CXLI–CXLII, British Library Additional MS 45208, CXLI, fol. 22.

63. A. Tindal Hart, *Country Counting House: The Story of Two Eighteenth-Century Clerical Account Books* (London: Phoenix House Ltd, 1962), 53.

64. Ibid., 102, 109.

65. Cole, *Blecheley Diary*, 275.

66. Ibid., 287.

67. Brockman Papers, fols 6, 46, 63.

68. Woodforde, *Diary*, vol. 1, 22–3.

69. Elizabeth Raper, *The Receipt Book of Elizabeth Raper*, ed. Bartle Grant (Soho: The Nonsuch Press, 1924), 19.

70. Robert Hooke, *Micrographia, or, some physiological descriptions of minute bodies made by magnifying glasses with observations and inquiries thereupon* (London, 1665), 6–7.

71. Oliver Goldsmith, *An History of the Earth and Animated Nature*, vol. 2 (London, 1779), 281–2.

72. Lisa T. Sarasohn has explained the intensification of disquiet about bedbugs in the context of shifting discourses of race and social status fuelled by a globalising eighteenth-century economy. Lisa T. Sarasohn, ' "That nauseous venomous insect": Bedbugs in Early Modern England', *Eighteenth-Century Studies* 46 (2013), 513–30.

73. Tryon, *A treatise of cleanness*, 5.

74. Horace Walpole, *Horace Walpole's Correspondence with Henry Seymour Conway, Lady Ailesbury, Lord and Lady Hertford, Lord Beauchamp, Henrietta Seymour Conway, Lord Henry and Lord Hugh Seymour*, vol. 39 of *The Yale Edition of Horace Walpole's Correspondence*, ed. W.S. Lewis, Lars E. Troide, Edwine M. Martz and Robert A. Smith (London and New Haven: Oxford University Press and Yale University Press, 1974), 285.

75. Richard Latham, *The Account Book of Richard Latham 1724–1767: Records of Social and Economic History*, vol. 15, ed. Lorna Weatherill (New York: published for the British Academy by Oxford University Press, 1990), 3, 80, 109. Cole, *Blecheley Diary*, 275. Pamela Sambrook, *A Country House at Work: Three Centuries of Dunham Massey* (London: The National Trust, 2003), 71. *The Workwoman's Guide*, 44, 200.

76. Amanda Vickery, *Behind Closed Doors: At Home in Georgian England* (New Haven and London: Yale University Press, 2009), 282.

77. John Southall, *A Treatise of Buggs* (London, 1730), 16. See also L.O.J. Boynton, 'The Bed-bug and the "Age of Elegance" ', *Furniture History* 1 (1965), v, 17–18.

78. The Morris family from Lewes, East Sussex, kept a notebook with recipes for keeping bedsteads free of 'London bugs'. Cited in Ponsonby, *Stories from Home*, 80.

79. 'A booke of divers receipts, c. 1660–c. 1750', Wellcome Trust Library (hereafter WT) MS 1322, fols 50–1.

80. Hannah Glasse, *The Servants' Directory, or the House-Keeper's Companion* (London, 1760), 42. *The Workwoman's Guide*, 228.

81. Anne Barker, *The Complete Servant Maid: or Young Woman's Best Companion* (London, 1770), 35. Similar advice appeared in *The Complete Man and Maid Servant* (London, 1764), 57–8.

82. *The Workwoman's Guide*, 185.

83. Glasse, *Servant's Directory*, 39–40. See also *The Universal Family Book: Or, A Necessary and Profitable Companion for all Degrees of People of Either Sex* (London, 1703), 197–8.

84. Glasse, *Servant's Directory*, 38–42, 427. See also Margaret Ponsonby, *Stories from Home*, 80.

85. Mary Fissell, 'Popular Medical Writing', 421, 426–7.

86. 'Book of Receites c. 1650–c. 1739', WT MS 144, fols 41, 48, 59.

87. 'Book of Receites c. 1650–c. 1739', WT MS 144, fol. 101. 'Receipt-Book c. 1635', WT MS 809192, fols 231. 232v. 'Collection of Medical Receipts c. 1748', WT MS 3295.

88. Alice Thornton, *The Autobiography of Mrs. Alice Thornton of East Newton, Co. York* (Durham, London and Edinburgh: Surtees Society, 1875), 333.

89. For a discussion of medical recipes as gift exchanges built on relationships of personal trust see Leong and Pennell, 'Recipe Collections', 133–4.

90. 'Receipt book of Elizabeth Okeover (& others), c. 1675–c. 1725', WT MS 3712, fol. 72.

91. 'Receipt book of Elizabeth Jacobs & others, 1654–1685', WT MS 3009, fol. 96.

92. Fissell notes that many recipe books were carefully itemised for ease of use. Fissell, 'Popular Medical Writing', 422.

93. Mary E. Fissell, 'The Marketplace of Print', in *Medicine and the Market in England and its Colonies c.1450–c.1850*, ed. Mark S.R. Jenner and Patrick Wallis (Basingstoke: Palgrave Macmillan, 2007), 114.

94. Ibid., 115; Fissell, 'Popular Medical Writing', 426–7.

95. Hannah Wolley, *The Accomplish'd lady's delight in preserving, physic, beautifying, and cookery* (London, 1675), 6.

96. John Gerard, *The Herball or Generall Historie of Plantes* (London, 1633), 850–3.

97. Joseph Blagrave, *Blagrave's Astrological Practice of Physick* (London, 1671), 109.

98. Gideon Harvey, *The family physician, and the house apothecary* (London, 1676), 4–5, 134–5. On the availability of individual ingredients see John Stobart, *Sugar and Spice: Grocers and Groceries in Provincial England, 1650–1830* (Oxford: Oxford University Press, 2012).

99. Josselin, *Diary*, 111.

100. 'English Receipt-Book', WT MS 634, fols 138, 151.

101. Josselin, *Diary*, 111–12, 214.

102. Willis, *Dr. Willis's practice of physick*, 137–43.

103. Elizabeth Grey, countess of Kent, *A choice manual of rare and select secrets in physic and chirurgery collected and practised by the Right Honorable, the Countesse of Kent* (London, 1653), 114, 118.

104. 'Boyle family recipe book, c. 1675–c. 1710', WT MS 1340, fols 17, 122, 132. See also 'Book of Receites', WT MS 144, fols 48, 59 and 'English Receipt-Book', WT MS 634, fol. 122.

105. *The Ladies Dispensatory, containing the natures, vertues, and qualities of all herbs, and simples usefull in physick reduced into a methodicall order* (London, 1651), 6–7.

106. 'Freke Papers', British Library Additional MS 45718, vol. 1, fol. 275.

107. Harvey, *The family physician*, 5, 43–4.

108. 'Trumbull Papers', British Library Additional MS 72516, fol. 19

109. Thomas Willis was one of many physicians who prescribed concoctions of chocolate for mental disorders. See Richard Sugg, *Mummies, Cannibals and Vampires: The History of Corpse Medicine from the Renaissance to the Victorians* (London and New York: Routledge, 2011), 57–9.

110. 'Trumbull Papers', BL Add. MS 72516, fol. 157.

111. Ibid., fols 161, 163.

112. Sugg, *Mummies, Cannibals and Vampires*, 2.

113. John French, *The Art of Distillation* (London, 1653), 91.

114. 'Trumbull Papers', BL Add. MS 72516, fol. 220.

115. William Ellis, *The Country Housewife's Family Companion* (London and Salisbury, 1750), 291.

Chapter 3: Faithful Slumber

1. John Evelyn, *The Diary of John Evelyn,* ed. E.S. de Beer, vol. 5 (Oxford: Clarendon Press, 2000), 400.

2. Alec Ryrie and Erin Sullivan have revealed how Protestant religious cultures shaped understandings and practices relating to sleep and dreams before 1640. Ryrie's work in particular has cemented bedtime prayers at the heart of household life. Alec Ryrie, 'Sleeping, Waking and Dreaming', 73–92. Alec Ryrie, *Being Protestant in Reformation Britain* (Oxford: Oxford University Press, 2013), 99–247, 363–408. Erin Sullivan, 'The Watchful Spirit', 14–35. On the significance of sleep, dreams and nocturnal visions in early America see Robert S. Cox, 'The Suburbs of Eternity: On Visionaries and Miraculous Sleepers', in *Worlds of Sleep,* ed. Brunt and Steger, 53–74 and Ann Kirschner, ' "Tending to Edify, Astonish, and Instruct": Published Narratives of Spiritual Dreams and Visions in the Early Republic', *Early American Studies* 1 (2003), 198–229.

3. Christopher Hill, 'The Spiritualization of the Household', in *Society and Puritanism in Pre-revolutionary England,* ed. Christopher Hill (London, 1964), 382–416. Charles E. Hambrick-Stowe, 'Practical Divinity and Spirituality', in *The Cambridge Companion to Puritanism,* ed. John Coffey and Paul C.H. Lim (Cambridge: Cambridge University Press, 2008), 191–205. Virginia Reinburg, 'Hearing Lay People's Prayer', in *Culture and Identity in Early Modern Europe (1500–1800),* ed. Barbara Diefendorf and Carla Hesse (Ann Arbor, MI: University of Michigan Press, 1993), 19–39. John Spurr, *English Puritanism, 1603–1689* (Basingstoke: Macmillan, 1998), 187–201. Alexandra Walsham, 'Holy Families: The Spiritualization of the Early Modern Household Revisited', in *Religion and the Household,* ed. John Doran, Charlotte Methuen and Alexandra Walsham (Woodbridge: published for the Ecclesiastical History Society by the Boydell Press, 2014), 122–60. Lauren F. Winner, *A Cheerful and Comfortable Faith: Anglican Religious Practice in the Elite Households of Eighteenth-Century Virginia* (London, 2010).

4. Ian Green, 'New for Old? Clerical and Lay Attitudes to Domestic Prayer in Early Modern England', *Reformation and Renaissance Review* 10 (2008), 219–21.

5. Psalms 121:4, King James Version (hereafter KJV).

6. Milton, *Paradise Lost* (4.776–80), ed. Leonard, 93.

7. Henry Newcome, *The Diary of the Rev. Henry Newcome, from September 30, 1661 to September 29, 1663,* ed. Thomas Heywood (Manchester: Chetham Society, 1849), 35.

8. For fuller exploration of the overlap between public liturgy and private devotions see Ian Green 'Varieties of Domestic Devotion in Early Modern English Protestantism', in *Private and Domestic Devotion,* ed. Martin and Ryrie, 9–31.

9. On the household as a site of subversion and worship for English and European Catholics see Walsham, 'Holy Families', 146–60.

10. *The Pious Country Parishioner* included a short form of morning prayer and specified the use of particular passages for children and servants. *The Pious Country Parishioner Instructed how to spend every day, through the whole course of his life, in a religious and acceptable manner* (London, 1753), 16. Thomas Ken's *Crown of Glory* was intended 'for the Use of a Noble Family'. Thomas Ken, *A Crown of Glory, The Reward of the Righteous* (London, 1725), title page.

11. Robert Warren, *The Daily Self-Examinant: or an Earnest Persuasive to the Duty of Daily Self-Examination* (London, 1720), iv, 54–5. See also *Crumbs of Comfort and Godly Prayers; with thankful remembrance of God's wonderful deliverances of this land* (London, 1726), 56.

12. *The New Practice of Piety: containing the necessary duties of a Christian Life* (London, 1749), 54, 88–91, 158, 456. Similar advice can be found in William Best, *An Essay on the Service of the Church of England, considered as a Daily Service* (London, 1794), 41 and *Christian Prudence: consisting of Maxims and Proverbs, Divine and Moral* (London, 1766), 70.

13. *Crumbs of Comfort and Godly Prayers*, 37–9. See also Symon Patrick, *The Devout Christian instructed how to pray and give thanks to God. Or, a Book of Devotions for families, and for particular persons, in most of the concerns of humane life* (London, 1759), 18, 50–1, 71, 267–8.

14. *The Pious Country Parishioner*, 167.

15. *Two East Anglian Diaries 1641–1729, Isaac Archer and William Coe*, ed. Matthew Storey (Woodbridge: Boydell & Brewer, 1994), 217, 219–21, 223, 226–30, 235, 238–9, 244, 250.

16. Edmund Harrold, *The Diary of Edmund Harrold, Wigmaker of Manchester 1712-15*, ed. Craig Horner (Aldershot: Ashgate, 2008), 11–12, 120.

17. Newcome, *Diary*, 132–4.

18. Richard Burdsall, *Memoirs of the Life of Richard Burdsall, shewing the mercy of God in Christ Jesus to a sinner* (Thetford, 1823), 36–7.

19. Thomas Tryon, *Wisdom's Dictates: or, Aphorisms and Rules Physical, Moral, and Divine, For Preserving the Health of the Body, and the Peace of the Mind* (1696), 87.

20. Ibid., 75.

21. Ralph Thoresby, *The Diary of Ralph Thoresby (1677–1724), now first published from the original manuscript*, ed. Joseph Hunter, vol. 2 (London: Henry Colburn and Richard Bentley, 1830), 152. On Thoresby's efforts to redeem time see David Wykes, ' "The Sabbaths spent . . . before in Idleness & the neglect of the word": The Godly and the Use of Time in Their Daily Religion', in *Studies in Church History: The Use and Abuse of Time in Christian History*, ed. R.N. Swanson, vol. 37 (2002), 211–21.

22. Newcome, *Diary*, 38.

23. Commonplace analogies between excess sleep, drowsiness and sin are also found in the writings of Samuel Ward, John Geree, Nehemiah Wallington and Richard Rogers. See Sullivan, 'Watchful Spirit', 15. Margo Todd, 'Puritan Self-Fashioning: The Diary of Samuel Ward', *Journal of British Studies* 31 (1992), 253. Tom Webster, 'Writing to Redundancy: Approaches to Spiritual Journals and Early Modern Spirituality', *Historical Journal* 39 (1996), 49.

24. On the quality of midnight devotions see Ryrie, 'Sleeping, Waking and Dreaming', 84–6.

25. Richard Baxter, *A Christian Directory, or, a summ of practical theologie and cases of conscience directing Christians how to use their knowledge and faith, how to improve all helps and means, and to perform all duties, how to overcome temptations, and to escape or mortifie every sin* (London, 1673), 404.

26. *The Meditations of Lady Elizabeth Delaval: written between 1662 and 1671*, ed. Douglas G. Greene (Gateshead: Publications of the Surtees Society, 1978), 5, 44, 82–3, 118.

27. Baxter, *A Christian Directory*, 405.

28. Newcome, *Diary*, 10, 31.

29. Ibid., 25–6.

30. John Wesley, *The Duty and Advantage of Early Rising. A Sermon on Ephesians v.16* (London, 1798), 2.

31. Henry Abelove, *The Evangelist of Desire: John Wesley and the Methodists* (Stanford: Stanford University Press, 1990), 96.

32. Wesley, *The Duty and Advantage of Early Rising*, 5.

33. John Wesley, *A Plain Account of Christian Perfection, as believed and taught by the Rev. Mr John Wesley, from the year 1725, to the year 1777* (Dublin, 1797), 72.

34. Phyllis Mack explored the link between Methodist conversion accounts and the preservation of sense perception through a well-regulated regimen of sleep. Phyllis Mack, *Heart Religion in the British Enlightenment: Gender and Emotion in Early Methodism* (Cambridge: Cambridge University Press, 2008), 234. Phyllis Mack, 'Does Gender Matter? Suffering and Salvation in Eighteenth-century Methodism', *Bulletin of the John Rylands University Library of Manchester* 85 (2003), 157–76. For similar themes in the mid-seventeenth century see *An Alarme to Awake Church-Sleepers* (London, 1644).

35. Wesley, *The Duty and Advantage of Early Rising*, 6–7, 11.

36. This relationship has been explored at length in Mack, *Heart Religion*.

37. Wesley, *The Duty and Advantage of Early Rising*, 11.

38. Cited in Mack, *Heart Religion*, 167–8.

39. 'John Henderson to Charles Wesley, February 26, 1787', John Rylands Library MS DDPr 1/36.
40. Evelyn, *Diary*, vol. 5, 268.
41. 2 Sam. 4:5–7; Judges 4:21, KJV.
42. John Brand, *Observations on popular antiquities: including the whole of Mr. Bourne's Antiquitates vulgares* (Newcastle upon Tyne, 1777), 63.
43. For a detailed discussion of the relationship between sleep-piety, death and the religious culture of late seventeenth-century England see Sasha Handley, 'From the Sacral to the Moral: Sleeping Practices, Household Worship and Confessional Cultures in Late Seventeenth-Century England', *Cultural and Social History* 9 (2012), 37–8. On the Christian symbolism of early rising see Ryrie, 'Sleeping, Waking and Dreaming', 75–8. On the association between sleep and death in an earlier period see Gabrielle Klug, 'Dangerous Doze', 31–52.
44. 'Elizabeth Chaddocke', The National Archives: Prerogative Court of Canterbury (hereafter TNA: PCC), PROB 3/47/1 (1747). Richard Allestree, *The whole duty of man laid down in a plain and familiar way for the use of all, but especially the meanest reader* (London, 1713), 383–4.
45. Thornton, *Autobiography*, 161.
46. Job 36:20, KJV.
47. Thomas Wilson, *Maxims of Piety and of Christianity* (London, 1789), 60.
48. *Christian Prudence*, 70–2.
49. Thomas Seaton, *The Devotional Life Render'd Familiar, Easy, and Pleasant, in Several Hymns Upon the Most Common Occasions of Human Life* (London, 1734), 67–8, 74–5.
50. William Bagshawe, *Essays on Union to Christ. Being the Substance of Several Sermons* (London, 1703), 366–7.
51. *The New Practice of Piety*, 158.
52. On the practice of 'watching' before burial see David Cressy, *Birth, Marriage, and Death: Ritual, Religion, and the Life-Cycle in Tudor and Stuart England* (Oxford: Oxford University Press, 1997), 425–31.
53. 'Mattress', Museum of English Rural Life, acc. no. 61/242 (1500–1800). For similar representations of these mattresses on English funeral monuments see Nigel Llewellyn, *Funeral Monuments in Post-Reformation England* (Cambridge: Cambridge University Press, 2000), 30, 78, 81, 103, 113, 126, 163, 178, 245, 298, 306, 327, 336, and Brian Kemp, *English Church Monuments* (London: B.T. Basford, 1980), 63, 107–8, 164.
54. My thanks go to Reverend Nigel Warner for deciphering this inscription and to Jennifer Morrison from Newcastle City Council for providing me with a copy of the Archaeological Watching Brief for the Haddon and Makepeace tomb.
55. John Valton, 'Diary, 1765', John Rylands Library: Methodist Church Archives (hereafter JRL: MCA), Diaries Collection, vol. 2, fols 84–5.
56. Valton, 'Diary, 1767', JRL: MCA, vol. 4, fol. 29.
57. Seaton, *The Devotional Life*, 10.
58. Norman Sykes, *Church and State in England in the XVIIIth Century* (Cambridge: Cambridge University Press, 1934), 276.
59. Evelyn, *Diary*, vol. 5, 400.
60. *Two East Anglian Diaries*, 267.
61. Elizabeth Johnson, *An Account of Mrs. Elizabeth Johnson, well known in the city of Bristol for more than half a century, for her eminent piety and benevolence. To which is added, an extract from her diary* (Bristol, 1799), 49.
62. Thomas Ken, *A morning, evening, and midnight hymn* (London, 1703), 5.
63. For alternative versions of the Paternoster see *Remaines of Gentilisme and Judaisme by John Aubrey, 1686–87*, ed. James Britten (London: Publications of the Folklore Society, 1881), 34. G.F. Northall, *English folk-rhymes; a collection of traditional verses relating to places and persons, customs, superstitions, etc* (London: Kegan Paul, Trench, Trubner & Co, 1892), 141–8.
64. John Wesley, *Sermons on Several Occasions*, vol. 9 (London, 1800), 195.
65. Ibid., 195–6.

66. Thomas Wilson, *A Short and Plain Instruction for the Better Understanding of the Lord's Supper* (London, 1740), 207.
67. On the vitality of belief in angels see Peter Marshall, 'Angels Around the Deathbed: Variations on a Theme in the English Art of Dying', in *Angels in the Early Modern World*, ed. Peter Marshall and Alexandra Walsham (Cambridge: Cambridge University Press, 2006), 83–103, and Laura Sangha, *Angels and Belief in England, 1480–1700* (London: Pickering & Chatto, 2012).
68. On this theme see Carolyn Steedman, *Master and Servant: Love and Labour in the English Industrial Age* (Cambridge: Cambridge University Press, 2007), 152–75. W.M. Jacob, *Lay People and Religion in the Early Eighteenth Century* (Cambridge: Cambridge University Press, 1996), 19.
69. Seaton, *The Devotional Life*, 75. A 1722 reprint of John Colet's *Daily devotions* begged God's assistance in 'A Prayer against evil Imaginations' from which acts of uncleanness might result during sleep. John Colet, *Daily devotions: or, the Christian's morning and evening sacrifice. Digested into prayers and meditations for every day in the week, and other occasions* (London, 1722), 151.
70. Newcome, *Diary*, 111.
71. Burdsall, *Memoirs*, 33–5.
72. William Hammond, *Psalms, Hymns and Spiritual Songs* (London, 1745), 215.
73. Josselin, *Diary*, 631.
74. Jacob, *Lay People and Religion*, 94. Earlier echoes of concerns about prayer posture can be found in Ryrie, *Being Protestant*, 171.
75. Newcome, *Diary*, 31.
76. Adam Eyre, 'A dyurnall, or, Catalogue of all my accions and expences from the 1ˢᵗ of January 1646–[7–]', in *Yorkshire diaries and autobiographies*, ed. H.J. Morehouse, vol. 1 (Durham: Surtees Society Publications, 1877), 53. Henry Lawrence's text *Of Our Communion and Warre with Angels* (London, 1646). Lawrence was a politician, appointed Lord Lawrence under the protectorate, with strong puritan beliefs.
77. Samuel Pepys, *The Diary of Samuel Pepys: A New and Complete Transcription*, ed. Robert Latham and William Matthews, vol. 9 (London: G. Bell and Sons Ltd, 1972), 371.
78. Many thanks to Christine and Michael Stone for bringing this 'moon-hole' to my attention and to Michelle Hill at the National Trust for providing me with a photograph. On the household venues for godly reading and different styles of godly reading in bedchambers see Andrew Cambers, *Godly Reading: Print, Manuscript and Puritanism in England, 1580–1720* (Cambridge: Cambridge University Press, 2011), 54–7.
79. Cockayne, *Hubbub*, 146–7.
80. Cited in Cambers, *Godly Reading*, 54. Newcome, *Diary*, 83.
81. *Arminian Magazine: consisting of extracts and original treatises on universal redemption*, vol. 7 (London: J. Fry & Co, 1778–97), 550. On 'shutting in', or locking up the household at night, see Amanda Vickery, 'An Englishman's Home is His Castle? Thresholds, Boundaries and Privacies in the Eighteenth-Century London House', *Past and Present* 199 (2008), 156, 169.
82. Newcome, *Diary*, 74, 81, 172.
83. Thornton, *Autobiography*, 191.
84. Pepys, *Diary*, vol. 9, 308. Harrold, *Diary*, 10, 22–3, 26–7, 43–4.
85. Jacqueline Pearson, *Women's Reading in Britain, 1750–1835: A Dangerous Recreation* (Cambridge: Cambridge University Press, 2005), 43–6.
86. Sarah Hurst, *The Diaries of Sarah Hurst 1759–1762: Life and Love in Eighteenth Century Horsham*, ed. Susan C. Djabri (Stroud: Amberley Publishing, 2009), 83, 94.
87. George Goodgion was also responsible for purchasing the countess's linen from which her bedsheets and pillowcases were made by local seamstress Margaret Montgomery, also from Penrith. Lady Anne Clifford, *The Diaries of Lady Anne Clifford*, ed. D.J.H. Clifford (Stroud: Alan Sutton, 1990), 235, 263–5.
88. Margaret Spufford, *Small Books and Pleasant Histories: Popular Fiction and its Readership in Seventeenth-Century England* (Cambridge: Cambridge University Press, 1985), 211.

89. James Janeway, *A Token for Children: being an exact account of the conversion, holy and exemplary lives, and joyful deaths, of several young children* (London, 1676). Ralph Houlbrooke, 'Death in Childhood: the Practice of the Good Death in James Janeway's "A Token for Children"', in *Childhood in Question: Children, Parents and the State*, ed. Anthony Fletcher and Stephen Hussey (Manchester: Manchester University Press, 1999), 37–56. On comparable reading for children see Ian Green, *Print and Protestantism in Early Modern England* (Oxford: Oxford University Press, 2000), 399–400.
90. Harrold, *Diary*, 21. Thomas Comber, *A Companion to the Temple: or, a Help to Publick and Private Devotion* (London, 1676).
91. 'Mrs Dodson's Account Book, 1746–1765', Museum of London, MS 80.7. Thomas Ken, *A Manual of Prayers for the Use of the Scholars of Winchester Colledge* (London, 1674). Green, *Print and Protestantism*, 635.
92. Ken, *Crown of Glory*, 179.
93. Elizabeth Beacon very likely owned a copy of John Foxe's *Actes and Monuments*, also commonly referred to as *The Book of Martyrs*, which was reprinted in full and abridged editions throughout the seventeenth and eighteenth centuries. 'Elizabeth Beacon, 1737', TNA: PCC PROB 3/37/21.
94. 'Mary Martin, 1668', TNA: PCC PROB 5/2377. 'Elizabeth Beacon, 1737', TNA: PCC PROB 3/37/21. 'Rebecca Weekes, 1730', TNA: PCC PROB 3/29/215. 'Richard Burford, 1738', TNA: PCC PROB 3/37/28.
95. William Burkitt also wrote the popular devotional text *The Poor Man's Help and Young Man's Guide*, which included a catechism, set prayers and advice on holy living (London, 1694). This work ran through twenty-two editions between the 1690s and 1730s. Green, 'New for Old?', 220.
96. 'Benjamin Coster, 1758', TNA: PCC PROB 3/57/7.
97. Beth Quitsland, 'Singing the Psalms for Fun and Profit', in *Private and Domestic Devotion*, ed. Martin and Ryrie, 237–58.
98. Jacob, *Lay People and Religion*, 95.
99. *The Book of Common Prayer: The Texts of 1549, 1559, and 1662*, ed. Brian Cummings (Oxford: Oxford University Press, 2011), 256.
100. On techniques for achieving secret prayer in busy households see Ryrie, *Being Protestant*, 154–63.
101. Early modern debates about the virtues and dangers of solitary prayers are explored in Erica Longfellow, ' "My now solitary prayers": *Eikon basilike* and Changing Attitudes toward Religious Solitude', in *Private and Domestic Devotion*, ed. Martin and Ryrie, 58–72. See also Ryrie, *Being Protestant*, 154–61.
102. Best, *Essay*, 29–31, 41.
103. Many thanks to Laura Sangha for sharing her research on Ralph Thoresby with me. On Thoresby's secret devotions see Ralph Thoresby, GB/0207/MS.26, Yorkshire Archaeological Society (1715), fols 252–3.
104. Thoresby, *Diary*, vol. 1, 410–12; vol. 2, 6, 12–13, 15, 94.
105. Josselin, *Diary*, 117.
106. Ibid., 603.
107. Thornton, *Autobiography*, 49, 122–3, 134.
108. Tara Hamling, *Decorating the 'Godly' Household: Religious Art in Post-Reformation Britain* (New Haven and London: Yale University Press, 2010), 166–74. Tara Hamling, 'Living with the Bible in Post-Reformation England: The Materiality of Text, Image and Object in Domestic Life', in *Religion and the Household*, ed. Doran, Methuen and Walsham, 217–24.
109. 'Young Bateman's ghost, or, a godly warning to all maidens' (London, 1760). On the visual iconography of early modern bedchambers as devotional supports see Hamling, *Decorating the 'Godly' Household*, 164–74.
110. William Stukeley, *The Family Memoirs of the Rev. William Stukeley M.D.*, ed. W.C. Lukis, R. Gale, S. Gale and G. Kneller, vol. 1 (London: Publications of the Surtees Society, 1882), 198.

111. Brand, *Observations on popular antiquities*, 366. 'Child's rattle, *c.* 1775–*c.* 1800', Victoria and Albert Museum, Object No. B.150-1997. 'Rattle, *c.* 1750', Victoria and Albert Museum, Object No. M.18-1996.

112. Marion Endt-Jones, 'A Monstrous Transformation: Coral in Art and Culture', in *Coral: Something Rich and Strange*, ed. Marion Endt-Jones (Liverpool: Liverpool University Press, 2013), 9, 11–12. Marion Endt-Jones, 'Coral Shrine from Trapani (*c.* 1650)', in *Coral*, ed. Endt-Jones, 59. Susannah Gibson, 'Living Rocks: The Mystery of Coral in the Eighteenth Century', in *Coral*, ed. Endt-Jones, 63.

113. On the nature and symbolism of coral see Marcia Pointon, *Brilliant Effects: A Cultural History of Gem Stones and Jewellery* (New Haven and London: Paul Mellon Centre for Studies in British Art, Yale University Press, 2009), 127–9.

114. Thomas Nicols, *Lapidary or, The History of Pretious Stones* (Cambridge, 1652), 102–7, 171–2.

115. John Pechey, *A general treatise of the diseases of infants and children* (London, 1697), 72. Brand, *Observations on popular antiquities*, 366. Sabino Perea Yébenes, 'Magic at Sea: Amulets for Navigation', in *Magical Practice in the Latin West*, ed. Richard L. Gordon and Francisco Marco Simón (Leiden: Brill, 2010), 467–9. William Henderson, *Notes on the Folk-Lore of the Northern Counties of England and the Borders* (London: W. Satchell, Peyton and Co., 1879), 14. Many thanks to Sarah Fox for providing me with this reference. For more examples of protective objects used to protect children and adults from diabolical dangers see Jennifer Spinks, Sasha Handley and Stephen Gordon, *Magic, Witches and Devils in the Early Modern World* (Manchester: The John Rylands Library, University of Manchester, 2016), 10–13.

116. Edward Rainbowe, *A Sermon preached at the funeral of the Right Honourable Anne Countess of Pembroke, Dorset and Montgomery* (1677), 40.

117. On the mnemonic function of household objects in Protestant culture see Tara Hamling, 'Old Robert's Girdle: Visual and Material Props for Protestant Piety in Post-Reformation England', in *Private and Domestic Devotion*, ed. Martin and Ryrie, 144–55.

118. Rainbowe, *A Sermon*, 42.

119. Many thanks to Timothy Easton for sharing his expertise, research and photography with me. This image shows part of the late-seventeenth-century candle-marked ceiling in an upstairs chamber from Great Barton, Suffolk. These letterforms are part of a recognisable group appearing from ceilings in several counties. On this ceiling are several representations of gridirons, crosses and the name of one of the occupants, Sarah Sugate, who was probably a teenager at the time. Her name appears several times, suggesting the ceiling may have been marked to neutralise some fear about her condition at the time, perhaps nightmares or sleepwalking, *c.* 1660–*c.* 1700. The fittings shown, the multi-angled lamp and the ventilation grid, are modern.

120. Timothy Easton, 'Candle Powers', *Cornerstone* 32 (2011), 56–60. I am grateful to Stephen Gordon for bringing this article to my attention and to Timothy Easton for sharing his wisdom.

121. Thornton, *Autobiography*, 261.

122. Woodforde, *Diary*, vol. 1, 33.

123. A window in St Edward's Chapel at St Chad's Cathedral in Birmingham depicts Henry Hodgetts in his bedstead as he was dying, shortly before he handed over the relics to the Jesuit Peter Turner. Michael W. Greenslade, *Catholic Staffordshire 1500–1800* (Leominster: Gracewing, 2006), xiv, 125–6.

124. Richard L. Williams, 'Forbidden Sacred Spaces in Reformation England', in *Defining the Holy: Sacred Space in Medieval and Early Modern Europe*, ed. Andrew Spicer and Sarah Hamilton (Aldershot and Burlington: Ashgate, 2005), 101, 108.

125. Pepys, *Diary*, vol. 5, 188.

126. Frances Gage, 'Teaching Them to Serve and Obey: Giulio Mancini on Collecting Religious Art in Seventeenth-Century Rome', in *Sacred Possessions: Collecting Italian Religious Art 1500–1900*, ed. Gail Feigenbaum and Sybille Ebert-Schifferer (Los Angeles: Getty Research Institute, 2011), 68–9.

127. On the acceptability and display of religious images in elite households see Hamling, *Decorating the 'Godly' Household*.

128. 'Elizabeth Dugdale, 1718', TNA: PCC PROB 3/17/5.

129. Easton, 'Candle Powers', 57.

130. Opie and Tatem, *Dictionary of Superstitions*, 361.

131. Ibid., 15–17.

132. Tryon, *Wisdom's Dictates*, 65.

133. On the decoration of bedsteads as prompts to prayer and meditation see Hamling, *Decorating the 'Godly' Household*, 169–74. A complementary relationship between household possessions and morality in nineteenth-century Britain is outlined in Deborah Cohen, *Household Gods: The British and Their Possessions* (New Haven and London: Yale University Press, 2006), 1–31.

134. Hamling, *Decorating the 'Godly' Household*, 170–2.

135. Cole, *Blecheley Diary*, 146, 244, 275, 280, 283, 324–6.

136. On domestic starching practices see Dolan, 'The Fabric of Life', 365.

137. Burdsall, *Memoirs*, 2.

138. 'Notebook containing manuscript copy letters in the hand of Charles Wesley', JRL: DDCW 8/15. *Arminian Magazine*, vol. 7, 549.

Chapter 4: Sleeping at Home

1. Pepys, *Diary*, vol. 7, 7.

2. On the emotional associations of 'home' see Amanda Vickery, *Behind Closed Doors: At Home in Georgian England* (New Haven and London: Yale University Press, 2009), 2.

3. On the varied and associated meanings of 'privacy' and its availability within eighteenth-century London homes see Vickery, 'An Englishman's Home', 147–73.

4. Important work by Elaine Tierney reveals the multifunctional uses of sheds in late seventeenth-century London when they were used for storage, to support commercial activities, as temporary residential shelters, and as semi-permanent or permanent dwellings for people in dire financial straits. Elaine Tierney, 'Dirty Rotten Sheds: Exploring the Ephemeral City in Early Modern London' (paper presented at the Lunchtime Seminar, University of Manchester, 2 December 2015). Makeshift London housing is also discussed in Derek Keene, 'Growth, Modernisation and Control: The Transformation of London's Landscape, *c.* 1500–*c.* 1760', in *Two Capitals: London and Dublin 1500–1840*, ed. Peter Clark and Raymond Gillespie (Oxford: published for the British Academy by Oxford University Press, 2001), 13. Elizabeth McKellar has calculated that the typical length of a London house lease between 1660 and 1720 was sixty-six years, a figure that rose to ninety-nine years by the end of the eighteenth century. Elizabeth McKellar, *The Birth of Modern London: The Development and Design of the City 1660–1720* (Manchester: Manchester University Press, 1999), 57–9.

5. Maxine Berg, *Luxury and Pleasure in Eighteenth-Century Britain* (Oxford: Oxford University Press, 2005). Crowley, *The Invention of Comfort*. Neil McKendrick, John Brewer and John Plumb, *The Birth of a Consumer Society: The Commercialization of Eighteenth-Century England* (London: Europa Publications, 1982). Carole Shammas, 'The Domestic Environment in Early Modern England and America', *Journal of Social History* 14 (1980), 3–24. *The Dress of the People: Gender, Taste, and Material Culture in Britain and North America 1700–1830*, ed. John Styles and Amanda Vickery (New Haven and London: Yale Center for British Art; Paul Mellon Centre for Studies in British Art, Yale University Press, 2006). Amanda Vickery, *The Gentleman's Daughter: Women's Lives in Georgian England* (New Haven and London: Yale University Press, 1998). Vickery, *Behind Closed Doors*. Lorna Weatherill, *Consumer Behaviour and Material Culture in Britain, 1660–1760* (London: Routledge, 1988).

6. On the cost of beds see Riello, 'Fabricating the Domestic', 49. Laura Gowing, ' "The Twinkling of a Bedstaff": Recovering the Social Life of English Beds 1500–1700', *Home Cultures* 11 (2014), 276.

7. Sasha Roberts, 'Lying Among the Classics: Ritual and Motif in Elite Elizabethan and Jacobean Beds', in *Albion's Classicism: The Visual Arts in Britain, 1550–1660*, ed. Lucy Gent (New Haven and London: Yale University Press, 1995), 325–58. Hamling, *Decorating the 'Godly' Household*, 166–74. Angela McShane and Joanne Bailey, 'Beds and the Making of the Domestic Landscape' (paper presented at 'The Body in Bed' seminar series, Royal Holloway Centre for the Study of the Body and Material Culture, University of London, 20 October, 2010).

8. Raffaella Sarti, *Europe at Home: Family Life and Material Culture 1500–1800* (New Haven and London: Yale University Press, 2002), 102.

9. Sarti, *Europe at Home*, 102. Ralph Treswell, *The London Surveys of Ralph Treswell*, ed. John Schofield (London: London Topographical Society, Publication No. 135, 1987), 11–15.

10. Cited in Wrightson, *Earthly Necessities*, 297. Weatherill, *Consumer Behaviour*, 6, 13. For an estimate of the income range of Weatherill's middle ranks see *Consumer Behaviour*, 101–2.

11. Peter King, 'Pauper Inventories and the Material Lives of the Poor in the Eighteenth and Early Nineteenth Centuries', in *Chronicling Poverty: The Voices and Strategies of the English Poor, 1640–1840*, ed. Tim Hitchcock, Peter King and Pamela Sharpe (Basingstoke: Macmillan, 1997), 179.

12. 'John Ellis, 1668', TNA: PCC PROB/5/100.

13. Frank E. Brown, 'Continuity and Change in the Urban House: Developments in Domestic Space Organisation in Seventeenth-Century London', *Comparative Studies in Society and History* 28 (1986), 558–90. Treswell, *London Surveys* 19–20.

14. 'Samuel Dennett, 1688', TNA: PCC PROB/5/510. 'Job Orchard, 1678', TNA: PCC PROB/5/552A. 'William Pease, 1668', TNA: PCC PROB/5/794. 'Honor Chew, 1698', TNA: PCC PROB/5/2893. 'Thomas Lloyd, 1758', TNA: PCC PROB 3/57/12.

15. Warming pans of different materials and values were listed amongst kitchen goods in fifty of the households examined. Peter King's analysis of Essex inventories from the late eighteenth century identifies warming pans stored in kitchens and butteries. King, 'Pauper Inventories', 185.

16. Weatherill, *Consumer Behaviour*, 11.

17. Brown, 'Continuity and Change', 589. Treswell, *London Surveys* 18.

18. Weatherill, *Consumer Behaviour*, 6.

19. Ibid., 159. Even some of the poorest households had designated chambers on the upper floors of their modest dwellings that were used for sleep. King, 'Pauper inventories', 184–6.

20. This calculation is based on a combined analysis of room location where it is directly specified in the inventories and room name based on the usual location of certain rooms as indicated in M. Bailey, 'Glossary of Names for Rooms', in *Culture and Environment: Essays in Honour of Sir Cyril Fox*, ed. I.L.L. Foster and L. Alcock (London: Routledge & Kegan Paul, 1963), 481–99.

21. The nature of servants' sleeping arrangements is explored in Amanda Flather, *Gender and Space in Early Modern England* (Woodbridge: Royal Historical Society/Boydell Press, 2007), 69–70. Barbara A. Hanawalt, *Growing Up in Medieval London: The Experience of Childhood in History* (Oxford: Oxford University Press, 1993), 180–1. Tim Meldrum, *Domestic Service and Gender 1660–1750: Life and Work in the London Household* (Harlow: Longman, 2000), 76–80, 100–8. Vickery, *Behind Closed Doors*, 38.

22. 'Richard Burford, 1738', TNA: PCC PROB/3/37/28 (1738).

23. 'Elizabeth Neale, 1758', TNA: PCC PROB 3/57/4.

24. On the building of one- and two-room plan houses in late seventeenth- and early eighteenth-century London see Peter Guillery, *The Small House in Eighteenth-Century London: A Social and Architectural History* (New Haven and London: Paul Mellon Centre for Studies in British Art, Yale University Press in association with English Heritage, 2004), 49–50, 146.

25. 'John Peach, 1738', TNA: PCC PROB/3/37/14.

26. The surviving oak box bedstead of yeoman Henry Hutchinson from Balderstone appears to have been specially commissioned to mark his marriage in 1712, but it may nevertheless offer an approximate guide to the size of similar bedsteads. Hutchinson's bedstead is 1918mm high and 1828mm wide. 'Box Bed, c. 1712', Courtesy of Beamish Museum.
27. 'William Peacocke, 1678', TNA: PCC PROB/5/438.
28. 'William Beeching, 1708', TNA: PCC PROB/5/2575.
29. 'Thomas Dullison, 1748', TNA: PCC PROB 3/47/18.
30. 'John Barrow, 1738', TNA: PCC PROB 3/31/2.
31. 'John Ellis, 1668', TNA: PCC PROB/5/1001.
32. 'Henry Clack, 1718', TNA: PCC PROB 5/9.
33. 'Elizabeth Cooper, 1758', TNA: PCC PROB 3/57/29.
34. 'John Lichford, 1718', TNA: PCC PROB/3/17/6.
35. On the internal boundaries and organisation of multi-occupancy households in London see Vickery, 'An Englishman's Home', 147–73.
36. 'Maria Barrett, 1728', TNA: PCC PROB 3/27/1.
37. 'William Lewis, 1748', TNA: PCC PROB 3/47/8.
38. 'John Darlinge, 1728', TNA: PCC PROB 31/58/350. For further examples of how sleeping spaces could be distinguished from living space see Vickery, Behind Closed Doors, 296.
39. In Norwich an estimated 87 per cent of parlour chambers from sixty-four surviving inventories were used for sleep with no indication that they functioned as sites for working or cooking. Ursula Priestley, P.J. Corfield and Helen Sutermeister, 'Rooms and Room Use in Norwich Housing, 1580–1730', Post-Medieval Archaeology 16 (1982), 107–9, 114.
40. Pamela Sambrook, A Country House at Work: Three Centuries of Dunham Massey (London: The National Trust, 2003), 70.
41. 'Sir Philip Harcourt, 1688', TNA: PCC PROB 5/704.
42. John Ellis's hall chamber included 'one skrene'. 'John Ellis, 1668', TNA: PCC PROB 5/1001. On the uses of linen as a physical and conceptual divider see Riello, 'Fabricating the Domestic', 62.
43. John Fransham, Memoirs of the Life, Character, Opinions and Writings of that Learned and Eccentric Man, John Fransham of Norwich, ed. W. Saint (Norwich, 1811), 148–9. 'Notebook containing manuscript copy letters in the hand of Charles Wesley', JRL: DDCW 8/15.
44. Flather, Gender and Space, 69.
45. Cited in Flather, Gender and Space, 71. On the sexual vulnerability of servants who slept in close proximity to their employers, see Gowing, ' "The Twinkling of a Bedstaff" ', 275–304.
46. On this point see Vickery, 'An Englishman's Home', 150–2.
47. Flather, Gender and Space, 72–3.
48. Horace Walpole, Horace Walpole's Correspondence with George Selwyn, Lord Lincoln, Sir Charles Hanbury Williams, Henry Fox, Richard Edgcumbe, vol. 30 of The Yale Edition of Horace Walpole's Correspondence, ed. W.S. Lewis and Robert A. Smith (London and New Haven: Oxford University Press and Yale University Press, 1961), 86–90
49. Peter Thornton and Maurice Tomlin, The Furnishing and Decoration of Ham House (London: Furniture History Society, 1980), 9, 39–41, 94–5. Peter Thornton, Seventeenth-Century Interior Decoration in England, France and Holland (New Haven and London: Paul Mellon Centre for Studies in British Art, Yale University Press, 1990), 59.
50. 'Notebook containing manuscript copy letters in the hand of Charles Wesley', JRL: DDCW 8/15.
51. The spatial separation of beds and their vertical relocation was not confined to England. Evidence from eighteenth-century Tuscany shows that beds were rarely found in ground-floor spaces. Sarti, Europe at Home, 137–9.

52. Woodforde, *Diary*, 263.
53. These figures are based on the incidence of the terms 'bedstead', 'bedsteed', 'steddle', 'pallet', 'truckle' or 'trundle'. References to 'settles', 'benches', 'squabs' and 'settees' have been excluded because these items of furniture served a dual purpose as seating furniture although they may also have been used for sleep on some occasions.
54. Overton, Whittle, Dean and Hann, *Production and Consumption*, 81.
55. For advice on the correct make-up of cradles see *The Workwoman's Guide*, 41–4.
56. Numerous references to 'matt and corde' appear in 'John Vaux, 1668', TNA: PCC PROB 5/965. See also 'John Beck, 1678', TNA: PCC PROB 5/595.
57. Cited in John Ashton, *Social life in the reign of Queen Anne* (London: Chatto & Windus, 1882), 58.
58. 'Thomas Moseley, 1688', TNA: PCC PROB 5/908. 'Thomas Holloway, 1668', TNA: PCC PROB 5/1385. See also 'Elizabeth Allen, 1678', TNA: PCC PROB 5/594; 'Thomas Alstone, 1678', TNA: PCC PROB 5/972; 'William James, 1678', TNA: PCC PROB 5/1031 and 'William Reed, 1678', TNA: PCC PROB 5/2304.
59. Hamling, *Decorating the 'Godly' Household*, 167–74. Elizabeth Sharrett, 'Beds as stage properties in English Renaissance drama: materializing the lifecycle', (PhD diss., University of Birmingham, 2014).
60. Many thanks to Sarah Fox for providing me with this image and to the Beamish Museum for allowing me to reproduce it.
61. This point has been made by scholars including McShane and Bailey, 'Beds'. Gowing, '"The Twinkling of a Bedstaff"', 282–4. Katie Barclay, 'Intimacy, Community and Power: Bedding Rituals in Eighteenth-Century Scotland', in *Emotion, Ritual and Power in Europe: 1200 to the Present*, ed. Katie Barclay and Merridee L. Bailey (Palgrave, forthcoming 2016). Many thanks to Angela McShane, Joanne Bailey and Katie Barclay for sharing their unpublished work with me.
62. Latham, *Account Book*, 3, 7, 9.
63. Dolan, 'The Fabric of Life', 360, 366.
64. 'Anne Blackburn, 1718', TNA: PCC PROB 5/1.
65. 'Ma'ttress' in Samuel Johnson, *A Dictionary of the English Language: in which the words are deduced from their originals, and illustrated in their different significations by examples from the best writers*, vol. 2 (London, 1755–6).
66. Cited in Clare Browne 'Making and Using Quilts in Eighteenth-century Britain', in *Quilts 1700–2010: Hidden Histories, Untold Stories*, ed. Sue Prichard (London: V&A Publishing, 2012) 25. See also Rosemary E. Allan, *Quilts & Coverlets: The Beamish Collections* (Co. Durham: Beamish Museum, 2007), 13.
67. This figure combines the use of the terms 'bed' and 'mattress' and divergent spellings of those two terms in the inventories. Down beds were listed in Thomas Alstone's 'Blew Chamber' and 'Best Chamber', 'Thomas Alstone, 1678', TNA: PCC PROB 5/972. A 'bead sack' appears in 'Samuel Dennett, 1688', TNA: PCC PROB 5/510.
68. *The Workwoman's Guide*, 198–9.
69. 'William Brewer, 1669', TNA: PCC PROB 5/1549.
70. 'December 1684, Trial of George Clark Mary Clark George Clark (t16841210-20)', and 'May 1693, Trial of Prudence Sanders Elizabeth Miller (t16930531-13)', accessed 16 May 2012, http://www.oldbaileyonline.org.
71. 'Edward Simpson, 1668', TNA: PCC PROB 11/327/553.
72. 'Margaretta Douglas, 1728', TNA: PCC PROB 31/58/348. 'Elizabeth Allen, 1678', TNA: PCC PROB 5/594.
73. Styles, 'Lodging at the Old Bailey', 61, 73.
74. 'Thomas Johnson, 1708', TNA: PCC PROB 5/1621.
75. Peter Thornton and Maurice Tomlin, *The Furnishing and Decoration of Ham House* (London: Furniture History Society, 1980), 12–13, 55–6. See also Anna Whitelock, *Elizabeth's Bed-Fellows*, 7–10.
76. 'truckle, v.', OED Online, Oxford University Press, accessed 13 July 2011, http://www.oed.com.
77. Pepys, *Diary*, vol. 8, 474.

78. Isaac Ware, *A complete body of architecture. Adorned with plans and elevations, from original designs* (London, 1767), 346–7. Tryon, *A treatise of cleanness*, 7–10. A mock song from 1675 also identified the truckle bed as a place of sexual vulnerability in narrating the misfortune of a young maidservant who was raped and impregnated by her lady's husband who had been lying in the 'High-bed' in the same room. Author of Westminster Drollery, *Mock Songs and Joking Poems* (London, 1675), 70–1. Similar versions of this story feature in Richard Head's *Nugae Venales, or, Complaisant Companion* (London, 1675), 33–4 and in William Hickes's *Coffee-House Jests* (London, 1686).

79. John Dryden, *The Wild Gallant* (London, 1669), 25. Possession of a bed was considered to be a fundamental unit of respectability for most early modern households. Steven King, *Poverty and Welfare in England, 1700–1850: A Regional Perspective* (Manchester: Manchester University Press, 2000), 1.

80. Edmund Bower, *Doctor Lamb Revived, or, Witchcraft condemn'd in Anne Bodenham* (London, 1653), 12–15.

81. George Sinclair, *Satan's Invisible World Discovered* (Edinburgh, 1685), 32–9, 146.

82. Samuel Butler, *Hudibras in Three Parts* (London, 1684), 186.

83. George Fox, *A New England Fire Brand Quenched* (London, 1678), 96. Norman Penney (ed.), *The First Publishers of Truth* (London: Headley, 1907), 93.

84. 'Christopher Wilson, 1728', TNA: PCC PROB 31/58/356. Rachel Fuller, 'Out of Sight, Out of Mind? The Meaning of the Linnenkast in the Material and Conceptual Landscape of the Seventeenth-Century Dutch Republic', (MA diss., Victoria and Albert Museum/Royal College of Art history of design programme, 2004).

85. *The Workwoman's Guide*, 181.

86. Maxine Berg, 'Women's Consumption and the Industrial Classes in Eighteenth-Century England', *Journal of Social History* 30 (1996), 415–34. For equivalent practices in early America see Laurel Thatcher Ulrich, *The Age of Homespun: Objects and Stories in the Creation of an American Myth* (New York: Alfred A. Knopf, 2001), 40.

87. A letter from Henry Seymour Conway to Horace Walpole confirmed that King William and Queen Mary slept with 'nothing but a single sheet of fine Holland over their persons'. Horace Walpole, *Horace Walpole's Correspondence with Henry Seymour Conway, Lady Ailesbury, Lord and Lady Hertford, Mrs Harris*, vol. 39 of *The Yale Edition of Horace Walpole's Correspondence*, ed. W.S. Lewis, Lars E. Troide, Edwine M. Martz and Robert A. Smith (London and New Haven: Oxford University Press and Yale University Press, 1974), 286. Lady Grisell Baillie, *The Household Book of Lady Grisell Baillie, 1692–1733*, ed. Robert Scott-Moncrieff (Edinburgh: Scottish History Society, 1911), 186.

88. 'William Brewer, 1668', TNA: PCC PROB 5/1549. 'Philip Harcourt, 1688', TNA: PCC PROB 5/704.

89. 'Elizabeth Mayne, 1698', TNA: PCC PROB 5/3613. 'Mary Griffin, 1688', TNA: PCC PROB 5/1181.

90. Many thanks to Susan North for her generous advice about thread counts. The Object Numbers of the eight sheets in the collections of the Victoria and Albert Museum are: T.54-1958; T.10-1914; T.295-1965; T.296-1965; T.152-1986; T.6-2002; T.161-1962; T.1-1986.

91. *The Workwoman's Guide*, 181–2.

92. The location of many blankets in the PCC inventories indicates that they were placed in storage at some times of the year, presumably to account for seasonal changes in temperature. The Queen's Bedchamber at Ham House had separate sets of bedding for summer and winter. Thornton and Tomlin, *Furnishing and Decoration*, 144–5.

93. 'Thomas Alstone, 1678', TNA: PCC PROB 5/972.

94. Baillie, *Household Book*, 179, 181, 186

95. John Vaux's 'Greate Chamber' in his Bedfordshire home listed blankets and rugs alongside each other in addition to the bedstead, matts, bed-cords and curtains. 'John Vaux, 1668', TNA: PCC PROB 5/965. 'rug' in Johnson, *Dictionary*, vol. 2.

96. *The Workwoman's Guide*, 200.

97. Samuel Johnson described a quilt as 'a cover made by stitching one cloth over another with some soft substance between them'. 'Quilt', in Johnson, *Dictionary*, vol. 2. On the large-scale importation of calico quilts from India in the late seventeenth century see

The British Cotton Trade 1660–1815 Part II International Trade and the Politics of Consumption 1690s–1730, ed. Beverly Lemire (London: Pickering & Chatto, 2010), 229.

98. On the role of the global textile trade in delineating the spatial and material boundaries of sleep see Beverly Lemire, 'Draping the Body', 87–91. Giorgio Riello, *Cotton: The Fabric that Made the Modern World* (Cambridge: Cambridge University Press: Cambridge and New York, 2013).

99. Rosemary E. Allan, *North Country Quilts & Coverlets: From Beamish Museum, County Durham* (Stanley: Beamish, North of England Open Air Museum, 1987), 171–2.

100. On the growing popularity of cotton bed coverings see John Styles, 'What Were Cottons for', 307–26. Beverly Lemire, *Fashion's Favourite: The Cotton Trade and the Consumer in Britain: 1660–1800* (Oxford: Oxford University Press, 1991). Erin Beeston, 'Unravelling Hidden Histories: Researching the Bolton Museum Caddow Quilt Collection', *Social History in Museums: Journal of the Social History Curators Group* 37 (2013), 60–9. Erin Beeston and Laurel Horton, 'Bolton's Cotton Counterpanes: Hand-Weaving in the Industrial Age', *Quilt Studies: the Journal of the British Quilt Studies Group* 14 (2013), 7–36.

101. *The Workwoman's Guide*, 192, 201, 216.

102. Cole, *Blecheley Diary*, 325.

103. Doctors recommend the use of such items to treat insomnia because they help to promote feelings of familiarity, belonging and relaxation. Steger, 'Cultures of Sleep', 71.

104. 'Reverend William Byatt, 1758', TNA: PCC PROB 3/57/38.

105. 'William Brewer, 1660', TNA: PCC PROB 5/1549.

106. 'Bed hanging, c. 1691–c. 1720', Museum of London, Object No. 68.57.

107. 'Abigail Pett bed hangings, c. 1680–c. 1700', Victoria and Albert Museum, Object No. T.13B&C-1929. On the tree-of-life design see Heather Audin, *Patchwork and Quilting in Britain* (Oxford: Shire Publications, 2013) 20.

108. The pattern for a local squire's quilt in Sussex was provided by the local schoolmaster, for which he was paid 10s 6d. Cited in Browne, 'Making and Using Quilts', 37.

109. See for example an embroidered and quilted cream linen bedcover and curtain that was possibly owned by the Hynde Cotton family of Madingley Hall, Cambridgeshire. 'Bedcover, c. 1725–c. 1750', Victoria and Albert Museum, Object No. T.386.A-1970.

110. John Styles suggests that woollen bedding textiles were commonplace in London lodgings in the mid-eighteenth century. Styles, 'Lodging at the Old Bailey', 75–85.

111. 'Pillowcase, c. 17th century', Victoria and Albert Museum, Object No. T.298-1965. 'Sheet, c. 17th century', Victoria and Albert Museum, Object No. T.295-1965. 'Sheet, c. 17th century', Victoria and Albert Museum, Object No. T.96-1965.

112. Emanuel Ford, *The Most Pleasant History of Ornatus and Artesia* (London, 1607), C2. I am grateful to Mary Brooks for this reference.

113. Catherine Hutton, *Reminiscences of a Gentlewoman of the Last Century: Letters of Catherine Hutton*, ed. C.H. Beale (Birmingham: Cornish Brothers, 1891), 213.

114. Susan Frye, *Pens and Needles: Women's Textualities in Early Modern England* (Philadelphia: University of Pennsylvania Press, 2010), 1–4. Thatcher Ulrich, *The Age of Homespun*, 40.

115. Latham, *Account Book*, 86, 105. Latham's account book shows that he relied on a dense network of local tradespeople to service his household needs.

116. Cole, *Blecheley Diary*, 146, 275, 283.

117. On 'quiltings' see Baumgarten and Smith Ivey, *Four Centuries of Quilts*, 7.

118. For an example of this see the composition of the 1718 patchwork coverlet from Wiltshire in Audin, *Patchwork and Quilting*, 14–16.

119. Joanne Bailey, 'Stitchers in Time and Space: Women in the Long Eighteenth Century', in *Quilts, 1700–2010*, 153–6.

120. Thomas Baker's play *Hampstead Heath* declared that 'Patchwork is the Fashion of this Age': cited in John Styles, 'Patchwork on the Page', in *Quilts*, 49–51.

121. Cited in Browne, 'Making and Using Quilts', 46–7.

122. On the composition of eighteenth-century quilts and the regulation of their fillings by the Worshipful Company of Upholders see Browne, 'Making and Using Quilts', 25, 27.

123. 'John Riddiough, 1698', TNA: PCC PROB 5/1270.

124. 'Richard Edward-Holmwood, 1688', TNA: PCC PROB 5/663.
125. 'Philip Harcourt, 1688', TNA: PCC PROB 5/704. *The Workwoman's Guide*, 200.
126. 'Elizabeth Dugdale, 1718', TNA: PCC PROB 3/17/5. 'Anne Blackburn, 1718', TNA: PCC PROB 5/1.
127. 'John Darlinge, 1728', TNA: PCC PROB 31/58/350. 'Richard Smith, 1758', TNA: PCC PROB 3/57/8.
128. Frances Gage, 'Teaching Them to Serve and Obey: Giulio Mancini on Collecting Religious Art in Seventeenth-Century Rome', in *Sacred Possessions: Collecting Italian Religious Art 1500–1900*, ed. Gail Feigenbaum and Sybille Ebert-Shifferer (Los Angeles: Getty Research Institute, 2011), 68–83. Frances Gage, 'The Air over There: Art, Travel and the Regulation of the Non-Naturals, c. 1580–1650', (paper presented at 'Healthy Living in Pre-modern Europe', Institute of Historical Research, September 2013). Frances Gage 'Exercise for Mind and Body: Giulio Mancini, Collecting, and the Beholding of Landscape Painting in the Seventeenth Century', *Renaissance Quarterly* 61 (2008), 1167–1207.
129. Shades of red often distinguished the most important rooms within many households including royal and noble residences. Vickery, *Behind Closed Doors*, 173–4. The heraldic significance of the colour red and the high cost of scarlet and crimson dyes are noted in David Mitchell, ' "My purple will be too sad for that melancholy room": Furnishings for Interiors in London and Paris, 1660–1735', *Textile History* 40 (2009), 7, 21.
130. Pastoureau cited in Mitchell, 'Furnishings', 23–5. Mitchell's analysis of the bedding textiles of London freemen shows that blue overtook green as the most popular colour for sleeping chambers in the late seventeenth century.
131. 'Benjamin Carter, 1728', TNA: PCC PROB 3/27/47.
132. 'Mary Martin, 1669', TNA: PCC PROB 5/2377. John Styles has shown how the poorer sorts exercised a degree of choice and agency over the objects to which they had indirect access. Styles, 'Lodging at the Old Bailey', 63. David Mitchell has noted the rising popularity of cheap printed stuff for bed furnishings amongst freemen in London between 1660 and 1735. Mitchell, 'Furnishings', 6–8.
133. The link between healthy sleep and feelings of satisfaction or reward is explained in Steger, 'Cultures of Sleep', 73.
134. Styles, 'Lodging at the Old Bailey', 73.
135. Vickery notes that green was the most commonly requested colour for bedrooms in her analysis of the letter-book of London upholsterers Trollope and Sons. Vickery, *Behind Closed Doors*, 174. Smith, *Key of Green*, 3, 171–8.
136. 'Philip Harcourt, 1688', TNA: PCC PROB 5/207. 'Margaretta Douglas, 1728', TNA: PCC PROB 31/58/348. Mitchell, 'Furnishings', 16.
137. Pepys, *Diary*, vol. 7, 257.
138. Peta Motture and Luke Syson, 'Art in the *casa*', in *At Home in Renaissance Italy*, ed. Marta Ajmar-Wollheim and Flora Dennis (London: V&A Publications, 2006), 283.
139. Pepys, *Diary*, vol. 7, 14.
140. Vickery, *Behind Closed Doors*, 175. *The Workwoman's Guide*, 192.
141. Italian sleeping chambers were replete with a plethora of symbolic colours and visual imagery that aimed to put their occupants in mind of procreation, to encourage fertility, and to safeguard pregnancy. Brenda Preyer, 'The Florentine *casa*', in *At Home in Renaissance Italy*, 40. Elizabeth Currie, *Inside the Renaissance House* (London: V&A Publications, 2006), 51–8.
142. Mitchell, 'Furnishings', 12–13.
143. 'George Ashbey, 1728', TNA: PCC PROB 5/2641. 'Benjamin Coster, 1758', TNA: PCC PROB 3/57/7.
144. Thornton, *Autobiography*, 249.
145. Ibid., 173, 261–2.
146. Auslander, 'Beyond Words', 1019.
147. On the creation of bedding textiles and other movable goods as markers of family history see Thatcher Ulrich, *The Age of Homespun*, 110–11, 135–8.
148. Latham, *Account Book*, 89.

149. 'George Ashbey, 1728', TNA: PCC PROB 5/2641.
150. Claire Smith, 'The Governor's Daughter', in *Quilts*, 54–5.
151. 'Dorothy Punnett, 1719', TNA: PCC PROB 5/41. Hutton, *Reminiscences*, 21.
152. James Daybell, *The Material Letter in Early Modern England: Manuscript Letters and the Culture and Practices of Letter-Writing, 1512–1635* (London: Palgrave Macmillan, 2012), 220–1. Vickery, 'An Englishman's Home', 147–8, 164, 166.
153. Such large items may not have been easily transportable between different parts of the house and some may well have been made within sleeping chambers, which reinforced the links between their production and intended use. Practising embroidery in sleeping chambers is suggested by the PCC inventories. The only pincushion in the home of Margaretta Douglas was listed in the red sleeping chamber in 1728. 'Margaretta Douglas, 1728', TNA: PCC PROB 31/58/348.
154. Sarti, *Europe at Home*, 119–120.

Chapter 5: Sleep and Sociability

1. Thomas Turner, *The Diary of Thomas Turner 1754–1765*, ed. David Vaisey (Oxford: Oxford University Press, 1985), 23.
2. Ibid., 130.
3. For a definition of 'beau monde' see Hannah Greig, *The Beau Monde: Fashionable Society in Georgian London* (Oxford: Oxford University Press, 2013), 3.
4. Thoresby, *Diary*, vol. 1, 55; vol. 2, 120.
5. Adam Fitz-Adam, *The World*, vol. 2, no. 74 (London, 1755–57), 130–1. Journal editor and novelist Edward Kimber likewise noted the intense flurry of nocturnal social interactions that characterised the associational culture of metropolitan clubs in *The Life and Adventures of Joe Thompson, a narrative founded on fact*, vol. 1 (London, 1775), 64–5.
6. Koslofsky, *Evening's Empire*, 1–18, 91–127. See also Ekirch, *At Day's Close*, 210–26.
7. *The Statutes at Large, from the twentieth year of the reign of King George the Second to the thirtieth year of the reign of King George the Second*, vol. 7 (London, 1764), 137. *An Act for the better enlightening the open places, streets, lanes, passages, and courts, and for the better regulating the nightly watch and bedels within the parish of Christ Church in the county of Middlesex* (London, 1738). Greig estimates that London's population was 575,000 in 1700 and 750,000 in 1750. Greig, *Beau Monde*, 8. See also Cockayne, *Hubbub*, 223.
8. For discussions of sociability in eighteenth-century culture see Gillian Russell, *Women, Sociability and Theatre in Georgian London* (Cambridge: Cambridge University Press, 2007). Neil McKendrick, John Brewer and John Plumb, *The Birth of a Consumer Society: The Commercialization of Eighteenth-Century England* (London: Europa Publications, 1982), 265–85. John Brewer, *The Pleasures of the Imagination: English Culture in the Eighteenth Century* (London: HarperCollins, 1997), 3–122.
9. *Tatler*, vol. 3, 330–4.
10. Ibid., 330–1.
11. William Ellis, *The Country Housewife's Family Companion* (London, 1750), ix. Lorna Weatherill suggests that midday was the usual time to take dinner amongst the middling sorts that she examined in *Consumer Behaviour*, 152–3.
12. Ashton, *Social Life*, 68–71.
13. Greig, *Beau Monde*, 32–98.
14. Horace Walpole, *Horace Walpole's Correspondence with Henry Seymour Conway, Lady Ailesbury, Lord and Lady Hertford, Mrs Harris*, vol. 39 of *The Yale Edition of Horace Walpole's Correspondence*, ed. W.S. Lewis, Lars E. Troide, Edwine M. Martz and Robert A. Smith (London and New Haven: Oxford University Press and Yale University Press, 1974), 436–8.
15. Richard Owen Cambridge, *An Elegy Written in an Empty Assembly-Room* (London, 1756), 11.
16. Adam Fitz-Adam, *The World*, vol. 2 (London, 1755–57), 134.

17. By the 1690s, a large proportion of gentry families spent at least six months of the year in London. See Susan Whyman, *Sociability and Power in Late Stuart England: The Cultural Worlds of the Verneys 1650–1720* (Oxford: Oxford University Press, 2002), 4. For details of new building projects in 'the town' see Greig, *Beau Monde*, 8–11.
18. Whyman, *Sociability and Power*, 94.
19. On the expansion of cultural activities in provincial centres see Peter Borsay, *The English Urban Renaissance: Culture and Society in the Provincial Town* (Oxford: Clarendon Press, 1991).
20. Nicholas Blundell, *Blundell's Diary, Comprising Selections from the Diary of Nicholas Blundell Esq. from 1702 to 1728*, ed. Rev. T. Ellison Gibson (Liverpool: Walmsley 1895), 27.
21. Ibid., 23, 27.
22. Ibid., 35.
23. Ibid., 38, 103, 198.
24. Hurst, *Diaries*, 94.
25. Paul Langford, *A Polite and Commercial People: England 1727–1783* (Oxford: Clarendon Press, 1992), 102. Frederick Alderson, *The Inland Resorts and Spas of Britain* (Newton Abbot: David and Charles Holdings Ltd, 1973).
26. Thoresby, *Diary*, vol. 2, 163. Katharine Glover, 'Polite Society and the Rural Resort: The Meanings of Moffat Spa in the Eighteenth Century', *Journal for Eighteenth-Century Studies* 34 (2011), 66.
27. 'Letters of Anne Dormer', British Library Add. MS 72516, fols 156, 192v.
28. Ibid., fol. 218v.
29. Blundell, *Diary*, 125.
30. Celia Fiennes, *The Journeys of Celia Fiennes*, ed. Christopher Morris (London: the Cresset Press, 1949), 1.
31. Ibid., 103.
32. Fiennes, *Journeys*, xxxii. *The Workwoman's Guide*, 108.
33. Fiennes, *Journeys*, 207.
34. Censure of irregular sleeping hours can be detected in a children's verse entitled 'The Sluggard' by independent minister Isaac Watts. Isaac Watts, *Divine Songs Attempted in Easy Language for the Use of Children* (London, 1716), 46–7.
35. Horace Walpole, *Horace Walpole's Correspondence with George Montagu, II*, vol. 10 of *The Yale Edition of Horace Walpole's Correspondence*, ed. W.S. Lewis and Ralph S. Brown Jr (London and New Haven: Oxford University Press and Yale University Press, 1941), 291–3.
36. Nathan Bailey, *Dictionarium Britannicum: or a more compleat universal etymological English dictionary than any extant* (London, 1737).
37. Lady Mary Wortley Montagu, *The Letters and Works of Lady Mary Wortley Montagu*, ed. Lord Wharncliffe, vol. 3 (London, 1837), 151–2.
38. Medical practitioners believed that the physical harm caused by late bedtimes intensified with age. Cogan, *The haven of health*, 233–4, 237–8.
39. Pepys, *Diary*, vol. 6, 147.
40. Baillie, *Household Book*, 333, 340, 374, 397.
41. Joseph Price, *A Kentish Parson: Selections from the Private Papers of the Revd Joseph Price Vicar of Brabourne, 1767–1786*, ed. G.M. Ditchfield and Bryan Keith-Lucas (Maidstone: Kent County Council, Arts & Libraries, 1991), 156. Horace Walpole, *Horace Walpole's Correspondence with Sir Horace Mann*, vol. 18 of *The Yale Edition of Horace Walpole's Correspondence*, ed. W.S. Lewis, Warren Hunting Smith and George L. Lam (London and New Haven: Oxford University Press and Yale University Press, 1955), 315.
42. Price, *Kentish Parson*, 157–8.
43. Alice Fairfax-Lucy, *Charlecote and the Lucys: The Chronicle of An English Family* (London: Oxford University Press, 1958), 205, 220.
44. 'Ann Eldridge, 19/7/1738', London Metropolitan Archives, DL/C/272, fol. 50. Cannon, *Chronicles*, Part 1, 129. Tryon, *A treatise of cleanness*, 5–7.

45. Horace Walpole warned George Montagu never to stay at Wellingborough: 'pray never lie there – the beastliest inn upon earth is there!' Walpole, *Correspondence with George Montagu*, 88.
46. Blundell, *Diary*, 165–8.
47. Tryon, *A treatise of cleanness*, 5.
48. Price, *Kentish Parson*, 29, 157–8, 160.
49. Hutton, *Reminiscences*, 118.
50. Pepys, *Diary*, vol. 6, 176–7.
51. Woodforde, *Diary*, 98, 134, 169, 305.
52. Adam Smith, *The Theory of Moral Sentiments* (London, 1759), 80–2.
53. Bernard Mandeville, *Aesop Dress'd, or a Collection of Fables* (London, 1704), 27–34.
54. Bernard Mandeville, *The Fable of the Bees, or, Private Vices, Public Benefits,* vol. 1 (Edinburgh, 1772), 108–9. David Hume, 'Essay II: Of Luxury', in *Essays and Treatises on Several Subjects* (London, 1758), 157–9. Hume was eager to strike a balance between 'innocent' and 'blameable' luxury, with the former defined as 'beneficial' to the public.
55. S.A.D. Tissot, *An Essay on the Disorders of People of Fashion* (London, 1771), 37–8.
56. Valangin, *A treatise on diet*, 273–9.
57. Benjamin Heller, 'Leisure and the Use of Domestic Space in Georgian London', *Historical Journal* 53 (2010), 623–5. Vickery, *Behind Closed Doors*, 14.
58. Blundell, *Diary*, 38, 45, 82, 98, 103, 131, 210, 219.
59. Hurst, *Diaries*, 71, 94, 175, 266. On the gendered nature of social interactions see Langford, *Polite and Commercial People*, 101
60. Benjamin Rogers, *The Diary of Benjamin Rogers, Rector of Carlton 1720–71*, ed. C.D. Linnell (Cambridge: Chadwyck-Healey, 1978), 9, 11, 44, 73.
61. Whyman, *Sociability and Power*, 90.
62. Cole, *Blecheley Diary*, 12.
63. Ibid., xxxiii.
64. Thoresby, *Diary*, vol. 1, 389. Anon., 'Of the Posture-Master', *Philosophical Transactions* 20 (1698), 262.
65. Newcome, *Diary*, 93.
66. Ibid., 13, 44, 56, 59, 137, 158.
67. *Two East Anglian Diaries*, 213–7, 226, 230, 235, 238–9, 250.
68. 'John Vaux, 1668', TNA: PCC PROB 5/965. Ponsonby, *Stories from Home,* 46.
69. Horace Walpole, *Horace Walpole's Correspondence with George Selwyn, Lord Lincoln, Sir Charles Hanbury Williams, Henry Fox, Richard Edgcumbe,* vol. 30 of *The Yale Edition of Horace Walpole's Correspondence,* ed. W.S. Lewis and Robert A. Smith (London and New Haven: Oxford University Press and Yale University Press, 1961) 165–6. See also Horace Walpole, *Horace Walpole's Correspondence with Hannah More, Lady Browne, Lady George Lennox, Lady Mary Coke, Anne Pitt, Lady Hervey, Lady Suffolk, Mary Hamilton,* vol. 31 of *The Yale Edition of Horace Walpole's Correspondence,* ed. W.S. Lewis, Robert A. Smith and Charles H. Bennett (London and New Haven: Oxford University Press and Yale University Press, 1961), 179.
70. Pepys, *Diary*, vol. 7, 241.
71. Crowley, *The Invention of Comfort*, 73–6. For an explanation of the bedding used by working people and tenants see Styles, 'Lodging at the Old Bailey', 71–5. Overton, Whittle, Dean and Hann, *Production and Consumption*, 81, 90–1, 108–10. Anne Blackburn kept a large stock of bedding in a store cupboard at the top of her staircase. 'Anne Blackburn, 1718', TNA: PCC PROB 5/1.
72. Hester C. Dibbits, 'Between Society and Family Values: The Linen Cupboard in Early-Modern Households', in *Private Domain, Public Inquiry: Families and Life-Styles in the Netherlands and Europe, 1550 to the Present*, ed. Anton Schuurman and Pieter Spierenburg (Hilversum: Verloren, 1996), 138.
73. 'Freke Papers', vol. 1, British Library Add. MS 45718, fol. 174.
74. 'Thomas Lloyd, 1758', TNA: PCC PROB 3/57/12. 'Richard Smith, 1758', TNA: PCC PROB 3/57/8. 'Benjamin Coster, 1758', TNA: PCC PROB 3/57/7. 'William Byatt, 1758', TNA: PCC PROB 3/57/38.

75. Ware, *Complete Body of Architecture*, 346–7.
76. 'Freke Papers', 180.
77. 'Richard Langricke, 1668', TNA: PCC PROB 5/694. 'Henry Mosse, 1688', TNA: PCC PROB 5/647.
78. 'Richard Edward-Holmwood, 1688', TNA: PCC PROB 5/663. 'Thomas Johnson, 1708', TNA: PCC PROB 5/1621.
79. *The Workwoman's Guide*, 197. Tryon, *A treatise of cleanness*, 6.
80. Fissell, 'Marketplace of Print', 108–32.
81. Pepys, *Diary*, vol. 8, 305, 584.
82. Ibid., vol. 4, 273.
83. Baillie, *Household Book*, 183, 186.
84. Pepys, *Diary*, vol. 8, 474.
85. Ibid., vol. 1, 139.
86. David Hill, 'James Pascall and the Long Gallery Suite at Temple Newsam', *Furniture History* 17 (1981), 70–4.
87. 'Soss' in Johnson, *Dictionary of the English Language*, vol. 2.
88. Thomas Chippendale, *The Gentleman and Cabinet-Maker's Director. Being a Large Collection of the Most Elegant and Useful Designs of Household Furniture in the Gothic, Chinese and Modern Taste* (London, 1754), 9.
89. Thornton and Tomlin, *Furnishing and Decoration*, 61–4, 149–51.
90. Ibid., 181–3.
91. Peter Thornton described the development of easy chairs in *Authentic Décor: The Domestic Interior 1620–1920* (London: Seven Dials, 2000), 52.
92. Elizabeth Freke and her husband used beds and chairs interchangeably as places of rest, particularly in times of illness. Elizabeth Freke, *The Remembrances of Elizabeth Freke, 1671–1714*, ed. Raymond A. Anselment (Cambridge: Cambridge University Press, 2001), 84, 196, 292.
93. Walpole, *Correspondence with Sir Horace Mann*, 377–8.
94. Sarah Fox noted writing letters whilst her husband dozed in his easy chair. Sarah Fox, *The Diary of Sarah Fox, née Champion, Bristol 1745–1802*, ed. Madge Dresser, vol. 55 (Bristol: Bristol Record Society, 2003), 169.
95. Charles Le Mercher de Longpré, baron d'Haussez, *Great Britain in 1833*, vol. 1, 102–3. Cited in Paul Langford, *Englishness Identified: Manners and Character, 1650–1850* (Oxford: Oxford University Press, 2000), 118.
96. Mary Leapor, 'Crumble Hall', in *Poems upon Several Occasions*, vol. 2 (London, 1751), 116.
97. Roger Schmidt, 'Caffeine and the Coming of the Enlightenment', *Raritan* 23 (2003), 147.
98. Alexander Pope, *Letters of Mr Pope, and Several Eminent Persons, from the year 1705, to 1735*, vol. 1 (London, 1735), 122.
99. Thomas Short, *A dissertation upon tea, explaining its nature and properties by many new experiments; and demonstrating from philosophical principles, the various effects it has on different constitutions* (London, 1730), 46.
100. Thomas Sheridan, *A general dictionary of the English language*, vol. 2 (London, 1780). The term also featured in Samuel Pratt, *Liberal Opinions, or the history of Benignus*, vol. 6 (London, 1777), 51, 64. 'Lucubratory', in Johnson, *Dictionary*, vol. 2.
101. John Ray, *A Collection of English Proverbs digested into a convenient method for the speedy finding any one upon occasion* (Cambridge, 1678), 34–5.
102. Cavallo and Storey, *Healthy Living*, 121–3.
103. Ray, *English Proverbs*, 34. Similar shifts in attitude towards daytime sleep, and signs of an emerging culture of napping, have been noted in the Italian context. Cavallo and Storey, *Healthy Living*, 121–3.
104. Newcome, *Diary*, 151.
105. Horace Walpole, *Horace Walpole's Correspondence with John Chute, Richard Bentley, The Earl of Strafford, Sir William Hamilton, the Earl and Countess Harcourt, George Hardinge*, vol. 35 of *The Yale Edition of Horace Walpole's Correspondence*, ed. W.S. Lewis

and A. Dayle Wallace and Robert A. Smith with the assistance of Edwine M. Martz (London and New Haven: Oxford University Press and Yale University Press, 1973), 590–1.

106. Pepys, *Diary*, vol. 1, 197.

107. Ibid., vol. 2, 147; vol. 6, 312.

108. Woodforde, *Diary*, vol. 1, 236.

109. Ibid., 131, 157.

110. Ibid., 153.

111. Walpole, *Correspondence with Henry Seymour Conway*, 284.

112. Maria, Lady Nugent, *A Journal of a Voyage to, and residence in, the Island of Jamaica, from 1801 to 1805, and of subsequent events in England from 1805 to 1811, in two volumes*, vol. 2 (London, 1839), 294–5.

113. On cleanliness and household reputation see Dolan, 'Fabric of Life', 355. Styles, *The Dress of the People*, 77–82. *The Workwoman's Guide*, 182, 200.

114. Horace Walpole, *Horace Walpole's Miscellaneous Correspondence*, vol. 41 of *The Yale Edition of Horace Walpole's Correspondence*, ed. W.S. Lewis and John Riely with the assistance of Edwine M. Martz and Ruth K. McClure (London and New Haven: Yale University Press and Oxford University Press, 1980), 37–9, 86, 125.

115. Walpole, *Correspondence with George Montagu*, 191–3. Henry Seymour Conway's wife timed her visit to Strawberry Hill according to the time needed to air her bed. Walpole, *Correspondence with Henry Seymour Conway*, 332–4, 562–3. Walpole, *Correspondence with Hannah More*, 234–5.

116. Families of the lower ranks commonly slept in the same bed out of necessity but this also ensured warmth and security. Ekirch, *At Day's Close*, 278–9.

117. Walpole, *Correspondence with Henry Seymour Conway*, 284.

118. Ralph Thoresby complained that sharing a bed and a chamber gave him insufficient time or privacy to perform his evening devotions. *Diary of Ralph Thoresby*, vol. 1, 412; vol. 2, 12–13, 15, 94.

119. The downside of sharing beds with strangers is explored in Cockayne, *Hubbub*, 149.

120. Turner, *Diary*, 286, 288, 295.

121. Pepys, *Diary*, vol. 6, 282, 285.

122. Ibid., vol. 6, 176–7.

123. Ibid., vol. 5, 189.

124. Ibid., vol. 1, 222.

125. Raper, *Receipt Book*, 16.

126. Cannon, *Chronicles*, Part 2, 424. Robert Forby, *The Vocabulary of East-Anglia; An Attempt to Record the Vulgar Tongue of the Twin Sister Counties of Norfolk and Suffolk as it existed in the last twenty years of the eighteenth century*, vol. 1 (London, 1830), 21.

127. Hurst, *Diaries*, 266.

128. Ibid., 175, 290–2. Sarah's poem was published in *The Lady's Magazine* in February 1760.

129. Ekirch, *At Day's Close*, 280–1.

130. Ibid., 282–4. On fears surrounding bedfellowship with strangers see Walpole, *Correspondence with John Chute*, 137.

131. Alan Bray, *The Friend* (Chicago and London: University of Chicago Press, 2003), 151–8.

132. For fuller discussion of medieval courtly gestures of bedfellowship and their meanings see John Gillingham, *Richard I* (New Haven and London: Yale University Press, 2002), 84. C. Stephen Jaeger, *Ennobling Love: In Search of a Lost Sensibility* (Philadelphia: University of Pennsylvania Press, 1999), 128–31.

133. Douglas Grant, *The Cock Lane Ghost*, (London: Macmillan and Company Limited, 1975), 10–11.

134. Turner, *Diary*, 266, 268, 270–1.

135. Woodforde, *Diary*, vol. 1, 112, 116, 149.

136. Simon Williams, 'Sleep and Health: Sociological Reflections on the Dormant Society', *Health* 6 (2002), 180.

Chapter 6: Sleep, Sensibility and Identity

1. Jane Austen, *Sense and Sensibility: a novel* (London, 1833), 71.
2. *The Encyclopaedia Britannica: or, a dictionary of arts, sciences, and miscellaneous literature on a plan entirely new*, vol. 17 (Dublin, 1790–98), 272.
3. On the popularisation of sensibility in medicine, literature and moral philosophy in eighteenth-century Britain and France see G.J. Barker-Benfield, *The Culture of Sensibility: Sex and Society in Eighteenth-Century Britain* (Chicago: University of Chicago Press, 1992). John Mullan, *Sentiment and Sociability: The Language of Feeling in the Eighteenth Century* (Oxford: Clarendon Press, 1988). Jessica Riskin, *Science in the Age of Sensibility: The Sentimental Empiricists of the French Enlightenment* (Chicago: University of Chicago Press, 2002). Janet Todd, *Sensibility: An Introduction* (London and New York: Methuen, 1986), 1–9. Ann Jessie van Sant, *Eighteenth-Century Sensibility and the Novel: The Senses in Social Context* (Cambridge: Cambridge University Press, 1993). Anne C. Vila, *Enlightenment and Pathology: Sensibility in the Literature and Medicine of Eighteenth-Century France* (Baltimore and London: The Johns Hopkins Press, 1998), 1–12.
4. The *Oxford English Dictionary* notes that the word 'sensibility' was rarely used until the mid-eighteenth century. Sensibility is here defined as 'Emotional consciousness' or 'quickness and acuteness of apprehension or feeling; the quality of being easily and strongly affected by emotional influences' and 'Capacity for refined emotion'. 'sensibility, n.', OED Online, Oxford University Press, accessed 11 October 2014, http://www.oed.com.
5. John Mullan, 'Feelings and Novels', in *Rewriting the Self: Histories from the Renaissance to the Present*, ed. Roy Porter (London and New York: Routledge, 1997), 122.
6. Martin Raymond and John Barresi have identified the long eighteenth century as the locus of a 'revolution in personal identity theory' whilst Dror Wahrman and Charles Taylor argue that this period witnessed the emergence of modern concepts of selfhood. Martin Raymond and John Barresi, *The Naturalization of the Soul: Self and Personal Identity in the Eighteenth Century* (London: Routledge, 2000). Dror Wahrman, *The Making of the Modern Self: Identity and Culture in Eighteenth-Century England* (New Haven and London: Yale University Press, 2006). Charles Taylor, *Sources of the Self: The Making of Modern Identity* (Cambridge: Cambridge University Press, 1989), 177–85. See also Alan Richardson, *The Neural Sublime: Cognitive Theories and Romantic Texts* (Baltimore: Johns Hopkins University Press, 2010), 11. See also Warner, *Fantastic Metamorphoses*, 209–10.
7. Turner, *Diary*, 26–7.
8. Lucia Dacome argues that the promotion of 'bodily domestication' drew succour from reactions against the threat of 'enthusiasm' in the early eighteenth century. Lucia Dacome, ' "To what purpose does it think?": Dreams, Sick Bodies and Confused Minds in the Age of Reason', *History of Psychiatry* 15 (2004), 396–7.
9. Anon., *A Treatise on Diseases of the Head, Brain & Nerves* (London, 1714), title page.
10. David Hartley, *Observations on Man, his Frame, his Duty, and his Expectations*, vol. 2 (London, 1749), 241.
11. James Boswell, *Boswell's Life of Johnson: Together with Boswell's Journal of a Tour to the Hebrides, and Johnson's Diary of a Journey into North Wales*, ed. George Birkbeck Hill, vol. 2 (Oxford: Clarendon Press, 1934), 440.
12. William Gerard Hamilton, *Four odes. I. On sleep. II. On beauty. III. On taste. IV. To the Right Hon. Lady *** on the death of her son* (London, 1750), 1–8.
13. William Congreve, *The story of Semele. As it is perform'd at the Theatre-Royal in Covent-Garden. Altered from the Semele of Mr. William Congreve. Set to musick by Mr. George Frederick Handel* (London, 1744), 21.
14. *Gentleman's Magazine*, vol. 7 (London, 1763), 90; vol. 33, 392.
15. Samuel Perrott, *Sermons on Practical Subjects* (Cork, 1798), 248, 250, 253, 257.
16. George Wright, *The Young Moralist consisting of Allegorical and Entertaining Essays, in Prose and Verse* (London, 1782), 47–9.

17. Seaton, *The Devotional Life*, 75.

18. Samuel Taylor Coleridge, *Collected Letters of Samuel Taylor Coleridge, 1785–1800*, ed. Earl Leslie Griggs, vol. 1 (Oxford: Clarendon Press, 1956), 455, 513.

19. John Trenchard, *A Natural History of Superstition* (London, 1709), 8, 23.

20. An appendix entitled 'A discourse of the causes, natures and cure of phrensie, madness or distraction' also appeared in Thomas Tryon ['Philotheos Physiologus'], *A Treatise of Dreams & Visions, wherein the causes natures and uses of nocturnal representations, and the communications both of good and evil angels, as also departed souls, to mankind, are theosophically unfolded; that is, according to the Word of God, and the Harmony of Created Beeings* (London, 1695).

21. See for instance Lucia Dacome, 'Resurrecting by Numbers in Eighteenth-Century England', *Past and Present*, 193 (2006), 73–110.

22. For further explanation see MacLehose, 'Fear, Fantasy and Sleep', 67–94. Rivière, 'Demons of Desire', 50. Owen Davies, 'The Nightmare Experience, Sleep Paralysis, and Witchcraft Accusations', *Folklore* 114 (2003), 187–8. Willem de Blécourt, 'Bedding the Nightmare: Somatic Experience and Narrative Meaning in Dutch and Flemish Legend Texts', *Folklore* 114:2 (2003), 227–45. Stephen Gordon, 'Medical Condition, Demon or Undead Corpse? Sleep Paralysis and the Nightmare in Medieval Europe', *Journal of the Social History of Medicine* 29 (2015), 425–44.

23. Tryon, *Treatise of Dreams*, 47–58. See also Jennifer Ford, 'Samuel Taylor Coleridge and "The pains of sleep"', in *Dreams and History*, ed. Pick and Roper, 105–24.

24. Tryon, *Treatise of Dreams*, 24–5.

25. John Bond, *An Essay on the Incubus, or Night-Mare. By John Bond M.D.* (London, 1753), 9–11. See also Laurence Heister, *A compendium of the practice of physic: by Laurence Heister, Senior Professor of Physic and Surgery in the University of Helmstad* (London, 1757), 338.

26. S.A.D. Tissot, *Advice to the people in general, with regard to their health: but more particularly calculated for those, who, by their distance from regular physicians, or other very experienced practitioners, are the most unlikely to be seasonably provided with the best advice and assistance, in acute diseases, or upon any sudden inward or outward accident* (London, 1765). Trenchard, *Natural History of Superstition*, 23.

27. John Locke, *An Essay Concerning Humane Understanding* (London, 1690), 40, 42.

28. Thomas Branch, *Thoughts on Dreaming. Wherein the notion of the sensory, and the opinion that it is shut up from the inspection of the soul in sleep, and that Spirits supply us with all our Dreams, are examined by Revelation and Reason* (London, 1738), 30, 80.

29. On the relationship between sensibility and quick-thinking see Barker-Benfield, *Culture of Sensibility*, 9–15.

30. On European investigations of somatic processes see Barbara Maria Stafford, *Body Criticism: Imaging the Unseen in Enlightenment Art and Medicine* (Cambridge, MA: MIT Press, 1993), 440–1.

31. Tryon, *Treatise of Dreams*, 19–23.

32. The related terms 'somnolent' and 'somnolencie' had circulated since the late fourteenth century; 'noctambulant', 'noct-ambler' and 'noctambulation' from the late seventeenth and early eighteenth centuries. It was in the second half of the eighteenth century that 'somnambulism' and 'somnambulist' moved into mainstream use. Definitions of 'somnambulism' and 'somnambuli' referenced entries for 'sleep-walker' in The *Encyclopaedia Perthensis; or Universal Dictionary of Knowledge*, vol. 21(Perth, 1796–1806), 159.

33. *Every Man Entertained: or select histories: giving an account of persons who have been most eminently distinguish'd by their virtues or vices, the perfections or defects, either of body or mind* (London, 1756), 236–41.

34. For examples of this advertisement see *The Times*, issue 2284 (London, England), 18 April 1792, 1. John Scot M.D. wrote a number of nerve-related medical treatises including *Histories of Gouty, Bilious, and Nervous Cases* (London, 1780), *An Enquiry into the Origin of the Gout* (London, 1780) and *Remarkable Cures, of Gouty, Bilious and Nervous Cases* (London, 1783).

35. *Weekly Entertainer; or Agreeable and instructive repository. Containing a collection of select pieces, both in prose and verse; curious anecdotes, instructive tales, and ingenious essays on different subjects*, vol. 14 (Sherborne, Dorset: 1783–1819), 154–6. *Aberdeen Magazine, Literary Chronicle and Review*, vol. 2 (Aberdeen, 1789), 680–5. *Scientific Magazine, and Freemasons' Repository,* vol. 2 (London, 1797), 176.

36. *Aberdeen Magazine*, vol. 2, 681.

37. Ibid., 173, 680–5.

38. Contemporary explanations of genius were formulated in Edward Young's *Conjectures on Original Composition* (London, 1759) and in William Duff's *Essay on Original Genius* (London, 1767).

39. *Scientific Magazine*, 175–6.

40. Cheyne, *The English Malady*, 262.

41. William Smellie, *The Philosophy of Natural History. By William Smellie, Member of the Antiquarian and Royal Societies of Edinburgh* (Edinburgh, 1790), 361, 363, 375.

42. James Boswell, *Scots Magazine* 51 (October 1789), 497–500. *Encyclopaedia Britannica; or, A Dictionary of Arts, Sciences, and Miscellaneous Literature*, vol. 17 (Dublin, 1790–98), 534–7.

43. *New Magazine of Knowledge*, vol. 1 (London, 1790–1), 282–5. The case was also reported in *Anecdotes, Historical and Literary* (London, 1796), 67–70.

44. Nathaniel Wanley, *The Wonders of the Little World: or, A General History of Man* (London, 1774), 624.

45. *Aberdeen Magazine*, vol. 1, 327.

46. Erasmus Darwin, *Zoonomia; or, The Laws of Organic Life*, vol. 1 (London, 1794–96), 202, 213, 221, 437.

47. Smellie, *Philosophy of Natural History*, 391–3. Sarah's sleepwalking, her failed love affair and frenzied emotional state were common refrains in gendered representations of nervous maladies. See Clark Lawlor, *Consumption and Literature: The Making of the Romantic Disease* (Basingstoke: Palgrave, 2006), 56.

48. Georges Louis Leclerc, comte de Buffon, *Natural History, General and Particular, by the Count de Buffon, translated into English*, vol. 3 (Edinburgh, 1780), 256–61. See also Tryon, *Treatise of Dreams*, 9.

49. *Gentleman's Magazine*, vol. 17 (London, 1747), 458–9.

50. Darwin, *Zoonomia*, 221.

51. Woodforde, *Diary*, vol. 1, 246.

52. *Gentleman's Magazine*, vol. 56 (1786), 712.

53. On gendered representations of disordered nerves see Stafford, *Body Criticism*, 445–50.

54. Laura Quinney, *William Blake on Self and Soul* (Cambridge, MA: Harvard University Press, 2010), 1–26. Jennifer Ford, *Coleridge on Dreaming: Romanticism, Dreams and the Medical Imagination* (Cambridge: Cambridge University Press, 1998), 4.

55. Percy Bysshe Shelley, *Prometheus Unbound. With Adonais, The Cloud, Hymn to Intellectual Beauty, and An Exhortation* (London, 1888).

56. Andrei Pop, 'Sympathetic Spectators: Henry Fuseli's Nightmare and Emma Hamilton's Attitudes', *Art History*, 34:5 (2011), 935.

57. *Morning Chronicle, and London Advertiser*, no. 4048, (9 May 1782), 2, col. C, cited in Pop, 'Sympathetic Spectators', 935.

58. 'Letter from R.A. Bromley, April 1794', in Henry Fuseli, *The Collected English Letters of Henry Fuseli*, ed. David H. Weinglass (New York: Kraus International Publications, 1982), 112.

59. Erasmus Darwin, *The Botanic Garden. Part II. Containing the loves of the plants. A poem.* (London, 1790), 101–3. On the reception of Fuseli's painting see Christopher Frayling, 'Fuseli's *The Nightmare*: Somewhere Between the Sublime and the Ridiculous', in *Gothic Nightmares: Fuseli, Blake and the Romantic Imagination*, ed. Martin Myrone (London: Tate Publishing, 2006), 9–20.

60. Neil Gregory Howe, 'The Politician in Caricature: The Case of Charles James Fox' (PhD diss., University of Nottingham, 2011). W.C. Butterfield, 'The Medical Caricatures

of Thomas Rowlandson', *Journal of the American Medical Association* 224 (1973), 113–17.

61. The capacious buttocks of Duke William's ghost may have been intended to presage the prince of Wales's fate. The duke became obese after suffering a leg wound at the Battle of Dettingen in 1743. He had a stroke in 1760 and died in 1765. James Gillray, 'Duke William's Ghost, 1799', National Portrait Gallery, image no. D13030. The warning is extended in the following works: Isaac Cruickshank, 'The ghost or second warning, 1799', British Museum, museum no. 1868,0808.6837; Isaac Cruickshank, 'The ghost or closet scene in Hamlet, 1799', British Museum, museum no. 1868,0808.12521; Charles Williams, 'The ghost, 1799', British Museum, museum no. 1868,0808.6836.

62. For additional satirical uses of the nightmare motif see Diana Donald, *The Age of Caricature: Satirical Prints in the Reign of George III* (New Haven and London: Yale University Press, 1996), 69–71.

63. Coleridge, *Collected Letters*, vol. 1, 352–3.

64. Ibid., 248–9.

65. Ibid., 539.

66. Ibid., 573.

67. Ibid., 649.

68. Alan Richardson, *British Romanticism and the Science of the Mind* (Cambridge: Cambridge University Press, 2001), 51–2. Dorothy A. Stansfield, *Thomas Beddoes M.D. 1760–1808* (Dordrecht: D. Reidel, 1984), 165–7. Mike Jay, *The Atmosphere of Heaven: The Unnatural Experiments of Dr Beddoes and His Sons of Genius* (New Haven and London: Yale University Press, 2009), 9, 116–121, 156.

69. Coleridge, *Collected Letters*, vol. 1, 459, 488–9.

70. Coleridge explained that the imagination was particularly excitable at night when the body was horizontal in bed since this posture allowed the blood to circulate with greater power and speed through the brain. Ford, *Coleridge on Dreaming*, 5. See also John Radcliffe, *Pharmacopoeia Radcliffeanna: or, Dr. Radcliffe's prescriptions, faithfully gather'd from his original recipe's* (London, 1718), 111; Bond, *Essay on the Incubus*, 19–20.

71. Ford, *Coleridge on Dreaming*, 164–5.

72. Coleridge, *Collected Letters*, vol. 1, 121, 152.

73. Ford, 'Samuel Taylor Coleridge', 105.

74. Tissot, *Essay on the Disorders of People of Fashion*, 37–8.

75. S.A.D. Tissot, *Onanism* (London, 1766), 123.

76. William Holland, *Paupers and Pig Killers: The Diary of William Holland, a Somerset Parson 1799–1818*, ed. Jack Ayres (Gloucester: Alan Sutton Publishing, 1984), 89, 99, 137–8.

77. Thoresby, *Diary*, vol. 2, 170–1.

78. 'Peregrine Bertie to his brother, the Earl of Lindsey, 3 June 1693', Lincolnshire Archives MS 8ANC9/11.

79. Harrold, *Diary*, 55.

80. Mrs Fay, *Original Letters from India; containing a narrative of a journey through Egypt, and the author's imprisonment at Calicut by Hyder Ally. To which is added an abstract of three subsequent voyages to India* (Calcutta, 1821), 127.

81. Fay, *Original Letters*, 182–3.

82. Nugent, *Journal of a Voyage*, vol.1, 428, 433.

83. Ibid., vol. 2, 304.

84. Ibid., vol. 1, 462, 465–7.

85. Ibid., vol. 1, 478–80; vol. 2, 69, 309.

86. Fox, *Diary*.

87. Harrold, *Diary*, 41, 55–6.

88. Nugent, *Journal of a Voyage*, vol. 1, 166, 313.

89. Ibid., 316.

90. Ibid., 428–9, 433–4.

91. 'Penelope Herne at Winchester to her mother, Lady Mordaunt at Grosvenor Street, 1729', Warwickshire County Record Office MS CR 1368, vol. 2/33.
92. Lady Mary Coke, *The Letters and Journals of Lady Mary Coke*, vol. 2 (Edinburgh: David Douglas, 1889), 145.
93. Coke, *Letters and Journals*, vol. 2, 147–8.
94. Thornton, *Autobiography*, 174–5.
95. 'Letter from Roger Hill to Rev. Nathaniel Resbury, 10 March 1692', Centre for Buckinghamshire Studies, MS D-W/76/14.
96. George Woodward, *A Parson in the Vale of the White Horse: George Woodward's Letters from East Hendred, 1753–1761*, ed. Donald Gibson (Gloucester: Alan Sutton Publishing Ltd, 1982), 147.
97. Coleridge, *Collected Letters*, vol. 1, 315–16.
98. Fox, *Diary*, 171.
99. Ibid., 184, 196.
100. Harrold, *Diary*, 77, 98.
101. Hurst, *Diaries*, 171.
102. Ibid., 77, 123.
103. Ibid., 120.
104. Ibid., 85.
105. Ibid., 137.
106. Ibid., 142.
107. Ibid., 76.
108. Ibid., 83.
109. Ibid., 118.
110. Ibid., 109.
111. Ibid., 78.
112. On the emergence of the 'cerebral subject' see Fernando Vidal, 'Brains, Bodies, Selves, and Science: Anthropologies of Identity and the Resurrection of the Body', *Critical Inquiry* 28 (2002), 930–74.

Conclusion

1. This is the working definition suggested by Lodewijk Brunt and Brigitte Steger who propose that it was the twentieth century that saw the 'medicalisation' of sleeping environments. Brunt and Steger, *Worlds of Sleep*, 11–14.
2. Pick and Roper (eds), *Dreams and History*, 6. Dreams and History: The Interpretation of Dreams from Ancient Greece to Modern Psychoanalysis, ed. Daniel Pick and Lyndal Roper (London and New York: Routledge, 2004), 6. Phyllis Mack, 'The Unbounded Self: Dreaming and Identity in the British Enlightenment', in *Dreams, Dreamers and Visions: The Early Modern Atlantic World*, ed. Ann Marie Plane and Leslie Tuttle, with a foreword by Anthony F.C. Wallace (Philadelphia: University of Pennsylvania Press 2013), 207–25.
3. Espie and Morgan advocate a psychologised approach to sleep management that fuses cognitive behavioural techniques with the management of sleep's temporal and material environments for those suffering from sleep disorders. Colin A. Espie, *Overcoming Insomnia and Sleep Problems: A Self-Help Guide Using Cognitive Behavioral Techniques* (London: Constable & Robinson Ltd, 2006), 103–22, 139–58. Kevin Morgan, 'Daytime Activity and Risk Factors for Late-Life Insomnia', *Journal of Sleep Research* 12 (2003), 231–8. See also Horne, 'Sleep Hygiene: Exercise and Other "Do's and Don'ts"', *Sleep Medicine* 15 (2014), 731–2, and Horne, *Sleepfaring*, 213, 216–17.
4. Bill MacLehose's work on medieval pathologies of sleep promises to deepen our knowledge of sleep's diverse phases of medicalisation. MacLehose, 'Fear, Fantasy and Sleep', MacLehose, 'Sleepwalking, Violence and Desire', 604–5.
5. Wilson and Nutt, *Sleep Disorders*, 34, 113–6.
6. Jonathan Crary, *24/7: Late Capitalism and the Ends of Sleep* (London and New York: Verso, 2013). Espie, *Overcoming Insomnia*, xvii–xviii, 139–58. Leon Kreitzman, Russell Foster and Lewis Wolpert, *Rhythms of Life: The Biological Clocks That Control the Daily*

Lives of Every Living Thing (London: Profile Books, 2004), 177–200. Arianna Huffington, *The Sleep Revolution: Transforming Your Life, One Night at a Time* (London: W.H. Allen, 2016). Steven W. Lockley and Russell G. Foster, *Sleep: A Very Short Introduction* (Oxford: Oxford University Press, 2012), 1–2, 117. Charles M. Morin and Colin A. Espie, 'Conclusion: Overview, Emerging Trends, and Future Directions in Sleep Research and Practice', in *The Oxford Handbook of Sleep and Sleep Disorders*, ed. Charles M. Morin and Colin A. Espie (Oxford: Oxford University Press, 2012), 864–70. See also Eluned Sumers-Bremner, *Insomnia: A Cultural History* (London: Reaktion Books, 2008), 7–11.

7. On technology as the key driver of changing sleeping practices and bedtimes see Ekirch, *At Day's Close*, and Ekirch, 'The Modernization of Western Sleep'. E.P. Thompson, 'Time, Work-Discipline, and Industrial Capitalism', *Past and Present* 38 (1967), 56–97.

SELECT BIBLIOGRAPHY

Manuscript Sources

British Library, London

'Brockman Papers: Household accompts of Anne, wife of Sir William Brockman', vols cxli–cxlii, Additional MS 45208.
'Culinary Receipts', MS Sloane 703.
'English Medical Receipt Book, c. 1635', Western MS 809.
'Francis Elcocke, List of diseases arranged astrologically', MS Sloane 2287.
'Freke Papers', vol. 1, Additional MS 45718.
'Letters of Anne Dormer', Additional MS 72516.

Centre for Buckinghamshire Studies

'Letter from Roger Hill to Rev. Nathaniel Resbury, 10 March 1692', MS D-W/76/14.

John Rylands Library, University of Manchester

'John Henderson to Charles Wesley, February 26, 1787', MS DDPr 1/36.
Methodist Church Archives Diaries Collection 'John Valton, Diary, 1765'.
'Notebook containing manuscript copy letters in the hand of Charles Wesley', DDCW 8/15.

Lincolnshire Archives

'Peregrine Bertie to his brother, the Earl of Lindsey, 3 June 1693', MS 8ANC9/11.

London Metropolitan Archives

'Ann Eldridge, 19/7/1738', DL/C/272.

Museum of London

'Mrs Dodson's Account Book, 1746–1765', MS 80.7.

Royal London Hospital Archives

'Ledger, June 1798–December 1807', LH/F/8/11.

The National Archives, London

Prerogative Court of Canterbury Probate Inventories 1668–1758, PROB 3, 5, 11, 31.

Warwickshire County Record Office

'Penelope Herne at Winchester to her mother, Lady Mordaunt at Grosvenor Street, 1729', vol. 2/33, MS CR 1368.

Wellcome Trust Library, London

'A booke of divers receipts, c. 1660–c. 1750', MS 1322.
'Book of Receites c. 1650–c. 1739', MS 144.
'Boyle family recipe book, c. 1675–c. 1710', MS 1340.
'Collection of Medical Receipts c. 1748', MS 3295.
'English Receipt Book', MS 634.
'Receipt book of Elizabeth Jacobs & others, 1654–1685', MS 3009.
'Receipt book of Elizabeth Okeover (& others), c. 1675–c. 1725', MS 3712.
'Receipt-Book c. 1635', MS 809192.

Yorkshire Archaeological Society, University of Leeds

'Ralph Thoresby, 1715', GB/0207/MS.26.

Museum Collections

Beamish Museum, County Durham
Museum of English Rural Life, University of Reading
Museum of London
National Trust Collections
Victoria and Albert Museum, London

Newspapers, Magazines and Periodicals

Aberdeen Magazine, Literary Chronicle and Review, vol. 2 (Aberdeen, 1789).
Annual Register, or a View of the History, Politics, and Literature for the Year 1777, vol. 20 (London, 1805).
Arminian magazine: consisting of extracts and original treatises on universal redemption, vol. 7 (London: J. Fry & Co, 1778–97).
Boswell, James, *The Scots Magazine* 51 (October 1789).
Encyclopaedia Britannica: or, a dictionary of arts, sciences, and miscellaneous literature on a plan entirely new, vol. 17 (Dublin, 1790–98).
Encyclopaedia Perthensis; or Universal Dictionary of Knowledge, vol. 21 (Perth, 1796–1806).
Fitz-Adam, Adam, *The World*, vol. 2, no. 74 (London, 1755–57).
Gentleman's Magazine, or, Monthly Intelligencer (London, 1747, 1763, 1786).
New Magazine of Knowledge, vol. 1 (London, 1790–91).
Scientific Magazine, and Freemasons' Repository, vol. 2 (London, 1797).
Spectator, ed. Donald F. Bond (Oxford: Clarendon Press, 1965).
Tatler, ed. Donald F. Bond (Oxford: Clarendon Press, 1987).
The Times, Issue 2284, 18 April 1792.

Printed Primary Sources

Adair, James Makittrick, *An essay on regimen, for the preservation of health, especially of the indolent, studious, delicate and invalid* (Air, 1799).
—— *Essays on fashionable diseases* (London, 1790).

Alexander, William, *Plain and easy directions for the use of Harrogate waters: adapted to the meanest capacity; and principally intended for the use of all who attend there* (Edinburgh, 1773).

Allen, John, *Dr Allen's Synopsis Medicinae*, vol. 2 (London, 1730).

Allestree, Richard, *The whole duty of man laid down in a plain and familiar way for the use of all, but especially the meanest reader* (London, 1713).

An Act for the better enlightening the open places, streets, lanes, passages, and courts, and for the better regulating the nightly watch and bedels within the parish of Christ Church in the county of Middlesex (London, 1738).

Andry de Bois-Regard, Nicolas, *Orthopaedia: or, the art of correcting and preventing deformities in children* (London, 1743).

Anon., *Account of the apprehending and taking six French prophets, near Hog-lane in Soho, who pretended to prophecy that the world should be at an end* (London, 1707).

Anon., *An Account of the trial, examination & conviction of the pretended French prophets* (London, 1707).

Anon., *An Alarme to Awake Church-Sleepers* (London, 1644).

Anon., *Anecdotes, Historical and Literary* (London, 1796).

Anon., *Aristotle's Secret of Secrets contracted; being the sum of his advice to Alexander the Great, about the preservation of health and government* (London, 1702).

Anon., *The Art of Nursing: or, the method of bringing up young children according to the rules of physick* (London, 1733).

Anon., *The Best and Easiest method of preserving uninterrupted health to extreme old age: established upon the justest laws of the animal oeconomy, and confirmed by the suffrages of the most celebrated practitioners among the ancients and moderns* (London, 1752).

Anon., *Christian Prudence: consisting of Maxims and Proverbs, Divine and Moral* (London, 1766).

Anon., *The Complete Man and Maid Servant* (London, 1764).

Anon., *Crumbs of Comfort and Godly Prayers; with thankful remembrance of God's wonderful deliverances of this land* (London, 1726).

Anon., *Every Man Entertained: or select histories: giving an account of persons who have been most eminently distinguish'd by their virtues or vices, the perfections or defects, either of body or mind* (London, 1756).

Anon., 'Of the Posture-Master', *Philosophical Transactions* 20 (1698).

Anon., *The Pious Country Parishioner Instructed how to spend every day, through the whole course of his life, in a religious and acceptable manner* (London, 1753).

Anon., *The true relation of two wonderfull sleepers* (London, 1646).

Anon., *The Universal Family Book: Or, A Necessary and Profitable Companion for all Degrees of People of Either Sex* (London, 1703).

Anon., *Young Bateman's ghost, or, a godly warning to all maidens* (London, 1760).

Archer, John, *Every Man his own Doctor* (London, 1671).

Aubrey, John, *Remaines of Gentilisme and Judaisme by John Aubrey, 1686–87*, ed. James Britten (London: Publications of the Folklore Society, 1881).

Austen, Jane, *Sense and Sensibility: a novel* (London, 1833).

Author of Westminster Drollery, *Mock Songs and Joking Poems* (London, 1675).

Bagshawe, William, *Essays on Union to Christ. Being the Substance of Several Sermons* (London, 1703).

Bailey, Nathan, *Dictionarium Britannicum: or a more compleat universal etymological English dictionary than any extant* (London, 1737).

Baillie, Lady Grisell, *The Household Book of Lady Grisell Baillie, 1692–1733*, ed. Robert Scott-Moncrieff (Edinburgh: Scottish History Society, 1911).

Barker, Anne, *The Complete Servant Maid: or Young Woman's Best Companion* (London, 1770).

Baxter, Richard, *A Christian Directory, or, a summm of practical theologie and cases of conscience directing Christians how to use their knowledge and faith, how to improve all helps and means, and to perform all duties, how to overcome temptations, and to escape or mortifie every sin* (London, 1673).

Best, William, *An Essay on the Service of the Church of England, considered as a Daily Service* (London, 1794).

Blagrave, Joseph, *Blagrave's Astrological Practice of Physick* (London, 1671).

Blake, William, *The Marriage of Heaven and Hell* (London, 1790).

—— *Milton's Paradise Lost. A new edition. Adorned with plates, engraved chiefly by F. Bartolozzi from designs by W. Hamilton and H. Fuseli* (London, 1802).

Blundell, Nicholas, *Blundell's Diary, Comprising Selections from the Diary of Nicholas Blundell Esq. from 1702 to 1728*, ed. Rev. T. Ellison Gibson (Liverpool: Walmsley 1895).

Boerhaave, Herman, *Boerhaave's Institutions in Physick*, trans. J. Browne (London, 1715).

Bond, John, *An Essay on the Incubus, or Night-Mare* (London, 1753).

The Book of Common Prayer: The Texts of 1549, 1559, and 1662, ed. Brian Cummings (Oxford: Oxford University Press, 2011).

Boorde, Andrew, *A Compendyous Regyment or a Dyetary of Healthe made in Mountpyllyer* (London, 1547).

Borsieri de Kanifeld, G., *The Institutions of the Practice of Medicine; delivered in a course of lectures, by John Baptist Burserius, De Kanifeld. Translated from the Latin by William Cullen Brown*, vol. 4 (Edinburgh, 1800–03).

Boswell, James, *Boswell's Life of Johnson: Together with Boswell's Journal of a Tour to the Hebrides, and Johnson's Diary of a Journey into North Wales*, ed. George Birkbeck Hill, vol. 2 (Oxford: Clarendon Press, 1934).

Bower, Edmund, *Doctor Lamb Revived, or, Witchcraft condemn'd in Anne Bodenham* (London, 1653).

Boyle, Robert, *Essays of the strange subtilty great efficacy determinate nature of effluviums* (London, 1673).

Branch, Thomas, *Thoughts on Dreaming. Wherein the notion of the sensory, and the opinion that it is shut up from the inspection of the soul in sleep, and that Spirits supply us with all our Dreams, are examined by Revelation and Reason* (London, 1738).

Brand, John, *Observations on popular antiquities: including the whole of Mr. Bourne's Antiquitates vulgares* (Newcastle upon Tyne, 1777).

Bullein, William, *Bulleins Bulwarke of Defence Against All Sicknes, Sornes, and Woundes that dooe daily assaulte mankinde* (London, 1562).

—— *The Government of Health* (London, 1558).

Burdsall, Richard, *Memoirs of the Life of Richard Burdsall, shewing the mercy of God in Christ Jesus to a sinner* (Thetford, 1823).

Burkitt, William, *The Poor Man's Help and Young Man's Guide* (London, 1694).

Butler, Samuel, *Hudibras in Three Parts* (London, 1684).

By a Lady, *The workwoman's guide, containing instructions . . . in cutting out and completing those articles of wearing apparel, &c. which are usually made at home* (London: Simpkin, Marshall, & Co., 1838).

By a physician, *A treatise of diseases of the head, brain & nerves* (London, 1714).

Cambridge, Richard Owen, *An Elegy Written in an Empty Assembly-Room* (London, 1756).

Cannon, John, *The Chronicles of John Cannon, Excise Officer and Writing Master*, ed. John Money, 2 vols (Oxford: published for the British Academy by Oxford University Press, 2010).

Carey, Henry, *Cupid and Hymen: or, a voyage to the isles of love and matrimony* (London, 1742).

Cheyne, George, *The English Malady: or, a treatise of nervous diseases of all kinds* (London, 1733).

—— *An Essay of Health and Long Life* (London, 1724).

Chippendale, Thomas, *The Gentleman and Cabinet-Maker's Director. Being a Large Collection of the Most Elegant and Useful Designs of Household Furniture in the Gothic, Chinese and Modern Taste* (London, 1754).

Clifford, Lady Anne, *The Diaries of Lady Anne Clifford*, ed. D.J.H. Clifford (Stroud: Alan Sutton, 1990).

Cogan, Thomas, *The haven of health chiefly gathered for the comfort of students* (London, 1636).

Coke, Lady Mary, *The Letters and Journals of Lady Mary Coke*, vol. 2 (Edinburgh: David Douglas, 1889).

Cole, William, *The Blecheley Diary of the Rev. William Cole, M.A., F.S.A., 1765–67*, ed. Francis Griffin Stokes (London, 1931).

Coleridge, Samuel Taylor, *Collected Letters of Samuel Taylor Coleridge, 1785–1800*, ed. Earl Leslie Griggs, 2 vols (Oxford: Clarendon Press, 1956).

Colet, John, *Daily devotions: or, the Christian's morning and evening sacrifice. Digested into prayers and meditations for every day in the week, and other occasions* (London, 1722).

Comber, Thomas, *A Companion to the Temple: or, a Help to Publick and Private Devotion* (London, 1676).

Congreve, William, *The story of Semele. As it is perform'd at the Theatre-Royal in Covent-Garden. Altered from the Semele of Mr. William Congreve. Set to musick by Mr. George Frederick Handel* (London, 1744).

Cullen, William, *Institutions of Medicine, Part I. Physiology. For the use of the Students in the University of Edinburgh* (Edinburgh, 1785).

—— *Synopsis Nosologiae Methodicae* (Edinburgh, 1769).

Culpeper, Nicholas, *Pharmacopoeia Londinensis: or the London Dispensatory* (London, 1653).

—— *A New Method of Physick* (London, 1654).

Darwin, Erasmus, *The Botanic Garden. Part II. Containing the loves of the plants. A poem.* (London, 1790).

—— *Zoonomia; or, The Laws of Organic Life*, 2 vols (London, 1794–96).

Delaval, Lady Elizabeth, *The Meditations of Lady Elizabeth Delaval: written between 1662 and 1671*, ed. Douglas G. Greene (Gateshead: Publications of the Surtees Society, 1978).

Dryden, John, *The Wild Gallant* (London, 1669).

Duff, William, *Essay on Original Genius* (London, 1767).

Ellis, William, *The Country Housewife's Family Companion* (London and Salisbury, 1750).

Elyot, Sir Thomas, *The Castel of Helthe gathered and made by Syr Thomas Elyot knyghte, out of the chiefe authors of physyke, wherby euery manne may knowe the state of his owne body, the preseruatio[n] of helthe, and how to instructe welle his physytion in syckenes that he be not deceyued* (London, 1539).

Evelyn, John, *The Diary of John Evelyn*, ed. E.S. de Beer, vol. 5 (Oxford: Clarendon Press, 2000).

Eyre, Adam, 'A dyurnall, or, Catalogue of all my accions and expences from the 1st of January 1646–[7–]', in *Yorkshire diaries and autobiographies*, ed. H.J. Morehouse, vol. 1 (Durham: Surtees Society Publications, 1877).

Fay, Mrs, *Original Letters from India; containing a narrative of a journey through Egypt, and the author's imprisonment at Calicut by Hyder Ally. To which is added an abstract of three subsequent voyages to India* (Calcutta, 1821).

Ficino, Marsilio, *Three Books on Life: A Critical Edition and Translation with Introduction and Notes by Carol V. Kaske and John R. Clark* (Tempe, Arizona: Arizona Center for Medieval and Renaissance Studies, in conjunction with the Renaissance Society of America, 2002).

Fiennes, Celia, *The Journeys of Celia Fiennes*, ed. Christopher Morris (London: the Cresset Press, 1949).

The First Publishers of Truth, ed. Norman Penney (London: Headley, 1907).

Forby, Robert, *The Vocabulary of East-Anglia; An Attempt to Record the Vulgar Tongue of the Twin Sister Counties of Norfolk and Suffolk as it existed in the last twenty years of the eighteenth century*, vol. 1 (London, 1830).

Ford, Emanuel, *The Most Pleasant History of Ornatus and Artesia* (London, 1607).

Fox, George, *A New England Fire Brand Quenched* (London, 1678).

Fox, Sarah, *The Diary of Sarah Fox, née Champion, Bristol 1745–1802*, ed. Madge Dresser (Bristol: Bristol Record Society, 2003).

Fransham, John, *Memoirs of the Life, Character, Opinions and Writings, of that Learned and Eccentric Man, John Fransham of Norwich*, ed. W. Saint (Norwich, 1811).

Freke, Elizabeth, *The Remembrances of Elizabeth Freke, 1671–1714*, ed. Raymond A. Anselment (Cambridge: Cambridge University Press, 2001).

French, John, *The Art of Distillation* (London, 1653).

Fuseli, Henry, *The Collected English Letters of Henry Fuseli*, ed. David H. Weinglass (New York: Kraus International Publications, 1982).

Gaule, John, *Pus-mantia the mag-astro-mancer, or, The magicall-astrologicall-diviner posed and puzzled* (London, 1652).

Gerard, John, *The Herball or Generall Historie of Plantes* (London, 1633).

Glasse, Hannah, *Servants' Directory, or House-Keeper's Companion* (London, 1760).

Goldsmith, Oliver, *An History of the Earth and Animated Nature*, vol. 2 (London, 1779).

Grey, Elizabeth, countess of Kent, *A choice manual of rare and select secrets in physic and chirurgery collected and practised by the Right Honorable, the Countesse of Kent* (London, 1653).

Hamilton, William Gerard, *Four odes. I. On sleep. II. On beauty. III. On taste. IV. To the Right Hon. Lady *** on the death of her son* (London, 1750).

Hammond, William, *Psalms, Hymns and Spiritual Songs* (London, 1745).

Harrold, Edmund, *The Diary of Edmund Harrold, Wigmaker of Manchester 1712–15*, ed. Craig Horner (Aldershot: Ashgate, 2008).

Hart, A. Tindal (ed.), *Country Counting House: The Story of Two Eighteenth-Century Clerical Account Books* (London: Phoenix House Ltd, 1962).

Hartley, David, *Observations on Man, his Frame, his Duty, and his Expectations*, 2 vols (London, 1749).

Harvey, Gideon, *The family physician, and the house apothecary* (London, 1676).

Head, Richard, *Nugae Venales, or, Complaisant Companion* (London, 1675).

Heister, Laurence, *A compendium of the practice of physic: by Laurence Heister, Senior Professor of Physic and Surgery in the University of Helmstad* (London, 1757).

Henderson, William, *Notes on the Folk-Lore of the Northern Counties of England and the Borders* (London: W. Satchell, Peyton and Co., 1879).

Heywood, Thomas, *A Curtaine Lecture* (London, 1637).

Hickes, William, *Coffee-House Jests* (London, 1686).

Hill, William, *A full account of the life and visions of Nicholas Hart* (London, 1711).

—— *The true and wonderful history of Nicholas Hart: or, a faithful account of the sleepy-man's visions* (London, 1711).

Holland, William, *Paupers and Pig Killers: The Diary of William Holland, A Somerset Parson 1799–1818*, ed. Jack Ayres (Gloucester: Alan Sutton Publishing, 1984).

Hooke, Robert, *Micrographia, or, some physiological descriptions of minute bodies made by magnifying glasses with observations and inquiries thereupon* (London, 1665).

Hume, David, 'Essay II: Of Luxury', in *Essays and Treatises on Several Subjects* (London, 1758).

Hurst, Sarah, *The Diaries of Sarah Hurst 1759–1762: Life and Love in Eighteenth Century Horsham*, ed. Susan C. Djabri (Stroud: Amberley Publishing, 2009).

Hutton, Catherine, *Reminiscences of a gentlewoman of the last century: letters of Catherine Hutton*, ed. C.H. Beale (Birmingham: Cornish Brothers, 1891).

Janeway, James, *A Token for Children: being an exact account of the conversion, holy and exemplary lives, and joyful deaths, of several young children* (London, 1676).

Johnson, Elizabeth, *An Account of Mrs. Elizabeth Johnson, well known in the city of Bristol for more than half a century, for her eminent piety and benevolence. To which is added, an extract from her diary* (Bristol, 1799).

Johnson, Samuel, *A Dictionary of the English Language: in which the words are deduced from their originals, and illustrated in their different significations by examples from the best writers*, 2 vols (London, 1755–56).

Josselin, Ralph, *The Diary of Ralph Josselin 1616–1683*, ed. Alan Macfarlane (London: published for the British Academy by Oxford University Press, 1976).

Ken, Thomas, *A Manual of Prayers for the Use of the Scholars of Winchester Colledge* (London, 1674).

—— *A morning, evening, and midnight hymn* (London, 1703).

Kimber, Edward, *The Life and Adventures of Joe Thompson, a narrative founded on fact*, vol. 1 (London, 1775).

Latham, Richard, *The Account Book of Richard Latham 1724–1767: Records of Social and Economic History*, vol. 15, ed. Lorna Weatherill (New York: published for the British Academy by Oxford University Press, 1990).

Lawrence, Henry, *Of Our Communion and Warre with Angels* (London, 1646).

Leapor, Mary, 'Crumble Hall', in *Poems upon Several Occasions*, vol. 2 (London, 1751).

Leclerc, Georges Louis, comte de Buffon, *Natural History, General and Particular, by the Count de Buffon, translated into English*, vol. 3 (Edinburgh, 1780).

Locke, John, *An Essay Concerning Humane Understanding* (London, 1690).

—— *Some thoughts concerning education* (London, 1693).

Lowe, Peter, *The Whole Course of Chirurgerie* (London, 1597).

Mandeville, Bernard, *Aesop Dress'd, or a Collection of Fables* (London, 1704).

—— *The Fable of the Bees, or, Private Vices, Public Benefits*, vol. 1 (Edinburgh, 1772).

Markham, Gervase, *Countrey Contentments, or The English Huswife* (London, 1623).

—— *The Dumbe Knight, A Historicall Comedy* (London, 1608).

Milton, John, *Paradise Lost*, ed. John Leonard (London: Penguin, 2000).

Montagu, Lady Mary Wortley, *The Letters and Works of Lady Mary Wortley Montagu*, ed. Lord Wharncliffe, vol. 3 (London, 1837).

The New Practice of Piety: containing the necessary duties of a Christian Life (London, 1749).

Newcome, Henry, *The Diary of the Rev. Henry Newcome, from September 30, 1661 to September 29, 1663*, ed. Thomas Heywood (Manchester: Chetham Society, 1849).

Nicols, Thomas, *Lapidary or, The History of Pretious Stones* (Cambridge, 1652).

Northall, G.F. *English folk-rhymes; a collection of traditional verses relating to places and persons, customs, superstitions, etc* (London: Kegan Paul, Trench, Trubner & Co., 1892).

Nugent, Maria, Lady, *A Journal of a Voyage to, and residence in, the Island of Jamaica, from 1801 to 1805, and of subsequent events in England from 1805 to 1811*, 2 vols (London, 1839).

Ovid, *Metamorphoses*, trans. David Raeburn (London: Penguin Books, 2004).

Partridge, John, *The treasurie of commodious conceits, and hidden secrets commonlie called The good huswiues closet of prouision, for the health of her houshold* (London, 1591).

Patrick, Symon, *The Devout Christian instructed how to pray and give thanks to God. Or, a Book of Devotions for families, and for particular persons, in most of the concerns of humane life* (London, 1759).

Pechey, John, *Collection of Chronical Diseases* (London, 1692).

—— *The Compleat Midwife's Practice enlarged in the most weighty and high concernments of the birth of man containing a perfect directory of rules for midwives and nurses* (London, 1698).

—— *A general treatise of the diseases of maids, bigbellied women, child-bed women, and widows* (London, 1696).

—— *A general treatise of the diseases of infants and children* (London, 1697).

Pepys, Samuel, *The Diary of Samuel Pepys: A new and complete transcription*, ed. Robert Latham and William Matthews, 11 vols (London: G. Bell and Sons Ltd, 1971).

Perrott, Samuel, *Sermons on Practical Subjects* (Cork, 1798).

Platter, Felix, Abdiah Cole and Nicholas Culpeper, *Platerus golden practice of physick* (London, 1664).

Pope, Alexander, *Letters of Mr Pope, and Several Eminent Persons, from the year 1705, to 1735*, vol. 1 (London, 1735).

Pratt, Samuel, *Liberal Opinions, or the history of Benignus*, vol. 6 (London, 1777).

Price, Joseph, *A Kentish Parson: selections from the private papers of the Revd Joseph Price Vicar of Brabourne, 1767–1786*, ed. G.M. Ditchfield and Bryan Keith-Lucas (Maidstone: Kent County Council, Arts & Libraries, 1991).

Radcliffe, John, *Pharmacopoeia Radcliffeanna: or, Dr. Radcliffe's prescriptions, faithfully gather'd from his original recipe's* (London, 1718).

Rainbowe, Edward, *A Sermon preached at the funeral of the Right Honourable Anne Countess of Pembroke, Dorset and Montgomery* (London, 1677).

Raper, Elizabeth, *The Receipt Book of Elizabeth Raper*, ed. Bartle Grant (Soho: The Nonsuch Press, 1924).

Ray, John, *A Collection of English Proverbs digested into a convenient method for the speedy finding any one upon occasion* (Cambridge, 1678).

Rogers, Benjamin, *The Diary of Benjamin Rogers, Rector of Carlton 1720–71*, ed. C.D. Linnell (Cambridge: Chadwyck-Healey, 1978).

Scot, John, *An Enquiry into the Origin of the Gout* (London, 1780).

—— *Histories of Gouty, Bilious, and Nervous Cases* (London, 1780).

—— *Remarkable Cures, of Gouty, Bilious and Nervous Cases* (London, 1783).

Seaton, Thomas, *The Devotional Life Render'd Familiar, Easy, and Pleasant, in Several Hymns Upon the Most Common Occasions of Human Life* (London, 1734).

Shakespeare, William, *King Henry IV, Part II*.

—— *Macbeth*.

—— *Richard III*.

Shelley, Percy Bysshe, *Prometheus Unbound. With Adonais, The Cloud, Hymn to Intellectual Beauty, and An Exhortation* (London, 1888).

Sheridan, Thomas, *A general dictionary of the English language*, vol. 2 (London, 1780).

Sherley, Thomas, *Theodor Turquet de Mayerne's Medicinal Councels, or Advices* (London, 1677).

Short, Thomas, *A dissertation upon tea, explaining its nature and properties by many new experiments; and demonstrating from philosophical principles, the various effects it has on different constitutions* (London, 1730).

Sinclair, George, *Satan's Invisible World Discovered* (Edinburgh, 1685).

Sinclair, John, *The Code of Health and Longevity or, A General View of the Rules and Principles Calculated for the Preservation of Health, and the Attainment of Long Life* (London, 1818).

Smellie, William, *The Philosophy of Natural History* (Edinburgh, 1790).

Smith, Adam, *The Theory of Moral Sentiments* (London, 1759).

Smythson, Hugh, *The Compleat Family Physician; or, Universal Medical Repository* (London, 1781).

Southall, John, *A Treatise of Buggs* (London, 1730).

Sowerby, Leonard, *The Ladies Dispensatory, containing the natures, vertues, and qualities of all herbs, and simples usefull in physick reduced into a methodicall order* (London, 1651).

Stanley, Thomas, *The History of Philosophy: containing the lives, opinions, actions and discourses of the philosophers of every sect* (London, 1750).

The Statutes at Large, from the twentieth year of the reign of King George the Second to the thirtieth year of the reign of King George the Second, vol. 7 (London, 1764).

Stukeley, William, *The Family Memoirs of the Rev. William Stukeley M.D.*, ed. W.C. Lukis, R. Gale, S. Gale and G. Kneller, vol. 1 (London: Publications of the Surtees Society, 1882).

Thoresby, Ralph, *The Diary of Ralph Thoresby (1677–1724), now first published from the original manuscript*, ed. Joseph Hunter, 2 vols (London: Henry Colburn and Richard Bentley, 1830).

Thornton, Alice, *The Autobiography of Mrs. Alice Thornton of East Newton, Co. York* (Durham, London and Edinburgh: Surtees Society, 1875).

Tissot, S.A.D., *Advice to the people in general, with regard to their health: but more particularly calculated for those, who, by their distance from regular physicians, or other very experienced practitioners, are the most unlikely to be seasonably provided with the best advice and assistance, in acute diseases, or upon any sudden inward or outward accident* (London, 1765).

—— *An Essay on the Disorders of People of Fashion* (London, 1771).

—— *Onanism* (London, 1766).

Trenchard, John, *A Natural History of Superstition* (London, 1709).

Treswell, Ralph, *The London Surveys of Ralph Treswell*, ed. John Schofield (London: London Topographical Society, Publication No. 135, 1987).

Trusler, John, *An Easy Way to Prolong Life, by a little attention to what we eat and drink* (London, 1775).

Tryon, Thomas, *A treatise of cleanness in meats and drinks of the preparation of food, the excellency of good airs and the benefits of clean sweet beds also of the generation of bugs and their cure* (London, 1682).

—— ['Philotheos Physiologus'], *A Treatise of Dreams & Visions, wherein the causes natures and uses of nocturnal representations, and the communications both of good and evil angels, as also departed souls, to mankind, are theosophically unfolded; that is, according to the Word of God, and the Harmony of Created Beeings* (London, 1695).

—— *Wisdom's dictates, or, Aphorisms & rules, physical, moral, and divine, for preserving the health of the body, and the peace of the mind* (London, 1693).

Turner, Thomas, *The Diary of Thomas Turner 1754–1765*, ed. David Vaisey (Oxford: Oxford University Press, 1985).

Two East Anglian Diaries 1641–1729, Isaac Archer and William Coe, ed. Matthew Storey (Woodbridge: Boydell & Brewer, 1994).

Valangin, Francis de, *A treatise on diet, or the management of human life; by physicians called the six non-naturals* (London, 1768).

Walpole, Horace, *The Yale Edition of Horace Walpole's Correspondence*, ed. W.S. Lewis et al., vols 10, 18, 22, 30, 31, 35, 39, 41 (London and New Haven: Oxford University Press and Yale University Press, 1941–1980).

Wanley, Nathaniel, *The Wonders of the Little World: or, A General History of Man* (London, 1774).

Ware, Isaac, *A complete body of architecture. Adorned with plans and elevations, from original designs* (London, 1767).

Warren, Robert, *The Daily Self-Examinant: or an Earnest Persuasive to the Duty of Daily Self-Examination* (London, 1720).

Watts, Isaac, *Divine Songs Attempted in Easy Language for the Use of Children* (London, 1716).

The Weekly Entertainer; or Agreeable and instructive repository. Containing a collection of select pieces, both in prose and verse; curious anecdotes, instructive tales, and ingenious essays on different subjects, vol. 14 (Sherborne, Dorset, 1783–1819).

Wesley, John, *The Duty and Advantage of Early Rising* (London, 1783).

—— *Duty and Advantage of Early Rising. A Sermon on Ephesians v.16* (London, 1798).

—— *A Plain Account of Christian Perfection, as believed and taught by the Rev. Mr John Wesley, from the year 1725, to the year 1777* (Dublin, 1797).

—— *Sermons on Several Occasions*, vol. 9 (London, 1800).

White, Charles, *A Treatise on the Management of Pregnant and Lying-in Women, and the means of curing, but more especially of preventing the principal disorders to which they are liable* (London, 1772).

Willis, Thomas, *The Anatomy of the Brain and Nerves; including facsimile reprint of the translation by Samuel Pordage, from the remaining medical works of Thomas Willis*, ed. William Feindel, vol. 1 (Montreal: University of McGill Press, 1965).

—— *Dr. Willis's practice of physick* (London, 1684).

—— *Two discourses concerning the soul of brutes which is that of the vital and sensitive of man* (London, 1683).

Wilson, Thomas, *Maxims of Piety and of Christianity* (London, 1789).

—— *A Short and Plain Instruction for the Better Understanding of the Lord's Supper* (London, 1740).

Wolley, Hannah, *The Accomplish'd lady's delight in preserving, physic, beautifying, and cookery* (London, 1675).

—— *The Compleat Servant-Maid: or, the Young Maiden's and Family's Daily Companion* (London, 1729).

Woodforde, James, *The Diary of a Country Parson, the Reverend James Woodforde, 1758–1781*, ed. John Beresford, 2 vols (Oxford: Oxford University Press, 1981).

Woodward, George, *A Parson in the Vale of the White Horse: George Woodward's Letters from East Hendred, 1753–1761*, ed. Donald Gibson (Gloucester: Alan Sutton Publishing Ltd, 1982).

Wright, George, *The Young Moralist consisting of Allegorical and Entertaining Essays, in Prose and Verse* (London, 1782).

Young, Edward, *Conjectures on Original Composition* (London, 1759).

Secondary Sources

Abelove, Henry, *The Evangelist of Desire: John Wesley and the Methodists* (Stanford: Stanford University Press, 1990).

Adam, Barbara, *Timescapes of Modernity: The Environment and Invisible Hazards* (London: Routledge, 1998).

Alderson, Frederick, *The Inland Resorts and Spas of Britain* (Newton Abbot: David and Charles Holdings Ltd, 1973).

Allan, Rosemary E., *North Country Quilts & Coverlets: From Beamish Museum, County Durham* (Stanley: Beamish, North of England Open Air Museum, 1987).

—— *Quilts & Coverlets: The Beamish Collections* (Co. Durham: Beamish Museum, 2007).

Andrews, Jonathan and Andrew Scull, *Undertaker of the Mind: John Monro and Mad-Doctoring in Eighteenth-Century England* (Berkeley and Los Angeles: University of California Press, 2001).

Ashmore, Paul, 'Bedtime Material: Recording Becoming Asleep', *Area* 43 (2010), 211–17.

Ashton, John, *Social life in the reign of Queen Anne* (London: Chatto & Windus, 1882).

Audin, Heather, *Patchwork and Quilting in Britain* (Oxford: Shire Publications, 2013).

Auslander, Leora, 'Beyond Words', *The American Historical Review* 110 (2005), 1015–45.

Bailey, Joanne, 'Stitchers in Time and Space: Women in the Long Eighteenth Century', in *Quilts 1700–2010: Hidden Histories, Untold Stories*, ed. Sue Prichard (London: V&A Publishing, 2012).

Bailey, M., 'Glossary of Names for Rooms', in *Culture and Environment: Essays in Honour of Sir Cyril Fox*, ed. I.L.L. Foster and L. Alcock (London: Routledge & Kegan Paul, 1963).

Barker-Benfield, G.J., *The Culture of Sensibility: Sex and Society in Eighteenth-Century Britain* (Chicago: University of Chicago Press, 1992).

Bate, Jonathan, *Shakespeare and Ovid* (Oxford: Clarendon Press, 1993).

Baumgarten, Linda and Kimberly Smith Ivey, *Four Centuries of Quilts: The Colonial Williamsburg Collection* (New Haven and London: Williamsburg: The Colonial Williamsburg Foundation in association with Yale University Press, 2014).

Beersma, Domien G.M., 'Models of Human Sleep Regulation', *Sleep Medicine Reviews* 2 (1998), 31–43.

Beeston, Erin, 'Unravelling Hidden Histories: Researching the Bolton Museum Caddow Quilt Collection', *Social History in Museums: Journal of the Social History Curators Group* 37 (2013), 60–9.

Beeston, Erin and Laurel Horton, 'Bolton's Cotton Counterpanes: Hand-Weaving in the Industrial Age', in *Quilt Studies: The Journal of the British Quilt Studies Group* 14 (2013), 7–36.

Ben-Ari, Eyal, ' "It's Bedtime" in the World's Urban Middle Classes: Children, Families and Sleep', in *Worlds of Sleep*, ed. Lodewijk Brunt and Brigitte Steger (Berlin: Frank & Timme, 2008).

Berg, Maxine, *Luxury and Pleasure in Eighteenth-Century Britain* (Oxford: Oxford University Press, 2005).

—— 'Women's Consumption and the Industrial Classes in Eighteenth-Century England', *Journal of Social History* 30 (1996), 415–34.

Biow, Douglas, *The Culture of Cleanliness in Renaissance Italy* (Ithaca and London: Cornell University Press, 2006).

Blécourt, Willem de, 'Bedding the Nightmare: Somatic Experience and Narrative Meaning in Dutch and Flemish Legend Texts', *Folklore* 114 (2003), 227–45.

Borbély, A.A., 'A Two-process Model of Sleep Regulation', *Human Neurobiology* 1 (1982), 195–204.

Borsay, Peter, *The English Urban Renaissance: Culture and Society in the Provincial Town* (Oxford: Clarendon Press, 1991).

Boynton, L.O.J., 'The Bed-bug and the "Age of Elegance" ', *Furniture History* 1 (1965).

Bray, Alan, *The Friend* (Chicago and London: University of Chicago Press, 2003).

Brewer, John, *The Pleasures of the Imagination: English Culture in the Eighteenth Century* (London: HarperCollins, 1997).

Brown, Frank E., 'Continuity and Change in the Urban House: Developments in Domestic Space Organisation in Seventeenth-Century London', *Comparative Studies in Society and History* 28 (1986), 558–90.

Browne, Clare, 'Making and Using Quilts in Eighteenth-century Britain', in *Quilts 1700–2010: Hidden Histories, Untold Stories*, ed. Sue Prichard (London: V&A Publishing, 2012).

Brunt, Lodewijk and Brigitte Steger (eds), *Worlds of Sleep* (Berlin: Frank & Timme, 2008).

Butterfield, W.C., 'The Medical Caricatures of Thomas Rowlandson', *The Journal of the American Medical Association* 224 (1973), 113–17.

Bynum, W.F., 'Cullen and the Nervous System', in *William Cullen and the Eighteenth Century Medical World*, ed. A. Doig, J.P.S. Ferguson, I.A. Milne and R. Passmore (Edinburgh: Edinburgh University Press, 1993).

Cambers, Andrew, *Godly Reading: Print, Manuscript and Puritanism in England, 1580–1720* (Cambridge: Cambridge University Press, 2011).

Cavallo, Sandra and Tessa Storey, *Healthy Living in Late Renaissance Italy* (Oxford: Oxford University Press, 2013).

Cockayne, Emily, *Hubbub: Filth, Noise & Stench in England 1600–1770* (New Haven and London: Yale University Press, 2007).

Cohen, Deborah, *Household Gods: The British and Their Possessions* (New Haven and London: Yale University Press, 2006).

Cowan Orlin, Lena, 'Fictions of the Early Modern Probate Inventory', in *The Culture of Capital: Properties, Cities and Knowledge in Early Modern England*, ed. H.S. Turner (London: Routledge, 2002).

Cox, Robert S., 'The Suburbs of Eternity: On Visionaries and Miraculous Sleepers', in *Worlds of Sleep*, ed. Lodewijk Brunt and Brigitte Steger (Berlin: Frank & Timme, 2008).

Crary, Jonathan, *24/7: Late Capitalism and the Ends of Sleep* (London and New York: Verso, 2013).

Cressy, David, *Birth, Marriage, and Death: Ritual, Religion, and the Life-Cycle in Tudor and Stuart England* (Oxford: Oxford University Press, 1997).

Crowley, John E., *The Invention of Comfort, Sensibilities & Design in Early Modern Britain and Early America* (Baltimore and London: Johns Hopkins University Press, 2001).

—— 'The Sensibility of Comfort', *The American Historical Review* 104 (1999), 749–82.

Currie, Elizabeth, *Inside the Renaissance House* (London: V&A Publications, 2006).

Dacome, Lucia, 'Resurrecting by Numbers in Eighteenth-Century England', *Past and Present,* 193 (2006), 73–110.

—— ' "To what purpose does it think?": Dreams, Sick Bodies and Confused Minds in the Age of Reason', *History of Psychiatry* 15 (2004), 395–416.

Dannenfeldt, Karl H., 'Sleep: Theory and Practice in the Late Renaissance', *Journal of the History of Medicine* 41 (1986), 415–41.

Davies, Owen, 'The Nightmare Experience, Sleep Paralysis, and Witchcraft Accusations', *Folklore* 114 (2003), 181–203.

Daybell, James, *The Material Letter in Early Modern England: Manuscript Letters and the Culture and Practices of Letter-Writing, 1512–1635* (London: Palgrave Macmillan, 2012).

Dibbits, Hester C., 'Between Society and Family Values: The Linen Cupboard in Early-Modern Households', in *Private Domain, Public Inquiry: Families and Life-Styles in the Netherlands and Europe, 1550 to the Present*, ed. Anton Schuurman and Pieter Spierenburg (Hilversum: Verloren, 1996).

Dolan, Alice, ' "The Fabric of Life": Time and Textiles in an Eighteenth-Century Plebeian Home', *Home Cultures* 11 (2014), 353–74.

Donald, Diana, *The Age of Caricature: Satirical Prints in the Reign of George III* (New Haven and London: Yale University Press, 1996).

Douglas, Mary, *Purity and Danger: An Analysis of Concepts of Pollution and Taboo* (London: Routledge, 2003).

Easton, Timothy, 'Candle Powers', *Cornerstone* 32 (2011), 56–60.

Edwards, Clive, *Turning Houses into Homes: A History of the Retailing and Consumption of Domestic Furnishings* (Aldershot: Ashgate, 2005).

Ekirch, A. Roger, *At Day's Close: Night in Times Past* (New York: W.W. Norton & Company Ltd, 2005).

—— 'The Modernization of Western Sleep: Or, Does Insomnia Have A History?', *Past and Present* 226 (2015), 149–92.

—— 'Sleep We Have Lost: Pre-Industrial Slumber in the British Isles', *The American Historical Review* 106 (2001), 343–86.

Endt-Jones, Marion (ed.), *Coral. Something Rich and Strange* (Liverpool: Liverpool University Press, 2013).

Espie, Colin A., *Overcoming Insomnia and Sleep Problems: A Self-Help Guide using Cognitive Behavioral Techniques* (London: Constable & Robinson Ltd, 2006).

Fairfax-Lucy, Alice, *Charlecote and the Lucys: The Chronicle of An English Family* (London: Oxford University Press, 1958).

Fissell, Mary E., 'The Marketplace of Print', in *Medicine and the Market in England and its Colonies c.1450–c.1850*, ed. Mark S.R. Jenner and Patrick Wallis (Basingstoke: Palgrave Macmillan, 2007).

—— 'Popular Medical Writing', in *The Oxford History of Popular Print Culture*, vol. 1 ed. Joad Raymond (Oxford: Oxford University Press, 2011).

Flather, Amanda, *Gender and Space in Early Modern England* (Woodbridge: Royal Historical Society/Boydell Press, 2007).

Ford, Jennifer, *Coleridge on Dreaming: Romanticism, Dreams and the Medical Imagination* (Cambridge: Cambridge University Press, 1998).

—— 'Samuel Taylor Coleridge and "The pains of sleep"', in *Dreams and History: The Interpretation of Dreams from Ancient Greece to Modern Psychoanalysis*, ed. Daniel Pick and Lyndal Roper (London and New York: Routledge, 2004).

Frayling, Christopher, 'Fuseli's *The Nightmare*: Somewhere Between the Sublime and the Ridiculous', in *Gothic Nightmares: Fuseli, Blake and the Romantic Imagination*, ed. Martin Myrone (London: Tate Publishing, 2006).

Frye, Susan, *Pens and Needles: Women's Textualities in Early Modern England* (Philadelphia: University of Pennsylvania Press, 2010).

Furdell, Elizabeth Lane, *Publishing and Medicine in Early Modern England* (Rochester, NY: University of Rochester Press, 2002).

Gage, Frances, 'Exercise for Mind and Body: Giulio Mancini, Collecting, and the Beholding of Landscape Painting in the Seventeenth Century', *Renaissance Quarterly* 61 (2008), 1167–207.

—— 'Teaching Them to Serve and Obey: Giulio Mancini on Collecting Religious Art in Seventeenth-Century Rome', in *Sacred Possessions: Collecting Italian Religious Art 1500–1900*, ed. Gail Feigenbaum and Sybille Ebert-Schifferer (Los Angeles: Getty Research Institute, 2011).

Gibson, Susannah, 'Living Rocks: The Mystery of Coral in the Eighteenth Century', in *Coral: Something Rich and Strange*, ed. Marion Endt-Jones (Liverpool: Liverpool University Press, 2013).

Gil Sotres, Pedro, 'The Regimens of Health', in *Western Medical Thought from Antiquity to the Middle Ages*, ed. M.D. Grmek (Cambridge, MA: Harvard University Press, 1998).

Gillingham, John, *Richard I* (New Haven and London: Yale University Press, 2002).

Glover, Katharine, 'Polite Society and the Rural Resort: The Meanings of Moffat Spa in the Eighteenth Century', *Journal for Eighteenth-Century Studies* 34 (2011), 65–80.

Gordon, Stephen, 'Medical Condition, Demon or Undead Corpse? Sleep Paralysis and the Nightmare in Medieval Europe', *Journal of the Social History of Medicine* 29 (2015), 425–44.

Gowing, Laura, '"The Twinkling of a Bedstaff": Recovering the Social Life of English Beds 1500–1700', *Home Cultures* 11 (2014), 275–304.

Grant, Douglas, *The Cock Lane Ghost* (London: Macmillan and Company Limited, 1975).

Green, Andrew and Alex Westcombe (eds), *Sleep: Multi-Professional Perspectives* (London and Philadelphia: Jessica Kingsley Publishers, 2012).

Green, Andrew, 'A Question of Balance: The Relationship Between Daily Occupation and Sleep', in *Sleep: Multi-Professional Perspectives*, ed. Andrew Green and Alex Westcombe (London and Philadelphia: Jessica Kingsley Publishers, 2012).

Green, Ian, 'New for Old? Clerical and Lay Attitudes to Domestic Prayer in Early Modern England', *Reformation and Renaissance Review* 10 (2008), 219–21.

—— *Print and Protestantism in Early Modern England* (Oxford: Oxford University Press, 2000).

—— 'Varieties of Domestic Devotion in Early Modern English Protestantism', in *Private and Domestic Devotion*, ed. Jessica Martin and Alec Ryrie (Farnham: Ashgate, 2012).

Greenslade, Michael W., *Catholic Staffordshire 1500–1800* (Leominster: Gracewing, 2006).

Greig, Hannah, *The Beau Monde: Fashionable Society in Georgian London* (Oxford: Oxford University Press, 2013).

Griffin, Patrick, 'The Pursuit of Comfort: The Modern and the Material in the Early Modern British Atlantic World' (Review of *The Invention of Comfort: Sensibilities and Design in Early Modern Britain and Early America* by John E. Crowley), *Reviews in American History* 30 (2002), 365–72.

Guerrini, Anita, *Obesity and Depression in the Enlightenment: The Life and Times of George Cheyne* (Norman: University of Oklahoma Press, 2000).

Guillery, Peter, *The Small House in Eighteenth-Century London: A Social and Architectural History* (New Haven and London: Paul Mellon Centre for Studies in British Art, Yale University Press in association with English Heritage, 2004).

Hambrick-Stowe, Charles E., 'Practical Divinity and Spirituality', in *The Cambridge Companion to Puritanism*, ed. John Coffey and Paul C.H. Lim (Cambridge: Cambridge University Press, 2008).

Hamling, Tara, *Decorating the 'Godly' Household: Religious Art in Post-Reformation Britain* (New Haven and London: Yale University Press, 2010).

—— 'Living with the Bible in Post-Reformation England: The Materiality of Text, Image and Object in Domestic Life', in *Religion and the Household*, ed. John Doran, Charlotte Methuen and Alexandra Walsham (Woodbridge: published for the Ecclesiastical History Society by the Boydell Press, 2014).

—— 'Old Robert's Girdle: Visual and Material Props for Protestant Piety in Post-Reformation England', in *Private and Domestic Devotion*, ed. Jessica Martin and Alec Ryrie (Farnham: Ashgate, 2012).

Hanawalt, Barbara A., *Growing Up in Medieval London: The Experience of Childhood in History* (Oxford: Oxford University Press, 1993).

Handley, Sasha, 'From the Sacral to the Moral: Sleeping Practices, Household Worship and Confessional Cultures in Late Seventeenth-Century England', *Cultural and Social History* 9 (2012), 27–46.

Heller, Benjamin, 'Leisure and the Use of Domestic Space in Georgian London', *Historical Journal* 53 (2010), 623–45.

Hill, Christopher, 'The Spiritualization of the Household', in *Society and Puritanism in Pre-Revolutionary England*, ed. Christopher Hill (London: Secker & Warburg, 1964).

Hill, David, 'James Pascall and the Long Gallery Suite at Temple Newsam', *Furniture History* 17 (1981), 70–4.

Hislop, J. and S. Arber, 'Understanding Women's Sleep Management: Beyond Medicalization–Healthicization?', *Sociology of Health and Illness* 25 (2003), 815–37.

Horne, Jim, 'Sleep Hygiene: Exercise and Other "Do's and Don'ts"', *Sleep Medicine* 15 (2014), 731–2.

—— *Sleepfaring. A Journey Through the Science of Sleep* (Oxford: Oxford University Press, 2006).

Houlbrooke, Ralph, 'Death in Childhood: the Practice of the Good Death in James Janeway's "A Token for Children"', in *Childhood in Question: Children, Parents and the State*, ed. Anthony Fletcher and Stephen Hussey (Manchester: Manchester University Press, 1999).

Huffington, Arianna, *The Sleep Revolution: Transforming Your Life, One Night at a Time* (London: W.H. Allen, 2016).

Jacob, W.M., *Lay People and Religion in the Early Eighteenth Century* (Cambridge: Cambridge University Press, 1996).

Jacobs, Stephen, 'Ambivalent Attitudes Towards Sleep in World Religions', in *Sleep: Multi-Professional Perspectives*, ed. Andrew Green and Alex Westcombe (London and Philadelphia: Jessica Kingsley Publishers, 2012).

Jaeger, C. Stephen, *Ennobling Love: In Search of a Lost Sensibility* (Philadelphia: University of Pennsylvania Press, 1999).

Jay, Mike, *The Atmosphere of Heaven: The Unnatural Experiments of Dr Beddoes and His Sons of Genius* (New Haven and London: Yale University Press, 2009).

Jones, Caroline H.D. and Helen L. Ball, 'Medical Anthropology and Children's Sleep: The Mismatch Between Western Lifestyles and Sleep Physiology', in *Sleep: Multi-Professional Perspectives*, ed. Andrew Green and Alex Westcombe (London and Philadelphia: Jessica Kingsley Publishers, 2012).

Keene, Derek, 'Growth, Modernisation and Control: The Transformation of London's Landscape, *c.* 1500–*c.* 1760', in *Two Capitals: London and Dublin 1500–1840*, ed. Peter Clark and Raymond Gillespie (Oxford: published for the British Academy by Oxford University Press, 2001).

Kemp, Brian, *English Church Monuments* (London: B.T. Basford, 1980).

King, Peter, 'Pauper Inventories and the Material Lives of the Poor in the Eighteenth and Early Nineteenth Centuries', in *Chronicling Poverty: The Voices and Strategies of the English Poor, 1640–1840*, ed. Tim Hitchcock, Peter King and Pamela Sharpe (Basingstoke: Macmillan, 1997).

King, Steven, *Poverty and Welfare in England, 1700–1850: A Regional Perspective* (Manchester: Manchester University Press, 2000).

Kirschner, Ann, '"Tending to Edify, Astonish, and Instruct": Published Narratives of Spiritual Dreams and Visions in the Early Republic', *Early American Studies* 1 (2003), 198–229.

Klug, Gabriele, 'Dangerous Doze: Sleep and Vulnerability in Medieval German Literature', in *Worlds of Sleep*, ed. Lodewijk Brunt and Brigitte Steger (Berlin: Frank & Timme, 2008).

—— *'Wol ûf, wir sullen slâfen gan!' Der Schlaf als Alltagserfahrung in der deutschsprachigen Dichtung des Hochmittelalters* (Frankfurt: Peter Lang, 2007).

Koslofsky, Craig, *Evening's Empire: A History of the Night in Early Modern Europe* (Cambridge: Cambridge University Press, 2011).

Kraftl, Peter and John Horton, 'Spaces of Every-Night Life: For Geographies of Sleep, Sleeping and Sleepiness', *Progress in Human Geography* 32 (2008), 509–24.

Kreitzman, Leon, Russell Foster and Lewis Wolpert, *Rhythms of Life: The Biological Clocks That Control the Daily Lives of Every Living Thing* (London: Profile Books, 2004).

Langford, Paul, *Englishness Identified: Manners and Character, 1650–1850* (Oxford: Oxford University Press, 2000).

—— *A Polite and Commercial People: England 1727–1783* (Oxford: Clarendon Press, 1992).

Lawlor, Clark, *Consumption and Literature: The Making of the Romantic Disease* (Basingstoke: Palgrave Macmillan, 2006).

Lemire, Beverly (ed.), *The British Cotton Trade 1660–1815, Part II: International Trade and the Politics of Consumption 1690s–1730*, (London: Pickering & Chatto, 2010).

—— 'Draping the Body and Dressing the Home: The Material Culture of Textiles and Clothes in the Atlantic World, *c.* 1500–1800', in *History and Material Culture: A Student's Guide to Approaching Alternative Sources*, ed. Karen Harvey (London and New York: Routledge, 2009).

—— *Fashion's Favourite: The Cotton Trade and the Consumer in Britain, 1660–1800* (Oxford: Oxford University Press, 1991).

Leong, Elaine and Sara Pennell, 'Recipe Collections and the Currency of Medical Knowledge in the Early Modern "Medical Marketplace"', in *Medicine and the Market in England and Its Colonies, c. 1450–c. 1650*, ed. Mark S.R. Jenner and Patrick Wallis (Basingstoke: Palgrave Macmillan, 2007).

Leong, Elaine, 'Making Medicines in the Early Modern Household', *Bulletin of the History of Medicine* 82 (2008), 145–68.

Levin, Carole, *Dreaming the English Renaissance: Politics and Desire in Court and Culture* (New York: Palgrave Macmillan, 2008).

Lindemann, Mary, *Medicine and Society in Early Modern Europe* (Cambridge: Cambridge University Press, 1990).

Llewellyn, Nigel, *Funeral Monuments in Post-Reformation England* (Cambridge: Cambridge University Press, 2000).

Lockley, Stephen W. and Russell G. Foster, *Sleep: A Very Short Introduction* (Oxford: Oxford University Press, 2012).

Longfellow, Erica, ' "My now solitary prayers": *Eikon basilike* and Changing Attitudes toward Religious Solitude', in *Private and Domestic Devotion*, ed. Jessica Martin and Alec Ryrie (Farnham: Ashgate, 2012).

Mack, Phyllis, 'Does Gender Matter? Suffering and Salvation in Eighteenth-century Methodism', *Bulletin of the John Rylands University Library of Manchester* 85 (2003), 157–76.

—— *Heart Religion in the British Enlightenment* (Oxford: Oxford University Press, 2008).

MacLehose, William, 'Fear, Fantasy and Sleep in Medieval Medicine', in *Emotions and Health, 1200–1700*, ed. Elena Carrera (Leiden: Brill, 2013).

—— 'Sleepwalking, Violence and Desire in the Middle Ages', *Culture, Medicine and Psychiatry* 37 (2013), 601–24.

Macnaghten, P. and J. Urry (eds), *Bodies of Nature* (London: Sage, 2001).

Marshall, Peter, 'Angels Around the Deathbed: Variations on a Theme in the English Art of Dying', in *Angels in the Early Modern World*, ed. Peter Marshall and Alexandra Walsham (Cambridge: Cambridge University Press, 2006).

McKellar, Elizabeth, *The Birth of Modern London: The Development and Design of the City 1660–1720* (Manchester: Manchester University Press, 1999).

McKendrick, Neil, John Brewer and John Plumb, *The Birth of a Consumer Society: The Commercialization of Eighteenth-Century England* (London: Europa Publications, 1982).

Meldrum, Tim, *Domestic Service and Gender 1660–1750: Life and Work in the London Household* (Harlow: Longman, 2000).

Merleau-Ponty, Maurice, *Phenomenology of Perception* (London: Routledge, 2013).

Mitchell, David, ' "My purple will be too sad for that melancholy room": Furnishings for Interiors in London and Paris, 1660–1735', *Textile History* 40 (2009), 3–28.

Morgan, Kevin, 'Daytime Activity and Risk Factors for Late-Life Insomnia', *Journal of Sleep Research* 12 (2003), 231–38.

Morin, Charles M. and Colin A. Espie, 'Conclusion: Overview, Emerging Trends, and Future Directions in Sleep Research and Practice', in *The Oxford Handbook of Sleep and Sleep Disorders*, ed. Charles M. Morin and Colin A. Espie (Oxford: Oxford University Press, 2012).

Motture, Peta and Luke Syson, 'Art in the *casa*', in *At Home in Renaissance Italy*, ed. Marta Ajmar-Wollheim and Flora Dennis (London: V&A Publications, 2006).

Mullan, John, 'Feelings and Novels', in *Rewriting the Self: Histories from the Renaissance to the Present*, ed. Roy Porter (London and New York: Routledge, 1997).

—— *Sentiment and Sociability: The Language of Feeling in the Eighteenth Century* (Oxford: Clarendon Press, 1988).

Newton, Hannah, ' "Nature Concocts & Expels": The Agents and Processes of Recovery from Disease in Early Modern England', *Social History of Medicine* 28 (2015), 465–86.

Opie, Iona and Moira Tate (eds), *A Dictionary of Superstitions*, (Oxford: Oxford University Press, 1989).

Overton, Mark, Jane Whittle, Darron Dean and Andrew Hann, *Production and Consumption in English Households, 1600–1750* (Abingdon: Routledge, 2004).

Paterson, Louise M., 'The Science of Sleep: What is it, What Makes it Happen and Why Do We Do it?', in *Sleep: Multi-Professional Perspectives*, ed. Andrew Green and Alex Westcombe (London and Philadelphia: Jessica Kingsley Publishers, 2012).

Paterson, Louise M., David J. Nutt and Sue J. Wilson, 'Sleep and its disorders in translational medicine', *Journal of Psychopharmacology* 25 (2011), 1226–8.

Pearson, Jacqueline, *Women's Reading in Britain, 1750–1835: A Dangerous Recreation* (Cambridge: Cambridge University Press, 2005).

Perea Yébenes, Sabino, 'Magic at Sea: Amulets for Navigation', in *Magical Practice in the Latin West*, ed. Richard L. Gordon and Francisco Marco Simón (Leiden: Brill, 2010).

Pick, Daniel and Lyndal Roper (eds), *Dreams and History: The Interpretation of Dreams from Ancient Greece to Modern Psychoanalysis* (London and New York: Routledge, 2004).

Plane, Ann Marie and Leslie Tuttle (eds), *Dreams, Dreamers, and Visions: The Early Modern Atlantic World* (Philadelphia: University of Pennsylvania Press, 2013).

Pointon, Marcia, *Brilliant Effects: A Cultural History of Gem Stones and Jewellery* (New Haven and London: Paul Mellon Centre for Studies in British Art, Yale University Press, 2009).

Ponsonby, Margaret, *Stories from Home: English Domestic Interiors 1750–1850* (Aldershot and Burlington: Ashgate, 2007).

Pop, Andrei, 'Sympathetic Spectators: Henry Fuseli's Nightmare and Emma Hamilton's Attitudes', *Art History* 35 (2011), 934–57.

Power, E.R., 'Domestic Temporalities: Nature Times in the House-as-Home', *Geogorum* 40 (2009), 1024–32.

Preyer, Brenda, 'The Florentine *casa*', in *At Home in Renaissance Italy*, ed. Marta Ajmar-Wollheim and Flora Dennis (London: V&A Publications, 2006).

Priestley, Ursula, P.J. Corfield and Helen Sutermeister, 'Rooms and Room Use in Norwich Housing, 1580–1730', *Post-Medieval Archaeology* 16 (1982), 93–123.

Quinney, Laura, *William Blake on Self and Soul* (Cambridge, MA: Harvard University Press, 2010).

Quitsland, Beth, 'Singing the Psalms for Fun and Profit', in *Private and Domestic Devotion*, ed. Jessica Martin and Alec Ryrie (Farnham: Ashgate, 2012).

Raymond, Martin and John Barresi, *The Naturalization of the Soul: Self and Personal Identity in the Eighteenth Century* (London: Routledge, 2000).

Reinburg, Virginia, 'Hearing Lay People's Prayer', in *Culture and Identity in Early Modern Europe (1500–1800)*, ed. Barbara Diefendorf and Carla Hesse (Ann Arbor, MI: University of Michigan Press, 1993).

Richardson, Alan, *British Romanticism and the Science of the Mind* (Cambridge: Cambridge University Press, 2001).

—— *The Neural Sublime: Cognitive Theories and Romantic Texts* (Baltimore: Johns Hopkins University Press, 2010).

Riello, Giorgio, *Cotton: The Fabric that Made the Modern World* (Cambridge: Cambridge University Press: Cambridge and New York, 2013).

—— 'Fabricating the Domestic: The Material Culture of Textiles and the Social life of the Home in Early Modern Europe', in *The Force of Fashion in Politics and Society: Global Perspectives from Early Modern to Contemporary Times*, ed. Beverly Lemire (Ashgate: Farnham, 2010).

Riley, James C., *The Eighteenth-Century Campaign to Avoid Disease* (New York: St. Martin's Press, 1987).

Riskin, Jessica, *Science in the Age of Sensibility: The Sentimental Empiricists of the French Enlightenment* (Chicago: University of Chicago Press, 2002).

Rivière, Janine, 'Demons of Desire or Symptoms of Disease? Medical Theories and Popular Experiences of the 'Nightmare' in Premodern England', in *Dreams, Dreamers, and Visions: The Early Modern Atlantic World*, ed. Ann Marie Plane and Leslie Tuttle (Philadelphia: University of Pennsylvania Press, 2013).

Roberts, Sasha, 'Lying Among the Classics: Ritual and Motif in Elite Elizabethan and Jacobean Beds', in *Albion's Classicism: The Visual Arts in Britain, 1550–1660*, ed. Lucy Gent (New Haven and London: Yale University Press, 1995).

Roenneberg, Till, *Internal Time: Chronotypes, Social Jet Lag, and Why You're So Tired* (Cambridge, MA: Harvard University Press, 2012).

Rose, Clare, 'The Manufacture and Sale of Marseilles Quilting in Eighteenth-Century London', *CIETA Bulletin* 76 (1999), 104–13.

Rousseau, George S., *Nervous Acts: Essays on Literature, Culture and Sensibility* (Basingstoke: Palgrave Macmillan, 2004).

Rublack, Ulinka, 'Fluxes: The Early Modern Body and the Emotions', *History Workshop Journal* 53 (2002), 1–16.

Russell, Gillian, *Women, Sociability and Theatre in Georgian London* (Cambridge: Cambridge University Press, 2007).

Ryrie, Alec, *Being Protestant in Reformation Britain* (Oxford: Oxford University Press, 2013).

—— 'Sleeping, Waking and Dreaming in Protestant Piety', in *Private and Domestic Devotion*, ed. Jessica Martin and Alec Ryrie (Farnham: Ashgate, 2012).

Sambrook, Pamela, *A Country House at Work: Three Centuries of Dunham Massey* (London: The National Trust, 2003).

Sangha, Laura, *Angels and Belief in England, 1480–1700* (London: Pickering & Chatto, 2012).

Sant, Ann Jessie van, *Eighteenth-Century Sensibility and the Novel: The Senses in Social Context* (Cambridge: Cambridge University Press, 1993).

Saper, C.B., T.E. Scammell and L. Lu, 'Hypothalamic Regulation of Sleep and Circadian Rhythms', *Nature* 437 (2005), 1257–63.

Sarasohn, Lisa T., '"That nauseous venomous insect": Bedbugs in Early Modern England', *Eighteenth-Century Studies* 46 (2013), 513–30.

Sarti, Raffaella, *Europe at Home: Family Life and Material Culture 1500–1800* (New Haven and London: Yale University Press, 2002).

Schmidt, Roger, 'Caffeine and the Coming of the Enlightenment', *Raritan* 23 (2003), 129–49.

Schwartz, B., 'Notes on the Sociology of Sleep', in *People in Places: The Sociology of the Familiar*, ed. A. Birenbaum and E. E. Sangrin (London: Nelson, 1973).

Sekules, Veronica, 'Spinning Yarns: Clean Linen and Domestic Values in Late Medieval French Culture', in *The Material Culture of Sex, Procreation, and Marriage in Premodern Europe*, ed. Anne L. McClanan and Karen Rosoff Encarnación (New York and Basingstoke: Palgrave, 2002).

Shammas, Carole, 'The Domestic Environment in Early Modern England and America', *Journal of Social History* 14 (1980), 3–24.

Sherman, William H., 'Shakespearean Somniloquy: Sleep and Transformation in *The Tempest*', in *Renaissance Transformations: The Making of English Writing (1500–1950)*, ed. Margaret Healy and Thomas Healy (Edinburgh: Edinburgh University Press, 2009).

Smith, Bruce R., *The Key of Green: Passion and Perception in Renaissance Culture* (Chicago: University of Chicago Press, 2008).

Spinks, Jennifer, Sasha Handley and Stephen Gordon, *Magic, Witches and Devils in the Early Modern World* (Manchester: The John Rylands Library, University of Manchester, 2016).

Spufford, Margaret, *Small Books and Pleasant Histories. Popular Fiction and its Readership in Seventeenth-Century England* (Cambridge: Cambridge University Press, 1985).

Spurr, John, *English Puritanism, 1603–1689* (Basingstoke: Macmillan, 1998).

Stafford, Barbara Maria, *Body Criticism: Imaging the Unseen in Enlightenment Art and Medicine* (Cambridge, MA: MIT Press, 1993).

Stansfield, Dorothy A., *Thomas Beddoes M.D. 1760–1808* (Dordrecht: D. Reidel, 1984).

Stearns, P., R. Perrin and L. Giarnella, 'Children's Sleep: Sketching Historical Change', *Journal of Social History* 30 (1996), 345–66.

Steedman, Carolyn, *Master and Servant: Love and Labour in the English Industrial Age* (Cambridge: Cambridge University Press, 2007).

Steger, Brigitte and Lodewijk Brunt (eds), *Night-time and Sleep in Asia and the West* (London and New York: RoutledgeCurzon, 2003).

Stobart, John, *Sugar and Spice: Grocers and Groceries in Provincial England, 1650–1830* (Oxford: Oxford University Press, 2012).

Styles, John, *The Dress of the People: Everyday Fashion in Eighteenth-Century England* (New Haven and London: Yale University Press, 2007).

——'Lodging at the Old Bailey: Lodgings and their Furnishing in Eighteenth-Century London', in *Gender, Taste and Material Culture in Britain and North America, 1700–1830*, ed. John Styles and Amanda Vickery (New Haven and London: Yale University Press, 2006).

—— 'Patchwork on the Page', in *Quilts 1700–2010: Hidden Histories, Untold Stories*, ed. Sue Prichard (London: V&A Publishing, 2012).

—— 'Picturing Domesticity: The Cottage Genre in Late Eighteenth-Century Britain', in *Imagined Interiors: Representing the Domestic Interior since the Renaissance*, ed. Jeremy Aynsley and Charlotte Grant, with assistance from Harriet McKay (London: V&A Publications, 2006).

—— 'What Were Cottons for in the Early Industrial Revolution', in *The Spinning World: A Global History of Cotton Textiles*, ed. Giorgio Riello and Prasannan Parthasarathi (Oxford: Oxford University Press/Pasold Research Fund, 2009).

Styles, John and Amanda Vickery (eds), *Gender, Taste, and Material Culture in Britain and North America 1700–1830* (New Haven and London: Yale Center for British Art, Paul Mellon Centre for Studies in British Art, Yale University Press, 2006).

Sugg, Richard, *Mummies, Cannibals and Vampires: The History of Corpse Medicine from the Renaissance to the Victorians* (London and New York: Routledge, 2011).

Suimin Bunka Kenkūjo (eds), *Netoko-jutsu* [The technique of the sleeping place] (Tokyo: Popura-sha 2005).

Sullivan Jr, Garrett A., 'Romance, Sleep and the Passions in Sir Philip Sidney's "The Old Arcadia"', *ELH* 74 (2007), 735–57.

—— *Sleep, Romance and Human Embodiment: Vitality from Spenser to Milton* (Cambridge: Cambridge University Press, 2012).

Sullivan, Erin, '"The Watchful Spirit": Religious Anxieties toward Sleep in the Notebooks of Nehemiah Wallington', *Cultural History* 1 (2012), 14–35.

Sumers-Bremner, Eluned, *Insomnia: A Cultural History* (London: Reaktion Books, 2008).

Sykes, Norman, *Church and State in England in the XVIIIth Century* (Cambridge: Cambridge University Press, 1934).

Taylor, Charles, *Sources of the Self: The Making of Modern Identity* (Cambridge: Cambridge University Press, 1989).

Thompson, E.P., 'Time, Work-Discipline, and Industrial Capitalism', *Past and Present* 38 (1967), 56–97.

Thornton, Peter and Maurice Tomlin, *The Furnishing and Decoration of Ham House* (London: Furniture History Society, 1980).

Thornton, Peter, *Authentic Décor: The Domestic Interior 1620–1920* (London: Seven Dials, 2000).

—— *Seventeenth-Century Interior Decoration in England, France and Holland* (New Haven and London: Paul Mellon Centre for Studies in British Art, Yale University Press, 1990).

Thunder, Moira, 'Deserving Attention: Margaretha Helm's Designs for Embroidery in the Eighteenth Century', *Journal of Design History* 23 (2010), 409–27.

Todd, Janet, *Sensibility: An Introduction* (London and New York: Methuen, 1986).

Todd, Margo, 'Puritan Self-Fashioning: The Diary of Samuel Ward', *Journal of British Studies* 31 (1992), 236–64.

Ulrich, Laurel Thatcher, *The Age of Homespun: Objects and Stories in the Creation of an American Myth* (New York: Alfred A. Knopf, 2001).

Venn, Susan and Sara Arber, 'Conflicting Sleep Demands: Parents and Young People in UK Households', in *Worlds of Sleep*, ed. Lodewijk Brunt and Brigitte Steger (Berlin: Frank & Timme, 2008).

Vickery, Amanda, 'An Englishman's Home is His Castle? Thresholds, Boundaries and Privacies in the Eighteenth-Century London House', *Past and Present* 199 (2008), 147–73.

—— *Behind Closed Doors: At Home in Georgian England* (New Haven and London: Yale University Press, 2009).

—— *The Gentleman's Daughter: Women's Lives in Georgian England* (New Haven and London: Yale University Press, 1998).

Vidal, Fernando, 'Brains, Bodies, Selves, and Science: Anthropologies of Identity and the Resurrection of the Body', *Critical Inquiry* 28 (2002), 930–74.

Vigarello, Georges, *Concepts of Cleanliness: Changing Attitudes in France since the Middle Ages*, trans. Jean Birrell (Cambridge: Cambridge University Press, 1988).

Vila, Anne C., *Enlightenment and Pathology: Sensibility in the Literature and Medicine of Eighteenth-Century France* (Baltimore and London: Johns Hopkins University Press, 1998).

Wahrman, Dror, *The Making of the Modern Self: Identity and Culture in Eighteenth-Century England* (New Haven and London: Yale University Press, 2006).

Walsham, Alexandra, 'Holy Families: The Spiritualization of the Early Modern Household Revisited', in *Religion and the Household*, ed. John Doran, Charlotte Methuen and Alexandra Walsham (Woodbridge: published for the Ecclesiastical History Society by the Boydell Press, 2014).

Warner, Marina, *Fantastic Metamorphoses, Other Worlds: Ways of Telling the Self* (Oxford: Oxford University Press, 2002).

Wear, Andrew, 'The Popularization of Medicine in Early Modern England', in *The Popularization of Medicine 1650–1850*, ed. Roy Porter (London and New York: Routledge, 1992).

Weatherill, Lorna, *Consumer Behaviour and Material Culture in Britain, 1660–1760* (London: Routledge, 1988).

Webster, Tom, 'Writing to Redundancy: Approaches to Spiritual Journals and Early Modern Spirituality', *Historical Journal* 39 (1996), 33–56.

Whitelock, Anna, *Elizabeth's Bedfellows: An Intimate History of the Queen's Court* (London: Bloomsbury, 2013).

Whyman, Susan, *Sociability and Power in Late Stuart England: The Cultural Worlds of the Verneys 1650–1720* (Oxford: Oxford University Press, 2002).

Williams, Richard L., 'Forbidden Sacred Spaces in Reformation England', in *Defining the Holy: Sacred Space in Medieval and Early Modern Europe*, ed. Andrew Spicer and Sarah Hamilton (Aldershot and Burlington: Ashgate, 2005).

Williams, Simon, 'Sleep and Health: Sociological Reflections on the Dormant Society', *Health* 6 (2002), 173–200.

—— *Sleep and Society: Sociological Ventures into the (Un)known* (London: Routledge, 2005).

Wilson, Sue and David Nutt, *Sleep Disorders* (Oxford: Oxford University Press, 2008).

Winner, Lauren F., *A Cheerful and Comfortable Faith: Anglican Religious practice in the Elite Households of Eighteenth-Century Virginia* (New Haven and London: Yale University Press, 2010).

Withey, Alun, *Physick and the Family: Health, Medicine and Care in Wales, 1600–1750* (Manchester: Manchester University Press, 2011).

Wrightson, Keith, *Earthly Necessities: Economic Lives in Early Modern Britain* (London: Penguin, 2002).

Wykes, David, ' "The Sabbaths spent . . . before in Idleness & the neglect of the word": The Godly and the Use of Time in Their Daily Religion', *Studies in Church History: The Use and Abuse of Time in Christian History*, ed. R. N. Swanson, vol. 37 (2002), 211–21.

Yoshida, Shuji, *Suimin bunka-ron* [Essays on Sleep Culture] (Tokyo: Heibonsha, 2001).

Unpublished Secondary Sources

Barclay, Katie, 'Intimacy, Community and Power: Bedding Rituals in Eighteenth-Century Scotland', in *Emotion, Ritual and Power in Europe: 1200 to the Present*, ed. Katie Barclay and Merridee L. Bailey (Basingstoke: Palgrave Macmillan, forthcoming 2016).

Fuller, Rachel, 'Out of Sight, Out of Mind? The Meaning of the Linnenkast in the Material and Conceptual Landscape of the Seventeenth-Century Dutch Republic' (MA diss., Victoria and Albert Museum/Royal College of Art history of design programme, 2004).

Gage, Frances, 'The Air over There: Art, Travel and the Regulation of the Non-Naturals, *c.* 1580–1650' (paper presented at 'Healthy Living in Pre-modern Europe', Institute of Historical Research, September 2013).

Howe, Neil Gregory, 'The Politician in Caricature: The Case of Charles James Fox' (PhD diss., University of Nottingham, 2011).

McShane, Angela and Joanne Bailey, 'Beds and the making of the Domestic Landscape' (paper presented at 'The Body in Bed' seminar series, Royal Holloway Centre for the Study of the Body and Material Culture, University of London, 20 October 2010).

North, Susan F., 'Dress and Hygiene in Early Modern England: a study of advice and practice' (PhD diss., Queen Mary, University of London, 2013).

Sharrett, Elizabeth, 'Beds as stage properties in English Renaissance drama: materializing the lifecycle' (PhD diss., University of Birmingham, 2014).

Tierney, Elaine, 'Dirty Rotten Sheds: Exploring the Ephemeral City in Early Modern London' (paper presented at the Lunchtime Seminar, University of Manchester, 2 December 2015).

Web Resources

Old Bailey Online: The Proceedings of the Old Bailey, 1674–1913, 2016, www.oldbaileyon line.org.

Oxford Dictionary of National Biography, Oxford University Press, 2016, www.oxforddnb. com.

Oxford English Dictionary, Oxford University Press, 2016, www.oed.com.

INDEX